Edited by

CORNELIUS KA~
RAYMOND LEVY

D1513185

ook ue for return on or before the last date shown below.

994

Delusi d Hallucinations
in Old

GASKELL

Gaskell is an imprint of the Royal College of Psychiatrists,
17 Belgrave Square, London SW1

British Library Cataloguing-in-Publication Data
Delusions and Hallucinations in Old Age
    I. Katona, C. L. E.   II. Levy, Raymond
    618.97

ISBN 0-902241-47-8

Distributed in North America
by American Psychiatric Press, Inc.
ISBN 0-880486-13-9

Publication of this book was made possible by the kind help
of Janssen Germany and the European Association for Geriatric
Psychiatry.

Phototypeset by Dobbie Typesetting Ltd., Tavistock, Devon
Printed in Great Britain by Bell and Bain Ltd., Glasgow

Contents

Part III. Organic disorders

Contributors

O. P. Almeida, Section of Old Age Psychiatry, Institute of Psychiatry, De Crespigny Park, London SE5 8AF, UK

R. C. Baldwin, Consultant Psychiatrist for the Elderly, Department of Psychiatry, York House, Manchester Royal Infirmary, Oxford Road, Manchester M13 9BX, UK

German E. Berrios, Consultant and University Lecturer in Psychiatry, Department of Psychiatry, University of Cambridge, Addenbrooke's Hospital, Hills Road, Cambridge CB2 2QQ, UK

Alistair Burns, Professor of Old Age Psychiatry, University of Manchester, Withington Hospital, West Didsbury, Manchester M20 8LR

J. P. Clément, Service Hospitalo-Universitaire de Psychiatrie, 15 rue du Docteur Marcland, 87025 Limoges, Cedex, France

A. F. Cooper, Consultant Psychiatrist, Leverndale Hospital, 510 Crookston Road, Glasgow G53 7TU, Scotland

José D. Cordeiro, Chair and Professor of Psychiatry, Faculty of Medicine of Lisbon, Hospital Sta. Maria, Avenue Prof. Egas Moniz, 1699 Lisboa Codex, Portugal

Anthony S. David, Senior Lecturer, Department of Psychological Medicine, King's College Hospital and the Institute of Psychiatry, Bessemer Road, Denmark Hill, London SE5 9RS, UK

A. Deister, Psychiatric Hospital of the University of Bonn, D-5300 Bonn, Germany

Hans Förstl, Central Institute of Mental Health, PO Box 122120, J5, W-6800 Mannheim 1, Germany, formerly Section of Old Age Psychiatry, Institute of Psychiatry, De Crespigny Park, London SE5 8AF, UK

Thomas Fuchs, Psychiatrische Klinik und Poliklinik der Technischen Universitat Munchen, Klinikum Rechts der Isar, Ismaninger Strasse 22, 8000 Munchen 80, Germany

E. Gabriel, Professor of Psychiatry, Medical Director, Psychiatrisches Krankenhaus der Stadt Wien, Baumgartner Hohe 1, 1145 Vienna, Austria

G. Le Goues, Vice President of the French Language Psychogeriatric Society, Hopital Rothschild, 33 Boulevard de Picpus, 75571 Paris, France

Lars Gustafson, Professor of Geriatric Psychiatry, Department of Psychogeriatrics, University Hospital, PO Box 638, S-22009, Lund, Sweden

R. Howard, Section of Old Age Psychiatry, Institute of Psychiatry, De Crespigny Park, London SE5 8AF, UK

Cornelius Katona, Professor of Psychiatry of the Elderly, Princess Alexandra Hospital, Hamstel Road, Harlow, Essex CM20 1QX, UK

Cornelius Kelly, Senior Registrar, Academic Unit of Psychiatry, St Charles Hospital, Exmoor Street, London.W10 6DZ, UK

Hans Lauter, Psychiatrische Klinik und Poliklinik der Technischen Universitat Munchen, Klinikum Rechts der Isar, Ismaninger Strasse 22, 8000 Munchen 80, Germany

J. M. Léger, Professor of Psychogeriatry, President of the French Language Psychogeriatric Society, Service Hospitalo-Universitaire de Psychiatrie, 15 Rue du Docteur Marcland, 87025 Limoges, Cedex, France

Raymond Levy, Professor of Old Age Psychiatry, Institute of Psychiatry, De Crespigny Park, London SE5 8AF, UK

Philip Lucas, Research Worker, Department of Psychological Medicine, King's College Hospital and the Institute of Psychiatry, Maudsley Hospital, Denmark Hill, London SE5 8AZ, UK

A. Marneros, Psychiatric Hospital of the University of Bonn, D-5300 Bonn, Germany

P. Pichot, Professor, 24 Rue des Fossés-Saint-Jacques, F-75005 Paris, France

Felix Post, 7 Leeward Gardens, London SW19 7QR and Emeritus Physician, The Bethlem Royal Hospital and the Maudsley Hospital, London

Jarl Risberg, Professor of Neuropsychology, Department of Psychogeriatrics, University Hospital, PO Box 638, S-22009, Lund, Sweden

A. Rohde, Psychiatric Hospital of the University of Bonn, D-5300 Bonn, Germany

Sir Martin Roth, Emeritus Professor of Psychiatry, Trinity College, Cambridge

G. Stadtmüller, Section of Old Age Psychiatry, Institute of Psychiatry, De Crespigny Park, Denmark Hill, London SE5 8AF, UK

Jean Wertheimer, Professor of Psychogeriatry, Psychogeriatrics Department of Lausanne University, Prilly Hospital, CH-1008 Prilly, Lausanne, Switzerland

Ken Woodhouse, Professor of Geriatric Medicine, University of Wales College of Medicine, Cardiff Royal Infirmary (West Wing), Newport Road, Cardiff CF2 1SZ

Introduction

CORNELIUS KATONA and RAYMOND LEVY

The cardinal features of psychosis – hallucinations and delusions – are commonly seen in a variety of psychiatric conditions in the elderly. It may therefore come as something of a surprise that they have not received the attention they deserve in contemporary European psychiatry. This was not always the case. During the 19th and early 20th century, many of the writings of the great figures of the period were taken up with the phenomenology, significance and possible mechanisms underlying these fascinating symptoms. At a time when psychiatry and its allied disciplines, and indeed the lay press, are placing so much emphasis on the exciting developments in the neurobiology of Alzheimer's disease, it behoves us to remember that Alzheimer's first case had delusions and hallucinations as well as problems of memory and orientation. More recently the 'cognitive paradigm' (Berrios, 1990) has reigned supreme in the realm of the dementias to the exclusion of other equally important symptoms. A parallel development has been seen in the area of depression where the 'affective paradigm' has made a successful takeover bid. These trends and the previous decline of interest in the paranoid psychoses of the elderly are beginning to show signs of modification. The realisation that it is the behaviour and not the cognitive component of the dementia which brings the patient to attention and that this is often linked to delusional ideation and to hallucinations has played a part in the change in perception. The development of newer techniques of neuroimaging, by opening up opportunities for the elucidation of underlying brain mechanisms, may also have made an important contribution to this change. In spite of this realignment, there remains a paucity of publications concerning these phenomena and we know of no recent book which attempts to bring together clinical descriptions, speculations and new research findings which are sometimes scattered in a wide diversity of journals.

The contributions which have been included in this volume were all presented in the course of a joint meeting of the European Association of Geriatric Psychiatry (EAG) and the Section for the Psychiatry of Old Age of the Royal College of Psychiatrists held in London. They reflect a wide range of approaches from contributors in seven European countries. We are delighted that Gaskell agreed to publish what is the first contribution from Old Age Psychiatry to its much sought after series and we hope that its symbolic appearance in 1992 will prove to be a fitting representation of our commitment to the European idea.

Finally we wish to thank Janssen Germany and the EAG for their financial contributions towards the cost of publication, Smith Kline Beecham for their sponsorship of the meeting on which it was based and our respective secretaries, Debbie Harrington and Margaret Derrick, for their patient assistance with the revision of chapters which either had to be retranslated or heavily edited.

Reference

BERRIOS, G. E. (1990) Memory and the cognitive paradigm of dementia during the 19th century: a conceptual history. In *Lectures on the History of Psychiatry* (eds R. M. Murray & T. A. Turner), pp. 194–211. London: Gaskell.

I. History, concepts and management

1 Psychotic symptoms in the elderly: concepts and models

GERMAN E. BERRIOS

This book will hopefully redress the neglect into which the study of psychotic symptoms in the elderly (particularly in the elderly with cognitive impairment) seems to have fallen in Great Britain (Berrios, 1989a). Until a few years ago, the 'cognitive paradigm' reigned supreme (Berrios, 1990a), and few researchers in Britain worried about the 'psychiatric', let alone 'psychotic' symptoms of dementia. In this chapter, the latter will be interpreted as meaning delusions and hallucinations, as other phenomena classifiable under this rubric (e.g. catatonia) are uncommon in the over-65s. It is believed that these two symptoms, whether or not in the presence of cognitive impairment, occur in the elderly at rates higher than expected (Ballinger et al, 1982; Burns et al, 1990; Cooper et al, 1991), and also that they may be more common (or at least more commonly reported) in women (Musalek et al, 1989; Berrios, 1990b). Whether or not these beliefs are based on fact is discussed by others in this book; this chapter focuses on concepts and models of delusions and hallucinations, particularly in the context of old age. Delusions are here defined as speech acts, unwarranted in logic and/or in reality, purporting to carry information about the world or the self (Berrios, 1991a), and hallucinations as verbal reports of 'sensory' experiences, with or without insight, not vouchsafed by a relevant stimulus (Berrios, 1985).

Delusions and hallucinations are often encountered in general psychiatric practice, and the issue of whether they are always pathological remains a recurrent nightmare for theoreticians. Literature on their nature and clinical meaning continues to grow at great pace; much selectivity has, therefore, been needed to write this chapter; not surprisingly, this has been governed by my ideas, and results of my own clinical research.

Two general hypotheses can be put forward to explain the putative increased prevalence of delusions and hallucinations in the elderly: one being that old people suffer more often from diseases which, at any age, would be accompanied by an increased incidence of such symptoms; the other that the CNS changes caused by ageing make the over-65s – irrespective of diagnosis – more prone to experiencing delusions and hallucinations (Pfersdorff, 1943; Pearlson *et al*, 1989). To be tested, these hypotheses need supplementary information on mechanisms. Those pertaining to delusions will be dealt with first.

Delusions in general

Delusions have been variously explained in organic (Mourgue, 1932; Arthur, 1964; Cummings, 1985), psychodynamic (Faure, 1971), and cognitive terms (Winters & Neale, 1983; Oltmanns & Maher, 1988), but only the first type of explanation is touched upon here. Currently, the clinical event in which identifiable brain changes seem to be causally related to delusions is dubbed 'organic delusional syndrome' (ODS) in DSM–III–R (American Psychiatric Association, 1987). The usefulness of this category is yet to be demonstrated, particularly in the elderly where functional and organic psychoses often coincide. As against a definitional injunction in DSM–III–R some authors have gone as far as diagnosing ODS in the presence of cognitive impairment and confusion or impaired sensorium (Cornelius *et al*, 1991); others have suggested that late paraphrenia may be a form of ODS (Miller *et al*, 1986).

The 19th century inherited the view that delusions were the hallmark of insanity (Berrios, 1991*a*). Thus, when after the 1840s the anatomo-clinical model of disease gained favour (Ackerknecht, 1967), it was assumed that insanity and delusions had to result from the same brain pathology (Ball & Ritti, 1881). After the 1860s, it was further assumed that delusions were linked to lesions in the 'thinking' areas of the brain, which by consensus were sited in the frontal lobes (Dening & Berrios, 1991). With the ascent of physiological concepts during the second half of the 19th century (López Piñero, 1983), explanations more detailed than the mere mentioning of anatomical loci were demanded. By the 1880s, two mechanisms were suggested: on the one hand, Tamburini (1990) proposed that seizural activation of engrammes might lead to mental contents being experienced with conviction (i.e. without insight) (Berrios, 1990*c*); on the other, Jackson (1894) saw delusions as resulting from the activation (and entry into consciousness) of thoughts normally kept dormant (or inhibited) in the nether levels of the CNS (Berrios, 1985*b*).

Modern versions of the Jacksonian model conceive of delusions as 'positive' symptoms generated in the temporal lobes (Berrios, 1991*b*). Since a similar model has been suggested for hallucinations, it is unclear what structures are differentially responsible for each symptom. Evidence linking delusions to the temporal lobe is based on a few significant correlations, for example, that short-lived delusional ideas may episodically occur in temporal lobe dysfunction (Tucker *et al*, 1986). Changing views on brain lateralisation have played a role in this view: thus, during the 1970s, attempts were made to link schizophrenia-like states to the dominant hemisphere (Trimble, 1984; Berrios, 1989*b*). Contradictory claims have also been marshalled, for example that by Peroutka *et al* (1982) that strokes affecting the non-dominant temporal lobe may lead to delusional experiences; more recently, Cutting (1990) has made a good case for a link between delusions (and the misidentification syndromes) and the non-dominant hemisphere. Finally, experiences held with conviction may also be evoked by cortical and subcortical stimulation to either side of the brain during neurosurgery for epilepsy (Halgren *et al*, 1978; Gloor *et al*, 1982). Recently, others have suggested that the frontal lobes may be a more plausible site for the generation of delusions (Benson & Stuss, 1990).

Delusions in the elderly

With regard to the increased presence of delusions in the elderly, three issues seem important. One concerns the epidemiological foundations of such a claim which seems based on a rich but nonetheless anecdotal historical database (Cabaleiro Goás, 1955; Cordeiro, 1970, 1972, 1973), and on more modern hospital-based case series (Liston, 1979; Ballinger *et al*, 1982; Berrios & Brook, 1985; Reisberg *et al*, 1986; Cummings *et al*, 1987; Merriam *et al*, 1988; Drevets & Rubin, 1989; Burns *et al*, 1990; Cooper *et al*, 1991), indeed, the fact has not yet been confirmed in community studies.

A second issue concerns the lack of information regarding the types of delusions involved, e.g. bizarre versus non-bizarre (Flaum *et al*, 1991) or primary versus secondary (Jaspers, 1963; Spitzer, 1990): in this regard, some studies do not even provide separate figures for delusions and hallucinations, let alone specify subtypes for the former (Cunha *et al*, 1985). However, the interesting problem arises here as to whether the traditional primary–secondary dichotomy still holds in the case of the deluded elderly. When made on independent phenomenological grounds this distinction is believed to have some diagnostic significance (Sims, 1988, p. 84); in practice, however, it requires the patient to have good powers of introspection and an intact cognition, because the 'primary perception' is often fleeting and unmemorable (Berrios, 1991*a*). A common clinical manoeuvre, therefore, has been to deduce type from diagnosis: for example, delusions seen in the context of what is believed to be (on different clinical grounds) a schizophrenic illness will be considered as 'primary', while those accompanying mania, involutional melancholia (Sims, 1988) or 'organic' states, are secondary (Cummings, 1985). But it is clear that using criteria other than those internal to the symptom itself biases the resulting decision and creates a question-begging loop. In the elderly with cognitive impairment, typing of delusions is harder to do, for the subject is likely to be suffering from brain disease, and hence it should conventionally be concluded that his/her delusions are secondary. The third issue relates to the relationship between cognitive impairment and delusions. In this regard it has been claimed that an adequate level of cognition may be relevant to both the appearance and maintenance of this symptom (Berrios & Brook, 1985); others have reported an increase in delusions as the illness worsens (Drevets & Rubin, 1989). In the elderly without cognitive impairment, delusions are found alone or combined with other mental symptoms; in either case, sensory deficits and a particular type of premorbid personality are said to play a role. Cases without affective or thought disorder, and where sensory deficits do not seem to play an important role, have a prevalence of about 8% and have been variously classed as late paraphrenia, paranoia, persecutory states, late onset schizophrenia, etc. (Post, 1966). No consistent causal factor seems to have been found for this group: even the role of sensory deficits remains unclear (Moore, 1981), although since Kraepelin (Cooper *et al*, 1974; Soni, 1988) it has been believed that, for example, deafness leads to delusions; the same doubts have been expressed with regard to the role of the 'hypersensitive' (Kretschmer, 1918; Rasmussen, 1978) or 'paranoid' personality (Schweighofer, 1982).

Delusions in the elderly can also be found constituting established diagnostic categories such as major (psychotic) depression, mania, and dementia. In this regard, and more for historical than clinical or neuro-biological reasons, specific delusional themes have been singled out for attention: e.g. Cotard's syndrome (Cotard, 1891), the misidentification states (MacCallum, 1984; Christodoulou, 1986), the solitary companion phenomenon (O'Mahoney *et al*, 1984; Léger *et al*, 1986), delusions of double mourning (Herrmann & Grek, 1988), the phantom boarders syndrome (Rowan, 1984), and symbiotic psychosis (Maier, 1985).

Significant correlations between delusions and social, iatrogenic, personality, psychodynamic, sex, age, general disease (Kivela *et al*, 1989), and organic (Miller *et al*, 1986) variables are often found and not surprisingly enshrined as risk factors. Thus, loneliness, multiple-drug therapy, being female, single or widowed, and living alone, having sexual adjustment difficulties earlier in life, etc. have all been considered as relevant (Berger & Zarif, 1978). Of these, however, organic factors seem to be the most important. An excess of brain tumours – particularly meningioma, glioma, and pituitary masses – has been noticed in elderly psychotics and depressives (Galasko *et al*, 1988), and late-life paraphrenia and delusional parasitosis, particularly in males, are reported as often being accompanied by organic disorder (Berrios, 1985c). With regard to biological markers, deluded subjects have been reported to have larger lateral cerebral ventricles and greater cognitive deficits (Naguib & Levy, 1987); on the other hand, an inverse relationship between cortical atrophy and paranoid delusions has also been reported (Jacoby & Levy, 1980). Kupfer *et al* (1989), in turn, have found it difficult to differentiate deluded elderly depressives from controls on the basis of sleep EEG. Delusions themselves have been found to be correlated with poor outcome and exposure to multiple medication (Wood *et al*, 1988); in this regard, a likely explanation is that the relevant delusions belonged to an organic delirium, and that the prediction of bad outcome was related to the latter.

Hallucinations in general

Based on the fact that no firm experimental evidence has yet become available that subjects reporting having a hallucination are necessarily experiencing or reading-off a percept, the existence of the symptom has occasionally been called into question, and the suggestion made that it may often be a form of 'sensory delusion' (Ey, 1973). This view is particularly applicable to 'true' or 'psychiatric' hallucinations, where the reported features of the 'percept' seem to violate the rules of perception (as, for example, in unilateral, extracampine or composite hallucinations). 'Organic' hallucinations, such as those accompanying delirium tremens or drug intoxication, i.e. what has been called for decades organic 'hallucinosis' in the Continental literature (Morsier, 1938; Berrios, 1985*a*) (and recently adopted by DSM–III–R) seem, on the other hand, a different phenomenon. Such hallucinations can be experimentally induced (Siegel & Jarvik, 1975) and have, since the last century, been related to dreaming breaking into consciousness (Lasègue, 1971 (first published 1881)).

Just as in the case of delusions, some hallucinations such as the so-called Lilliputian, peduncular, functional, extracampine, heautoscopic, negative, verbal, and unilateral hallucinations (Berrios, 1985*a*) have been singled out as separate types in terms of their phenomenological features; this has rarely led to the identification of a firm clinical predictor.

On account of the fact that organic mechanisms are often in operation in the elderly, the distinction between psychiatric and organic hallucinosis becomes less clear-cut. The type of hallucinations often seen in this age group also leads to another clinical problem, namely, that of separating hallucinations occurring in sense modalities related to public (vision and audition) and private stimuli (touch and propioception), for example, that of differentiating between a real and a hallucinated itch. This is particularly problematic when cognitive impairment is present.

Hallucinations in the elderly

Hallucinations in the elderly involve all sense modalities, and remain a cause of concern among caregivers (Haley *et al*, 1987). Prevalence figures, once again based on hospital samples, range from 15 % (Eastwood & Corbin, 1983) to 30 % (Berrios & Brook, 1984). The differential strength of risk factors such as age, premorbid personality, sensory deficits, and sex remains unclear. However, a recent study suggests that visual hallucinations increase with age (Anonymous, 1990). With regard to premorbid personality, Eastwood & Corbin (1983) reported that hallucinators tended to be single, to have been living alone before admission, and have an 'independent' or 'reclusive' personality. Other reports suggest that sensory deficits (Slade, 1976) and being female (Berrios, 1990*b*) increase the risk of hallucinations.

Conventional classifications of hallucinations by sense modality, disease, presence of insight, and/or accompanying symptoms may be less adequate in the elderly for, as mentioned above, a shift has taken place in this age group towards the organic end of the causal continuum. In order to construct a proper database in this area, it would seem advisable simply to describe the hallucination and its context. The latter may range from states of apparent cerebral normality, in which case clinicians have been given to call it Charles Bonnet syndrome, to those where there is clear brain pathology. With regard to the Charles Bonnet syndrome (Berrios & Brook, 1982; Podoll *et al*, 1989) much confusion remains; for example, recent American work suggests that some believe that sensory deprivation is the essence of this phenomenon, so that an apparently 'normal' elderly subject who hallucinates but has no eye-sight troubles is denied the appellative (Schenck, 1990). The issue remains, however, whether visual impairment alone is a sufficient and necessary cause for hallucinations in subjects otherwise showing no evidence of neurological or psychiatric disease: the main problem with this view is that declarations of normality, based on the sensitivity of current instruments, are notoriously unreliable; yet another problem is the discrepancy between the high frequency of peripheral visual defect in the elderly and the rarity of the Charles Bonnet phenomenon. It is likely, therefore, that a second, central factor is in operation; what this factor may be is conjectural, and may range from some unknown genetic tendency to hallucinate – coded, say, by what one could speculate to be a hallucinator's gene – to the more likely presence of (undetected) cerebral pathology.

'Provoked' or drug-induced hallucinations are common in the elderly, as attested by papers reporting toxic hallucinations – both simple and formed – and in all sense modalities (Brown *et al*, 1980; Sonnenblick *et al*, 1982; Gardner & Hall, 1982; Chinisci, 1985). It is in the nature of anecdotal clinical reporting that these studies are uncontrolled and hence suggest little in the way of risk factors. For example, is the triggering of hallucinations dose-related? What are the relevant host variables? etc.

Yet a third dichotomous group of hallucinations concerns those found either as a single symptom, as in delusional parasitosis (Berrios, 1982; 1985*c*; Bourgeois *et al*, 1986) or the hallucinations of widowhood (Olson *et al*, 1985) or as one among many other symptoms (as in Alzheimer's disease). With regard to the latter, it is not widely known that the first 'case' exhibited auditory hallucinations (Berrios & Freeman, 1991). Recent interest in the 'psychiatric aspects' of Alzheimer's disease (Wragg & Jeste, 1989) has led to a string of papers, some suggesting that senile dementia of the Lewy body type (SDLT) is more often accompanied by visual hallucinations than Alzheimer's disease (Perry *et al*, 1990*a*), and that reduction in cortical choline acetyltransferase is more marked among hallucinators (Perry *et al*, 1990*b*). This finding ties in well with what is known of the role of acetylcholine in the control of rapid eye movement (REM) activity and dreaming.

Finally, the issue of causal models must be dealt with. Hallucinations in the elderly are likely to be multidetermined. Current explanations are of two types: those originated in experimental psychology (Bentall, 1990) and neurobiology, albeit attractive, are articulated at a high level of generality, and hence are not readily applicable to the individual case; explanations originated in clinical psychiatry tend to be anecdotal and mostly based on casual correlations. There are various reasons for this divorce between the theoretical and clinical approach: firstly, since the 19th century, no real improvement has taken place in the quality of the concepts marshalled to examine hallucinatory phenomena (Mourgue, 1932; Paulus, 1941; Berrios, 1982); secondly, the major advances made on the experimental psychology (Slade & Bentall, 1988) and neurobiology of perception have only been partially tried in the field of hallucinations (indeed, a great specialist in the physiology of perception once told me that hallucinations had little to do with his field of inquiry!); and thirdly, the type of statistical analysis used in most psychiatric studies does not allow one to draw any causal connections. Finally even the putative relevance to diagnosis of sensory modality and/or theme (e.g. is it necessary to separate hallucinations from pseudohallucinations?) has been called into question (Lowe, 1973).

Strangely, most explanatory models seem to apply to the elderly with hallucinations. This is, for example, the case with the views put forward by Jackson (Marrazzi, 1962; West, 1962) according to which the release of 'lower' centres and consequent 'experiencing' of hallucinations might be due to a loss of inhibition; and also with the deafferentation model suggested by Fischer (1969) (Fischer *et al*, 1970) and based on the view that hallucinations result from a loss of balance between sensory/sensory or sensory/motor inputs: in this regard, the elderly present the best examples of cases where there is a decline in both sensory input (caused by deficits in the windows of perception) and motor activity (caused by physical disabilities). Equally applicable to the elderly is the model according to which hallucinations result from mechanical and/or electrical irritation of relevant brain sites (Tamburini, 1990; Miller *et al*, 1987); indeed, there is some evidence that strokes, tumours, and epileptic foci play a role in this regard (Berrios, 1990*b*).

Conclusions

With regard to the putative increased incidence of delusions and hallucinations in the elderly, the conclusions outlined below can be made.

(a)   There seems to be an increased incidence and prevalence of delusions and hallucinations, regardless of whether cognitive impairment is present; the effect may be more marked in women.

(b)   Apart from a few series, the literature in this field remains anecdotal and hence insufficient to solve problems pertaining to mechanisms.

(c)   No concepts specially tailored for the elderly are available; so far, those developed in younger age groups have been extrapolated. This may lead to a biased understanding.

(d)   Delusions and hallucinations in the elderly share a number of clinical and neurobiological markers.

(e)   Two grand hypotheses are available to explain their high frequency in the elderly. One says that delusions and hallucinations are disease-related, the other that they are ageing-related. It is likely that both are contributory factors.

(f)   Models developed to explain delusions and hallucinations in the young seem to apply to the elderly; these include the mechanisms of release, deafferentation, loss of balance between sensory and motor inputs, and irritation.

(g)   Organic models seem particularly relevant to the elderly. Of late there has been, once again, a return to the frontal lobes, particularly in relation to delusions. It is unlikely that this is due to a genuine accumulation of data but to the fact that frontal lobes are back in fashion, as attested by similar claims made in clinical fields such as dementia, schizophrenia and obsessive–compulsive disorder.

References

ACKERKNECHT, E. H. (1967) *Medicine at the Paris Hospital 1794–1848*. Baltimore: Johns Hopkins Press.

ANONYMOUS (1990) Psychiatrische Symptomatologie en Leeftijdsafhankelijkheid. Een preliminaire A.M.D.P. IV Studie Bij 140 Psychogeriatrische Patienten. *Acta Neuropsychiatrica*, **3**, 55–60.

AMERICAN PSYCHIATRIC ASSOCIATION (1987) *Diagnostic and Statistical Manual of Mental Disorders* (3rd edn, revised) (DSM–III–R). Washington DC: APA.

ARTHUR, A. Z. (1964) Theories and explanations of delusions: a review. *American Journal of Psychiatry*, **121**, 105–115.

BALL, B. & RITTI, A. (1881) Délire. In *Dictionnaire Encyclopédique des Sciences Médicales* (eds A. Dechambre & L. Lereboullet), pp. 315–343. Paris: Masson, Asselin et Houzeau.

BALLINGER, B. R., REID, A. H. & HEATHER, B. B. (1982) Cluster analysis of symptoms in elderly demented patients. *British Journal of Psychiatry*, **140**, 257–262.

BENSON, D. F. & STUSS, D. T. (1990) Frontal lobe influences on delusions: a clinical perspective. *Schizophrenia Bulletin*, **16**, 403–411.

BENTALL, R. P. (1990) The illusion of reality: a review and integration of psychological research on hallucinations. *Psychological Bulletin*, **107**, 82–95.

BERGER, K. S. & ZARIT, S. H. (1978) Late life paranoid states: assessment and treatment. *American Journal of Orthopsychiatry*, **48**, 528–537.

BERRIOS, G. E. (1982) Tactile hallucinations: conceptual and historical aspects. *Journal of Neurology, Neurosurgery, and Psychiatry*, **45**, T285–293.

—— (1985a) Hallucinosis. In *Handbook of Clinical Neurology, Vol 2 (46): Neurobehavioural Disorders* (ed. J. A. M. Fredericks), pp. 561–572. Amsterdam: Elsevier.

—— (1985b) Positive and negative symptoms and Jackson. *Archives of General Psychiatry*, **42**, 95–97.

—— (1985c) Delusional parasitosis and physical disease. *Comprehensive Psychiatry*, **26**, 395–403.

—— (1989a) Non-cognitive symptoms and the diagnosis of dementia. Historial and clinical aspects. *British Journal of Psychiatry*, **154** (suppl. 4), 11–16.

—— (1989b) Epilepsia y Psiquiatría: aspectos generales y su relación con la depresión. *Revista de Psiquiatría Facultad de Medicina Barna*, **16**, 35–43.

—— (1990a) Memory and the cognitive paradigm of dementia during the 19th century: a conceptual history. In *Lectures on the History of Psychiatry* (eds R. M. Murray & T. A. Turner), pp. 194–211. London: Gaskell.

—— (1990b) Musical hallucination. A historical and clinical study. *British Journal of Psychiatry*, **156**, 188–194.

—— (1990c) A theory of hallucinations. *History of Psychiatry*, **1**, 145–150.

—— (1991a) Delusions as "wrong beliefs": a conceptual history. *British Journal of Psychiatry*, **159** (suppl. 14), 6–13.

—— (1991b) French views on positive and negative symptoms: a conceptual history. *Comprehensive Psychiatry*, **32**, 395–403.

—— & BROOK, P. (1982) The Charles Bonnet syndrome and the problem of visual perceptual disorders in the elderly. *Age and Ageing*, **11**, 17–23.

—— & —— (1984) Visual hallucinations and sensory delusions in the elderly. *British Journal of Psychiatry*, **144**, 662–664.

—— & —— (1985) Delusions and psychopathology of the elderly with dementia. *Acta Psychiatrica Scandinavica*, **72**, 296–301.

—— & FREEMAN, H. L. (eds) (1991) *Alzheimer and the Dementias*. London: Royal Society of Medicine.

BOURGEOIS, M., RAGER, P., PEYRE, F., *et al* (1986) Frequence et aspects du syndrome d'Ekbom enquête auprés des dermatologues franais. *Annales Médico-Psychologiques*, **144**, 659–668.

BROWN, M. J., SALMON, D. & RENDELL, M. (1980) Clonidine hallucinations. *Annals of Internal Medicine*, **93**, 456–457.

BURNS, A., JACOBY, R. & LEVY, R. (1990) Psychiatric phenomena in Alzheimer's disease. 1: Disorders of thought content. *British Journal of Psychiatry*, **157**, 72–76.

CABALEIRO GOÁS, M. (1955) Los síndromes psicóticos de la presenilidad. *Actas Luso-Españolas de Neurología y Psiquiatría*, **14**, 17–26.

CHINISCI, R. A. (1985) Auditory and visual hallucinations as a medication side effect: recognition and management. *Clinical Gerontologist*, **3**, 71–73.

CHRISTODOULOU, G. N. (ed.) (1986) *The Delusional Misidentification Syndromes*. Basel: Karger.

COOPER, A. F., CURRY, A. R., KAY, D. W. K., *et al* (1974) Hearing loss in paranoid and affective psychoses of the elderly. *Lancet*, **ii**, 852–854.

COOPER, J. K., MUNGAS, D., VERMA, M., *et al* (1991) Psychotic symptoms in Alzheimer's disease. *International Journal of Geriatric Psychiatry*, **6**, 721–726.

CORDEIRO, J. D. (1970) Les ideés delirantes de prejudice. *Annales Médico Psychologiques*, **128**, 719–734.

—— (1972) *Les états délirants tardifs*. Geneve: Editions Médicine et Hygiène.

—— (1973) Etats délirants du troisième age. *L'Encephale*, **62**, 20–55.

CORNELIUS, J. K., DAY, N., FABREGA, H. JR., *et al* (1991) Characterizing organic delusional syndrome. *Archives of General Psychiatry*, **48**, 749–753.

COTARD, J. (1891) *Etudes sur les maladies cérébrales et mentales*. Paris: Baillière et fils.

CUMMINGS, J. L. (1985) Organic delusions: phenomenology, anatomical correlations, and review. *British Journal of Psychiatry*, **146**, 184–197.

——, MILLER, B., HILL, M. A., *et al* (1987) Neuropsychiatric aspects of multi-infarct dementia and dementia of the Alzheimer type. *Archives of Neurology*, **44**, 389–393.

CUNHA, V. G., BARROS, O. & SIQUEIRA, A. L. (1985) Levantamento epidemiológico psicogeriátrico em Asilos. *Jornal Brasileiro de Psiquiatria*, **34**, 389–394.

CUTTING, J. (1990) *The Right Cerebral Hemisphere and Psychiatric Disorders*. Oxford: Oxford University Press.

DENING, T. R. & BERRIOS, G. E. (1991) The vascular dementias. In *Alzheimer and the Dementias* (eds G. E. Berrios & H. L. Freeman), pp. 69–76. London: Royal Society of Medicine.

DREVETS, W. C. & RUBIN, E. H. (1989) Psychotic symptoms and the longitudinal course of senile dementia of the Alzheimer type. *Biological Psychiatry*, **25**, 39–48.

EASTWOOD, M. R. & CORBIN, S. (1983) Hallucinations in patients admitted to a geriatric psychiatry service: review of 42 cases. *Journal of the American Geriatrics Society*, **31**, 593–597.

EY, H. (1973) *Traité des Hallucinations, 2 Vols*. Paris: Masson.

FLAUM, M., ARNDT, S. & ANDREASEN, N. C. (1991) The reliability of "bizarre" delusions. *Comprehensive Psychiatry*, **32**, 59–65.

FAURE, H. (1971) *Les Appartenances du Délirant*. Paris: Presses Universitaires de France.

FISCHER, R. (1969) The perception–hallucination continuum. *Diseases of the Nervous System*, **30**, 161–171.

——, KAPPELER, T., WISECUP, P., *et al* (1970) Personality trait dependent performance under psilocybin. *Diseases of the Nervous System*, **31**, 91–101.

GALASKO, D., KWO ON YUEN, P. F. & THAL, L. (1988) Intracranial mass lesions associated with late onset psychosis and depression. *Psychiatric Clinics of North America*, **11**, 151–166.

GARDNER, E. R. & HALL, R. C. W. (1982) Psychiatric symptoms produced by over the counter drugs. *Psychosomatics*, **23**, 186–190.

GLOOR, P., OLIVIER, A., QUESNEY, L. F., *et al* (1982) The role of the limbic system in experiential phenomena of temporal lobe epilepsy. *Annals of Neurology*, **12**, 129–144.

HALEY, W. E., BROWN, S. L. & LEVINE, E. G. (1987) Family caregiver appraisals of patient behavioral disturbance in senile dementia. *Clinical Gerontologist*, **6**, 25–34.

HALGREN, E., WALTER, R. D., CHERLOW, D. G., *et al* (1978) Mental phenomena evoked by electrical stimulation of the human hippocampal formation and amygdala. *Brain*, **101**, 83–117.

HERRMANN, N. & GREK, A. (1988) Delusional double mourning: a complication of bereavement in dementia. *Canadian Journal of Psychiatry*, **33**, 851–852.

JACKSON, H. (1894) The factors of insanities. *Medical Press and Circular*, **ii**, 615–625.

JACOBY, R. J. & LEVY, R. (1980) Computed tomography in the elderly: II. Senile dementia: diagnosis and functional impairment. *British Journal of Psychiatry*, **136**, 256–269.

JASPERS, K. (1963) *General Psychopathology* (Translated by J. Hoenig and M. W. Hamilton). Manchester: Manchester University Press.

KIVELA, S. L. & PAHKALA, K. (1989) Delusional depression in the elderly: a community study. *Zeitschrift für Gerontology*, **22**, 236–241.

KUPFER, D. J., REYNOLDS, C. F. & EHLERS, C. L. (1989) Comparison of EEG sleep measures among depressive subtypes and controls in older individuals. *Psychiatry Research*, **27**, 13–21.

KRETSCHMER, E. (1818) *Der sensitive Beziehungswahn*. Berlin: Springer.

LASÈGUE, C. (1971) *Ecrits psychiatriques*. Toulouse: Privat.

LÈGER, J. M., GAROUX, R., TESSIER, J. F., *et al* (1986) Le compagnon tardif et l'objet non animé du sujet dément sénile. *Annales Médico-Psychologiques*, **144**, 341–355.

LISTON, E. H. (1979) The clinical phenomenology of presenile dementia. *Journal of Nervous and Mental Disease*, **167**, 329–336.

LÓPEZ PINERO, J. M. (1983) *Historical Origins of the Concept of Neurosis*. (Translated by D. Berrios). Cambridge: Cambridge University Press.

LOWE, G. R. (1973) The phenomenology of hallucinations as an aid to differential diagnosis. *British Journal of Psychiatry*, **123**, 621–633.

MACCALLUM, W. A. (1984) A syndrome of misinterpreting role changes as changes of person. *British Journal of Psychiatry*, **144**, 649–650.

MAIER, CH. (1985) Ein bemerkenswerter Fall von symbiontischer Psychose. *Psychiatrische Praxis*, **12**, 200–202.

MARRAZZI, A. S. (1962) Pharmacodynamics of Hallucination. In *Hallucinations*, (ed. L. J. West), pp. 36–49. New York: Grune & Stratton.

MERRIAM, A. E., ARONSON, M. K., GASTON, P., *et al* (1988) The psychiatric symptoms of Alzheimer's disease. *Journal of the American Geriatrics Society*, **36**, 7–12.

MILLER, B. L., BENSON, D. F., CUMMINGS, J. L., *et al* (1986) Late life paraphrenia: an organic delusional syndrome. *Journal of Clinical Psychiatry*, **47**, 204-207.
MILLER, F., MAGEE, J. & JACOBS, R. (1987) Formed visual hallucinations in an elderly patient. *Hospital and Community Psychiatry*, **38**, 527-529.
MORSIER DE, G. (1938) Les hallucinations. *Revue d'Oto-Neuro-Ophthalmologie*, **16**, 244-352.
MOORE, N. C. (1981) Is paranoid illness associated with sensory defects in the elderly? *Journal of Psychosomatic Research*, **25**, 69-74.
MOURGUE, R. (1932) *Neurobiologie de L'hallucination*. Bruxelles: Maurice Lamertin.
MUSALEK, M., BERNER, P. & KATSCHNIG, H. (1989) Delusional theme, sex and age. *Psychopathology*, **22**, 260-267.
NAGUIB, M. & LEVY, R. (1987) Late paraphrenia: neuropsychological impairment and structural brain abnormalities on computed tomography. *International Journal of Geriatric Psychiatry*, **2**, 83-90.
O'MAHONEY, M., SHULMAN, K. & SILVER, D. (1984) Roses in December: imaginary companions in the elderly. *Canadian Journal of Psychiatry*, **29**, 151-159.
OLSON, P.R., SUDDETH, J. A., PETERSON, P. J., *et al* (1985) Hallucinations of widowhood. *Journal of the American Geriatrics Society*, **33**, 543-547.
OLTMANNS, T. F. & MAHER, B. A. (eds) (1988) *Delusional Beliefs*. New York: Wiley.
PAULUS, J. (1941) *Le problème de l'hallucination et l'évolution de la psychologie: d'Esquirol à Pierre Janet*. Bibliothèque de la Faculté de Philosophie et Letters de l'Université de Liège XCI. Paris: Les Belles Lettres.
PEROUTKA, S. J., SOHMER, B. H., KUMER, A. J., *et al* (1982) Hallucinations and delusions following a right temporoparieto-occipital infarction. *Johns Hopkins Medical Journal*, **151**, 181-185.
PEARLSON, G. D., KREGER, L., RABINS, P. V., *et al* (1989) A chart review study of late onset and early onset schizophrenia. *American Journal of Psychiatry*, **146**, 1568-1574.
PERRY, R. H., IRVING, D., BLESSED, G., *et al* (1990a) Senile dementia of Lewy body type. A clinically and neuropathologically distinct form of Lewy body dementia in the elderly. *Journal of Neurological Sciences*, **95**, 119-139.
PERRY, E. K., MARSHALL, E., PERRY, R. H., *et al* (1990b) Cholinergic and dopaminergic activities in senile dementia of Lewy body type. *Alzheimer Disease Association Disorders Journal*, **4**, 87-95.
PFERSDORFF, C. (1943) L'influence de l'age sur la symptomatologie des psychoses. *Annales Médico-Psychologiques*, **101**, 248-258.
PODOLL, K., OSTERHEIDER, M. & NOTH, J. (1989) Das Charles Bonnet Syndrom. *Fortschritte Neurologie und Psychiatrie*, **57**, 43-60.
POST, F. (1966) *Persistent Persecutory States of the Elderly*. Oxford: Pergamon Press.
RASMUSSEN, S. (1978) Sensitive delusion of reference, 'sensitiver Beziehungswahn'. *Acta Psychiatrica Scandinavica*, **58**, 442-448.
REISBERG, B., BORENSTEIN, J., FRANSSEM, E., *et al* (1986) Remediable behavioural symptomatology in Alzheimer's disease. *Hospital and Community Psychiatry*, **37**, 1199-1201.
ROWAN, E. L. (1984) Phantom boarders as a symptom of late paraphrenia. *American Journal of Psychiatry*, **141**, 580-581.
SCHENCK, J. M. (1990) Visual hallucinations as grief reaction without the Charles Bonnet syndrome. *New York State Journal of Medicine*, **90**, 216-217.
SCHWEIGHOFER, F. (1982) Der Fall Schreber. *Psychotherapie Psychosomatische Medizine Psychologie*, **32**, 4-8.
SIEGEL, R. K. & JARVIK, M. E. (1975) Drug-induced hallucinations in animals and man. In *Hallucinations* (eds R. K. Siegel & L. J. West), pp. 81-162. New York: Wiley & Sons.
SIMS, A. (1988) *Symptoms in the Mind*. London: Baillière Tindal.
SLADE, P. (1976) Hallucinations. *Psychological Medicine*, **6**, 7-13.
—— & BENTALL, R. P. (1988) *Sensory Deception*. London: Croom Helm.
SONI, S. D. (1988) Relationship between peripheral sensory disturbance and onset of symptoms in elderly paraphrenics. *International Journal of Geriatric Psychiatry*, **3**, 275-279.
SONNENBLICK, M., WEISSBERG, N. & ROSIN, A. J. (1982) Neurological psychiatric side effects of cimetidine. Report of 3 cases with review of the literature. *Postgraduate Medical Journal*, **58**, 415-418.

SPITZER, M. (1990) On defining illusions. *Comprehensive Psychiatry*, **31**, 377–397.
TAMBURINI, A. (1990) A theory of hallucinations. *History of Psychiatry*, **1**, 145–156.
TRIMBLE, M. (1984) Interictal psychoses of epilepsy. *Acta Psychiatrica Scandinavica*, **69** (suppl. 313), 9–20.
TUCKER, G. J., PRICE, T. R. P., JOHNSON, V. B., *et al* (1986) Phenomenology of temporal lobe dysfunction: a link to atypical psychosis. A series of cases. *Journal of Nervous and Mental Disease*, **174**, 348–356.
WEST, L. J. (1962) *Hallucinations*. New York: Grune & Stratton.
WINTERS, K. C. & NEALE, J. M. (1983) Delusions and delusional thinking in psychotics: a review of the literature. *Clinical Psychology Review*, **3**, 227–253.
WOOD, K. A., HARRIS, M. J., MORREALE, A., *et al* (1988) Drug-induced psychosis and depression in the elderly. *Psychiatric Clinics of North America*, **11**, 167–193.
WRAGG, R. R. & JESTE, P.V. (1989) Overview of depression and psychosis in Alzheimer's disease. *American Journal of Psychiatry*, **146**, 577–587.

2 History of the concepts of functional disorders in the elderly

P. PICHOT

Before surveying the history of the concepts of functional disorders in the elderly, some preliminary considerations seem necessary. The functional disorders will be restricted to the pathological entities:

(a) whose symptoms are of a nature and/or an intensity which can be described as psychotic in the present classifications such as the DSM-III-R or the ICD-10
(b) which do not belong to the organic mental syndromes and disorders.

The term elderly has no uniform definition. Since the 19th century it has been customary to describe two periods. The first is variously named 'decline of life' (Maudsley), 'presenium' or 'period of involution'. Its beginning is marked in women by the menopause (climacterium) and the age of 45 is commonly mentioned. In men, the concept and the limit are more vague. The second is true old age, the senium, the *Greisesalter* in German or the *vieillesse* in French, now often named 'the third age' beginning at 65, or at 60 for some authors. The terminology varies. Some German psychiatrists have used *Umbildungsalter* (age of transformation) instead of *Involutionsalter* (age of involution) and *Rückbildungsalter* (age of regression) instead of *Greisesalter* (senium). Additional subdivisions have been proposed, such as the 'fourth age' beginning at 80. The indistinctness of the limits and the constantly stressed fact that disorders appearing in the period of involution can also appear later, suggest that the whole complex must be included in any study of old-age disorders.

Old-age disorders are of two types: some have had their first manifestations during the young or middle ages, and their evolution, which may be chronic or phasic, has continued into the period considered; others appear in patients, previously mentally normal, after the age of 45. We shall restrict our discussion to the history of the latter disorders. It must however, be recognised that the situation is made less schematic by the constantly

recurring suggestion that the late-appearing disorders may not be autonomous, but belong to the entities manifesting themselves earlier, the eventual
specificity of symptoms and course being attributed to the pathoplastic effect
of age. An additional difficulty in the delimitation of our subject is connected
with the relationships which often exist in the elderly between functional
and organic disorders.

For the sake of clarity, the history of the functional disorders in the elderly
will be divided somewhat arbitrarily into four periods. The first is before 1896;
the second, dominated by the work of Kraepelin, extends from 1896 until about
1919; the third spans the years between the two World Wars; the last
corresponds to the evolution since 1945. During each period the two main
poles of the discussions have been the mood (or affective) disorders on the
one side, and the delusional disorders in the broad meaning of the word
on the other, many points of contact existing between the two categories.

Before 1896

The study of old-age mental disorders begins with Esquirol (1814) who,
clarifying Pinel's classification, defined dementia as an acquired intellectual
deficit, and described, among other types, senile dementia. In his later
works he recognised that, in the elderly, 'functional' disorders could also
be observed, such as "manias occurring even after eighty", which "could
sometimes be cured". Other isolated descriptions can be found in the
following decades, the best known being that of the 'climacteric melancholia'
by Maudsley (1895). Maudsley pointed out the role both of 'physiological
changes' and 'moral causes', the latter being 'sometimes predominant'. He
mentioned that the illness could, despite the name he coined, occur in men
and that it was marked by intense delusional ideas, suicide impulses, 'paroxysms
of excited anguish', hypochondriasis and, in a special clinical form, by
'insane jealousy'. He concluded that the "common but mistaken notion that
these patients did not recover" was false, since "as many as half get well
eventually". In fact, the first general study of the mental disorders in the
elderly, based on 62 cases, was published in Switzerland by Wille (1873).
Under the term 'simple psychotic processes' he described disorders "not
complicated by psychic weakness" which included acute delirium, mania,
melancholia and delusional states of depressive or expansive colouring. He
claimed that they did have the same prognosis as the disorders of an identical
aspect occurring in younger subjects and, although a heightened mortality
could be observed owing to the age of the patients, "they exhibit very
satisfactory healing conditions". A more detailed study with similar conclusions came from Furstner (1889) who described 95 cases observed at the
Heidelberg Clinic, 81 presenting with functional disorders. They were
divided into melancholia (54%), mania (11%), confusional states (*Verworrenheit*)

(13.5%) and 'more or less abortive forms of madness' (*Verrücktheit*), i.e. delusional disorders (8.5%). At the 1895 Congress of French Psychiatrists and Neurologists, 'psychosis of the old age' was the main theme and Ritti (1896) analysed the whole previous literature in a detailed report, which can be considered as the concluding synthesis of the works of the first period. He dealt successively with mania, melancholia, confusional states, delusional states (divided into persecutory and expansive forms). 'instinctive madness' (kleptomania, erotic behaviour, etc.) and 'senile hysteria', its final optimistic viewpoint being that "the prognosis is not unfavourable, the insanity of old people being very often curable".

1896 to 1919

As in other domains of psychiatry, the work of Kraepelin occupies a central place in the history of the mental disorders of the elderly. In the eight successive editions of his *Manual* (the 9th published after his death was written almost entirely by his pupil Lange) he created progressively a nosological system whose broad lines have remained the basis of our present day conceptions. We shall consider only the relevant elements of four editions, the 5th (1896), the 6th (1899), the 7th (1904) and the 8th (1909–1915). The 5th will be taken as a starting point, since it was considered by Kraepelin as an expression of the radical change from the syndromic point of view to the 'concept of disease' (*Krankheitsbegriff*) based essentially on the "conditions of appearance, evolution and termination". In 1896 Kraepelin described the 'deterioration processes' including as separate entities, dementia praecox (equivalent to Hecker's hebephrenia), catatonia, and the dementia paranoides, as well as the 'constitutional mental disorders' with two categories, 'periodic insanity' with manic, depressive and circular forms, and 'madness' (*Verrücktheit*) or paranoia, this last category having broad limits and including hallucinatory forms. In the special chapter on the "Insanity of the age of regression" no precise limits are given between the 'period of involution' and old age proper, both being marked by a lowering of the vital processes. By far the most frequent illness of the period of involution is the 'melancholia'. The disease is, for Kraepelin, completely distinct from the depressive form of periodic insanity, its main length of evolution is about one year (with the possibility of more chronic courses), 55% of the patients recover completely or partially, a quarter have a chronic course and one-fifth exhibit signs of deterioration after two years. In the period of involution are also observed "special forms of paranoia" which are probably specific illnesses. In true old age 'depressive states' are also the most common disorders, the other ones during that period being 'excitatory states' and 'delirious states' with confusional features with an eventually favourable evolution.

The 6th edition, as is well known, is marked by the synthesis of the dementia praecox with its three forms, hebephrenic (the dementia praecox of the former edition), catatonic, and paranoid, by the introduction of 'manic–depressive insanity' which replaces 'periodic insanity' and which includes depressive, manic and, for the first time, mixed forms, and finally by the restriction of the limits of the paranoia, many of the previous cases being attributed to the paranoid form of dementia praecox. Among old-age disorders, two new entities appear. 'Presenile delusion of prejudice' (*präseniler Beeinträchtigungswahn*) is a relatively uncommon incurable disease, slowly progressing in an otherwise clear mind, distinct from paranoia by the structure of the delusions, and from the paranoid form of dementia praecox by the absence of later deterioration. The second entity is 'senile delusion of persecution' (*seniler Verfolgungswahn*) also chronic and without deterioration, no sharp boundaries existing between the two.

The 7th edition is roughly similar to the 6th. Kraepelin maintains melancholia as a distinct entity, although he begins to have doubts about its possible relationship with manic–depressive insanity. More generally he stresses now that "it is certain that in old age illnesses appear which do not differ clinically from the forms of the young" and he mentions the existence of a 'late catatonia'. The far reaching changes which characterise the 8th edition, whose four volumes appeared between 1908 and 1915, can only be briefly summarised. In a chapter on 'endogenous deteriorations' Kraepelin introduces, next to dementia praecox, the 'paranoid forms' tentatively separated from paranoid dementia praecox, for which he proposes the name of paraphrenias, used by older authors in a different meaning. They are distinguished, in the modern terminology, by the absence of negative symptoms and by a chronic course, final deteriorations being exceptional and, in any case, minimal. The nature of paranoia is also seen in a new light: it is no longer a processual endogenous disease, but a slow psychotic development of a personality, and never exhibits hallucinations among its symptoms. In the chapter now entitled "senile and presenile insanity" the paragraph on 'presenile insanity' offers a completely new aspect. The most striking change is the disappearance of melancholia. Kraepelin has been convinced by a study of Thalbitzer (1905) and especially by the book of his pupil Dreyfus (1907) based on a catamnestic study of all the cases diagnosed in Munich as melancholia that the disorder was not a special entity, and that the patients belonged to the manic–depressive insanity. Dreyfus had shown *inter alia* that the relatively frequent evolution towards an intellectual deficit was in fact due to the concomitant and unrelated existence of arteriosclerotic brain changes. Kraepelin now sees "the domain of presenile psychoses as perhaps the most obscure of the whole psychiatry". He enumerates a series of pathological aspects, either related to the affective disorders the 'anxious excitation states' with a frequent lethal evolution, the 'excitation states with protracted evolution towards deterioration', or connected with the delusional disorders; 'late catatonia'; 'depressive madness' (*Depressiver Wahnsinn*), an entity proposed by Thalbitzer, in which delusional and hallucinatory symptoms are associated with a secondary depression; the 'anxious delusional states with evolution towards deterioration' and finally 'presenile delusions of persecution'. Kraepelin, conscious of the uncertainties of his new classification, mentions for example that "anxious excitation may be a particular psychosis, evolved from several other psychoses, or be the same disease as delirium appearing in old age proper". The new classification of the non-affective psychoses in the elderly, in conjunction with Kraepelin's new views on paranoia and with his description of the paraphrenias, stimulated original concepts. E. Kleist (1912, 1913) proposed to subdivide the delusional states appearing in old age into two categories:

(a) late manifestations of the paranoid form of dementia praecox
(b) a new entity he named 'late paranoia' (*Spätparanoia*).

The first was, in his opinion, not homogeneous, and Kleist suggested that part of it belonged possibly to the paraphrenias just described by Kraepelin. Late paranoia was completely different. It was basically the development, beginning usually around age 50, possibly under the influence of endocrine modifications, of a well organised system of delusions, in subjects presenting previously a 'hypoparanoic personality' (*hypoparanoische Konstitution*). The delusional system, constantly associated with hallucinations (a point which differentiates late paranoia from Kraepelin's delusions of prejudice) becomes fully developed when the patient reaches the age of 60 and then remains stationary. Kleist pointed out the similarities between Kraepelin's ideas expressed in the 8th edition and his own regarding the psychopathology of paranoia, although his 'late paranoia' differs from Kraepelin's 'early paranoia' by the age of appearance as well as by other aspects: late paranoia is seen predominantly in women, and hallucinations are present, but both can be considered as "autochthonous increments of an hypoparanoic constitution". Serko (1919) reformulated the same problem. Accepting Kleist's description of late paranoia and his suggestion about the heterogeneity of the paranoid delusional states in old age, he isolated among them a new entity: 'late paraphrenia', appearing in a relatively acute manner from the age of 45 on, but sometimes much later, generally in women, whose symptoms were characterised by polymorphic delusional ideas of prejudice, but also of grandeur, by many hallucinations, and by a chronic course never leading to the 'disintegration of personality' seen in paranoid schizophrenia. Serko stresses the differences between late paraphrenia and Kraepelin's delusion of prejudice (late paraphrenia exhibits more hallucinations) and senile delusion of persecution (late paraphrenia has a more polymorphic delusional system and more ideas of grandeur).

1919 to 1945

The period between the two World Wars was marked by a development, largely specific to the German psychiatry, which is mainly expressed in the volumes of the *Handbuch der Geisteskrankheiten* edited by Bumke. In this work, Lange (1928) surveys the 'endogenous and reactive mood diseases' and accepts the position taken by his teacher Kraepelin in the 8th edition. Although he includes a short paragraph on involutional depression, he follows Bumke's opinion according to which depressive states appearing in old age result from a combination of endogenous and psychological factors, but does not claim that they represent a special entity and, in the Chapter on 'pathoplastic factors', speaks in general terms of 'the influence of old age'. On the other hand, Kraepelin's tentative isolation of paraphrenia was short lived. Already in 1921, W. Mayer had shown in a catamnestic study that a large proportion of the cases so diagnosed ended in a typical schizophrenic deterioration and, from now on, schizophrenia, which was considered by the influential Heidelberg School to be an endogenous processual disease, took a monopolistic position. It tended even to incorporate paranoia, Kolle (1931) having shown in a catamnestic study that many cases exhibit schizophrenic symptoms at one time or another. Kurt Schneider (1987) considered it, under the name of paraphrenia that Kolle had proposed to reserve for this syndrome, as an extremely rare marginal form of schizophrenia. In such a situation, the specific features of the delusional disorders appearing in old age are seen as the result of the pathoplastic influences of age on a general process, and not as the expression of specific entities. In Bumke's handbook, Mayer-Gross, in the volume on schizophrenia (1932) takes more or less this position, and Runge, in the chapter on the 'Psychoses of the age of regression'' (1930) satisfies himself by quoting Kleist and Serko. However, the trends of German psychiatry were not followed elsewhere. This is especially true for involutional depression. In the international literature, there is no general acceptance of Kraepelin's 8th edition. For example, in the UK Henderson & Gillespie, in their manual (1944) criticise the 'Kraepelin–Dreyfus position' and give a traditional description of 'involutional melancholia' as a separate disease. Most of the textbooks of the period took the same position.

1945 onwards

Since the end of World War II, a new focus of interest has appeared: the reversibility of the disorders in the elderly. Although the relatively favourable prognosis of some clinical types, especially of the mood disorders, had often been mentioned by older authors, the generally held idea was that the special features of old-age psychoses were linked with biological changes, as implied in the term involution. The frequent co-morbidity with arteriosclerotic and/or degenerative brain changes, encouraged the widespread pessimistic view that many of the apparently functional psychoses of old age were in fact symptomatic of early organic dementia and shared its incurability. The introduction of electroconvulsive therapy (ECT) in the therapy of depression provided a powerful argument against those ideas (Mayer-Gross, 1945). A number of catamnestic studies (Roth & Morissey, 1952; Roth 1955; Kay, 1962; Post, 1962) suggested that "mood disorders are practically never premonitory signs of senile dementia" (Post, 1972), a position already held by Dreyfus in 1907. The problem was complicated by the fact that old-age depressions often exhibited symptoms suggesting organic changes. The concept of 'pseudodementia' was introduced by Kiloh (1961) for cases "in which the picture of dementia may be closely mimicked" and, although the term 'dementia syndrome of depression' has been subsequently preferred, its frequency and importance are now recognised (Pichot, 1990).

The history of involutional depression has been reviewed elsewhere (Pichot & Pull, 1981). Schematically, at the beginning of the period, the disorder was still, except for the followers of Kraepelin's late views, considered as a special illness with specific symptoms, developing on a particular type of personality, with aetiological factors both genetic and psychological, differing from those responsible for manic–depressive psychosis. Progressively, its originality was more and more contested and the term finally disappeared in the 9th edition of the *International Classification of Diseases* (ICD–9; World Health Organization, 1978) and the Third Edition of the *Diagnostic and Statistical Manual of Mental Disorders* (DSM–III; American Psychiatric Association, 1980). Involutional depression is now included in the unipolar form of the mood disorders, its special aspects, which are not even mentioned in the classifications, being eventually attributed to the pathoplastic effect of age, a return to the 8th edition of Kraepelin's *Manual*.

A similar evolution of ideas took place in relation to the non-affective delusional psychoses. American psychiatry had initially taken an original position. In DSM–I (Committee on Nomenclature and Statistics of the American Psychiatric Association, 1952) they were described under the name 'involutional psychotic reaction' a single disorder encompassing both the 'depression occurring in the involutional period' and the 'cases characterised by paranoid ideas'. This syncretic concept was short lived. Kay & Roth (1961) revived the term 'late paraphrenia' created by Serko in 1919 and their proposal gained wide acceptance. In 1968, DSM–II (Committee on Nomenclature and Statistics of the American Psychiatric Association, 1968) described an 'involutional paraphrenia' as completely distinct from the 'involutional depression'. But the trend initiated in Germany in the 1920s, which tended to incorporate into schizophrenia most of the related disorders, gained strength. Although both DSM–III–R (American Psychiatric Association, 1987) and ICD–10 (World Health

Organization, 1988) maintain schizophrenia and delusional disorders in separate chapters, no mention is made of special categories specific to old age. Modern surveys of the problem still use the term 'chronic delusion of persecution' (Post, 1972) and the concept of 'senile paraphrenia' (Post, 1987) describing three clinical forms of the latter (Post, 1966), the third of which is indistinguishable from paranoid schizoprenia. Although it is considered that previous personality and exogenous factors, especially deafness, seem to play a role, and although the genetic loading is less conspicuous than in cases of schizoprenia of earlier onset, the present general trend seems, as in the case of the mood disorders, to be not to make special entities out of the delusional disorders of the elderly, but to consider 'late schizophrenia' (Grahame, 1984) as a clinical form of a general diagnostic category and to explain the special features by pathoplastic influences.

Conclusion

The history of the functional psychoses in the elderly has been centred around two main chapters, the recent evolution having been influenced by the progresses of the biological therapies. The first chapter deals with the competition between two perspectives. According to the first, illnesses specific to old age, such as involutional depression, presenile delusion of prejudice, senile delusion of persecution, late paranoia, and late paraphrenia, to name a few, are autonomous, whereas, according to the second, the aspects observed are the result of pathoplastic influences, the same functional psychoses being responsible for the different pathological pictures observed before and during old age. Kraepelin hesitated between the two but the second seems now to have gained the upper hand, although conflicting views are still expressed. The second chapter concerns the role of somatic factors, such as a diffuse 'involution of the brain and its function' or, more precisely, of arteriosclerotic and/or degenerative brain lesions, the problem being mostly discussed today in terms of techniques allowing a valid differential diagnosis between functional and organic mental disorders. It is obvious that the present situation in which modern nosological systems solve the questions raised by not mentioning them, is not satisfactory, and the future will probably add new chapters to this history.

References

AMERICAN PSYCHIATRIC ASSOCIATION (1980) *Diagnostic and Statistical Manual of Mental Disorders* (3rd edn) (DSM–III). Washington, DC: APA.
—— (1987) *Diagnostic and Statistical Manual of Mental Disorders* (3rd edn, revised) (DSM–III–R). Washington, DC: APA.
BUMKE, O. (1928) *Handbuch der Geisteskrankheiten*. Berlin: Springer.

COMMITTEE ON NOMENCLATURE AND STATISTICS OF THE AMERICAN PSYCHIATRIC ASSOCIATION (1952) *Diagnostic and Statistical Manual. Mental Disorders.* Washington, DC: American Psychiatric Association Mental Hospital Service.

—— (1968) *DSM-II. Diagnostic and Statistical Manual of Mental Disorders* (2nd edn). Washington, DC: APA.

DREYFUS, G. L. (1907) *Die Melancholie, ein Zustandsbild des manisch-depressiven Irreseins.* Iena: G. Fischer.

ESQUIROL, J. E. D. (1814) Demence. In *Dictionnaire des Sciences Medicales* t.VIII, pp. 280-294. Paris: C. L. F. Panckouke.

FÜRSTNER, K. (1889) Ueber die Geistesstorungen des Senium. *Archiv fur Psychiatrie und Nervenkrankheiten*, **20**, 458-472.

GRAHAME, P. S. (1984) Schizophrenia in old age (late paraphrenia). *British Journal of Psychiatry*, **145**, 493-495.

HENDERSON, D. K. & GILLESPIE, R. D. (1944) *A Textbook of Psychiatry for Students and Practitioners* (Sixth edition). London: Oxford University Press.

KAY, D. W. K. (1962) Outcome and cause of death in mental disorders of old age: a long-term follow-up of functional and organic psychoses. *Acta Psychiatrica Scandinavica*, **38**, 249-276.

—— & ROTH, M. (1961) Environmental and hereditary factors in the schizophrenia of old age ("late paraphrenia") and their bearing on the general problem of causation in schizophrenia. *Journal of Mental Science*, **107**, 649-686.

KILOH, L. G. (1961) Pseudo-dementia. *Acta Psychiatrica Scandinavica*, **37**, 336-351.

KLEIST, E. (1912) Uber chronische wahnbildende Psychosen des Rückbildungsalters, besonders im Hinblick auf deren Beziehungen sum manisch-depressiven Irresein. *Allgemeine Zeitschrift fur Psychiatrie*, **69**, 705-707.

—— (1913) Die Involutionsparanoia. *Allgemeine Zeitschrift fur Psychiatrie*, **70**, 1-134.

KOLLE, K. (1931) *Die primare Verrucktheit.* Leipzig: Thieme.

KRAEPELIN, E. (1896) *Psychiatrie. Ein Lehrbuch fur Studirende und Aerzte.* Funfte Auflage. Leipzig: Johann Ambrosius Barth.

—— (1899) *Psychiatrie. Ein Lehrbuch fur Studirende und Aerzte.* Sechste Auflage. Leipzig: Johann Ambrosius Barth.

—— (1903-1904) *Psychiatrie. Ein Lehrbuch fur Studirende und Ärzte.* Siebente Auflage. Leipzig: Johann Ambrosius Barth.

—— (1909-1915) *Psychiatrie. Ein Lehrbuch fur Studirende und Ärzte.* Achte Auflage. Leipzig: Johann Ambrosius Barth.

LANGE, J. (1928) Die endogenen und reaktiven Gemütserkrankungen und die manisch-depressive Konstitution. In *Handbuch der Geisteskrankheiten.* (ed. O. Bumke) Sechster Band, Spezieller Teil II, pp. 1-231. Berlin: Springer.

MAUDSLEY, H. (1895). *The Pathology of Mind. A Study of the Distempers, Deformities and Disorders.* London: MacMillan.

MAYER, W. (1921) Uber paraphrene Psychosen. *Zeitschrift fur die gesamte Neurologie und Psychiatrie*, **71**, 186-206.

MAYER-GROSS, W. (1932) Die Klinik. In *Handbuch der Geisteskrankheiten* (ed. O. Bumke) Neunter Band, Spezieller Teil V, pp. 293-578. Berlin: Springer.

—— (1945) Electro-convulsive treatment in patients over sixty. *Journal of Mental Science*, **91**, 101-103.

PICHOT, P. (1990) Symptomatology and diagnosis of depression in later life. In *Psychogeriatrics. Biomedical and Social Advances.* (eds K. Hasegawa & A. Homma), pp. 311-319. Amsterdam: Excerpta Medica.

—— & PULL, C. (1981) Is there an evolutional depression? *Comprehensive Psychiatry*, **22**, 2-10.

POST, F. (1962) *The Significance of Affective Symptoms in Old Age.* Maudsley Monograph No 10. London: Oxford University Press.

—— (1966) *Persistent Persecutory States in the Elderly.* Oxford: Pergamon Press.

—— (1972) Spezielle Alterspsychiatrie. In *Psychiatrie der Gegenwart. Forschung und Praxis* (eds K. P. Kisker, J. E. Meyer, M. Müller, *et al*) Band II: Klinische Psychiatrie, Teill 2, Zweite Auflage, pp. 1077-1101. Berlin: Springer.

—— (1987) Depression, alcoholism and other functional psychoses. In *Psychogeriatrics: An International Handbook* (ed M. Bergener), pp. 222-250. New York: Springer.

RITTI, A. (1896) Les psychoses de la vieillesse. In *Congrès des Médecins Aliénistes et Neurologistes de France et des Pays de Langue Francaise. Sixieme session. Bordeaux 1-7 Aout 1895* (ed. E. Regis) Volume 1, pp. 3-48. Paris: Masson.

ROTH, M. (1955) The natural history of mental disorder in old age. *Journal of Mental Science*, **101**, 280-301.

—— & MORISSEY, J. D. (1952) Problems in the diagnosis and classification of mental disorder in old age; with a study of case material. *Journal of Mental Science*, **98**, 66-80.

RUNGE, W. (1930) Die Geistesstörungen des Umbildungsalters und der Involutionszeit. Die Geistesstörungen des Greisesalters. In *Handbuch der Geisterskrankheiten* (ed. O. Bumke) Achter Band. Spezieller Tiel IV. pp. 542-597, 597-668. Berlin: Springer.

SCHNEIDER, K. (1987) *Klinische Psychopathologie*. 12. Auflage. Stuttgart: Georg Thieme.

ŠERKO, A. (1919) Die Involutionsparaphrenie. *Monatsschrift fur Psychiatrie*, **45**, 245-286, 334-364.

THALBITZER, S. (1905) Melancholie und Depression. *Allgemeine Zeitschrift fur Psychiatrie*, **62**, 715-786.

WILLE (1873-1874) Die Psychosen des Greisenalters. *Allgemeine Zeitschrift fur Psychiatrie*, **30**, 269-294.

WORLD HEALTH ORGANIZATION (1978) *Mental disorders: Glossary and Guide to their Classification in Accordance with the Ninth Revision of the International Classification of Diseases (ICD-9)*. Geneva: World Health Organization.

—— DIVISION OF MENTAL HEALTH (1988) *ICD-10. 1988 Draft of Chapter V Categories F00-F99. Mental, Behavioural and Developmental Disorders. Clinical Descriptions and Diagnostic Guidelines*. Geneva: World Health Organization.

3 A review of late paraphrenia and what is known of its aetiological basis

SIR MARTIN ROTH and A. F. COOPER

The history of the concept

The history of the paranoid psychoses of middle age and late life has been marked from its earliest beginning by differences and polarities in viewpoint about the diagnosis, classification and pathogenesis of these disorders. The subject continues to be controversial. Kraepelin (1909), who originally coined the term 'paraphrenia' ultimately concurred with the view of his pupils Kolle (1931) and Mayer (1921) that 'paranoia' and 'paraphrenia' were essentially schizophrenic in their genetic origins, clinical course and long-term outcome.

On the basis of intensive clinical investigations of the mass murderer Wagner over a long period, and exploration of his personality and family background, Gaupp (1914, 1920) dissented from this view. His observations of Wagner, which were sustained over a period of 25 years, led him to conclude that the murderer's chronic paranoid psychosis had been psycho-dynamically determined, having evolved in a manner comprehensible through empathy in the setting of a hypersensitive, hostile and paranoid personality.

Gaupp was followed by his pupil Kretschmer (1918) who formulated the concept of a reactive psychosis that developed in the setting of a specific personality and constitution; those affected were sensitive, thin-skinned and introverted persons who laboured under constant emotional tension. It was the impact of a 'key event' on the vulnerable Achilles' heel in their personality that precipitated the psychotic disorder. Evidence in support of this conception of the illness could be elicited by exploration of the developmental history, personality structure and social adaptation of those affected.

Kretschmer's work was one of the main starting points of the concept of 'psychogenic psychosis' which remains influential in Scandinavian countries at the present time. In the view of some Scandinavian workers this embraces the paraphrenic and paranoid psychoses of later life (Retterstol, 1966, 1970). The paraphrenic group of disorders is regarded as essentially schizophrenic (and the appellation of 'late paraphrenia' as superfluous) by some workers,

25

as conforming to 'delusional disorder' as defined in DSM–III–R (American Psychiatric Association, 1987) by others, as a form of 'reactive' psychosis by some Scandinavian authors and as an organic form of late-life psychosis by a number of those who have found evidence of cerebral lesions in a proportion of cases.

The view adopted in the present paper and in previous publications by the authors (Kay & Roth, 1963; Roth, 1987, 1989) is that while late paraphrenia has to be regarded as a variant of schizophrenia on grounds of biological and phenomenological criteria, it deserves separate status by virtue of a different sex distribution and the presence of a number of specific aetiological factors. It also differs from ordinary schizophrenia in course and outcome. It is considered that fresh light might be shed on the schizophrenic group of disorders by systematic comparison of those variants that are manifest in early adult life with those that make their appearance in middle life and in old age.

The evidence for this concept of the disorder will now be examined under separate headings.

Evidence for kinship of late paraphrenia with schizophrenia

In respect of phenomenology, there are indubitable first-rank symptoms and others of high diagnostic value including auditory hallucinations in clear consciousness, passivity feelings such as experiences of sexual assault by occult means, thought withdrawal, or other ideas of influence on mental or bodily functions by apparatus operated at a distance, bizarre delusions sometimes of a 'primary' character, absence of insight and, in a proportion of cases, thought disorder. In paranoid psychoses without hallucinations, delusional ideas defended by a topsy-turvy logic and organised into a closely knit system of ideas that distort reality and fundamentally alter behaviour provide phenomenological links with schizophrenia. These cases also share with hallucinated patients some of the other variables cited in this section.

With respect to hereditary factors, there is a smaller morbid risk of psychosis in first-degree relatives than in schizophrenia but those family members affected become schizophrenic or paraphrenic (Kay, 1959; Kay & Roth, 1961).

A high proportion of patients exhibit schizoid personalities or prominent schizoid traits before breakdown. As in the premorbid phase of schizophrenia in earlier life there is a low rate of marriage, low fertility, poor sexual adjustment, high divorce rate and poor mothering (Kay & Roth, 1961, 1963; Kay, 1963).

Studies of treatment of late paraphrenia (LP) have shown there is a satisfactory response to neuroleptic drugs. The remissions induced are at least as good or better in quality and duration than those in schizophrenia of early onset (Post, 1966; Raskind *et al*, 1979; Rabins *et al*, 1984).

As far as course and outcome are concerned, until the advent of neuroleptics LP was a chronic psychotic illness associated in most cases with life-long hospital care. In those who refuse or abandon treatment, the psychosis still pursues a chronic course. However, the great majority of treated patients are now enabled to live in the community with the aid of neuroleptic drugs and supportive treatment.

Summary of the features that differentiate late paraphrenic and paranoid disorders from schizophrenic psychosis

Late paraphrenia shows a marked predominance of females, contrasting with schizophrenia in earlier adult life which affects mainly males. Deterioration of personality, as seen in schizophrenia of early adult life, is very rare. The premorbid personality, whether schizoid features are present or absent, remains essentially unchanged in the course of the disease. Hereditary factors, although homologous with those in schizophrenia, make a smaller contribution to causation in LP.

A number of exogenous factors contribute. The prevalence of deafness has been found to be twice as great in late paraphrenics (45%) than in patients with late affective disorder (22%). The aetiology of deafness also differs in the paraphrenic group (Cooper *et al*, 1974; Cooper, 1976). There is also a significant excess of visual impairment (Cooper & Porter, 1976).

Lifetime premorbid 'schizoid' or 'paranoid' personality features are present in the majority of patients. Although the disease is chronic it is now rare for long-term hospital care to be required.

The main lines of evidence for and against a kinship between late paraphrenia and schizophrenia will now be considered individually in greater detail.

Phenomenology

The condition usually begins after a period of six to 18 months of increasing suspiciousness, irritability and hostile attitudes in seclusive, cold, querulous, litigious persons. The psychotic illness evolves rapidly and in some cases in an abrupt stepwise manner. The patient complains of being under hostile scrutiny by neighbours or others, who are determined to oust her from her house. 'Atomic apparatus', X-rays, or other torture machines are used in neighbouring houses to keep them awake at night and submit them to shameful insults. Electrical sensations are felt in the perineum, and sexual assault by occult means is committed nightly by influential politicians, ordinary acquaintances, and others erotically interested in the patient. Men and boys enter freely through the bedroom walls. The patient complains of being photographed in her bathroom by special cameras which can be heard clicking from rooms in adjacent houses. Her thoughts are read and sometimes anticipated by hallucinatory voices which criticise and mock the patient, making obscene suggestions. One or more persons can be heard and they may discuss her in the third person, or the voice of one may threaten to attack or harm her. Poisonous fumes are pumped through the floorboards and the walls.

A recent patient introduced at a social gathering to a man who had been superficially acquainted with her years previously inferred from his manner of looking at her that he was in love with her and had infected her by some means with 'virulent syphilis'.

There is no insight into the illusory nature of these experiences nor any awareness that they originate from an illness.

The paranoid psychosis of Wagner

These florid psychoses are not necessarily those with the most unfavourable prognoses. We may take as an example the paranoid state without hallucinations from the writings of Gaupp (1914, 1920) who described the notorious mass murderer Wagner. He was a well educated and scholarly school master, poet and novelist who, on the night of 3rd/4th September 1913, killed his wife and four children by cutting their throats while they slept. He then travelled by train and bicycle from Stuttgart to Muhlhausen. On the following night he started four fires in the sleeping village and when the inhabitants tried to escape from their houses, he fired shots from two pistols at all the male inhabitants, killing eight and severely wounding twelve others.

He was then brought down by some inhabitants who prevented him from completing his entire plan. This was to murder his brother's family, to set fire to other houses in the village and to escape to the neighbouring castle where he was to commit a dramatic Wagnerian suicide by shooting himself. He had planned these murders in secret for a decade. Wagner was committed to an asylum where he spent the rest of his life and was observed by Gaupp for 25 years.

The illness had begun abruptly against a background of circumscribed paranoid traits of personality after he had committed a number of acts of indecency with animals while making his way from a public house to his home in a drunken state. Almost immediately afterwards he began to observe others commenting and laughing at him, and heard them discussing his behaviour in contemptuous terms. As he was convinced that the whole population of Muhlhausen knew about his perverted conduct he left to take up a post in Stuttgart. He planned to murder his enemies out of revenge and to kill his family out of compassionate concern for their future sufferings.

Despite the acute onset of deranged behaviour the psychosis pursued a chronic course. But the delusions remained unshakeable, except for intervals in which they would recede only to be replaced by a fresh delusional system. He felt persecuted by Jews whom he detected all around him, and accused Franz Werfel, a novelist of Jewish origin, of plagiarising his works. He welcomed the advent of the Nazi regime and its racial policies with joyous satisfaction. Despite the chronicity of the illness there was no impairment of intellect, or personality deterioration. He remained quick witted, powerful in argument, and verbally fluent until his death from tuberculosis. Eugen Bleuler believed that Wagner suffered from paranoid schizophrenia. In fact, two of his maternal relatives were clearly schizophrenic and one uncle suffered from delusional ideas of self-reference centring around masturbation. This was reminiscent of the earlier stages of the development of Wagner's psychosis. This case exemplifies well both kinship with schizophrenia, and the difference, in certain respects. There was an apparent psychogenic origin following a 'key event' followed by a wide ranging delusional system which became chronic, but no deterioration of personality was manifest over a period of 25 years.

Evidence from heredity

Kay's inquiry (Kay, 1959) revealed a morbid risk for schizophrenia significantly higher than that in control subjects but lower than that observed in younger schizophrenics. Similar findings have been recorded in a number of other investigations (e.g. Herbert & Jacobsen, 1967). Women predominate in late paraphrenic and paranoid psychoses, and the hereditary and other aspects reflect the more benign prognosis and lower genetic predisposition of women than men to a schizophrenic illness.

The late paraphrenias provide the most extreme illustration of the postponement of age of onset for schizophrenia and also its benign character in women. These cases make up a substantial part of the shortfall in schizophrenics of female sex in earlier life. The life-time morbid risk is the same in the two sexes. In marked contrast to the primary degenerative dementias those patients with late paraphrenia have a normal life expectancy.

Sexual adaptation

There is an over-representation of unmarried and divorced persons among late paraphrenics. One of our patients left her husband three weeks after marrying him and immediately afterwards reverted to her maiden name by deed poll. As is characteristic of early life schizophrenia the fertility of female paraphrenics is significantly lower than that of control women. In Sweden, Kay (1959, 1962) found that married paraphrenic women had an average of 1.2 children per patient (Swedish average 3.8 children) and married patients an average of 1.9 per marriage compared with an average of 3.0 children born to those with affective disorder and 2.7 to those with organic psychoses. This low fertility rate is similar to that found in schizophrenia of early life.

Late paraphrenic patients make cold and unaffectionate wives and unmaternal mothers liable to inflict trauma on their offspring through their incapacity for emotional attachment and devotion. The findings provide evidence of abnormal reproductive behaviour in a variant of schizophrenic illness before the appearance of definite psychotic symptoms.

Personality

The personality characteristics of those with late paraphrenia have been described in such terms as serious, solitary, reserved, hostile to relatives, unsympathetic, suspicious, quarrelsome, and cold.

In an investigation some years ago (Kay *et al*, 1976*a*), the premorbid personality of patients and their relationships with others were examined by interviewing independently the patient and a close relative or friend using a semi-structured clinical interview. This had been designed to cover a wide range of premorbid personality traits thought to be common in paranoid and affective psychoses.

Product-moment correlations between diagnosis and each personality item were calculated for both patient self-ratings and the relative's ratings in late paraphrenic and late affective disorders. It was found that patients suffering from paranoid psychosis were rated by themselves and their relatives more highly than the affectives on certain items relating to their emotional characteristics, their attitudes to others and their ability to form interpersonal relationships before illness. They had been more solitary, shy and reserved, touchy and suspicious, had less interest in others and fewer social contacts, and were less able to display sympathy or emotion (Tables 3.1 and 3.2). The only item that showed a positive correlation with affective illness was patient self-ratings on high premorbid anxiety.

TABLE 3.1
Personality data (self-ratings): significant correlations with diagnosis (n = 111)

Variable	Correlation coefficient
Unemotional	0.41***
Detached/unsympathetic	0.25**
Solitary interests	0.29**
Little interest in other people	0.26**
Undemonstrative	0.23*
Sensitive and touchy	0.22*
Anxious	− 0.21*
Relatives not friendly to patient	0.21*
Patient not friendly to relatives	0.19*

*** = $P<0.001$; ** = $P<0.01$; * = $P<0.05$; − sign indicates correlation with affective psychosis. (From Kay *et al*, 1976*a*)

TABLE 3.2

Personality data (relatives' ratings): significant correlations with diagnosis (n = 107)

Variable	Correlation coefficient
Solitary interests	0.34***
Little interest in other people	0.33***
Patient hostile to relatives	0.29**
Relatives hostile to patient	0.26**
Detached/unsympathetic	0.25**
Serious natured	0.25**
Few social contacts	0.24*
Shy and reserved	0.24*
Undemonstrative	0.24*
Suspicious	0.22*
Few friends	0.20*

*** = $P<0.001$; ** = $P<0.01$; * = $P<0.05$. (From Kay *et al*, 1976*a*)

There is a remarkable similarity between the hierarchical order of the personality features elicited from patients and relatives or friends. A principal-component analysis of self-rated traits and traits rated by relatives was undertaken. The general component consisted largely of deviating traits (unsociability, suspiciousness, hostility) which were construed as describing a schizoid-paranoid/prepsychotic personality. The scores obtained on this factor by affective and paranoid patients were plotted. Figure 3.1 shows that paranoid patients obtained higher mean scores on the schizoid factor, the difference between the mean scores of the paranoid and affective groups proving highly statistically significant ($P = 0.01$).

A discriminant function analysis (Kay *et al*, 1976*a*), with diagnosis as the dependent variable, was undertaken on the social and biological features which were found on preliminary analysis to distinguish paranoid and affective groups. Only five features discriminated significantly between these diagnostic groups. The presence of any kind of precipitating factor and family history of affective disorder predicted affective illness and low social class; few surviving children and deafness predicted paranoid illness. Being unmarried, living alone, and a family history of schizophrenia added little to discrimination.

The role of personality factors was evaluated in a separate investigation which estimated the contribution of a personality score derived from principal-components analysis, along with the contribution of the five features listed above. This showed 'schizoid personality' to have made the largest contribution to the prediction of diagnosis. Further reference is made to this analysis in the next section.

It is noteworthy that no significant correlations were found between personality score and low social class, the unmarried state, or living alone. It was therefore unlikely that these characteristics could have originated, to more than a limited extent, from abnormalities of personality.

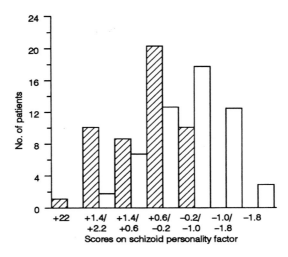

Fig. 3.1. Distribution of scores on a 'schizoid' personality factor in paranoid (▨) and affective (▢) groups (Kay et al, 1976a)

The contribution of deafness to causation of the paranoid psychosis of late life

Cooper *et al* (1974) studied two unselected samples of elderly patients admitted to hospital suffering from paranoid and affective psychoses. The clinical diagnostic criteria were clearly defined, age was taken into account, the different forms of deafness were categorised with the aid of audiometry, and the relationship of deafness to the onset of psychosis was established as accurately as possible.

Clinical assessment of social deafness revealed hearing deficits in 25 of the 54 paranoid and 12 of the 57 affective patients studied, a difference which was statistically significant. Audiometry and otological examination showed that this difference was largely accounted for by the presence of significantly more bilateral conductive and mixed forms of deafness in the paranoid group.

In a larger sample of deaf paranoid and deaf affective patients, Cooper & Curry (1976) drew attention to the long duration of hearing impairment in the paranoid patients as compared with the affective group. For example, in the 60–69 age range, the mean duration of deafness in the paranoid group was 39.7 years and in the affective group 12.0 years – a statistically significant difference. Audiometric testing showed that the deaf paranoid group had a significantly greater mean hearing loss than the deaf affectives. The authors suggested that factors related to long duration and severity of deafness were of greater importance in the aetiology of paranoid illness than the quality of hearing loss.

In order to investigate the significance of deafness as a possible contributory factor to paranoid illness, Kay *et al* (1976*a*) compared the premorbid characteristics of the groups of patients already referred to (Cooper *et al*, 1974). Using discriminant function analysis, it was shown that the two diagnostic groups were significantly differentiated from each other by six independent variables. Of these, scores on a 'schizoid' personality factor, few surviving children, social deafness at onset of psychosis and low social class were each found to make independent and significant contributions to the prediction of a diagnosis of paranoid psychosis.

Deafness, therefore, appeared to be an important independent contributory factor in the onset of paranoid psychosis in the middle aged and elderly. The chronic middle ear disease which Cooper *et al* (1974, 1976) found in about one-fifth of the patients bore no relationship to social class in the samples studied. It is difficult to conceive how impairment of hearing could have resulted from the same genetic or environmental factors that predispose to paranoid illness. Deafness was much more likely to have been accidental but capable of exerting pathogenic effects on its own. Indeed, the paranoid patients whose deafness began before the age of 45 were thought to constitute a distinct subgroup, having fewer deviating personality traits and possibly reduced genetic loading for paranoid illness (Cooper *et al*, 1976). In these patients in particular, deafness may have played a significant and perhaps a crucial role in the development of psychosis.

In the light of these findings, early identification and treatment of conductive deafness in middle age might well make a significant contribution to the prevention of paranoid psychoses in a substantial proportion of patients at risk for the development of the illness in late life. Evidence that such treatment might indeed prove effective as a prophylactic measure is presented later in this chapter.

Same-sex concordance

Attention has been drawn by several authors to the fact that in families which contain more than one schizophrenic, two siblings who both have a psychotic disorder are more likely to be of the same sex than could be expected by chance. Crow (Crow, 1988; Crow *et al*, 1989) has adduced evidence for the hypothesis that the major dominant gene responsible for the transmission of schizophrenia and other psychotic disorders may be in the 'pseudo-autosomal' region of the X-chromosome. This refers to those distal segments of the short arms of these chromosomes in which there is cross-over and therefore genetic exchange between the X and Y chromosomes during meiosis. There is no evidence for sex-linked transmission of schizophrenia or affective psychosis. But any gene in the pseudoautosomal region would be transmitted in an apparently autosomal manner. The hypothesis suggested by Crow is being submitted to further scientific investigation.

There is an alternative, simpler explanation for same-sex concordance in men in particular. In males, schizophrenia tends to develop in the second or third decade, is often severe, and frequently pursues a chronic or relapsing course, whereas females tend to have a later age of onset and a better prognosis. Therefore any predisposed male sibling of a male schizophrenic would be likely to develop a first illness in the same period as his brother.

In females of the same sibship similarly predisposed to schizophrenia, however, the first psychotic breakdown would be likely to occur at a later age. The condition tends to be more benign or to be manifest in a more ambiguous form. Alternatively, the genetic predisposition may remain unexpressed. Part of the explanation for the shortfall of female cases of schizophrenia in early life may be that in some predisposed persons the disease makes its first appearance in the form of paraphrenia or paranoid psychosis in middle age or late life. At the age of 45, 62% of the total risk for developing schizophrenia has been passed in men but only 47% in women (Slater & Roth, 1977). As these figures were gathered at a time when late paraphrenia was not included among schizophrenic disorders, the actual disparity in incidence between men and women may differ from that reflected in these figures. There is in fact some excess of female to female pairs of siblings in schizophrenia, but it cannot be explained in terms of a pseudoautomosal locus.

In the case of manic–depressive disorder there is an explanation for the tendency to female same-sex concordance along similar lines in terms of a difference in the mean age of onset. In the second and third decades there is a considerable preponderance of women among manic–depressives. But after middle age the relative proportion of men shows a steep upward incline. By the age of 40 years only 33% of the risk of developing manic–depressive and related psychoses has been passed in the case of men. Hence, female to female concordance would be expected to be manifest for a considerable part of the lifespan. From some figures available for first admission rates between 1952 and 1960 (Slater & Roth, 1977) first admission rates per million are twice as high in females than in males between the ages of 15 and 45. Thereafter this imbalance is redressed so that in those aged 75 and over first admission rates per million are almost equal in men and women. As a high proportion of bipolar patients are nowadays treated outside hospital, epidemiological data would be required to provide a contemporary picture.

The benign character of late paraphrenia is reflected most clearly in the fact that those affected live through the greater part of their adult lives without falling ill. The advantages of a late onset of such a destructive mental disorder are obvious. How the women predisposed by heredity and abnormal personality traits to schizophrenia manage to escape illness until late life is unknown. Comparative studies of late paraphrenic patients with siblings who have fallen ill at an earlier age might shed light on factors that protect against early expression of schizophrenia and perhaps also those that promote it.

The relevance of the Charles Bonnet syndrome and musical hallucinosis

The views expressed in this section are prompted by the chapter on this subject by Fuchs & Lauter which is included in this volume. Their findings have implications for theories of possible causation of the late paraphrenic and related psychoses.

The Charles Bonnet syndrome

The age of onset of Charles Bonnet syndrome (CBS) in the series of patients reviewed by Fuchs & Lauter varied between 59 and 92 years. The condition was equally distributed between the sexes. They quote other series in which there was a marked predominance of females. The sensory impairment consists of marked but variable loss of vision in 80% of patients. Cataract and glaucoma were the most common underlying causes.

The condition begins suddenly and in most cases some months or years after the onset of visual impairment. The episodes of hallucinations last for seconds or minutes, occur several times daily and predominate in the evening and night. They are located in external space and in a proportion, to the side of poorest vision. The hallucinations are intense in quality and perceived in vivid and distinct form. Their content comprises geometric patterns or occasionally other abstract forms, but in the course of time they change into more complex forms such as human figures, and, less commonly, animals, plants, or inanimate objects. These are fragmented, frequently comprising isolated parts of the body or of other objects. '*Déjà-vu*' experiences are rare and only a minority of patients recognise the human hallucinations as acquaintances.

After some time the hallucinations change to present as scenically moving objects or human figures which may be seen as gliding across the room. The same phantoms present repeatedly, creating the impression of a continual procession.

The patients seem capable of modifying hallucinations by voluntary acts such as moving or turning the eyes, closing the lids or, in rare instances, by ordering the figures to disappear. Insight into the illusory nature of the hallucinations is present in the majority of patients, but recognition that these experiences are due to some disorder of visual perception is achieved in some patients only after a period of uncertainty and exploration to check the authenticity or otherwise of the visions.

Musical hallucinations

Musical hallucinations (MH) resemble CBS in certain respects but differ from it in others. Most patients experience them continually, obtaining relief only while asleep. As in CBS the hallucinations are intense in quality. Instrumental and vocal music are the most frequent sounds but plain human voices uttering words or phrases may be heard instead. They are nearly always familiar and never threatening or disturbing. The melodies have usually been known to the patients from childhood years. As in CBS the hallucinations are repetitive and devoid of interest. The disorder continues for months or years and some emotional disorder may follow after a long period of endurance. In CBS also, a long period of continuous hallucinations may be associated with emotional distress and mild paranoid reactions. But the phenomena are qualitatively different from the complex, ever-changing, threatening and terrifying life-like experiences of those with late paraphrenic psychosis.

One of the most interesting factors in Fuchs & Lauter's review relates to the results of treatment. Successful cataract operation caused hallucinations to disappear in six out of seven cases of CBS and an otosclerosis operation gave relief to a patient with musical hallucinations.

The explanations that have been advanced to explain CBS and MH are summarised by Fuchs & Lauter. A number of workers have stressed the imbalance in normal perception created by the elimination of its afferent component. Thus realistic images stored in the relevant central sensory system are not inhibited by the flow of incoming sensory stimuli. The centrifugal component that is normally integrated with afferent input to fashion perception is released spontaneously so creating spurious percepts. Such explanations are incomplete, but further inquiries into CBS and MH may shed light on certain problems of normal as well as morbid human perception.

The similarities between the two groups of conditions consist of the presence in both of significant sensory impairment. Both defects of hearing and impairment of vision have been shown to be present in a proportion of patients with paraphrenia. They have been found in the great majority of patients with CBS and MH. What reasons can be defined for the almost total absence of any psychotic development or any other form of psychiatric disorder in CBS and MH, and the development of a chronic psychosis in the paraphrenic patients?

The clinical features differ in certain respects. The hallucinations of patients with paraphrenia are never of the simple monotonous kind observed in CBS & MH. They are wide ranging, variable and rich in content. This parallels the wealth of delusional symptoms manifest in these patients. Yet there is some measure of overlap as illustrated by the following cases.

Case reports

Case 1:   A 73-year-old woman suffering from paraphrenia had been hard of hearing for about 35 years as a result of otosclerosis. She said she received messages through the night about events which were about to happen, e.g. a tornado in Canada and trouble over Russian trawlers spying. She described auditory hallucinations – hearing voices through the night, music, songs she learned at school, a lady singing in a high-pitched voice, head noises and a 'thud, thud, thud'. The recrudescence of childhood memories and the element of repetitiveness are noteworthy.

Case 2: An 80-year-old man suffering from paraphrenia had been slightly deaf for about three years before the onset of psychosis. However, he had suffered from poor vision due to severe lens opacities for some years before the onset of psychosis and had undergone cataract extraction. He complained that he had been bothered by a family of Pakistanis who, he said, had moved into his old people's bungalow with him. He claimed they walked in and out through walls and doors day and night but never spoke. He saw them but was unable to touch them. He believed it was the man living across the road who had brought them. Visual hallucinations ceased in hospital but paranoid delusions regarding the Pakistanis persisted and he became convinced that they had removed money and possessions from his house in his absence. The silent procession of strangers is reminiscent of experiences in CBS.

Case 3: A lady aged 79 with visual impairment owing to glaucoma complained that her garden was regularly invaded by a large group of young men clad in jerseys and shorts worn by footballers of the Newcastle United team, who would climb silently over her garden walls. They would steal vegetables and flowers and despoil her garden. She also described rumbling noises that seemed to emanate from adjacent houses. They could be heard at anytime but were more frequent at night. She believed neighbours who were seeking to dispossess her of her home were responsible.

Personality factors

Nothing is currently known about the personalities of patients with CBS and MH, but a large proportion of patients with paraphrenia are characterised by schizoid personality profiles which appear to have been lifelong. A possible explanation for the difference in the clinical picture of the two groups of disorders therefore emerges. The simple monotonous hallucinatory phenomena experienced with insight by patients with CBS and MH may be complications of severe sensory deficits in individuals whose personality characteristics fall within the normal range. Late paraphrenia may differ from these two groups on account of an interaction between sensory deficits and a schizoid or kindred personality constitution; these patients are oversensitive, hostile, unfriendly, suspicious, uninterested in others and so liable to misconstrue events in the outside world and the behaviour of others towards them. In terms of one of the theories for hallucinosis cited by Fuchs & Lauter, there might also be not only exaggeration of the corticofugal component of normal perception but a subjective distortion of it in schizoid personalities whose internal models of the world may be misshapen.

Comparative studies of patients with CBS or MH, paraphrenic patients, and normal elderly subjects might serve to substantiate or to refute a hypothesis along these lines. Comparative studies should investigate the aetiological basis of the sensory deficits in all groups and the presence of concomitant cerebral lesions which have been demonstrated in a proportion of patients with paraphrenia and to a limited extent in CBS and MH.

The relevance of cerebral lesions

Cerebral lesions were present in some 5% of late paraphrenic patients in whom post-mortem studies were undertaken as reported in early inquiries (Kay & Roth, 1961; Kay, 1963). Evidence of damage was found in a higher proportion in some other early series (Post, 1966) but some patients in whom paranoid symptoms had presented in a setting of organic psychiatric features had been included.

The subject has attracted growing interest in recent years. In an investigation of 29 patients with schizophrenia commencing after the age of 44, the mean ventricle to brain ratio was found to be significantly higher than in 23 age-matched normal subjects, and smaller than the ratio estimated for 23 patients with Alzheimer's disease, in whom hallucinations and delusions were manifest (Rabins *et al*, 1984).

In an investigation of patients who had developed their first psychotic illness after the age of 45 years, inquiries were conducted by magnetic resonance imagery (MRI) and comprehensive neuropsychological testing; comparisons were made with 72 healthy elderly subjects (Miller *et al*, 1990). The case material comprised schizophreniform, paraphrenic and 'not otherwise specified' cases diagnosed by DSM–III criteria (American Psychiatric Association, 1980).

Although the history and neurological examination did not suggest structural disease, MRI detected brain abnormalities in over 40% of patients. The mean area of temporal white matter lesions was more than six times greater in patients than in controls. For occipital and frontal lesions there was a four-fold increase in pathology in the patients. These differences had arisen mainly from a subgroup of patients with a large amount of white matter pathology.

In addition to the 41% who showed structural pathology, a further 16% appeared to have metabolic disorders.

The psychotic patients performed worse than controls on neuropsychological tests that assessed frontal-lobe function and verbal memory. It was noteworthy, however, that no significant difference was found in respect of neuropsychological performance in patients with and without structural lesions.

These findings do not differentiate late paraphrenia from schizophrenia: observations in recent years have established the presence of circumscribed structural lesions in a substantial minority of those with schizophrenia in early adult life. Diminution of the volume of periventricular and limbic structures and hippocampus and parahippocampal gyrus in particular have been reported by Bogerts (1988). He considers these lesions originate from dysplasias due to obstetric complications and other perinatal lesions.

Lewis *et al* (1988) reported a history of obstetric complications in 17% of 207 schizophrenic patients compared with 8% of 748 patients with other psychiatric disorders. Some workers consider that negative symptoms predate the development of schizophrenic psychopathology in these patients (Murray *et al*, 1988). Other characteristics comprising prepsychotic intellectual impairment and poor social outcome suggest an affinity with the patients Kraepelin described in the syndrome 'dementia praecox'. In the paraphrenic group of patients, however, negative symptoms (other than premorbid schizoid personality features in a proportion of cases) are conspicuous by their absence. Late paraphrenics also respond well to treatment and have a favourable prognosis as far as their psychosis is concerned.

Those with lesions detected by imaging methods or post-mortem do not differ in performance in neuropsychological tests from those without lesions. Dementia has been reported as a late development in a proportion of paraphrenic patients, but this outcome has not materialised in large representative samples at greater than chance expectation (Kay & Roth, 1961). There is a favourable response to neuroleptic treatment in a high proportion of paraphrenic patients (Rabins *et al*, 1984). As they also have a normal life expectancy, late paraphrenia without concomitant organic psychiatric features at onset will rarely prove the first manifestation of a dementing process.

Cerebral lesions may make some limited contribution to causation in a small proportion of patients with late paraphrenia. This is not proven, and lesions cannot be regarded as either a sufficient or a necessary cause of the syndrome. The same statement holds in the present state of knowledge for the schizophrenic group of disorders as a whole.

Summary and conclusions

A review of the clinical features and contributory aetiological factors shows late paraphrenia to have a close affinity with schizophrenic illness in earlier adult life. It also defines certain differences between these conditions and schizophrenia. Further comparison of the two conditions may shed fresh light on the aetiological basis of schizophrenic illness.

In respect of phenomenology the presenting clinical picture is characterised by first rank and other features which discriminate schizophrenia from other psychoses. Certain clinical features distinctive for paraphrenia may be regarded as pathoplastic in origin: delusions of sexual assault and threat of dispossession may be linked with the predominance of females who are often single, divorced, isolated and sexually maladapted.

The hereditary basis of paraphrenia is homologous with that of schizophrenia, but the morbid risk in first-degree relatives is intermediate between that of normal persons and that of schizophrenic illness that starts in earlier decades. The psychotic and personality disorders in first-degree relatives of paraphrenic patients deserve further investigation.

There is evidence that the increased prevalence of deafness and, to a lesser extent, of impaired visual acuity among paraphrenic patients contributes to the genesis of the psychosis in a substantial proportion of cases. In a high proportion of patients personality profile has been found to be the best discriminator between paraphrenic and affective disorders in late life. Certain features such as deficiency of affect, social withdrawal and impoverishment of social relationship precede the development of delusions and hallucinations in late paraphrenia by several decades.

In so far as late paraphrenia can be regarded as a late-life form of schizophrenia it is consistent with that view which considers certain negative symptoms and impairments to antedate the development of positive symptoms and to continue into the chronic phase of the disease (Wing, 1987; Murray *et al*, 1988). But the premorbid schizoid traits of paraphrenic patients are often associated with outstanding positive assets of drive, determination, ego-strength and at times high achievement. These are manifest alongside poor adjustment in sexual and social relationships, low rate of marriage and, within marriage, low fertility, poor mothering, and high divorce rate. Questions are posed regarding the factors that have enabled late paraphrenic persons to avoid breakdown for the greater part of the lifespan notwithstanding personality defects.

Until the advent of neuroleptics, paraphrenia was associated with lifelong hospital treatment in most cases. In those who refuse or abandon treatment, psychosis continues to pursue a chronic course. A high proportion of patients respond well to neuroleptic drugs and the majority are able to live outside hospitals and other institutions, in the community.

Comparison of benign hallucinations such as the Charles Bonnet syndrome (CBS) and Musical Hallucinosis (MH), and late paraphrenia defines a number of problems for inquiry. All the syndromes occur in late life. Women predominate in all groups. There is visual impairment in most cases of CBS and loss of hearing in MH. Both types of deficit (but mainly deafness) occur in late paraphrenia. The illusory nature of hallucinations is appreciated with insight in the great majority of patients with CBS and MH. In late paraphrenia it is associated with a florid chronic psychosis in which insight is totally absent in most cases.

One possible explanation for the disparity is that in the first two groups we deal with individuals with sensory deficits that develop in a setting of personalities within the normal range. There may be other factors. The decisive importance of the sensory defects is reflected in the recoveries that have been recorded following successful treatment of blindness and deafness in CBS and MH.

In late paraphrenia, sensory deficits occur in the setting of a schizoid or schizotypal premorbid personality determined in part by hereditary causes. Is it this personality factor that constitutes the critical difference in the benign and psychotic forms of hallucinosis? A limited amount of evidence in favour of this hypothesis is available from comparisons of deaf patients with those of sound hearing.

Comparative studies of patients with CBS and MH and late paraphrenics with or without sensory deficits may shed light on the commonest form of chronic paranoid psychosis among the elderly. The results of such inquiries may provide insight into some of the causes of the schizophrenic family of disorders as a whole.

References

AMERICAN PSYCHIATRIC ASSOCIATION (1980) *Diagnostic and Statistical Manual of Mental Disorders* (3rd edn) (DSM–III). Washington, DC: APA.
—— (1987) *Diagnostic and Statistical Manual of Mental Disorders* (3rd edn, revised) (DSM–III–R). Washington, DC: APA.
BOGERTS, B. (1988) Limbic and paralimbic pathology in schizophrenia: interaction with age and stress related factors. In *Proceedings of the first International Congress of Schizophrenia Research* (eds S. C. Schulz & T. A. Tamminga). New York: Oxford University Press.
COOPER, A. F. (1976) Deafness and psychiatric illness. *British Journal of Psychiatry*, **129**, 216–226.
——, KAY, D. W. K., CURRY, A. R., *et al* (1974) Hearing loss in paranoid and affective psychoses of the elderly. *Lancet*, ii, 851–860
—— & CURRY, A. R. (1976) The pathology of deafness in the paranoid and affective psychoses of later life. *Journal of Psychosomatic Research*, **20**, 97–105.
—— & PORTER, R. (1976) Visual acuity and ocular pathology in the paranoid and affective psychoses of later life. *Journal of Psychosomatic Research*, **20**, 107–114.
——, GARSIDE, R. F. & KAY, D. W. K. (1976) A comparison of deaf and non-deaf patients with paranoid and affective psychoses. *British Journal of Psychiatry*, **129**, 532–538.
CROW, T. J. (1988) Sex chromosomes and psychosis: the case for a pseudoautosomal locus. *British Journal of Psychiatry*, **153**, 675–683.
CROW, T. J., DELISI, L. E. & JOHNSTONE, E. C. (1989) Concordance by sex in sibling pairs with schizophrenia is paternally inherited: evidence for a pseudoautosomal locus. *British Journal of Psychiatry*, **155**, 92–97.
FUCHS, T. & LAUTER, H. (1992) Charles Bonnet syndrome and musical hallucinations in the elderly. In *Delusions and Hallucinations in Old Age* (eds C. Katona & R. Levy), pp. 187–198. London: Gaskell.
GAUPP, R. (1914) *Zur Psychologie des Massenmordes*. Berlin: Hauptlehrer Wagner von Degerloch.
—— (1920) Der Fall Wagner. Eine Katamnese, zugleigh ein Beitrag zur Lehre von Paranoia. *Zeitschrift fur Gesamte Neurologie und Psychiatrie*, **60**, 312–327.
HERBERT, M. & JACOBSEN, S. (1967) Late paraphrenia. *British Journal of Psychiatry*, **113**, 461–469.

KAY, D. W. K. (1959) Observations on the natural history and genetics of old age psychoses: Stockholm material 1931–1937 (abridged). *Proceedings of the Royal Society of Medicine*, **52**, 791–794.

—— (1962) Outcome and cause of death in mental disorders of old age: a long-term follow-up of functional and organic psychoses. *Acta Psychiatrica Scandinavica*, **38**, 249–276.

—— (1963) Outcome and cause of death in mental disorders of old age: a long-term follow-up of functional and organic psychoses. *Acta Psychiatrica Scandinavica*, **39**, 159–169.

—— & ROTH, M. (1961) Environmental and hereditary factors in the schizophrenia of old age (''late paraphrenia'') and their bearing on the general problem of causation in schizophrenia. *Journal of Mental Science*, **107**, 649–686.

—— & —— (1963) Schizophrenias of old age. In *Processes of Aging: Social and Psychological Perspectives* (eds R. Williams, C. Tibbits & W. Donahue), pp. 402–488. New York: Atherton Press/Prentice-Hall.

——, COOPER, A. F., GARSIDE, R. F., *et al* (1976a) The differentiation of paranoid from affective psychoses by patients' premorbid characteristics. *British Journal of Psychiatry*, **129**, 207–215.

——, GARSIDE, R. F., ROTH, M., *et al* (1976b) Schizophrenics' families. *British Journal of Psychiatry*, **128**, 510–511.

KOLLE, K. (1931) *Die Primare Verrucktheit*. Leipzig: George Thieme.

KRAEPELIN, E. (1909–1915) *Psychiatrie. Ein Lehrbuch fur Studierende und Ärzte*, 8th ed. Leipzig: Aufl. J. A. Barth.

KRETSCHMER, E. (1918) *Der Sensitive Beziehungswahn*. Berlin: Julius Springer.

LEWIS, S. W., MURRAY, R. M. & OWEN, M. (1988) Obstetric complications in schizophrenia. Methodology and mechanisms. In *Proceedings of the First International Congress of Schizophrenia Research* (eds S. C. Schulz & T. A. Tamminga). New York: Oxford University Press.

MAYER, W. (1921) Der paraphrene psychosen Zentralblalt fur diegesante. *Neurologie und Psychiatrie*, **71**, 187–216.

MILLER, B. L. & LESSER, I. M. (1988) Late-life psychosis and modern neuroimaging. *Psychiatric Clinics of North America*, **11**, 33–44.

——, ——, BOONE, K. B., *et al* (1990) Brain lesions and cognitive function in late-life psychosis. *British Journal of Psychiatry*, **158**, 76–82.

OPJOURDSMOEN, S. (1986) Long-term follow-up of paranoid psychoses. *Psychopathology*, **19**, 44–49.

POST, F. (1966) *Persistent Persecutory States of the Elderly*. Oxford: Pergamon Press.

RABINS, P. V., PAUKER, S. & THOMAS, J. (1984) Can schizophrenia begin after age 44? *Comprehensive Psychiatry*, **25**, 290–294.

RASKIND, M., ALVAREZ, C. & HERLIN, R. N. (1979) Fluphenzine enanthate in the outpatient treatment of late paraphrenia. *Journal of the American Geriatrics Society*, **27**, 459–463.

RETTERSTOL, N. (1966) *Paranoid and Paranoiac Psychoses*. Oslo: Universitetsforlaget.

—— (1970) *Prognosis in Paranoid Psychoses*. Springfield, Ill.: Charles C. Thomas.

ROTH, M. (1987) Late paraphrenia: phenomenology and etiological factors and their bearing upon problems of the schizophrenic family of disorders. In *Schizophrenia & Aging* (eds N. E. Miller & G. D. Cohen), pp. 217–234. New York, London: The Guilford Press.

—— (1989) Delusional (paranoid) disorders. In *Treatments for Psychiatric Disorders. A Task Force Report of the American Psychiatric Association. Vol. 2* (ed. T. B. Karasu), pp. 1609–1652. Washington, DC: APA.

SLATER, E. & ROTH, M. (1977) *Clinical Psychiatry* (revised third edition). London: Bailliere, Tindall & Cassell.

WING, J. K. (1987) Has the outcome of schizophrenia changed? In *Recurrent and Chronic Psychoses* (ed. T. J. Crow). *British Medical Bulletin*, **43**, 741–753.

4 Changing concepts: persistent delusions

FELIX POST

This contribution on changing concepts of delusions and hallucinations in old age will be limited to the small proportion of patients who in their late 50s, but more often during the seventh or eighth decades of their lives or even later, begin to be deluded or hallucinate, singly or in combination. Their symptoms are not associated with transitory brain syndromes or affective psychoses, nor are they part and parcel of a chronic brain syndrome, for example one of the dementias of old age. Moreover, these patients' symptoms persist to the end of their days unless they are suppressed or ameliorated by treatment with major tranquillising drugs.

Paraphrenia

Involutional paranoia was probably first conceptualised by Kleist (1913). He found that on follow-up into their 60s and 70s patients with this condition did not deteriorate like cases of either dementia praecox or dementia senilis, and he wondered whether they might not be similar to a group of younger patients recently classed as paraphrenics by Kraepelin (1913). For reasons summarised by, among others, Mayer-Gross (1932), Kraepelin soon abandoned a diagnosis of paraphrenia, which increasingly fell into disrepute. It was resurrected as late or senile paraphrenia by Roth (1955) as applying in a purely descriptive fashion to some 10% of patients first admitted to a mental hospital after the age of 60 with delusions and/or hallucinations in clear consciousness, of recent onset, and without either cerebral-organic deterioration or any additional schizophrenic symptoms or defects.

Undeterred by various critical voices, Kay & Roth (1961) went on to propose that senile paraphrenia was the mode in which schizophrenia manifested itself in late life. In a follow-up study of personal cases admitted for the first time after the age of 60 with paranoid delusions and/or hallucinations, Post (1966) found that only one-third of patients exhibited Schneider's first rank symptoms for a diagnosis of schizophrenia; they were in many ways indistinguishable from younger paranoid schizophrenics. Another third of patients were also severely disturbed by their symptoms, but these were not of first rank according to Schneider's criteria. Finally, there remained patients who were relatively calm and undisturbed because their delusions and, occasionally, hallucinations were confined to one or two themes. The validity of these three types of paranoid illness was later confirmed by Grahame (1984), who found an insignificantly larger proportion of Schneider-positive cases, possibly because unlike Post's series, his study also included compulsorily admitted and probably more severely ill patients. Post (1966) did not accept Kay & Roth's (1961) concept of senile paraphrenia as a late mode of schizophrenia, but preferred to see the persistent persecutory states of late life as a congery of partial schizophrenias, which in the great majority of cases had been foreshadowed by abnormal, usually 'schizoid' personality characteristics. However, against expectation, the most completely schizophrenic, Schneider-positive, patients were not differentiated from the rest by a significantly higher incidence of schizophrenic family histories nor, as might be expected, by a less frequent association with dubious or confirmed cerebral–organic changes. Other variables, like deafness or response to drug treatments, also did not differ between Post's three syndromes at a statistically significant level, and on the basis of this 1966 series of patients with persistent persecutory states, the concept of partial schizophrenia was not supported.

More recently changing concepts

To judge by the Anglo-Saxon literature, no further attempts were made to examine the concept of late paraphrenia until the paper by Grahame (1984), referred to above. On the basis of his findings and their long and thoughtful discussion, Grahame concluded very confidently that late paraphrenia was the form of expression of schizophrenia in old age.

However, Holden (1987) came to a rather different conclusion. From case registers of a hospital catchment area covering the years 1971 to 1975 he pulled out the case notes of 47 patients with persistent paranoid psychoses who, on their original presentation, had been regarded as cognitively intact. The patients were followed for 10 years or to earlier death, and the results were based on re-examinations, interviews and/or various records. It emerged that for various reasons ten cases had been wrongly diagnosed at their original presentation, but that the remaining 37 patients did satisfy Roth's (1955) criteria for late paraphrenia. However, 13 of these patients had clearly started to dement early into the follow-up period, i.e. during the first three years, and five had suffered at least one episode of clearly affective illness, and had to be reclassified as schizoaffective. Of the original 37 patients initially satisfying Roth's criteria, only 19 patients were left with confirmed late paraphrenia, only ten of whom were Schneider-positive. The results of Holden's analysis need not detain us here, except to note that the 13 patients who had turned out to be dementing pursued, quite apart from their earlier deaths, a much less favourable course in comparison with the 24 who had remained 'functional'. Holden suggested that late paraphrenia was a heterogeneous syndrome giving the appearance of overlapping conditions with paranoid delusions.

In a prospective study, Hyams *et al* (1989) compared late paraphrenics with age-matched healthy control subjects. The patients had been carefully selected by members of the research team, and over a follow-up period of an average 3.7 years no changes of diagnosis were required, except that two of the 31 surviving patients were thought to be dementing, compared with only one of the controls. In addition, on inception, the patients had been significantly inferior to the controls on their Mental Test Score (Hodkinson, 1973) performance, and the patients' scores further declined slightly, but significantly, during the follow-up period. In keeping with this finding, the paraphrenics as a group had, in terms of factors of the Geriatric Mental State Schedule (Copeland *et al*, 1976), declined on several cognitive functions, while registering considerable improvements, presumably due to treatment, of their delusions and hallucinations. These workers suggested that there was an organic substrate of late paraphrenia, but conjectured that the cerebral changes were relatively subtle and slowly progressive because ventricular size on the CT scans had not been a predictor of outcome.

However, Miller *et al* (1991) employing magnetic resonance imaging scans found that 25% of patients with late-life psychoses had cortical or white matter infarctions compared with 79 of their controls. A little later, Flint *et al* (1991*a*) announced that they had also discovered, by means of CT scans, cerebral infarctions mostly affecting the frontal subcortical system in 31% of 33 neurologically and cognitively intact patients. The presence of infarcts was found to correlate negatively with that of long-recognised risk factors for late paraphrenia, such as failure to marry and social isolation. This suggested that subclinical strokes were a potent mechanism in the pathogenesis of the illness. In addition, Flint *et al* (1991*b*) criticised previous investigators for not having treated paranoid patients with delusions only, i.e. without any hallucinations, separately. They divided their 33 cases into 21 with both hallucinations and delusions and 12 patients who were only deluded, and whose condition they equated with Kraepelin's paranoia. This bold decision might be criticised because the delusions of late paraphrenics are not anything like well systematised, and in contrast to paranoiacs they often reflect themes from the patients' immediate environment (theft of property, deprivation of home, etc.) rather than systematic persecutions by a person or group of the general population. All the same, in the case of the 16 patients who had CT scans, those suffering from delusions without hallucinations more often had evidence for cerebral infarcts. These 'paranoia' patients also responded less well to treatment, presumably because they could not tolerate sufficiently high doses of major tranquillisers. In view of the small numbers, these workers emphasised that their findings, which split off an organic delusional syndrome from late paraphrenia, were only tentative and preliminary. The same has to be said about the results of an investigation of genetic markers, which would deal a death blow to the concept of senile paraphrenia as a late-life manifestation of schizophrenia if it were to be confirmed. Naguib *et al* (1987) investigated genetic markers for susceptibility to late paraphrenia as presented by certain antigens of the human leucocyte antigen (HLA) complex. One of them (HLA-A9) had been found with virtually complete consistency to be associated with paranoid schizophrenia of any age at onset. This antigen was not found in association with late paraphrenia in assays on 31 carefully diagnosed patients. Instead there were (at first sight significant) associations with three other antigens. However, at least 105 patients would be needed to remove all reasonable doubts from these findings. They would, if confirmed, indicate clearly that paranoid schizophrenia and late paraphrenia were biologically different illnessses, keeping in mind that HLA profiles do not change due to ageing.

Persistent delusions of psychiatrists

To a purist adept in psychopathology, the delusions of late paraphrenics, as against those of paranoiacs or of schizophrenics would not be true delusions, but only delusional ideas (summarised by Post, 1982). The erroneous beliefs of psychiatrists are not even delusional, but merely overvalued ideas. In the present context, we shall be concerned only with psychiatrists' overvalued ideas on diagnosis and on the concept of schizophrenia.

Although really we know better, few of us can rid ourselves of the false belief that by making a diagnosis we imply any scientific understanding of the nature of a psychiatric illness. By-and-large, diagnoses do, of course, in most cases, direct doctors towards the most appropriate forms of management, and precise and agreed diagnostic classification of patient groups is essential for communication between researchers and for epidemiological inquiries. At the present time, however, psychiatric diagnoses, except where they refer to conditions associated with well established cerebral causes, are only provisional and operational. Internationally, we have failed even at this operational level of labelling cases for world-psychiatric purposes, as there are, in parallel use, the World Health Organization's (1979) *International Classification of Diseases* (ICD–9) and the American Psychiatric Association's (1987) *Diagnostic and Statistical Manual of Mental Disorders* (DSM–III–R) competing with one another.

The North Americans have never accepted the concept of late paraphrenia, and that schizophrenia could manifest itself for the first time in life after the age of 45 was only conceded in the current DSM-III-R (1987). So now patients of all ages falling ill with persistent mood incongruent paranoid delusions, in a setting of intact brain functioning, can be diagnosed either as paranoid schizophrenics, or as cases of delusional paranoid disorder, a diagnosis restricted to patients with no or few hallucinations, or other disorders of experiencing or conduct usually seen in schizophrenia. ICD-9 did indeed include a diagnosis of late paraphrenia, but it is now proposed to delete it from the 10th revision. Persistent delusional states without cerebral-organic features would have to be registered either as paranoid schizophrenia or as one of three kinds of delusional state. Employing the guide lines attached to one of the drafts circulated by the WHO for field studies, Quintal *et al* (1991) reviewed the case notes of a series of patients who had originally been given an ICD diagnosis of late paraphrenia. Two independent raters achieved complete agreement in rediagnosing some 70% as paranoid schizophrenics and some 30% as cases with various delusional states. This would seem highly satisfactory for communication between clinicians. However, the investigators thought that the WHO guide lines gave an undue hierarchical preponderance to schizophrenia, and by making the criteria for schizophrenia more restrictive, one of the raters reduced the proportion of paranoid schizophrenics to 37%, and the other to 39%. Also, they recommended that, to facilitate the retrieval of cases for research, the proposed ICD revision should allow for coding age of onset. However, it seems likely that, whichever suggestions are adopted, future researchers into persistent persecutory states employing the ICD system will be dealing with patients who are not identical to those investigated by North American workers, unless the World Health Organization and the American Psychiatric Association can come to an agreement on the criteria for the category of paranoid schizophrenia.

Turning to overvalued ideas concerning schizophrenia, we have seen that from Kay & Roth (1961) onwards most researchers have been preoccupied with trying to discover whether or not, or to what extent, senile paraphrenia was a late form of schizophrenia. These workers, the present writer included, had failed to remain fully aware that the whole concept of schizophrenia other than in a purely operational sense was a nebulous one, so that there was little hope of discovering its relevance to the genesis of late paraphrenia.

More recently, the results of investigations (too numerous and too various to quote here) have begun to demonstrate that schizophrenics (to refer to only two psychodynamic tenets) were not victims of traumatic early family experiences nor of an ostracising society, but that their condition was related to cerebral abnormalities. It is worth remembering this was one of the few opinions shared by fathers of biological psychiatry, like Griesinger and Kraepelin, and the most important founder of dynamic psychiatry, Sigmund

Freud. All the same, the search for coarse brain changes and for metabolic abnormalities affecting brain functioning has remained largely without success. A hereditary factor has been generally accepted, but its mode of operating remains controversial. Recent investigators have reported faulty arrangements of cortical neurons in certain areas of the brain in some schizophrenics, and it has been suggested that these were due to faulty directions during foetal development. The faults could be heredo-genetic, mutational, or environmentally caused, e.g. by a virus infection suffered by the mother during a crucial stage of her pregnancy. Further, it has been speculated that the resultant miniscule cerebral abnormalities made the affected individuals prone to break down with schizophrenic symptoms during adolescence or the earlier years of adult life. Now, we saw that subtle brain changes (in this instance due to ageing or small infarcts) have also begun to be suspected in elderly patients with persistent delusions and hallucinations of recent onset. It would be foolhardy to indulge in further speculations, but suggestions on the way in which future research ought to be conducted may be tentatively indicated.

A not-so-modest proposal

Clinicians should study the nature of delusions and hallucinations occurring in old age far more intensively and with more sophistication than in the past and, regardless of the absence or presence of confirmed cerebral pathology or of affective components, it might be possible to categorise patients in terms of the finer characteristics of their delusions and hallucinations, going beyond a preoccupation with Schneiderian or other criteria of schizophrenia. The results should then be submitted to experts in areas like modern genetics, molecular biology, and neurohistology to investigate possible correlations with the clinical findings.

Such multidisciplinary research would have to be prospective and based on a much larger case material than was available in the prospective studies recently reported. Individual psychiatrists see far too few patients over a limited timespan for the conduct of investigations of the proposed depth and extent. Workers will, therefore, have to pool their patients in future projects, and probably at a national or even international level. Is that a Utopian idea?

References

AMERICAN PSYCHIATRIC ASSOCIATION (1987) *Diagnostic and Statistical Manual of Mental Disorders* (3rd edn, revised) (DSM–III–R) Washington, DC: APA.

COPELAND, J. R. M., KELLEHER, M. J., KELLET, J. M., *et al* (1976) A semi-structured clinical interview for the assessment of diagnosis and mental state in the elderly: The Geriatric Mental State Schedule: 1. Development and reality. *Psychological Medicine*, **6**, 439–449.

FLINT, A., RIFAT, S. & EASTWOOD, R. (1991a) Brain lesions and cognitive function in late-life psychosis. *British Journal of Psychiatry*, **158**, 866.

———, ——— & ——— (1991b) Late onset paranoia: distinct from paraphrenia? *International Journal of Geriatric Psychiatry*, **6**, 103–109.

GRAHAME, P.S. (1984) Schizophrenia in old age (late paraphrenia). *British Journal of Psychiatry*, **145**, 493–495.

HODKINSON, H. M. (1973) Mental impairment in the elderly. *Journal of the Royal College of Physicians of London*, **7**, 305–317.

HOLDEN, N. L. (1987) Late paraphrenia or the paraphrenias? A descriptive study with a 10-year follow-up. *British Journal of Psychiatry*, **150**, 635–639.

HYAMS, N., NAGUIB, M. & LEVY, R. (1989) Late paraphrenia – a follow-up study. *International Journal of Geriatric Psychiatry*, **4**, 23–29.

KAY, D. W. K. & ROTH, M. (1961) Environmental and hereditary factors in the schizophrenias of old age ('late paraphrenia') and their bearing on the general problem of causation in schizophrenia. *Journal of Mental Science*, **107**, 649–686.

KLEIST, K, (1913) Die Involutionsparanoia. *Allgemeine Zeitschrift fuer Psychiatrie*, **70**, 1–134.

KRAEPELIN, E. (1913) *Klinische Psychiatrie, Vol.III, Part II* (8th edn). Leipzig: Barth.

MAYER-GROSS, W. (1932) Die Schizophrenie (IV Die Klinik, V Erkennung und Differentialdiagnose) In *Bumke Handbuch der Geisteskrankheiten*. Berlin: Springer.

MILLER, B. L., LESSER, I. M., BOONE, K. B., *et al* (1991) Brain lesions and cognitive functions in late-life psychosis. *British Journal of Psychiatry*, **158**, 76–82.

NAGUIB, M., MCGUFFIN, P., LEVY, R., *et al* (1987) Genetic markers in late paraphrenia: a study of HLA antigens. *British Journal of Psychiatry*, **150**, 124–127.

POST, F. (1966) *Persistent Persecutory States of the Elderly*. Oxford: Pergamon Press.

——— (1982) Paranoid disorders. In *Handbook of Psychiatry 3* (eds J. K. Wing & L. Wing), pp. 22–27. Cambridge: Cambridge University Press.

QUINTAL, M., DAY-CODY, D. & LEVY, R. (1991) Late paraphrenia and ICD-10.

ROTH, M. (1955) The natural history of mental disorders in old age. *Journal of Mental Science*, **101**, 281–301.

WORLD HEALTH ORGANIZATION (1978) *Mental Disorders: Glossary and Guide to their Classification in Accordance with the Ninth Revision of the International Classification of Diseases* (ICD–9). Geneva: WHO.

5 Late-onset delusional states: mechanisms and understanding

G. LE GOUES

The reference model

As Beresin (1988) has shown, delusional states are the commonest mental disorders in old age. Despite their poor prognosis in 25% of cases, they are unfortunately too often ignored by physicians. Doctors, in fact, may refer mistakenly to 'confusion', a confusion more often imagined than real, because of the difficulty in correctly identifying true delusional states in late life.

From a developmental perspective, it would be appropriate to review the characteristic symptoms and signs that enable a diagnosis to be made. Since, however, this is not my purpose here, I will restrict myself to reminding the reader of the existence of abnormalities of thought that are sometimes observed before the onset of full-blown delusions. Concerning these disorders, Lipowski (1967) specifies that the onset of delusions in old age is often preceded by a decline in associative thought, bizarre ideas, and a rich variety of abnormal images and fantasies, alternating with moments of lucidity. As the delusion develops, perceptual illusions merge with hallucinations. The projection of thoughts and ideas can be confounded by loss of perception, an added difficulty for the doctor. Rather than describing the clinical manifestations of delusions, I will limit myself to citing the work of Manus & Monfort (1991) who restrict the term 'late onset delusional state' to episodes with first onset in old age. In consequence, elderly patients with schizophrenia and those with chronic delusional states are excluded, while confusional states and dementias are marginally classified under the heading of psycho-organic symptoms (Loo & Zarifian, 1982).

In this paper, I am concerned with the dementias because their late-onset decompensation is hardly ever preceded by a psychosis and the emergence of a delusional idea within a non-psychotic framework forces us to re-examine our understanding of psychic functioning.

This choice may seem questionable to classical psychiatry which has been more concerned with involutional melancholia, delusions of loss, late paraphrenia and hypochondriasis rather than those problems with a neurological component. Let me assure you, however, that my choice is not the result of a determination to seek out the difficult. It is aimed simply to relaunch an attempt at understanding from a more general standpoint: nothing happens in the body without the psychic apparatus having to find a way to understand it. The question of how and where this psychic understanding can take place as the brain degenerates is the focus of my research.

In placing the emphasis on the patient's mental productions, we seek to enrich the clinical model that has been in operation since the time of Sydenham. One must remind oneself that Sydenham tried to "reduce all illnesses to specified types with the same care and the same exactitude that the botanists have employed in the Treatise on Plants" (Foucault, 1972). This is a project which has shown considerable heuristic value in the field of clinical anatomy but which remains notoriously inadequate in the psychological domain.

Essentially, where a human being is the author of his own performance, a botanical description of his function will never tell us anything about his way of thinking. To discover the intimate detail of his psychic world, we have to gain his confidence, and obtain his freely granted collaboration. Once we have attained this, we discover that the patient gives meaning to events according to the organisation of his personality and the nature of his defence mechanisms. The psychological model to which I refer involves:

(a) the patient's personality
(b) the mechanisms of defence
(c) the reactions of those around him.

Only the mechanisms of defence and the reactions of other people are truly amenable to interference and may be changed more or less profoundly according to the technique employed.

In elderly people, only a limited number of psychological stances are available. Dias Cordeiro (1973) distinguishes three which are outlined below.

(a) The elderly subject manages to accept his lot and experiences a normal ageing process.
(b) He suffers multiple losses which accumulate around him and in him to a greater extent than can be tolerated: he becomes depressed.
(c) He endures everything but does not become truly depressed (perhaps because of the impossibility of tolerating depression for a long time). His depression, having failed to develop, forces him to become deluded: in other words, to choose a psychotic defence against depression. He develops a delusional state.

In this chapter, I put forward the opinion of a psychoanalyst faced with delusions and hallucinations in elderly patients.

Delusional mechanisms

In order to do this I am going to start with a number of examples drawn from my clinical experience. Before this, it may be useful to remind the reader that, according to the psychoanalytic theory of delusions (Nacht & Racamier, 1958) delusional ideas are not merely abnormal productions. They are also an effort to defend oneself against a narcissistic wound or an object loss. For example, Dias Cordeiro says "a patient with dementia finds it less difficult to accuse a thief than to acknowledge that he is losing his faculties". In a demented patient, delusions preserve the defensive apparatus and protect narcissism, but place them in a new context since in dementia the psychological apparatus can reorganise itself around a perceptive centre.

During adult life, the human being thinks, thanks to increasingly detailed and abstract representations. In the dementing process, these detailed representations are the first to disappear. As deterioration progresses, only images are left to tie together ideas and produce a thought. In essence, the thinking of a demented person returns to a figurative level. It must be understood that it is consciousness which detects these representations. According to Freud, consciousness is assimilated to a sensorium which receives stimuli from the outside world and is alerted by the inner world. Consciousness is two-faced and, as representations become impoverished and grow scarce, creating a mental void, the psychic apparatus has no other option than to try to construct some meaning from perceptions, i.e. images and sounds, in other words to return to a perceptive focus.

To the extent that the quality of sensory input is adequate to feed thought, the perceptive link continues to function. As perception itself deteriorates, the patient wanders into mental chaos with no clearly defined inside and outside. It is at this point that he becomes deluded.

Many clinicians have noticed that paranoid states in old age are often associated with hearing loss (Bridge & Wyatt, 1980). Some have postulated that sensory deficit is the basis for the delusional idea. It is certainly basic, but one must also consider the thinking process. For myself, I am inclined to think that the delusional idea is manifest at the point where the psychological hold on reality becomes dependent only on perception. In other words, the richer the thinking process, and the more the elderly patient is involved with it, the less the risk of delusions. On the other hand, the more impoverished the thinking process, the less important it is to the patient, and the greater his dependence on perception. Although all demented patients may become deluded one day they do not all do so at the same time.

Perception preserves some degree of organisational ability in the demented patient's thinking. He can maintain his interest through music or imagery. The identity of his thinking quietly crumbles, however, and he relies increasingly on perceptual identity. When no longer able to call upon his memory, he questions his appearance in the mirror or as others see him. In doing so, he accomplishes a probably rather complicated psychic task. The effort involved in this can, in the long term, overtax the patient. The concept of hypersensitivity to sensory stimuli is already accepted in the clinical study of old-age delusions (Lishman, 1978). This hypersensitivity may be seen prodromally. From the point of view of over-investment, it represents the patient's last attempt to control his experiences before being overwhelmed by them and becoming deluded. Thus the patient uses whatever means are still available to attain some order in his chaos.

Forms of organisation

As far as specific methods of organisation are concerned, I will restrict myself to:

(a) over-investment in the concrete
(b) hallucination of desire
(c) projection outside the self of an intolerable element.

Over-investment in the concrete

This is found in subjects whose thought is so near to perception or to perceptual memory that one can ask oneself if things have not always been so. Here is an example where thought has become reorganised on the basis of the reconstruction of a tape.

The patient remembers an encounter during which someone offered him a drink of . . . of . . . (the word escapes him). "What does one drink in the cellars at Reims? . . . What is it called?" He searches for the word for a long time, without success, and then gives up. A little later, he describes a family scene: "When my nephew comes to my house", he explains, "we drink champagne". Surprise, surprise: "Hang on! I found it!". The word has surfaced within a pleasant train of thought. It is as if the pleasant feeling has found the word, and has linked it up to the memory of the thing.

This kind of mental boost reflects a large and more complex mental task than a simple relearning of words, since all the patient's experience is mobilised. His way of reconstructing an image from fragments is similar to that of an archaeologist deducing the shape of a vase from scattered fragments. Logical functioning takes the form of operational thinking centred more on external events than on being tuned in to interior life. Patients equipped with this way of functioning and maintaining a strong relationship with external reality, seem for a long time to be less vulnerable to delusions than others. In common with those who turn actively towards their mental processes, they have a powerful investment in thinking, whether it be operational or abstract. In such cases, thinking forms a barrier against delusions in that it lets the patient fight against depression, that is, to endure solitude without too much harm. One may reformulate the problem by raising the question of the economic value of sublimation. The more creative the human being, the better he survives adversity.

Hallucination of desire

Hallucinations within dementia syndromes are distinct from psychotic hallucinations in a number of respects. For example, psychotic hallucinations are harrowing, whereas hallucinations in dementia are not always so. Indeed a demented patient may find his hallucinations pleasant and say happily: "My mother is up there, she is going to come and see me soon". The psychological process is here subjugated to the pleasure principle, in a dream-like state, to be dealt with positively or negatively as a hallucination. A positive attitude is found most frequently. For example, an elderly demented patient one day refused to let a nurse in, despite knowing her well. Coming naked towards her he declared without any embarrassment "Leave me be, I am in bed with my daughter!". This caricatured formulation reveals a contra-oedipal fantasy freed from all censure. In this sense, the dementia has decapitated any moral authority. An idea that had been habitually repressed is presented here as a reality. The patient can also hallucinate an absence by announcing, for example, that his child is dead and he has had to bury him. As he says so he cries as if he were just coming back from the burial. From a structural perspective, the hallucination of a demented subject seems to involve a regression like that within hypnosis, during which an 'internal perception' is superimposed upon 'external perception'.

Projection

This consists of the attempt to expel from the self an aspect that is judged bad, intolerable and incompatible with the self's ideal. To define this mechanism Green (1987) says that projection is a drive transformed into a wish, transformed into a perception. It is, in effect, experienced as a perception since in the patient's eyes it involves a wish which comes from outside. Successful projection is easily identified both by the observer and by the patient during lucid moments. "Just eight days ago" a patient told me, "I came back from a pleasant walk with my sister. I observed that my room had been burgled. Immediately I worked out what was going on and went to find the hall porter. 'Sir, I have been robbed. The building is not being guarded adequately', 'Please calm down Sir, you know this is just your illness' . . . I am 'the robbed man'. It is as if an imbecile had taken charge of my possessions, of my speech and was using them without my knowledge to pervert them." In this example, the patient remains able to assess his own abnormal thoughts. He can distinguish clearly between inside and outside. The limits of his personality hold good.

But as these limits become blurred, confusion results, a confusion with a psychic origin. For example: an elderly lady sees a man coming out of her television screen. She panics, screams and calls for help. The burglar is there in her house, he is going to rob her! Internal and external psychological spaces have become mixed up. The intrusion takes place in the flat (inside) although he is in the television set (outside). It invades the patient's psychic space, in which nothing differentiates inside and outside. Mental limits are abolished, and anxiety is intense. The bad object inflicts a persecution in which the patient defends herself very badly. She tries to expel it but her attempt peters out.

In order to identify the nature and specificity of these experiences, they must be described in a way common to all the dementias and characterised by the importance of imitation and suggestion.

A mode of being common to all

Imitation

The demented patient recycles sounds heard round him by means of echolalia, of repetition and of imitation without any reshaping. The patient's conversation seems empty and mechanical. Despite this, one must always be wary of any mobilisation of affect. The word which one thought had been reduced to an empty sound can reawaken a pain. The connection between word and affect can suddenly be re-established, albeit momentarily. This explains the impression gained by many clinicians and by carers that the demented person can understand some of our interpretations very well indeed.

I believe that personal contact can be re-established, albeit transiently. If this does happen, I think that the affective tone of the interaction is much more important than the words themselves. In dementia, reconstruction of affect can bring a word back into memory (gerontophasia): in schizophrenia the opposite occurs: the word triggers the affect (schizophasia). Imitation has one disadvantage however: it encourages the patient to repeat what we say. We risk finding in the patient what we have ourselves put there.

Suggestibility

A demented patient may enter another's conversation without any appropriate cue. If the other participant is deluded he takes on the same delusions. Nurses are familiar with these situations where, when one subject within a ward is deluded everyone else becomes deluded with him. It is a very contagious and very changeable habit. As soon as the first person is quiet everyone else resumes his normal mental content. I should add that these intrusions into the consciousness of another have a mainly perceptual basis. They are quick and fleeting. The real question is to know the extent to which people with dementia use mechanisms of identification, imitation or simple suggestion.

To the extent that the demented patient shows himself to be very perceptive, he rapidly gathers either good will or hostility. This does not mean that he remains able to maintain organised emotions until late into the disease. In general, observed changes last no longer than the length of an interview, which supports the argument that any intervention can be mediated by no more than suggestion. In repeated sessions, however, one can observe the development of an affective memory through which the patient can remember the setting, the interviewer's voice, some of the interviewer's facial features – all as if a memory itself were the measure of the affective context.

In conclusion, I would like to remind the reader that, according to psychoanalytic theory:

(a) delusions begin at the point where a new sensory deficit occurs, when the patient's thinking is already focused on perceptions

(b) since the demented patient uses images and sounds instead of words to try and make sense of his feelings, contact with him is easier to establish through the use of sensory supports than through speech

(c) since no one can be in clinical practice without some capacity to be astonished and without gaining pleasure from discovery we should allow ourselves to be guided by the demented person in order to understand him and to understand his delusions. In essence we must give him the floor.

Acknowledgements

Thanks to my colleagues in "Seminaire de Rothschild", and specially to Marion Peruchon. Their suggestion and friendly criticism are a constant enrichment; their ideas contribute to this paper.

References

BERESIN, E. V. (1988) Delirium in the elderly. *Journal of Geriatric Psychiatry and Neurology*, **1**, 127–143.

BRIDGE, T. P. & WYATT, R. J. (1980) Paraphrenia: paranoid states of late life. I. European research. *Journal of the American Geriatrics Society*, **28**, 193–200.

DIAS CORDEIRO, J. C. (1973) Etats Delirants du troisieme age. *L'Encephale*, **1**, 65–79.

FOUCAULT, M. (1972) *Histoire de la Folie a l'Age Classique*, p. 206. Paris: Gallimard.

GREEN, A. (1987) La representation de chose entre pulsion et langage. *Psychanalyse à l'Université*, **12**, 357–371.

KENDLER, K. S. (1980) The nosologic validity of paranoia (simple delusional disorder). *Archives of General Psychiatry*, **37**, 699–706.

LIPOWSKI, Z. (1967) Delirium, clouding of consciousness and confusion. *Journal of Nervous and Mental Diseases*, **145**, 227–255.

LISHMAN, W. A. (1978) *Organic Psychiatry: The Psychological Consequences of Cerebral Disorder*. Oxford: Blackwell Scientific.

LOO, H. & ZARIFIAN, E. (1982) *Precis de Psychiatrie*. Paris: Flammarion.

MANUS, A. & MONFORT, J. C. (1991) Les etats delirants tardifs. *Psychogeriatrie*, **9**, 23–26.

NACHT, S. & RACAMIER, P. C. (1958) La theorie psychanalytique de delire. *Revue Francaise de Psychanalyse*, **22**, 417–532.

NEYRAUT, M. (1974) *Le Transfert*. Paris: Presses Universitaries de France.

6 Neurological models of auditory hallucinations

ANTHONY S. DAVID and PHILIP LUCAS

"The disorders of inner speech [may] . . . be understood from the point of view of a relaxation of the relations between idea and actual speech. By this destruction of inner concatenation and causation, the whole of active life receives the stamp of the incalculable, the incomprehensible, and the distorted."
(Kraepelin, 1919)

Auditory hallucinations (AHs), particularly where the person hears a voice, sometimes called verbal hallucinations (VHs), are one of the fundamental features of mental illness (Goodwin *et al*, 1971). The prevalence of auditory hallucinations in schizophrenia has been calculated by Slade & Bentall (1988), based on 16 published reports including 2924 cases, as occurring in 60.2%. In the International Pilot Study of Schizophrenia (Wing *et al*, 1974), 74% of 306 schizophrenics had this symptom.

Psychiatrists emphasise aspects of the form of hallucinations. Are they experienced as real or unreal, inside the head or outside? Do they consist of meaningful sounds or noises? If they are verbal, is the voice known? Is it male or female? What of the grammatical form – does the voice refer to the subject in the second or third person (Schneider, 1959)? Such considerations are of considerable diagnostic significance. Less attention has been given to the content of the hallucination (Larkin, 1979), such as whether it is critical or supportive, whether the content is unpleasant, sexual, violent, neutral, etc.

There are numerous experiential phenomena which resemble VHs. These are usually placed under the rubric of auditory imagery, a specific variety of which is inner speech. This phenomenon is of course normal and, presumably, universal. As the above quotation illustrates, the resemblance between inner speech and VHs has been noted for at least a century. In a wide-ranging review, Hoffman (1986) drew attention to this once again. Our contention is that inquiry into the nature of VHs would profit from a brain-based functionalist approach common in cognitive neuropsychological research. That is, we believe that VHs ultimately rely on brain processes but

57

C

can be best understood in functional, psychological terms. First, we examine whether cerebral insult is either necessary or sufficient to cause VHs, in terms of neurological inputs or 'the mind's ear' and then in terms of the 'mind's voice'. Next, we move on to a more psychological perspective, that of inner speech. From this we look at the relevance of structural and functional cerebral abnormality for AHs in psychosis, reviewing work in neuroimaging. Finally we argue that VHs must be viewed as heterogeneous with respect to form, content and origin. We suggest that research should focus on the functioning of a complex normal mechanism underlying inner speech whose normal in-built control mechanisms may be distorted, by a focal brain abnormality, and offer a preliminary model.

Neurological input models

Auditory experiences during electrical brain stimulation

A series of famous experiments were carried out by Penfield and co-workers in Montreal (Penfield & Perot, 1963). Early work showed that stimulation of the primary auditory areas resulted in crude 'noises' while more complex sounds followed stimulation of 'secondary' association areas. Out of 1132 stimulation studies – 520 of the temporal lobes (TLs) – only 40 resulted in 'experiential hallucinations' including complex auditory–visual experiences, 'voices' and music. Auditory responses were produced in 24 patients from 66 stimulation points. Going through each of these in turn, one is struck by how dissimilar the reports are to auditory hallucinations seen in psychiatric settings. The descriptions often mention voices muttering, shouting or whispering, not the distinct, repetitive statements schizophrenic patients experience. In two-thirds of cases, the patient reports ''a voice from the past'' that is the memory of an actual phrase spoken to them – usually by a close relative. Having a vision of a person who speaks to the subject as in a dream was a frequent occurrence, one which would be regarded as a 'dissociative hallucination' by most psychopathologists rather than a 'true' hallucination (see Wing *et al*, 1974).

Verbal hallucinations whose content was clear enough to be recorded verbatim were limited to five cases. These consisted of a voice calling the patient's name, one calling the patient's husband's name, one saying ''vite, vite'' (French), another saying ''Yes, get out'' and later ''Tokyo, Tokike'' (sic) and finally a voice instructing the patient to ''Bend down . . .''. Penfield & Perot localised the auditory experiences to the lateral and superior surface of the first temporal convolution, more often on the right.

Bancaud *et al* (1976) carried out 521 stimulations of the anterior cingulate gyrus on 83 patients. Only two experienced auditory sensations. A careful study by Halgren *et al* (1978) of 3495 deep temporal lobe stimulations in 36 psychomotor epileptics, evoked no formed verbal hallucinations. Memory-like episodes were elicited in three cases, after stronger stimulation and hence wider activations. All three were found to be predisposed to aberrant perceptual experiences as assessed by the Minnesota Multiphasic Personality Inventory (MMPI; Hathaway & McKinley, 1967). The authors argue that their inability to produce experiential responses as readily as Penfield may be explained by the weaker and more precise application of current and that such experiences are the indirect result of extensive electrical disruption of the TLs. This would fit with the frequency of hallucinatory experiences occurring post/inter-ictally in epileptics rather than during the ictus (see later). More sophisticated studies have since been conducted using stereotactically placed electrodes (Gloor *et al*, 1982). Unlike Halgren *et al* (1978) these authors found that experiential phenomena could be elicited by limbic (e.g. amygdala) stimulation alone. Again, purely auditory as opposed to visual hallucinations were found in just two of 35 patients, perhaps because of the privileged access of input in the visual modality to the amygdala. Gloor (1990) has discussed mechanisms based on concepts of parallel distributed processes which might explain experiential phenomena. Clearly, early notions that they represent a replay of past experience are not consistent with current theories of cognition.

In summary, brain stimulation experiments, despite their promise, have failed to provide a plausible model of functional auditory hallucinations.

Verbal hallucinations during seizures

The experience of a complex auditory hallucination during a seizure (or coinciding with an EEG record of seizure activity) appears to be extremely rare. This must be distinguished from hallucinations and a range of other psychiatric phenomena occurring in the post-ictal period or, alternatively, associated with a long-standing diagnosis of epilepsy (Ferguson & Rayport, 1984; Trimble, 1990). For example, a detailed study by So *et al* (1990) using continuous stereotactic depth and epidural EEG confirmed that a young man's hallucination of a voice accusing him of being homosexual was a post-ictal phenomenon. While such an association is of considerable importance in suggesting an aetiology for 'functional psychosis', it does not help us understand the genesis of the hallucination itself.

A study of 90 patients with temporal lobe epilepsy (TLE) by Bingley (1958) showed 18% experienced "auditory illusions and hallucinations" at some time. A larger survey of 666 patients revealed that 16% had auditory–sensory components to the attack, which were five times more likely to be 'crude' than 'elaborate' (Currie *et al*, 1971). The elaborate ones often included automatisms and sensations in more than one sensory modality, so these do not provide an ideal analogy for 'functional' auditory hallucinations. The only other cases in the literature were collected by Hécaen & Ropert (1959) who collected 34 cases over more than a decade. Only in two cases did the AHs occur in the absence of either sensory impairment or

TABLE 6.1
Verbal hallucinations of patients with demonstrable cerebral lesions

Case no.	Mechanism	Content and comments
6	Post-ictal	"Oui" and "Eva"
1	Post-ictal	"I'm coming back, I'm coming back . . ."
7	Epileptic aura	A phrase in Latin and 'écho de la pensée'. "Not like hearing people speaking".
14	Epileptic aura	"Genevieve, you are going to vanish . . ."
10	L temporal glioma	Palinacousis
27	L temporo-parietal discharges on EEG	Sister's voice e.g. "Tata Lène". Knew it was "in her brain".

Adapted from Hécean & Ropert, 1959.

perceptual disturbances in other modalities. Complex verbal hallucinations occurred in six cases (see Table 6.1). The authors' found an association between complex musical or verbal hallucinations and left temporal lesions.

One rare example which comes nearer to demonstrating EEG abnormalities coincident with hallucinations was reported by Wieser (1980) by whom epileptic discharges were recorded from a 22 year-old woman in her right gyrus of Heschl, accompanied by the hallucination of songs (but not speech; see also Keshavan *et al*, 1992). Finally, a case of epilepsy due to an arterio-venous malformation in which unspecified auditory hallucinations occurred as an aura was studied using positron emission tomography (PET) (De Reuck *et al*, 1989). A decrease in blood flow and oxygen metabolism was demonstrated behind the left insular region malformation, 14 days after the event.

Verbal hallucinations due to static brain lesions in the absence of seizures

Again, we are making the distinction between brain lesions found in association with an entire clinical syndrome of which AHs may be a part (69% of 150 cases reviewed by Davison & Bagley (1969)), and the acute, isolated production of hallucinations. The latter is extremely rare. Courville (1928) examined the records of 412 verified cases of brain tumour. Of 99 TL lesions, four had AHs, and of 98 frontal lesions, six had AHs, but these were invariably combined with experiences in other modalities. A different collection of 110 cases of TL tumours contained only four cases with AHs, two of whom had complex experiences, one of which was of Irish folk songs and the other was associated with "crude visual hallucinations and a dreamy state" (Keschner *et al*, 1936). A more recent study of 61 TL tumours found no instances of AHs (Gal, 1958). Despite these inconsistencies, if a brain region were to be chosen as the seat of AHs from this data it would probably be the TLs, although the only significant, but weak ($r = 0.29$), correlation found by Davison & Bagley for AHs was with diencephalic lesion sites (Davison & Bagley, 1969).

One category of AH which should be considered separately is unilateral hallucinations. This again is uncommon although it may follow contralateral brain lesions. Bergman (1965) reported in brief 12 such cases of unilateral auditory hallucinations but states "intelligible speech was not reported by any patient". Of more interest is the patient described by Tanabe *et al* (1986) who had a left superior temporal gyrus infarction and experienced transient aphasia and voices, of a female TV announcer, coming from the right ear.

To complicate matters, another cause of unilateral AHs is ear disease. This has been recognised for decades (e.g. Morel, 1936) and was re-emphasised by Gordon (1987). The mechanism of peripheral sensory disruption leading to hallucinations is an important one which must operate in some cases. It is particularly relevant in musical hallucinations (Berrios, 1990). In a recent review, ear disease was associated with musical hallucinations in at least 38 out of 59 cases (Keshavan *et al*, 1992). In schizophrenia it may represent co-morbidity. Collicut & Hemsley (1981) have shown that auditory perception is neither better nor worse in schizophrenic hallucinators.

In conclusion, VHs as a direct and immediate consequence of brain lesions, both irritative and destructive, are rare. If such hallucinations occur, they may be unilateral. Unilateral VHs in functional psychosis will be discussed later in this chapter, as will EEG and brain stimulation studies of psychotic, usually schizophrenic, patients.

Neurological output models

In considering the neurological origins of auditory–verbal hallucinations it seems important to broaden the scope of the discussion to encompass speech production. As will be discussed in the context of inner speech, a disturbance manifesting in hearing voices could arise from any point in an inner voice–inner ear circuit. Brain stimulation experiments assume that exogenous stimulation at the input stage (auditory association cortex or 'inner ear') will mimic AH. Equally plausible is that abnormal production of speech or at least a motor programme which would normally precede speech (i.e. an 'inner voice') might, if redirected, produce the experience of hearing a voice in the absence of an external stimulus. This assumes that the inner voice uses, in part, the same mechanism as that for speech output (see Green & Preston, 1981).

Following this reasoning and stated simply, the origin of speech in the brain may be the origin of verbal hallucinations. The "seat of articulate language", after Broca, is usually located around the 3rd inferior frontal convolution of the left hemisphere, although other regions such as the supplementary motor area and more anterior frontal areas are implicated in the initiation of speech (Ojemann, 1983). Speech production can be studied in a variety of ways such as during brain stimulation and epilepsy.

Brain stimulation and epilepsy

Penfield & Roberts (1959) were unable to produce anything other than 'crude vocalization' during their brain stimulation experiments to either of the precentral cerebral areas. This was in contrast to the wide areas which, when stimulated, led to speech arrest. Recent work by Ojemann *et al* (1990) on 117 patients undergoing left frontotemporoparietal craniotomies has aimed at mapping language areas by assessing picture naming during electrical stimulation. While discrete areas underlying this function were located in individuals, as a group, localisation was highly variable.

Turning to epileptic disturbances of speech, Serafetinides & Falconer (1963) surveyed 100 cases of TLE and found 34 with dysphasic disturbances and 38 with speech automatisms. This concurs with Bingley's (1958) figure of 39% for automatisms. The dysphasic group more often had left hemisphere discharges while those with automatisms had more on the right. They divided the utterances into five sub-types: warning – e.g. "I feel funny"; recurrent – e.g. "I must go, I must go"; irrelevant – described as of "conversational character" but "out of context"; emotional – e.g. swear words and "I don't care what you do to me"; perplexity – e.g. "Why not? Who are you? Where am I?" In bilinguals, some utterances were in the patient's mother tongue. Similar speech fragments occur in severe aphasics (Code, 1987). All of these examples would fit into Hughlings Jackson's category of non-propositional speech (1874/1932).

To some extent, these utterances, single words, and inane, often repetitive, phrases, in the patient's first language (Jaspers, 1913; Hoffman, 1986), are reminiscent of some types of AHs in functional disorders. Obscenities are commonly reported – although data are not available on the relative proportion of AHs of different content. Therefore, the topic deserves fuller investigation.

Right hemisphere speech?

Jackson's dichotomy between propositional and non-propositional speech carried an anatomical division – the left and right hemispheres respectively. To what extent do speech automatisms and other recurrent utterances reflect right hemisphere (RH) activity? We will review briefly the evidence on this with additional information from left hemispherectomy and commissurotomy cases as well as studies on intact subjects.

As already mentioned, ictal and electrically induced speech is more common after RH activation and the implication from recurrent utterances from aphasics is that it is their intact RHs which are doing the talking. Support for this comes from a number of studies of aphasics who, following a second lesion to the RH, suffer dramatic deterioration in language output (see e.g. Basso *et al*, 1989). Secondly, experiments by Kinsbourne (1971) using the Wada technique (Intracarotid amytal injection) showed that temporary anaesthesia of the two aphasic patients' LHs showed similar, although reversible effects.

The Wada test was devised to establish cerebral dominance before temporal lobe surgery. The inability to speak while the left hemisphere (LH) is temporarily out of action remains the most reliable index. Branch *et al* (1964) showed that only 4% of right-handers could speak under these circumstances compared with 15% of left-handers. It should be remembered that the subjects involved cannot be considered normal since they all suffered from intractable epilepsy. However, the data are consistent with the effects of stroke in previously well individuals in terms of aphasia in right- and left-handers (see McCarthy & Warrington, 1990), that is, dextrals seldom become aphasic following RH damage while sinistrals may do. Further studies by Milner (1975) have clarified the role of handedness and early brain injury in determining lateralisation for speech. In a study of 109 subjects who had sustained early LH damage, 19% of 31 right-handers had right or bilateral language representation while 70% of 78 non-right-handers had right or bilateral language.

A possible intermediary factor is the corpus callosum thickness. O'Kusky *et al* (1988) performed a magnetic resonance imaging (MRI) study which revealed that increased callosal thickness predicted RH speech independently of handedness in epileptic subjects. Some authors have found an association between left-handedness and increased callosal dimensions while others have not (Raine *et al*, 1990). Similar claims have been made for gender effects. While no firm conclusions can be reached at present it is possible to state that in all the circumstances where RH language is suspected to be more developed than 'normal', such as in females and left-handers, some studies have found increased callosal size. This finding is important in the light of studies of the corpus callosum in schizophrenia.

Studies of commissurotomy – the 'split-brain' operation – have revealed a wide range of comprehension abilities in the separated RH (Zaidel, 1985). However, after more than 30 years of testing, none of the original Bogen-Vogel West Coast series have demonstrated communicative speech from the RH (Gazzaniga & Hillyard, 1971). By way of contrast, two subjects from the East coast series, operated in two stages and sparing the anterior commissure, studied by Gazzaniga and colleagues, have experienced the emergence of some RH speech (Sitdis *et al*, 1981; Gazzaniga *et al*, 1984). The output is simple and 'agrammatic' – that is, mainly content words without connections between them. The question of why these subjects should have this ability while none of the others do is still debated (Gazzaniga, 1983; Zaidel, 1983). One likely explanation is the influence of early LH damage, which led the RH to develop a greater than usual, although latent, language competence.

Support for this position comes from hemispherectomy. Early left hemispherectomy has been shown to be compatible with a full range of linguistic ability (Bishop, 1983). However, patients who have undergone the same operation after childhood language acquisition remain severely limited in verbal expression. Smith (1966) described an adult case. Post-operatively he struggled to utter a few isolated words often exclaiming "Goddamit!" in frustration. However, over the ensuing weeks he would occasionally manage brief phrases and by six months replied to the question "Is it snowing outside?", with "What do you think I am? A mind reader?" More recently Patterson *et al* (1989) described in detail the linguistic ability of an adolescent girl operated on because of Rassmusen's encephalitis. The following speech sample was given: Q: What do you particularly like to eat? "I like . . . er . . . you know . . . the . . . I can't say it now . . . well, I like . . . I don't like chips a lot but . . . I like bolognaise".

A profile of RH language has been formulated as follows: it has better comprehension of speech than reading, it has limited access to abstract words in the lexicon. Phonology in the RH is very rudimentary so that rhyme judgements are poor, as are tasks requiring written word-to-sound (grapheme–phoneme) correspondence. This profile is derived from left hemispherectomy, split brain and certain aphasic syndromes such as deep dyslexia (Zaidel, 1985; Coltheart *et al*, 1987). In these respects, the LH has much greater facility.

To summarise, there is convergence from various sources in the literature that the RH seldom has the ability to speak (< 5%) despite significant language comprehension capacity. This ceases to pertain so strongly when the LH has undergone early disruption and/or when the subject is left-handed. This situation is important as it figures prominently in various psychiatric theories which nominate the RH as the origin of AHs.

The right cerebral hemisphere and auditory hallucinations

We have established that the RH can swear and make non-propositional statements. VHs are often described as having a similar content (Hill, 1936). The RH's language output increases in the absence of the LH and more commonly, when the LH is subject to insults in development and when the usual pattern of cerebral asymmetry is altered. With and without this knowledge base, various authors have proposed theories linking the RH with AHs, particularly VHs. The first was anthropologist Julian Jaynes (1976) who argued that in early civilisations, man frequently experienced 'voices' which he then attributed to divine powers but which in fact arose from a relatively autonomous RH. With evolution, the separateness or 'bicamerality' of the hemispheres has broken down leading to a reduction in VHs in ordinary people. One group which is an exception to this view is, according to Jaynes, psychotics, whose RH language system remains unintegrated with the left's except for a link via the anterior commissure. Randall (1983) put forward a neurodevelopmental account in which mis-connections between brain regions, including right and left language areas, lead to VHs as well as other schizophrenic symptoms such as thought insertion and withdrawal. A related theory was put forward by Nasrallah (1985) which explained the same cluster of symptoms in terms of 'partial disconnection' of the hemispheres. All of these accounts invoke interhemispheric communication as a key element. The evidence for this will be discussed later.

Cutting (1990) proposed a novel theory which comes out of his view that underactivity of the RH is fundamental to schizophrenia. He suggests that verbal thoughts, presumably arising from the LH, lack their "accustomed tone . . . which stamps them as uniquely ours, . . . because of the loss of the right hemisphere's prosodic contribution" (p. 264). Hence they are given non-self status. So far, this attractive notion has not been subject to empirical verification. Indirect support would be provided by an account from a patient with RH damage reporting loss of prosody of their inner voice. Such an account is awaited.

In conclusion, the RH is a plausible site for the origin of AHs where their content is rudimentary and 'non-propositional'. However, where there has been early brain damage, an alteration in cerebral asymmetry and/or an increase in interhemispheric communication, the RH may have the capacity to support even complex VHs.

Neuropsychological models – inner speech

To many, the relationship between inner speech and VH as noted over many years, is self-evident (see Johnson, 1978, for review). Unfortunately, this intuitive correspondence has seldom led to testable hypotheses since the experimental paradigms required have only recently been devised and validated.

Phenomenology, reading and memory

Our own introspections form a useful starting point. We do not have to think using an inner voice but we often do. Our thoughts tend to be experienced in our own (external) voice, although this may not quite accord with how it sounds to others. Reading is frequently accompanied by a vivid inner voice which may be identified with the writer if he/she is known. We may become especially aware of the inner voice when reading a difficult passage which we do not immediately understand. Sub-vocal muscular activity is sometimes detected, especially in poor readers who tend to mouth the words more obviously (Dooley & George, 1988). Certain aspects of reading would seem to rely on an inner voice such as deriving the correct meaning from the sentence containing the word *tear*: "Her dress had a tear in it" v. "Her eye had a tear in it" (Ellis & Young, 1988). Similarly, how do we know that BRANE (a pseudohomophone) sounds like a real word and rhymes with TAYNE and REIGN? And that T42 is the title of a popular song?

Evidence for this intuition comes from experiments which utilise articulatory suppression. This entails subjects repeating a meaningless phrase or word (e.g. the-the-the), so occupying inner speech, while reading words, letter strings or sentences (see Baddeley & Lewis (1981) and Besner (1987) for a discussion of this field). While it is quite possible to understand even complex sentences under conditions of articulatory suppression, detecting rhyme is impaired (Richardson, 1987) as is the detection of anomalous sentences where a homophone replaces the correct word (e.g. The king sat in his *thrown* room) (Coltheart *et al*, 1990). This work provides a number of paradigms which could be employed in the study of the relationship between VHs and inner speech.

Neuroimaging

Early research measuring cerebral blood flow confirmed classical neurological expectations in showing left anterior increases during speech (Ingvar & Schwartz, 1974). However, automatic speech appears to coincide with much wider areas of activation in addition to speech centres and involving both hemispheres (Ryding *et al*, 1987). Inner speech has not been specifically studied using positron emission tomography (PET) but work by Petersen and colleagues (Petersen *et al*, 1988), on word recognition, is of relevance here. Using multiple scans and the subtraction method it is possible to localise specific cognitive processes to changes in blood flow. They found that phonological recoding was not a necessary aspect of reading but that phono-logical coding activated temporal cortical regions bilaterally and in temporal–parietal cortex on the left. Speech involved peri-sylvian areas bilaterally and the left prefrontal region. Work by Wise and colleagues (Wise *et al*, 1991) suggests that the supplementary motor area, in association with left auditory association cortex, is crucially involved in a verb retrieval task which was presumed to involve sub-vocal rehearsal.

Studies in patients with brain damage

A traditional source of information on normal psychological processes is provided by the study of patients who have lost the faculty of interest following brain damage.

Levine *et al* (1982) described just such a patient who, following a presumed left hemisphere stroke, was unable to "speak to himself" other than through visual imagery. When reading he would only " 'see' words as ideas not sounds". Among his many deficits, he could not detect whether words rhymed, nor could he select homophones from an array.

The classical aphasiological view is that a two-way connection links input and output language centres. Damage to this interconnection results in the loss of ability to repeat verbal sequences (e.g. digit span). This has been called 'conduction aphasia' although current views stress the impairment of short-term memory (STM) (Baddeley, 1986; Vallar & Shallice, 1990). As well as having a characteristic pattern of performance on STM tests, some individuals with this deficit do not seem to have the experience of inner speech (Feinberg *et al*, 1986). A detailed study by Howard & Franklin (1990) provides good evidence for a mechanism underpinning rehearsal of phonological items which can be disrupted following brain disease. This patient had a variety of language difficulties alongside a markedly reduced STM span and was unable to evoke a phonologically or speech–sound-based representation of written language. His performance was best explained by an inability to rehearse internally.

Another case that bears upon this issue is that described by Ellis *et al* (1989). This patient experienced 'natterings' or 'persistent inner speech vocalisations' plus musical fragments, inside her head, due to bilateral cerebrovascular brain disease. She was noted to have reduced STM (3 digits) following a left thalamic haematoma, but the uncontrollable inner speech began after a subsequent lesion in the right basal ganglia. The authors suggest that their patient's damaged STM system not only lost some of its capacity but also the ability to regulate its contents – allowing entry to unwanted memories presumed to arise from the damaged RH. Unlike most schizophrenic patients, Ellis *et al*'s patient retained her ability to label the voices as her own. But like them, she lost her hallucinations when speaking or listening to speech (see Margo *et al*, 1981). This suggests the phonological store is open to inappropriate activation, possibly from the right hemisphere, perhaps due to a gating failure at a subcortical level (see Ojemann, 1978). When activity engages the system, other inputs are inhibited. Normally, some control mechanism of the cognitive system can also prohibit internally derived information from entering STM.

Studies in psychotics

Phenomenology

The phenomenological distinction between inner speech and VHs has drawn comment from many noted phenomenologists (Jaspers, 1913). Sedman (1966) attempted to distinguish inner speech from both auditory pseudohallucination and 'true' AH. The criteria for this were based on ego-compatibility and inner subjective space, and the 'insight' into the un-reality of the experience. Current thinking is now inclined towards a less categorical view of psychotic phenomena (Strauss, 1969; David, 1990) and regards them as lying on a continuum. Support for this comes from a survey of schizophrenic patients' self-ratings of AHs on a number of dimensions (Junginger & Frame, 1985). The majority of patients regarded their hallucinations as 'inside the head' despite the classical view that these should be clearly outside, to be counted as hallucinations. In our experience, many patients struggle with notions of whether the 'voices' are under their control or outside their head, and that the nature of the experience changes according to course of illness, mood and how willing the patient is to discuss their AHs with staff.

From data currently being collected by workers from the Department of Psychological Medicine, Institute of Psychiatry, London (Jones, personal communication) of consecutive psychotic admissions from a defined

TABLE 6.2
Frequency of different types of auditory hallucination – PSE item 65

	Non-schizophrenic psychotics	Schizophrenics	All
No hallucinations	57	50	107 (49.8%)
Pseudohallucinations	9	17	26 (12.1%)
True hallucinations	9	16	25 (11.6%)
Both together	29	28	57 (26.5%)
Total	104	111	215 (100%)

Data courtesy of Dr P. Jones (Institute of Psychiatry, London) from consecutive admissions with psychosis from defined catchment area in South London.
PSE = Present State Examination (Wing *et al*, 1974).

catchment area, the rates are available on various forms of VH, classified according to the Present State Examination (PSE; Wing *et al*, 1974). The incidence of pseudo-hallucinations ('within the mind'), true hallucinations ('through the ears'), and both types together are shown for DSM–III schizophrenics and a combined group of schizophreniform, schizoaffective and affective patients (see Table 6.2).

Lateralisation of auditory hallucinations

Localisation in space is an aspect of the heterogeneity of auditory hallucinations which may also bear upon the anatomical site of brain processes. Lateralisation of abnormal visual and somatic sensations occurs more often to the left side of the body (Taylor & Fleminger, 1981; Cutting, 1989). By way of contrast, VHs in schizophrenia are usually un-lateralised and poorly localised (Bracha *et al*, 1985). In a series of 54 subjects with a variety of diagnoses, localising of a voice to the right side of the subject was associated with higher scores on the Hamilton rating scale for depression (Gruber *et al*, 1984). Where AHs are clearly located to one hemispace, the neurological literature (Hécaen & Ropert, 1959; Bergman, 1965; Tanabe *et al*, 1986) suggests a contralateral temporal lobe lesion or, alternatively, ipsilateral ear disease (Morel, 1936; Gordon, 1987). Hence, study of these, admittedly atypical, patients using neuroimaging techniques, would allow unambiguous testing of the neurological/audiological hypotheses, already confirmed once by Notardonato *et al* (1989).

Form and content

Crude hallucinations, odd noises, sound fragments and indistinct whispers etc, were frequently elicited by Penfield by brain stimulation (Penfield

& Perot, 1963) and have been shown to be associated with (contralateral) cerebral lesions (Morel, 1936; Hécean & Ropert, 1959). While these are not commonly reported in schizophrenia, they do occur. From the Institute of Psychiatry data, 33 (13.4%) out of 247 patients experienced 'non-verbal' hallucinations (PSE item 60); 19 (7.7%) were music, tapping, engines etc. and 14 (5.7%) were mutterings or whisperings. Only nine (3.6%) patients reported hearing their name as the sole hallucinatory symptoms (PSE item 61, rating = 1). Again, given the neurological work reviewed earlier, these phenomena would make a suitable target for separate neurophysiological study, particularly of the primary auditory areas of the brain.

We would expect the different types of hallucination to have different pathogeneses: thought echo is plausibly connected to inner speech; non-verbal hallucinations may be the result of cortical irritation, perhaps right more than left, from unknown cause; 3rd person VHs, being less common than 2nd person and pseudohallucinations would be expected to represent a more severe and specific disturbance of inner speech control.

EEG recordings in hallucinating patients

Despite the lack of empirical support, the notion that sporadic psychotic phenomena such as AHs are the products of seizure discharges remains compelling for psychiatric researchers. The most systematic studies have been carried out by Stevens and her colleagues (Stevens *et al*, 1979) who concluded that while EEG abnormalities were found in around 40% of 40 patients, ''The abnormal waveforms . . . seldom coincided with episodes of blocking, stereotypy, or other abnormal behaviours'' (which included AHs). Stevens & Livermore (1982) later described differences in power spectra derived from scalp EEGs. These patterns, which resembled 'ramps' when charted graphically, were seen during a range of abnormal behaviours and 'hallucinatory periods'. However, Serafetinides *et al* (1986) found that the results were substantially altered when patients' self-report rather than observer rating of hallucinations was used. It appears that the 'ramps' were more likely to occur between periods of hallucination.

Studies using depth electrodes for recording and brain stimulation in schizophrenic subjects have seldom been carried out, presumably because of their invasiveness. A Japanese study (Ishibashi *et al*, 1964) was conducted on 17 patients. As in normal subjects, complex AHs were seldom evoked (three cases only) during electrical stimulation of the temporal cortex. The authors make the important observation that the hallucinations produced in this way ''greatly differ from those of schizophrenic hallucinations''. Again, the brain stimulation/epilepsy model for VHs in functional disorders, fails to find support.

Single photon emission computerised tomography (SPECT) and positron emission tomography (PET) in the study of auditory hallucinations

Background

While the newer techniques of radio-imaging cannot yet obtain readings from ambulant psychotics, they are superior tools for brain localisation than surface EEG. In contradistinction to computerised tomography (CT) and magnetic resonance imaging (MRI) which provide information about brain structure, PET is the most powerful tool available for the investigation of *in-vivo* brain function. As cerebral blood flow is physiologically coupled to neuronal activation, and as spatial resolution of less than 7 mm and temporal resolution of about 40 seconds can now be obtained with PET, changes in regional neuronal activity in response to specified mental activities can be followed.

A number of studies have been undertaken with, it appears, the rather naive aim of localisation within the brain of 'the hallucination' itself. Since the phenomena are inherently neither mental nor physical, the search for the site of 'the hallucination' becomes an attempt to identify and characterise the brain processes specific to hallucinating individuals.

Before considering experimental data in such individuals, some of the difficulty inherent in this endeavour can be conveyed by a consideration of observations obtained from normal subjects. For example, the importance of anticipation in the neuronal activation response to a given stimulus has recently been demonstrated by Corbetta *et al* (1990) who used PET to measure changes in regional cerebral blood flow (rCBF) of subjects while they were discriminating different attributes of the same set of visual stimuli. Using a different PET technique (^{18}F-fluorodeoxyglucose uptake), Reivich *et al* (1984) observed asymmetrically increased neuronal activity in the right inferior parietal lobule of subjects directing attention to external sensory stimulation (visual or auditory) compared with those not so attending. They also report that anxiety increased metabolic asymmetry between cerebral hemispheres (right greater than left). PET studies have also indicated that anticipatory anxiety may lead to changes in TL blood flow in normal subjects (Reiman *et al*, 1989).

Given the wide spectrum of responses to hallucinations, from outright terror during the acute phase of a first psychotic episode on the one hand, to the studied indifference of a therapeutically sophisticated chronic sufferer on the other, these observations are of obvious relevance. Indeed, in a discussion of their failure to find specific regions in which brain metabolism differed between hallucinating and non-hallucinating patients, Cleghorn and colleagues (1990) suggest that the subjects may have ceased to "attend to their voices". Unless factors such as attention and anxiety are taken into account, difficulties in interpretation will arise. A PET study by DeLisi *et al* (1989) of TL glucose metabolic rate in schizophrenic patients illustrates the problem. Their subjects were receiving brief electrical stimuli ranging in intensity "from barely perceptible to unpleasant". It is difficult to escape the conclusion that significant anxiety must have been engendered, potentially confounding the aims of the study.

Patient studies

While much effort has been expended to define the site of abnormal brain activity in psychosis, the results of ten years of PET studies have been contradictory (Bench *et al*, 1990). Heterogeneity of psychopathology (and presumably associated brain pathology) is likely to be responsible. Furthermore, patient selection is influenced by the nature of the technology, with violent and highly aroused subjects being avoided. The techniques have themselves developed and improved considerably over the last decade, and consequently problems arise in comparing results of earlier studies with those carried out more recently (Fox *et al*, 1988). Such considerations at least partly explain the bewildering variety of findings in studies of schizophrenic subjects with at least three main brain areas suggested to be abnormal, the frontal lobes, basal ganglia and temporal lobes (Buchsbaum, 1990).

By a factor analytic technique, Liddle (1987) provided evidence for three separate sub-syndromes within subjects diagnosed as schizophrenic of which the major features were respectively positive symptoms, negative symptoms and disordered thought. The same group has recently succeeded in demonstrating three corresponding distinct rCBF profiles (Liddle *et al*, 1992). Of interest here is the association between increased left parahippocampal flow and 'reality distortion' – which includes hallucinations.

Musalek *et al* (1989) have also focused on phenomenology, without emphasising diagnosis. They observed two distinct patterns, one associated with auditory, the other with tactile hallucinatory activity by means of SPECT. They reported lower frontal activity and higher basal ganglia rCBF, in both groups of hallucinators compared with normal subjects but those with auditory hallucinations (7 schizophrenic, 4 affective, 3 uncertain) manifested increased flow in the amygdala, hippocampus and parahippocampus – bilaterally; those with tactile hallucinations (9 affective, 2 organic) had decreased flow to the inferior temporal region compared with normal subjects.

Using similar technology but scanning the same subjects in both the hallucinating and non-hallucinating state, preliminary observations of McGuire & Murray (1991) have suggested significantly greater flow to the middle part of the left lateral temporal lobe during auditory hallucinatory activity. Few studies have attempted such repeated measurements but there is some evidence that abnormal patterns of rCBF may depend on the subjects' clinical state (see Table 6.3). Warkentin *et al* (1990) used the ^{133}Xe inhalation method with which Ingvar & Franzen (1974) first observed hypo-frontality in chronic schizophrenic patients. They observed normal relative frontal flow during the acute attack with relative hypofrontality on remission.

TABLE 6.3

Single case studies using SPECT in patients with auditory hallucinations

Author	Technique	Diagnosis	Results
Matsuda *et al* (1988*a*)	[123]I Iodoamphetamine	schizophrenia	Accumulation in L superior & inferior temporal gyrus
Matsuda *et al* (1988*b*)	[123]I Iodoamphetamine	alcoholic hallucinosis	Accumulation in L superior temporal lobe
Notardonato *et al* (1989)	[123]I Iodoamphetamine	schizophrenia (L sided hallucinations)	↑ uptake caudate nuclei bilaterally & R temporal lobe (normalised after treatment)
Hawton *et al* (1990)	[99]Tc[m] HMPAO	schizophrenia (prominent hallucinations)	↓ Frontal blood flow during psychosis and relapse. Reperfusion during remission

Their findings are in agreement with those of Géraud *et al* (1987) but directly contradictory of those of Hawton *et al* (1990) who carried out serial SPECT scans in an individual patient with schizophrenia at the time of two successive psychotic episodes and during the period of remission between. Unlike Warkentin *et al* and Géraud *et al*, they observed hypoperfusion of frontal regions during the acute episode only. The reasons for these differences are unclear, although medication may have been a confounding variable.

Several investigators have analysed their results in terms of correlations between the degree of symptomatic abnormality of their subjects and the extent of the abnormality of part of the brain (Table 6.4). Leaving aside the statistically problematic question of multiple testing, the significant correlations involving degrees of hallucinatory experience have not resulted in much clarification. Most studies have employed the Brief Psychiatric Rating Scale (BPRS; Overall & Gorham, 1962) to quantify the hallucinatory experience. Mathew *et al* (1982) reported inverse correlations between hallucinatory experience and blood flow in the left parietal and TL as well as right temporoparietal and occipital lobes. Volkow *et al* (1987) reported a positive correlation between right temporal glucose metabolism and hallucination scores. When an eye-tracking task was performed during testing, the correlation coefficient increased from 0.49 to 0.72. Measurement of glucose metabolism rate with PET was employed by DeLisi *et al* (1989) who reported a positive correlation between the ratio of left to right superior temporal lobe metabolic rates and AHs. As discussed above, the validity of these findings is vitiated by an experimental protocol involving the delivery of random electrical stimuli. Weiler *et al* (1990) report an inverse correlation between left caudate glucose metabolism and extent of hallucinatory activity. Using the rating scale for hallucinations of the Schizophrenia Assessment,

TABLE 6.4
SPECT and PET studies in patients with auditory hallucinations

Authors	Technique	Subjects	Results
Mathew et al (1982)	^{133}Xe inhalation	23 schizophrenics 18 normal controls	Hallucinations – BPRS: negative correlations ($0.34 < r < 0.45$) with L temporal/parietal; R. temporo-parietal/occipital blood flow
Erbaş et al (1990)	^{99}Tc^m HMPAO	20 schizophrenics (all with auditory hallucinations) 11 normal controls	reduced frontal:occipital blood flow ratios
Kurachi et al (1985)	^{133}Xe inhalation	16 schizophrenics (8 hallucinators) 20 normal controls	↑ L temporal blood flow in hallucinators ↓ bilateral frontal flow in patients
Volkow et al (1987)	^{11}C-deoxyglucose Resting and activation scans	18 schizophrenics 12 normal controls	Hallucinations – BPRS: positive correlation ($r = 0.49$) with R temporal metabolism. Hypofrontality
DeLisi et al (1989)	^{18}F Fluorodeoxy-glucose	21 schizophrenics off medication 19 normal controls	Hallucinations – BPRS: positive correlation ($r = 0.47$) with R : L superior temporal flow ratio
Musalek et al (1989)	^{99}Tc^m HMPAO	28 hallucinators: 17 auditory, 11 tactile. 28 normal controls	Auditory: ↑ hippocampus amygdala, parahippocampus R & L. Tactile: ↓ inferior temporal bilaterally
Weiler et al (1990)	^{18}F Fluorodeoxy-glucose	Combined data on: 49 schizophrenics 30 awake normal & 12 REM-sleep controls	Hallucinations – BPRS: negative correlation ($r = -0.45$) with L caudate activity
Cleghorn et al (1990)	^{18}F Fluorodeoxy-glucose	19 schizophrenics: 9 with hallucinations 10 normal controls	Hallucinations – SAPS: positive correlation ($r = 0.82$) anterior cingulate activity. High intercorrelations between frontal language areas L & R

Positive Symptoms (SAPS), Cleghorn et al (1990) found a high correlation between glucose metabolism in the anterior cingulàte region, and AHs.

From the data presented, it can be seen that if sought, support from PET studies may be found for a range of competing theories seeking to explain hallucinations. In particular both hemispheres have been implicated.

It must also be noted that PET and SPECT studies addressing a variety of hypotheses have proved negative. For example, in the PET study cited above, Weiler *et al* (1990) found no evidence for postulated similarities between rapid eye movement (REM) sleep and brain processes in psychosis. Similarly, a SPECT study by Walter *et al* (1990) found only differences between the observations associated with AHs in schizophrenia and those induced by hypnosis in normal subjects.

Comparison with obsessive–compulsive disorder

Within the sphere of psychiatric disorders, obsessive–compulsive disorder (OCD) has recently been investigated by PET. In this condition, thoughts which are recognised as originating in the sufferer's mind nonetheless intrude unwelcome into consciousness in a manner which might in some respects be akin to that of auditory hallucinations. Abnormally increased metabolic activity in the orbital frontal cortex and the caudate nucleus has been reported in OCD (Baxter *et al*, 1988). It is noteworthy that significantly increased left globus pallidus activity has recently been reported in a well designed study of never-medicated patients with schizophrenia (Early *et al*, 1987). Perhaps more relevantly in the present context, Musalek *et al* (1989), observed significantly increased basal ganglia activity in hallucinators. From their findings in OCD, Baxter *et al* postulate that orbital cortical overactivity in some way overwhelms the caudate's capacity to maintain its integrative role. This is reminiscent of Ojemann's suggestion (1978) that the thalamus acts as a gate for language-related activity in the cortex. It is not impossible that a similar mechanism might contribute to the genesis of the brain processes corresponding to an AH.

In summary, some of the conceptual and methodological difficulties involved in PET studies of the brain processes associated with AHs have been considered. While we have noted that the comparison of groups of schizophrenic patients with normal subjects has, on the whole, proved unproductive, the enormous potential of PET is evident. It is unlikely that further progress in determining the brain processes underlying AH can be made without detailed and repeated study of individual patients with particular emphasis on the precise phenomenology of their hallucinations and of their mental states at the time of study.

Inner speech, subvocal activity and verbal hallucinations

Several studies over the last 40 years (Gould, 1948), offer tantalising evidence for a direct relationship between subvocal processes and VHs. It is assumed that the kind of activity recorded (somewhat crudely) is epiphenomenal to the hallucination, representing a kind of motor overflow from an inner speech command, which is proximal to the motor output. A review of these studies by Green & Kinsbourne (1990) has pointed to a number of methodological problems. Firstly, it appears that subvocal speech does not occur in all hallucinators. Secondly, it is important to control for higher background muscle tension – due to anxiety, medication etc. – which can contaminate the EMG. Even if this work does not lead to a full account of the origin of VHs it has been important for other reasons. This includes new treatment strategies (Bick & Kinsbourne, 1987; Green & Kinsbourne, 1989), and the possibility, as yet unexploited, to combine subvocal recordings with techniques such as EEG and PET in order to facilitate a more accurate mapping of active hallucinations with cerebral activity.

Structural brain imaging

The huge number of CT scan studies of psychotic patients will not be reviewed here. Suffice it to say that, in general, the only finding of relevance to the present discussion has been the negative correlation between ventricle–brain ratio and auditory hallucinations (Owens *et al*, 1985). One interpretation of this pattern is that the more elaborate hallucinations depend on there being 'intact' cerebral tissue (this applies to psychosis in both elderly and young psychotics (Förstl *et al*, this volume, pp. 153–170).

While MRI provides information about brain structure rather than brain function, some observations may be relevant to the explanation of the nature of hallucinations. Barta *et al* (1990) have reported a reduction in volume of the left superior temporal gyrus and amygdala in schizophrenic subjects, findings which are part of a growing body of data implicating these regions in the schizophrenic process. Moreover, they claim a highly significant correlation ($r = 0.70$, $P < 0.005$) between the degree of reduction in volume of the left superior temporal gyrus and the extent of hallucinatory experience as recorded in the case records. Unfortunately, if one non-hallucinating subject (SAPS score = 0) is excluded from the analysis, the correlation is less impressive ($r = 0.54$, $P < 0.05$).

Deafness and auditory hallucinations

There appears to be a higher prevalence of longstanding sensory deficits in older patients with paranoid – although not necessarily hallucinatory – disorders (Cooper *et al*, 1974). The most common auditory and visual deficits were conductive deafness and cataracts respectively, emphasising the potential for corrective treatment and possible amelioration of the mental state. Auditory hallucinations have been reported in association with progressive deafness (Thomas, 1981) and may be consequent on relative sensory deprivation. Some sort of 'seepage' into consciousness of mental activity that is normally preconscious and inhibited by external stimulation is the common feature of theories linking sensory restriction with the origin of hallucinations.

Although attractive as a mechanism, there is little evidence to suggest that such AHs are implicated in the higher risk of paranoid psychosis in elderly deaf subjects. It is also important to stress that while deafness appears to be a vulnerability factor for the development of paranoid illness, the elderly, who form the vast majority of individuals with acquired sensory deficits, generally do not develop psychopathology (Corbin & Eastwood, 1986).

Theoretical integration

Monitoring and verbal hallucinations

Current theories which take 'unintendedness' and the feeling of alien influence as their central focus, are the monitoring and discourse planning theories of Frith (1987; Frith & Done, 1988) and Hoffman (1986), respectively. Frith takes an information processing approach and argues that the primary abnormality is a failure of feed-forward or 'corollary discharge' by which a central 'monitor' can anticipate and so label correctly intended acts. Hoffman has a psycholinguistic perspective in which he links thought disorder, essentially disordered speech output, and VHs, to disordered inner speech which is ''nonconcordant with cognitive goals''. Both of these models have received some empirical support, albeit indirect. Hoffman found an association between VHs and thought disorder in a group of psychotic patients, and Frith & Done (1988) found a lack of rapid error correction in a video-game task which they took to indicate a failure of internal monitoring. Researchers have not tackled the intermittent nature of VHs by examining cognitive processes during the hallucination.

Following Gray (1982), Frith & Done suggest the hippocampus as the likely anatomical site of the 'monitor' and propose that monitoring failures arise through interruptions to certain inputs thereto. The prefrontal cortex, the site of initiation of spontaneous action (Goldberg, 1985), is linked to the hippocampus via the cingulate and the parahippocampal cortex: it is disorder in these connections which is postulated in psychosis. This hypothesis might be thought to gain support from the findings cited above. Cleghorn *et al* (1990) report an abnormal pattern of correlations between glucose metabolism in different parts of the brain which distinguishes hallucinating from non-hallucinating schizophrenic patients. Activity in the left TL lobe, for example, was abnormally highly correlated with that in the anterior cingulate gyrus, and Broca's area was abnormally highly correlated with its right hemisphere homologue. The latter observation might also be held consistent with the hypothesis that auditory hallucinations somehow originate in the right hemisphere (see also Volkow *et al*, 1987). However, the most parsimonious interpretation of these data is consistent with the view that VHs are directly linked with the activity of language production and reception systems in the brain, a view which concurs with Frith and Hoffman's basic assumptions about their internal origin.

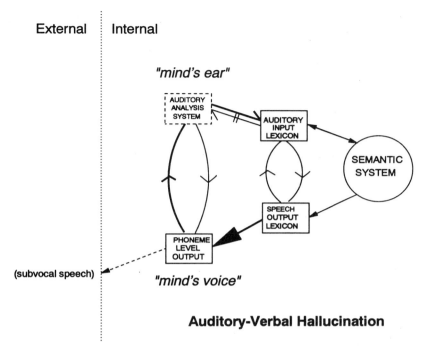

External : Internal

"mind's ear"

(subvocal speech)

"mind's voice"

Auditory-Verbal Hallucination

Fig. 6.1. Diagram (after Ellis & Young, 1988) of a preliminary cognitive neuropsychological model of auditory–verbal hallucinations. Inputs usually reach the semantic system through the auditory–analysis module and thence the auditory–input lexicon (a store of all known (heard) words). Speech output arises from the semantic system, then activating items in the speech output lexicon (a store of all known (spoken) words). Then, a programme for producing speech sounds is initiated at the phoneme level, and eventually a word is spoken. There is feedback and feed forward between all input and output levels. Increased activation from the speech output system is fed to the auditory analysis system which is not expecting an internal input. This leads to the experience of an auditory hallucination.

A preliminary neuropsychological model

The following scheme is an attempted integration of the neuropsychological evidence reviewed above and the kind of model provided by Frith (see Fig. 6.1). It takes as its basis a cognitive neuropsychological model of language perception and production summarised by Ellis & Young (1988) (see also Monsell, 1987). The model points to a failure of 'feed-forward' at a relatively peripheral level, namely the auditory analysis system which is taken to correspond to the 'mind's ear'. The hallucination arises from the semantic system but without an intended thought or idea. This triggers certain contents of the speech output lexicon which are at a higher level of activation, such as obscene and anxiety-provoking words. This overflows to the phoneme level output, analogous to the 'mind's voice'; depending on the strength of activation, this may produce subvocal speech. The output is picked up by the auditory analysis system which is primed by default to interpret input as that coming from outside. The result is the experience of an auditory-verbal hallucination. There are a number of questions arising from this model which is simply an attempt to link VH to current neuropsychological theories and is by no means a definitive account of the phenomena. One question is why do the 'thoughts' arise from the semantic system in the first place? Perhaps it is a subsidiary system, possibly within the RH, which acts in this autonomous way. The essence of the model is the assumption that AHs will only come to be understood by viewing them as the products of a normal set of systems rather than the random out-pourings from a diseased brain.

Conclusion

Neurological input models do not provide a compelling account of verbal hallucinations. Neurological output models seem more promising and can accommodate right hemisphere theories. This may explain simple verbal hallucinations but not complex ones which are likely to involve inner speech. Inner speech is a phenomenon capable of being studied scientifically from a neuropsychological perspective. Such an approach, combined with advances in neuroimaging may yet shed light upon one of psychiatry's most intriguing problems.

References

BADDELEY, A. D. (1986) *Working Memory*. Oxford: Oxford University Press.
——— & LEWIS, V. J. (1981) Inner active processing in reading: the inner voice, the inner ear and the inner eye. In *Interactive Processes in Reading* (eds A. M. Lesgold & C. A. Perfetti). Hillside, NJ: Lawrence Erlbaum Associates.
BANCAUD, J., TALAIRACH, J., GEIER, S., *et al* (1976) Manifestations comportementales induites par la stimulation électrique du gyrus congulaire antérieur chez l'homme. *Revue Neurologique*, **132**, 705–724.
BARTA, P. E., PEARLSON, G. D., POWERS, R. E., *et al* (1990) Auditory hallucinations and smaller superior temporal gyral volume in schizophrenia. *American Journal of Psychiatry*, **147**, 1457–1462.
BASSO, A., GARDELLI, M., GRASSI, M. P., *et al* (1989) The role of the right hemisphere in recovery from aphasia. Two case studies. *Cortex*, **25**, 555–566.
BAXTER, L. R., SCHWARTZ, J.M., MAZZIOTTA, J. C., *et al* (1988) Cerebral glucose metabolic rates in obsessive compulsive disorder. *American Journal of Psychiatry*, **145**, 1560–1563.
BENCH, C. J., DOLAN, R. J., FRISTON, K. J., *et al* (1990) Positron emission tomography in the study of brain metabolism in psychiatric and neuropsychiatric disorders. *British Journal of Psychiatry*, **157** (suppl.9), 82–95.
BERGMAN, P. S. (1965) Unilateral auditory hallucinations. *Transactions of the American Neurological Association*, **90**, 226–227.
BERRIOS, G. E. (1990) Musical hallucinations: a historical and clinical study. *British Journal of Psychiatry*, **156**, 188–194.
BESNER, D. (1987) Phonology, lexical access in reading, and articulatory suppression: a critical review. *Quarterly Journal of Experimental Psychology*, **39A**, 467–478.

BICK, P. A. & KINSBOURNE, M. (1987) Auditory hallucinations and subvocal speech in schizophrenia patients. *American Journal of Psychiatry*, **144**, 222–225.

BINGLEY, T. (1958) Mental symptoms in temporal lobe epilepsy and temporal gliomas. *Acta Psychiatrica et Neurologica Scandinavica*, **33** (suppl. 120), 1–151.

BISHOP, D. V. N. (1983) Linguistic impairment after left hemidecortication for infantile hemiplegia?: reappraisal. *Quarterly Journal of Experimental Psychology*, **35A**, 199–207.

BRACHA, H. S., CABRERA, F. J., KARSON, C. N., *et al* (1985) Lateralization of visual hallucinations in chronic schizophrenia. *Biological Psychiatry*, **20**, 1132–1136.

BRANCH, C., MILNER, B. & RASMUSSEN, T. (1964) Intracarotid sodium amytal for the lateralization of cerebral speech dominance. *Journal of Neurosurgery*, **21**, 399–405.

BUCHSBAUM, M. S. (1990) The frontal lobes, basal ganglia and temporal lobes as sites for schizophrenia. *Schizophrenia Bulletin*, **16**, 379–389.

CLEGHORN, J. M., GARNETT, E. S., NAHMIAS, C., *et al* (1990) Regional brain metabolism during auditory hallucinations in chronic schizophrenia. *British Journal of Psychiatry*, **157**, 562–570.

CODE, C. (1987) *Language, Aphasia and the Right Hemisphere*. Chichester: John Wiley & Sons.

COLLICUTT, J. R., & HEMSLEY, D. R. (1981) A psychophysical investigation of auditory functioning in schizophrenia. *British Journal of Clinical Psychology*, **20**, 199–204.

COLTHEART, M., PATTERSON, K. & MARSHALL, J. C. (1987) *Deep Dyslexia* (2nd edn). London: Routledge & Kegan Paul.

——, ARONS, S. E. & TROLLOPE, J. (1990) Articulatory suppression and phonological codes of reading for meaning. *Quarterly Journal of Experimental Psychology*, **42A**, 375–399.

COOPER, A. F., KAY, D. W., CURRY, A. R., *et al* (1974) Hearing loss in paranoid and affective psychoses in the elderly. *Lancet*, *ii*, 851–854.

CORBETTA, M., MIEZIN, F. M., DOBMEYER, S., *et al* (1990) Attentional modulation of neural processing of shape, colour and velocity in humans. *Science*, **248**, 1556–1559.

CORBIN, S. L. & EASTWOOD, M. R. (1986) Sensory deficits and mental disorders of old age: causal or coincidental associations? *Psychological Medicine*, **16**, 251–256.

COURVILLE, C. B. (1928) Auditory hallucinations provoked by intracranial tumours. *Journal of Nervous and Mental Disease*, **67**, 265–272

CURRIE, S., HEATHFIELD, K. W. G., HENSON, R. A., *et al* (1971) Clinical course and prognosis of temporal lobe epilepsy – a survey of 666 patients. *Brain*, **92**, 173–190.

CUTTING, J. (1989) Body image disorder: comparison between unilateral hemisphere damage and schizophrenia. *Behavioural Neurology*, **2**, 201–210.

—— (1990) *The Right Cerebral Hemisphere and Psychiatric Disorders*. Oxford: Oxford University Press.

DAVID, A. S. (1990) Insight and psychosis. *British Journal of Psychiatry*, **156**, 798–808.

DAVISON, K. & BAGLEY, C. R. (1969) Schizophrenia-like psychoses associated with organic disorders of the central nervous system. In *Current Problems in Neuropsychiatry* (ed. R. N. Herrington) British Journal of Psychiatry Special Publication No 4. Ashford, Kent: Headley Brothers.

DE LISI, L. E., BUCHSBAUM, M. S., HOLCOMB, H. H., *et al* (1989) Increased temporal lobe glucose use in chronic schizophrenic patients. *Biological Psychiatry*, **25**, 835–851.

DE REUCK, J., VAN AKEN, J., VAN LANGDEGEM, S., *et al* (1989) Positron emission tomography studies of changes in cerebral blood flow and oxygen metabolism in arteriovenous malformation of the brain. *European Neurology*, **29**, 294–297.

DOOLEY, C. & GEORGE, R. E. (1988) A single case study illustrating the reduction in subvocalisation with electromyography. *Behavioural Psychotherapy*, **16**, 231–240.

EARLY, T. S., REIMAN, E. M., RAICHLE, M. E., *et al* (1987) Left globus pallidus abnormality in never-medicated patients with schizophrenia. *Proceedings of the National Academy of Sciences (USA)*, **84**, 561–563.

ELLIS, A. W. & YOUNG, A. W. (1988) *Human Cognitive Neuropsychology*. New Jersey: Lawrence Erlbaum Associates.

——, —— & CRITCHLEY, E. M. R. (1989) Intrusive automatic or nonpropositional inner speech following bilateral cerebral injury. *Aphasiology*, **3**, 581–585.

ERBAŞ, B., KUMBASAR, H., ERBENGI, G., *et al* (1990) Tc-99m HMPAO/SPECT determination of regional cerebral blood flow changes in schizophrenics. *Clinical Nuclear Medicine*, **12**, 904–907.

FEINBERG, F. E., GONZALEZ ROTHI, L. J. & HEILMAN, K. M. (1986) 'Inner speech' in conduction aphasia. *Archives of Neurology*, **43**, 591–593.

FERGUSON, S. M. & RAYPORT, M. (1984) Psychosis in epilepsy. In *Psychiatric Aspects of Epilepsy* (ed. D. Blummer). Washington DC: American Psychiatric Press Inc.

FOX, P. T., MINTUN, M. A., REIMAN, E. M., et al (1988) Enhanced detection of focal brain responses using intersubject averaging and change distribution analysis of subtracted PET images. *Journal of Cerebral Blood Flow and Metabolism*, **8**, 642–653.

FRITH, C. D. (1987) The positive and negative symptoms of schizophrenia reflect impairments in the perception and initiation of action. *Psychological Medicine*, **17**, 631–648.

—— & DONE, D. J. (1988) Towards a neuropsychology of schizophrenia. *British Journal of Psychiatry*, **153**, 437–443.

GAL, P. (1958) Mental symptoms in cases of tumor of the temporal lobe. *American Journal of Psychiatry*, **115**, 157–160.

GAZZANIGA, M. S. (1983) Right hemisphere language following brain bisection: a 20-year perspective. *American Psychologist*, **38**, 525–537.

—— & HILLYARD, S. A. (1971) Language and speech capacity of the right hemisphere. *Neuropsychologia*, **9**, 273–280.

——, SMYLIE, C. S., BAYNES, K., et al (1984) Profiles of right hemisphere language and speech following brain bisection. *Brain and Language*, **22**, 206–220.

GÉRAUD, G., ARNE-BES, M. C., GUELL, A., et al (1987) Reversibility of hemodynamic hypofrontality in schizophrenia. *Journal of Cerebral Blood Flow and Metabolism*, **7**, 9–12.

GLOOR, P. (1990) Experiential phenomena of temporal lobe epilepsy. *Brain*, **113**, 1673–1694.

——, OLIVIER, A., QUESNEY, L. F., et al (1982) The role of the limbic system in experiential phenomena of temporal lobe epilepsy. *Annals of Neurology*, **12**, 129–144.

GOLDBERG, G. (1985) Supplementary motor area structure and function: review and hypotheses. *Behavioural and Brain Sciences*, **8**, 567–616.

GOODWIN, D. W., ALDERTON, P. & ROSENTHAL, R. (1971) Clinical significance of hallucinations in psychiatric disorders. *Archives of General Psychiatry*, **24**, 76–80.

GOULD, L. N. (1948) Verbal hallucinations and activity of vocal musculature. *American Journal of Psychiatry*, **105**, 367–372.

GORDON, A. G. (1987) Letter to the editor. *Acta Psychiatrica Scandinavica*, **75**, 664–668.

GRAY, J. A. (1982) *The Neuropsychology of Anxiety*. Oxford: Oxford University Press.

GREEN, M. F. & KINSBOURNE, M. (1989) Auditory hallucinations in schizophrenia: does humming help? *Biological Psychiatry*, **25**, 633–635.

—— & —— (1990) Subvocal activity and auditory hallucinations: clues for behavioral treatments? *Schizophrenia Bulletin*, **16**, 617–625.

GREEN, P. & PRESTON, M. (1981) Reinforcement of vocal correlates of auditory hallucinations by auditory feedback: a case study. *British Journal of Psychiatry*, **139**, 204–208.

GRUBER, L. N., MANGAT, B., BALMINDER, S., et al (1984) Laterality of auditory hallucinations in psychiatric patients. *American Journal of Psychiatry*, **141**, 586–588.

HALGREN, E., WALTER, R. D., CHERLOW, D. G., et al (1978) Mental phenomena evoked by human electrical stimulation of the human hippocampal formation and amygdala. *Brain*, **101**, 83–117.

HATHAWAY, S. R. & McKINLEY, J. C. (1967) *Minnesota Multiphasic Personality Inventory: Manual for Administration and Scoring*. New York: Psychological Corporation.

HAWTON, K., SHEPSTONE, B., SOPER, N., et al (1990) Single-photon emission computerised tomography (SPECT) in schizophrenia. *British Journal of Psychiatry*, **156**, 425–427.

HÉCAEN, H. & ROPERT, R. (1959) Hallucinations auditives au cours de syndromes neurologiques. *Annales Médico-Psychologiques*, **1**, 257–306.

HILL, J. M. (1936) Hallucinations in psychosis. *Journal of Nervous and Mental Disease*, **83**, 402–421.

HOFFMAN R. E. (1986) Verbal hallucinations and language production processes in schizophrenia. *The Behavioral and Brain Sciences*, **9**, 503–548.

HOWARD, D. & FRANKLIN, S. (1990) Memory without rehearsal. In *Neuropsychological Impairments of Short-Term Memory* (eds G. Vallar & T. Shallice). Cambridge: Cambridge University Press.

INGVAR, D. H. & FRANZEN, G. (1974) Abnormalities of cerebral blood flow distribution in patients with chronic schizophrenia. *Acta Psychiatrica Scandinavica*, **50**, 425–462.

—— & SCHWARTZ, M. S. (1974) Blood flow patterns induced in the dominant hemisphere by speech and reading. *Brain*, **96**, 274–288.

ISHIBASHI, T., HORI, H., ENDO, K., *et al* (1964) Hallucinations produced by electrical stimulation of the temporal lobes in schizophrenic patients. *Tohuku Journal of Experimental Medicine*, **82**, 124–139.

JACKSON, J. H. (1874/1932) *Selected Writings of John Hughlings Jackson*, Vol 2. (ed. J. Taylor). London: Hodder & Stoughton.

JASPERS, K. (1913) *General Psychopathology* (transl. 1963). Manchester: Manchester University Press.

JAYNES, J. (1979) *The Origins of Consciousness in the Breakdown of the Bicamecal Mind*. Boston: Houghton-Mifflin Co.

JOHNSON, F. (1978) *The Anatomy of Hallucinations*. Chicago: Melson Hall.

JUNGINGER, J. & FRAME, C. L. (1985) Self-report of the frequency and phenomenology of verbal hallucinations. *Journal of Nervous and Mental Disease*, **173**, 149–155.

KESCHNER, M., BENDER, M. B. & STRAUSS, I. (1936) Mental symptoms in cases of tumour of the temporal lobe. *Archives of Neurology and Psychiatry*, **35**, 572–596.

KESHAVAN, M. S., DAVID, A. S., STEINGARD, S., *et al* (1992) Musical hallucinations: a review and synthesis. *Neuropsychiatry, Neuropsychology & Behavioral Neurology* (in press).

KINSBOURNE, M. (1971) The minor cerebral hemisphere as a source of aphasic speech. *Archives of Neurology*, **25**, 302–306.

KRAEPELIN, E. (1919) *Manic Depressive Insanity and Paranoia*. Edinburgh: Livingstone.

KURACHI, M., KOBAYASHI, K., MATSUBARA, R., *et al* (1985) Regional cerebral blood flow in schizophrenic disorders. *European Neurology*, **24**, 176–181.

LARKIN, A. R. (1979) The form and content of schizophrenic hallucinations. *American Journal of Psychiatry*, **136**, 940–943.

LEVINE, D. N., CALVINO, R. & POPOVICS, A. (1982) Language in the absence of inner speech. *Neuropsychologia*, **20**, 391–409.

LIDDLE, P. (1987) The symptoms of chronic schizophrenia: a reexamination of the positive–negative dichotomy. *British Journal of Psychiatry*, **151**, 145–151.

——, FRISTON, K. J., FRITH, C. D., *et al* (1992) Patterns of cerebral blood flow in schizophrenia. *British Journal of Psychiatry*, **160**, 179–186.

LOWE, G. R. (1973) The phenomenology of hallucinations as an aid to differential diagnosis. *British Journal of Psychiatry*, **123**, 621–633.

MARGO, A., HEMSLEY, D. R. & SLADE, P. D. (1981) The effects of varying auditory input on schizophrenic hallucinations. *British Journal of Psychiatry*, **139**, 122–127.

MATHEW, R. J., DUNCAN, G. C., WEINMAN, M. L., *et al* (1982) Regional cerebral blood flow in schizophrenia. *Archives of General Psychiatry*, **39**, 1121–1124.

MATSUDA, H., GYOBU, T. M. & HISADA, K. (1988*a*) Iodine-123 Iodoamphetamine brain scan in a patient with auditory hallucination. *Journal of Nuclear Medicine*, **29**, 558–560.

——, ——, MASAYASU, I., *et al* (1988*b*) Increased accumulation of N-isopropyl-(I-123) p-iodoamphetamine in the left auditory area in a schizophrenic patient with auditory hallucinations. *Clinical Nuclear Medicine*, **13**, 53–55.

MCCARTHY, R. A. & WARRINGTON, E. K. (1990) *Cognitive Neuropsychology: a Clinical Introduction*. London: Academic Press Inc.

MCGUIRE, P. K. & MURRAY, R. (1991) Auditory hallucinations and regional cerebral blood flow in schizophrenia. (Abstract). *International Congress on Schizophrenia Research*, Tucson, Arizona.

MILNER, B. (1975) Psychological aspects of focal epilepsy, and its neurological management. *Advances in Neurology*, **8**, 299–321.

MONSELL, S. (1987) On the relation between lexial input and output pathways for speech. In *Language Perception and Production: Relationships between Listening, Speaking, Reading and Writing* (eds D. G. Allport, W. Mackay, W. Prinz, *et al*). London: Academic Press.

MOREL, F. (1936) Des bruits d'oreille des bourdonnements des hallucinations auditives élémentaires, communes et verbales. *Encephale*, **31**, 81–95.

MUSALEK, M., PODREKA, I., WALTER, H., *et al* (1989) Regional brain function in hallucinations: a study of regional cerebral blood flow with 99M Tc HMPAO–SPECT in patients with auditory hallucinations, tactile hallucinations and normal controls. *Comprehensive Psychiatry*, **30**, 99–108.

NASRALLAH, H.A. (1985) The unintegrated right cerebral hemispheric consciousness as alien intruder. *Comprehensive Psychiatry*, **26**, 273–282.

NOTARDONATO, H., GONZALEZ-AVILEZ, A., VAN HEERTUM, R. L., *et al* (1989) The potential value of serial cerebral SPECT scanning in the evaluation of psychiatric illness. *Clinical Nuclear Medicine*, **14**, 319–321.

OJEMANN, G. A. (1978) Organization of short-term verbal memory in language areas of human cortex: evidence from electrical stimulation. *Brain and Language*, **5**, 331–340.

—— (1983) Brain organization for language from the perspective of electrical stimulation mapping. *The Behavioral and Brain Sciences*, **6**, 189–230.

——, OJEMANN, J., LETTICH, B. A., *et al* (1990) Cortical language localization in left, dominant hemisphere. *Journal of Neurosurgery*, **71**, 316–326.

O'KUSKY, J., STRAUSS, E., KOSAKA, B., *et al* (1988) The corpus callosum is larger with right-hemisphere cerebral dominance. *Annals of Neurology*, **24**, 379–383.

OVERALL, J. & GORHAM, D. (1962) The Brief Psychiatric Rating Scale. *Psychological Reports*, **10**, 799–812.

OWENS, D. G. C., JOHNSTONE, E. C., CROW, T. J., *et al* (1985) Lateral ventricular size in schizophrenia: relationship to the disease process and its clinical manifestations. *Psychological Medicine*, **15**, 27–41.

PATTERSON, K., VARGHA-KHADEM, F. & POLKEY, C. E. (1989) Reading with one hemisphere. *Brain*, **112**, 39–63.

PENFIELD, W. & ROBERTS, L. (1959) *Speech and Brain Mechanisms*. Princeton, NJ: Princeton University Press.

—— & PEROT, P. (1963) The brain's record of auditory and visual experience: a final summary and conclusion. *Brain*, **86**, 595–696.

PETERSEN, S. E., FOX, P. T., POSNER, M. I., *et al* (1988) Positron emission tomographic studies of the cortical anatomy of single-word processing. *Nature*, **331**, 585–589.

RANDALL, P. L. (1983) Schizophrenia, abnormal connection and brain evolution. *Medical Hypotheses*, **10**, 247–280.

RAINE, A., HARRISON, G. N., REYNOLDS, G. P., *et al* (1990) Structural and functional characteristics of the corpus callosum in schizophrenics, psychiatric controls, and normal controls. *Archives of General Psychiatry*, **47**, 1060–1064.

REIVICH, M., ALAVI, A. & GUR, R. C. (1984) Positron emission tomographic studies of perceptual tasks. *Annals of Neurology*, **15** (suppl), 561–565.

REIMAN, E. M., FUSSELMAN, M. J., FOX, P. T., *et al* (1989) Neuroanatomic correlates of anticipatory anxiety. *Science*, **243**, 1071–1074.

RICHARDSON, J. T. E. (1987) Phonology and reading: the effects of articulatory suppression on homophony and rhyme judgements. *Language and Cognitive Processes*, **2**, 229–244.

RYDING, E., BRÅDVIK, B. & INGVAR, D. H. (1987) Changes of regional cerebral blood flow measured simultaneously in the right and left hemisphere during automatic speech. *Brain*, **110**, 1345–1358.

SCHNEIDER, K. (1959) *Clinical Psychopathology*. New York: Grune & Stratton.

SEDMAN, G. (1966) Inner voices: phenomenological and clinical aspects. *British Journal of Psychiatry*, **112**, 485–490.

SERAFETINIDES, E. A. & FALCONER, M. A. (1963) Speech disturbances in temporal lobe seizures: a study of 100 epileptic patients submitted to temporal lobectomy. *Brain*, **86**, 333–346.

——, COGER, R. W. & MARTIN, J. (1986) Different methods of observation affect EEG measurements associated with auditory hallucinations. *Journal of Psychiatric Research*, **17**, 73–74.

SIDTIS, J. J., VOLPE, B. T., WILSON, D. H., *et al* (1981) Variability in right hemisphere language function after callosal section: evidence for a continuum of generative capacity. *International Journal of Neuroscience*, **1**, 323–331.

SLADE, P. D. & BENTALL, R. P. (1988) *Sensory Deception: a Scientific Analysis of Hallucinations*. London: Croom Helm.

SMITH, A. (1966) Speech and other functions after left (dominant) hemispherectomy. *Journal of Neurology, Neurosurgery and Psychiatry*, **49**, 159–187.

SO, N. K., SAVARD, G., ANDERMANN, F., *et al* (1990) Acute postictal psychosis: a stereo EEG study. *Epilepsia*, **31**, 188–193.

STEVENS, J. R., BIGELOW, L., DENNEY, D., *et al* (1979) Telemetered EEG–EOG during psychotic behaviours of schizophrenia. *Archives of General Psychiatry*, **36**, 251–262.

——— & LIVERMORE, A. (1982) Telemetered EEG in schizophrenia: spectral analysis during abnormal behaviour episodes. *Journal of Neurology, Neurosurgery and Psychiatry*, **45**, 385–395.

STRAUSS, J. S. (1969) Hallucinations and delusions as points on continua function. *Archives of General Psychiatry*, **21**, 581–586.

TANABE, H., SAWADA, T., ASAI, H., *et al* (1986) Lateralisation phenomenon of complex auditory hallucinations. *Acta Psychiatrica Scandinavica*, **74**, 178–182.

TAYLOR, P. & FLEMINGER, J. J. (1981) The lateralization of symptoms in schizophrenia. *British Journal of Medical Psychology*, **54**, 59–65.

THOMAS, A. J. (1981) Acquired deafness and mental health. *British Journal of Medical Psychology*, **54**, 219–229.

TRIMBLE, M. R. (1990) First-rank symptoms of Schneider: a new perspective? *British Journal of Psychiatry*, **156**, 195–200.

VALLAR, G. & SHALLICE, T. (1990) *Neuropsychological Impairments of Short-Term Memory*. Cambridge: Cambridge University Press.

VOLKOW, N. D., WOLF, A. P., VAN GELDER, P., *et al* (1987) Phenomenological correlates of metabolic activity in 18 patients with chronic schizophrenia. *American Journal of Psychiatry*, **144**, 151–158.

WALTER, H., PODREKA, I., STEINE, M., *et al* (1990) A contribution to classification of hallucinations. *Psychopathology*, **23**, 97–105.

WARKENTIN, S., NILSSON, A., RISBERG, J., *et al* (1990) Regional cerebral blood flow in schizophrenia: repeated studies during a psychotic episode. *Psychiatry Research: Neuroimaging*, **35**, 27–38.

WING, J. K., COOPER, J. E. & SARTORIUS, N. (1974) *Measurement and Classification of Psychiatric Symptoms*. Cambridge: Cambridge University Press.

WEILER, M. A., BUCHSBAUM, M. S., GILLIN, J. C., *et al* (1990) Explorations in the relationship of dream sleep to schizophrenia using positron emission tomography. *Biological Psychiatry*, **23**, 109–118.

WIESER, H. G. (1980) Temporal lobe or psychomotor status epilepticus. *Electroencephalography and Clinical Neurophysiology*, **48**, 558–572.

WISE, R., CHOLLET, F., HADAR, U., *et al* (1991) Distribution of cortical neural networks involved in word comprehension and word retrieval. *Brain*, **114**, 1805–1817.

ZAIDEL, E. (1983) A response to Gazzaniga: language in the right hemisphere, convergent perspectives. *American Psychologist*, **38**, 542–546.

——— (1985) Language in the right hemisphere. In *The Dual Brain* (eds D. F. Benson & E. Zaidel). New York: Guilford Press.

7 The pharmacology of major tranquillisers in the elderly

KEN WOODHOUSE

Major tranquillisers are widely used in elderly disturbed patients, both to alleviate psychotic symptoms and to treat behavioural disturbances. Despite this, relatively little is known of their age-related pharmacology. These agents are undoubtedly effective, but they generate significant side-effects in older patients; partly because of age-related changes in kinetics, partly because of impaired homeostatic response, and partly because of alterations in nervous system receptors, especially dopamine receptors. This chapter reviews these changes, with emphasis on the inter-relationships between kinetics, dynamics, homeostatic failure and concurrent disease.

Pharmacokinetics in the elderly: general principles

Pharmacokinetics describes the fate of a drug in the body ('what the body does to the drug') and comprises: absorption, first pass elimination, distribution and protein building, and hepatic and renal elimination. All of these factors may be potentially modified by the ageing process, although the clinical relevance of these changes is often minor.

Absorption

Various age-related changes do occur within the gastrointestinal tract, including reduced gastric acid output and altered gut motility. These could theoretically affect drug absorption, but in practice there is no good evidence that the absorption of drugs across the gut wall is significantly reduced in the elderly. Some authors have suggested absorption may be a little slower, possibly due to delayed gastric emptying; it is, however, just as complete as in younger subjects (Castleden et al, 1977; Cusack et al, 1979).

First-pass metabolism

After absorption across the gut, drugs are transported in the portal circulation to the liver. For many drugs, particularly lipid-soluble agents with a high extraction ratio, uptake into the liver during this 'first pass' is enormous (90% +) resulting in greatly reduced bioavailability. There is now good data showing that first pass metabolism is markedly impaired, even in relatively 'normal' elderly people, resulting in increased availability of drugs, higher plasma concentrations, and adverse side-effect profiles (Castleden & George, 1979; Robertson *et al*, 1988). The exact mechanisms underlying these changes are as yet unclear.

Distribution and protein binding

Various physiological changes occur with ageing, which may modify drug distribution; body water decreases, with a concurrent increase in body fat. For drugs which are polar, and distributed to water, apparent volume of distribution will fall (Vestal *et al*, 1977; Redolfi *et al*, 1979); by contrast, non-polar compounds distributed to body fats have a larger distribution volume (Christensen *et al*, 1981).

Similarly, changes in plasma proteins occur, which may modify protein binding, and hence free-drug fraction. Plasma albumin falls a little with ageing – the free fraction of albumin bound (acidic) drugs (e.g. diazepam) is slightly higher. Basic drugs tend to bind to $alpha_1$ acid glycoprotein, and the level of this does not change with age *per se*, being more influenced by concurrent disease states (Veering *et al*, 1990).

Although these physiological changes are of theoretical interest, their clinical relevance is minor, because at steady state the plasma concentration of free (biologically active) drug depends principally upon free-drug clearance by kidney or liver rather than protein concentration or distribution volume (Woodhouse & James, 1990).

Renal clearance

The kidney is one organ that declines in function markedly with age. Reductions in glomerular filtration rate, effective renal plasma flow, and tubular function have all been reported (Davies & Shock, 1950). The clearance of many drugs by this route is consequently impaired, resulting in higher plasma drug concentrations and the development of dose-dependent adverse drug reactions. This is particularly important for drugs used in medical rather than psychiatric practice – and care needs to be taken with compounds such as digoxin, aminoglycoside antibiotics, and water soluble beta-blockers (Lumholtz *et al*, 1974; Barber *et al*, 1981). However, lithium, which is renally excreted, is being used more widely once again in psychiatric therapy, and can cause significant problems in elderly patients (Hewick *et al*, 1977).

It should be noted that the changes mentioned above describe populations, not individuals – there is marked variation between ageing humans with respect to renal function – some maintain almost 'normal' renal function until advanced old age, whereas others suffer severe impairment. Such increased inter-individual variability is a very typical feature of the ageing process, and highlights the need for dose titration within each patient, based on clinical response and adverse event profile.

Liver metabolism

The systemic clearance of drugs metabolised by the liver tends to decline with ageing. An enormous number of compounds metabolised by a variety of biotransformation pathways have now been studied; and extensive reviews written (Woodhouse & James, 1990; Woodhouse & Wynne, 1991). Reduced clearance will of course lead to high steady-state plasma concentrations, and to the development of adverse reactions. The mechanisms underlying reduced hepatic drug clearance have only been clarified in the last few years. Early animal-based studies, using elderly rodents, suggested that the activities of some enzymes of drug metabolism, notably the cytochrome P450-dependent microsomal mono-oxygenases, were reduced with ageing. It is now clear that this is primarily a phenomenon of the ageing male rat, affecting only male-specific cytochrome P450 isozymes (Schmucker, 1985), and that these changes are probably not seen in primates, including humans (Woodhouse & James, 1990; Schmucker *et al*, 1990). Although indirect *in vivo* evidence implies that a few, very specific P450 isozymes may be lost in ageing people (Posner *et al*, 1987; Woodhouse & James, 1990; Woodhouse & Wynne, 1991), this has not been confirmed by *in vitro* studies, and further clarification is awaited.

The major age-related changes which occur in the liver are morphological and physiological, rather than biochemical. For example, liver size, corrected for body weight, declines by 20–40% between the third and ninth decade of life. Similar decrements in hepatic blood flow have been observed (Wynne *et al*, 1989). Simultaneous measurements of drug clearance and liver size, using the oxidised acetanilide and the conjugated paracetamol as marker substrates, have clearly shown that an age-related reduction in the systemic elimination of both of these compounds can be accounted for entirely on the basis of a smaller liver (Woodhouse & James, 1990; Wynne *et al*, 1990; Woodhouse & Wynne, 1991).

As with renal function, it is important to consider interindividual variation in hepatic drug elimination. Even in healthy young people, the rates of elimination of some compounds (such as tricyclic antidepressants) may vary by as much as an order of magnitude between individuals, and this variance tends to increase with ageing. Dose titration is, again, crucial.

Pharmacodynamics and homeostasis in the elderly: general principles

Pharmacodynamics describes the effect of a drug on a specific target organ ('what the drug does to the body'), and is a major determinant of the sensitivity of an individual to a drug. Sensitivity to drugs may also be related to adaptive and homeostatic responses, and this is particularly important in old people as failure of adaptation is one of the typical features of the ageing process.

Orthostatic blood pressure control

Rising from the supine to the upright position results in a series of cardiovascular reflexes designed to maintain blood pressure. On rising, an initial fall in blood pressure is noted by baroreceptors in the carotid bodies and elsewhere, resulting in a reflex tachycardia, and subsequent peripheral vasoconstriction. Similar reflexes occur after administration of vasodilator drugs. In the elderly, this series of events is often blunted, if not lost; reflex tachycardia is less marked, and peripheral vasoconstriction is slower (Johnson *et al*, 1965; Robertson *et al*, 1988). The net result is the frequent occurrence of postural hypotension in the elderly, particularly after vasodilating agents (Robertson *et al*, 1988).

Temperature control

A fall in core body temperature results in a series of events designed to maintain body temperature. These include a perception of cold leading to behavioural changes (putting on the fire, donning a pullover); and physiological changes such as increased metabolic rate, skin vasoconstriction and shivering to generate heat. There is evidence that elderly subjects who are prone to accidental hypothermia have lost some or all of these responses (Collins *et al*, 1977). This may be important with regard to major tranquillisers as some of these drugs blunt thermoregulatory reflexes even more, resulting in the development of accidental hypothermia, especially in the elderly (Caird & Scott, 1986; Woodhouse, 1991).

Postural control

Postural control is an important homeostatic mechanism, and can be conveniently measured using body sway as a marker. Body sway increases with normal ageing, and is much more marked after the administration of any drug with sedative properties (Sheldon, 1963). Impaired postural control may be a major contributory factor to falls in old people given major tranquillisers.

Receptor changes

Many authors have studied the relationship between the ageing process and the density and affinity of drug receptors. Results have often been conflicting, largely because ageing seems to affect different receptors differently; and interspecies differences may be important. The beta-adrenergic nervous system has been most extensively studied, and ageing seems to be associated with a reduction in the density and affinity of these receptor populations. For example, the chronotropic effect of isoprenaline is less in the aged, greater doses being required to produce a 25% increase in heart rate in the old compared with the young. Similarly, older persons seem to be relatively resistant to beta-blockade. Similar changes appear to occur with respect to beta$_2$-receptors (Bylund *et al*, 1977; Vestal *et al*, 1979; Feldman *et al*, 1984).

Central nervous system dopaminergic receptors are more relevant to the pharmacology of major tranquillisers. Classical teaching suggests that the two most important sub-types of dopamine receptors with respect to this group of drugs are D_1 and D_2. D_1 receptors seem to be linked to adenylate cyclase and the antipsychotic effect of these drugs seems to be due to their interaction with and blockade of D_1 receptors in the limbic area. By contrast, D_2 receptors are more related to motor function, and blockade of striatal D_2 receptors by major tranquillisers is important in the development of extrapyramidal side effects (Borison *et al*, 1981; Rifkin, 1983; Walker *et al*, 1988; Wolters *et al*, 1989).

Initial reports suggested that ageing was primarily associated with a loss of D_2 receptor sub-types (hence the increased susceptibility of the elderly to Parkinsonian type reactions to neuroleptics) (DeBlasi & Mennini, 1982; O'Boyle & Waddington, 1984). However, recent animal data has suggested that both D_1 and D_2 receptor populations are reduced with age (Henry *et al*, 1986). Furthermore, the turnover of receptors also seems to decline in elderly individuals. These changes are clearly important for the pharmacology of major tranquillisers.

The fact that different dopamine receptor populations are responsible for the therapeutic and adverse effects of this group of drugs has lead to significant advances recently. For example, the dibenzapine derivative clozapine has been shown to be relatively specific for dopamine D_1 receptors, and this is likely to account for its low propensity for extrapyramidal effects and tardive dyskinesias (Wolters *et al*, 1989).

Major tranquillisers in the elderly: pharmacokinetics

As noted above, the major tranquillisers are generally dopamine-receptor antagonists, with differing affinities for different dopamine-receptor subpopulations. Their chemical structure is varied; a classification is given in Table 7.1. Although there are exceptions (e.g. sulpiride), most of these

TABLE 7.1
Some common neuroleptic drugs

Main class	Subdivision	Drug
Phenothiazines	Aliphatic side chain	chlorpromazine promazine
	Piperidine side chain	thioridazine pericyazine
	Piperazine side chain	fluphenazine trifluoperazine perphanazine prochlorperazine
Diphenylbutylpiperides		pimozide fluxpiriline penfluridol
Benzamide derivatives		sulpiride
Thioxanthenes		thiothixine flupenthixol clopenthixol
Butyrophenones		haloperidol benperidol droperidol trifluperidol

TABLE 7.2
Kinetics of major tranquillisers in relation to age

Drug	Kinetic changes with ageing	Reference
Chlorpromazine	Younger age associated with lower plasma levels	Rivera-Calimlin *et al*, 1977
Thiothixine	Plasma concentrations correlate with age No very elderly studied (oldest = 53 years)	Yesavage *et al*, 1981
Thioridazine	Plasma concentrations 1.5 to 2 times higher in old (mean 76 years) than young (mean 28 years)	Cohen & Sommer, 1988
Thioridazine metabolites	Findings as with thioridazine	Cohen & Sommer, 1988
Haloperidol	Tendency (statistically non-significant) to increasing concentrations with age	Forsman & Ohman, 1977

drugs are well absorbed from the gastrointestinal tract, usually undergo first pass metabolism, and are eliminated by hepatic metabolism. On first principles, it could be predicted that steady-state plasma concentrations of these drugs would tend to be larger in the aged. In fact, few studies of the pharmacokinetics of neuroleptic drugs are available; Table 7.2 summarises

D

some of the studies that are available. Plasma concentrations of thioridazine, thiothixine and possibly chlorpromazine and haloperidol are higher in the elderly, and apparent oral clearance may be lower. Further detailed kinetic–dynamic studies are urgently required.

Adverse reactions to major tranquillisers in the aged: general

Postural hypotension may occur with neuroleptics, as many of these drugs have anticholinergic or vasodilatory properties. Some, for example, are mild alpha-adrenoceptor antagonists. This, coupled with impaired baroreceptor function with ageing (Feldman *et al*, 1984), may result in a fall in blood pressure on standing, with a tendency to falls. Falls may also be associated with impaired postural control – many of these agents have marked sedative effects, increasing body sway and impairing postural reflexes (Sheldon, 1963). Finally, the central effects of these drugs blunt hypothalamic thermoregulatory mechanisms, and this, coupled with potentially poor temperature control as a result of ageing *per se*, may lead to the development of accidental hypothermia, particularly in the presence of other risk factors such as underlying illness, low environmental temperatures, alcohol abuse and co-prescription of other drugs (Woodhouse, 1991).

An important but poorly recognised complication of neuroleptic treatment in the elderly is neuroleptic malignant syndrome. This is a condition comprising an uncontrolled heat reaction, similar to malignant hypoporexia, but in general slightly less dramatic. It involves hyperthermia, muscle rigidity, fluctuating consciousness and autonomic disturbance such as labile blood pressure, tachycardia, incontinence, dystonia, and sweating. The condition tends to occur after physical exertion or dehydration, and has been described with haloperidol, thiothixine and piperazine phenothiazines. The likelihood is that it can be precipitated by most neuroleptics. The syndrome may persist for five to 10 days after stopping the drug, much longer if depot preparations have been used. Mortality may approach 20% (Woodhouse, 1991; Caroff, 1980; Moore *et al*, 1990; Nicklason *et al*, 1991).

It may well be that dopamine receptor modulation is an important factor in the pathogenesis of the condition. The author has seen at least two patients with a similar but milder clinical picture following abrupt withdrawal of levodopa.

Adverse reactions to major tranquillisers in the aged: extrapyramidal

Extrapyramidal adverse effects from neuroleptics are well described. The various types of reactions and their age dependence are shown in Table 7.3.

TABLE 7.3
Extrapyramidal reactions to neuroleptics

Type of reaction	Ages most at risk	Reference
Acute dystonia	Young (teens and early twenties)	Ayd, 1961; Bateman *et al*, 1989
Akathisia	Middle aged	Ayd, 1961
Tardive dyskinesia	Middle aged and elderly	Blain & Lane, 1991
Parkinsonism	Elderly	Stephen & Williamson, 1984; Bateman *et al*, 1989.

An early, although often ignored, review of drug-induced extrapyramidal reactions appeared in 1961 (Ayd, 1961), and gave a clue as to the frequency of the problem; of 3775 patients prescribed major tranquillisers who were studied, 1472 (38.9%) had suffered some form of extrapyramidal reaction – 21% had akathisia, 15.4% Parkinsonism, and 2.3% an acute dystonia. The occurrence of tardive dyskinesia was not documented. Females seemed to be more at risk than males and this was particularly marked in older patients suffering Parkinsonism. These age and sex differences have been noted by other authors, who have also reported a high frequency of adverse reactions. For example, Bateman and colleagues (1989) have shown that the risk of Parkinsonism in a patient given a prescription for prochlorperazine is one in 159 in those over 60 and only one in 1555 in those under this age. Drug-induced Parkinsonism (DIP) may be a major public-health problem in elderly people in the United Kingdom. For example, Stephen & Williamson (1984) studied the frequency of DIP in aged patients seen in an Edinburgh Geriatric Unit. They found that of 95 newly diagnosed cases of Parkinsonism, 48 (51%) were associated with prescribed drugs. Of these, 25% were immobile when seen, and 45% required hospital admission. Resolution occurred in only two-thirds of patients, symptoms persisting in 17%, whereas in others (11%) initial resolution was followed by subsequent relapse.

The duration of treatment required before onset of extrapyramidal symptoms varies with the type of reaction. Acute dystonia occurs early (within a few days), whereas akathisia and DIP occur later – 50% of cases having occurred by 30 to 40 days, and 90% by 70 to 75 days (Ayd, 1961; Bateman *et al*, 1989).

As its name implies, tardive dyskinesia occurs late – often after many years of treatment. It is common in patients who have received long-term neuroleptics. It comprises chewing movements of the jaw, rolling or smacking of the tongue, and twisting of the fingers. Although distressing to watch, many patients seem relatively untroubled (Blain & Lane, 1991).

Treatment of neuroleptic-induced extrapyramidal disorders varies. Acute dystonias respond well to drug withdrawal and anticholinergic agents. Drug-induced Parkinsonism and akathisia may respond to similar methods. Tardive dyskinesia is notoriously difficult to treat, anticholinergics have been tried with limited success. Abnormal movements may be reduced, paradoxically, by a temporary increase in drug dosage, but they recur fairly soon thereafter (Blain & Lane, 1991).

Conclusions

Major tranquillisers may be a useful group of drugs in the elderly, but adverse reactions, particularly extrapyramidal syndromes, are a frequent problem. Current knowledge of their pharmacokinetics and pharmacodynamics in the elderly is inadequate. A greater research effort is needed in this area so that these helpful drugs may be used more rationally in older populations, and adverse events minimised.

References

AYD. F. J (1961) A survey of drug-induced extrapyramidal reactions. *Journal of the American Medical Association*, **175**, 1054–1060.

BARBER, H. E., HAWKSWORTH, G. M., PETRIE, J. C., *et al* (1981) Pharmacokinetics of atenolol and propranolol in young and elderly subjects. *British Journal of Clinical Pharmacology*, **12**, 118P.

BATEMAN, D. N., DARLING, W. M., BOYS, R., *et al* (1989) Extrapyramidal reactions to metoclopramide and prochlorperazine. *Quarterly Journal of Medicine*, New Series 71, **264**, 307–311.

BLAIN, P. G. & LANE R. J. M. (1991) Neurological disorders. In *Textbook of Adverse Drug Reactions (Fourth Edition)* (ed. D. M. Davies), pp. 535–566. New York: Oxford University Press.

BORISON, R. L., FIELD, J. Z. & DIAMOND, B. I. (1981) Site-specific blockade of dopamine receptors by neuroleptic agents in human brain. *Neuropharmacology*, **76**, 182–187.

BYLUND, D. M., TELLEZ-INON, M. H. & HOLLENBERG, M. D. (1977) Age-related parallel decline in beta adrenergic receptors, adenylate cyclase and phosphodiesterase activity in rat erythrocyte membranes. *Life Sciences*, **21**, 403–410.

CAIRD, F. I. & SCOTT, P. J. W. (1986) *Drug Induced Diseases in the Elderly*. Amsterdam: Elsevier.

CAROFF, S. N. (1980) The neuroleptic malignant syndrome. *Journal of Clinical Psychiatry*, **41**, 79–83.

CASTLEDEN, C. M., VOLANS, G. N. & RAYMOND, K. (1977) The effect of ageing on drug absorption from the gut. *Age and Ageing*, **6**, 138–143.

—— & GEORGE C. (1979) The effect of ageing on hepatic clearance of propranolol. *British Journal of Clinical Pharmacology* **7**, 49–54.

CHRISTENSEN, J. H., ANDREASON, F. & JANSEN, J. A. (1981) Influence of age and sex on the pharmacokinetics of thiopentone. *British Journal of Anaesthesia*, **53**, 1189–1195.

COHEN, B. & SOMMER, B. (1988) Metabolism of thioridazine in the elderly. *Journal of Clinical Psychopharmacology*, **8**, 336–339.

COLLINS, K. J., DOVE, C. & EXTON-SMITH, A. N. (1977) Accidental hypothermia and impaired temperature homeostasis in the elderly. *British Medical Journal*, i, 353–356.

CUSACK, B., KELLY, J., O'MALLEY, K., *et al*, (1979) Digoxin in the elderly: pharmacokinetic consequences of old age. *Clinical Pharmacology and Therapeutics*, **25**, 772–776.

DAVIES, D. F. & SHOCK, N. W. (1950) Age changes in glomerular filtration rate, effective renal plasma flow and tubular excretory capacity in adult males. *Journal of Clinical Investigations*, **29**, 1950.

DEBLASI, A. & MENNINI, T. (1982) Selective reduction of one class of dopamine receptor binding sites in the corpus striatum of aged rats. *Brain Research*, **242**, 361–364.

FELDMAN, R. D., LIMBIRD, L. E. & NADEAU, J. L (1984) Alterations in leukocyte beta receptor affinity with ageing. A potential explanation for altered beta adrenergic sensitivity in the elderly. *New England Journal of Medicine*, **310**, 815–819.

FORSMAN, A. & OHMAN, R. (1977) Applied pharmacokinetics of haloperidol in man. *Current Therapeutic Research*, **21**, 396–411.

HENRY, J. M., FILBURN, C., JOSEPH, J., *et al* (1986) Effect of ageing on striatal dopamine receptor subtypes in WISTAR rats. *Neurobiology of Ageing*, **7**, 357–361.

HEWICK, D. S., NEWBURY, P., HOPWOOD, S., *et al* (1977) Age as a factor affecting lithium therapy. *British Journal of Clinical Pharmacology*, **4**, 201–205.

JOHNSON, R. H., SMITH, A. C. & SPALDING, J. M. K. (1965) The effect of posture on blood pressure in elderly patients. *Lancet*, *i*, 731–733.

LUMHOLTZ, B., KAMPMANN, J., SIERSBACK-NIELSEN, K., *et al* (1974) Dose regimen of kanamycin and gentamycin. *Acta Medica Scandinavia*, **190**, 521–524.

MOORE, A. P., MACFARLANE, I. A. & BLUMHARDT, L. D. (1990) Neuroleptic malignant syndrome and hypothyroidism. *Journal of Neurology, Neurosurgery and Psychiatry*, **53**, 517–518.

NICKLASON, F., FINUCANE, P., PATHY, M. S. J., *et al* (1991) Neuroleptic malignant syndrome – an unrecognised problem in elderly patients with psychiatric illness? *International Journal of Geriatric Psychiatry*, **6**, 171–175.

O'BOYLE, K. M. & WADDINGTON, J. L. (1984) Loss of rat striatal dopamine receptors with ageing is selective for D_2 but not D_1 site. *European Journal of Pharmacology*, **105**, 171–174.

POSNER, J., DANHOF, M. & TEUNISSEN, M. W. E. (1987). The disposition of antipyrine and its metabolites in young and elderly healthy volunteers. *British Journal of Clinical Pharmacology*, **24**, 51–55.

REDOLFI, A., BORGOGELLI, E. & LODOLA, E. (1979) Blood level of cimetidine in relation to age. *European Journal of Clinical Pharmacology*, **15**, 257–261.

RIFKIN, A. (1983) *Schizophrenia and Affective Disorders*. Boston: Wright-PSG.

RIVERA-CALIMLIN, L., NASRALLAH, H. & GIFT, T. (1977) Plasma levels of chlorpromazine: Effect of age, chronicity of disease and duration of treatment. *Clinical Pharmacology and Therapeutics*, **21**, 115–116.

ROBERTSON, D. R. C., WALLER, D. G., RENWICK, A. G., *et al* (1988) Age-related changes in the pharmacokinetics and pharmacodynamics of nifedipine. *British Journal of Clinical Pharmacology*, **25**, 297–305.

SCHMUCKER, D. C. (1985) Ageing and drug disposition. An update. *Pharmacological Reviews*, **37**, 133–148.

————, WOODHOUSE, K. W., WANG, R. K., *et al* (1990) Effects of age and gender on in vitro properties of human liver microsomal monooxygenases. *Clinical Pharmacology and Therapeutics*, **48**, 365–374.

SHELDON, J. H. (1963) The effect of age on the control of sway. *Gerontology*, **5**, 129–138.

STEPHEN, P. J. & WILLIAMSON, J. (1984) Drug-induced Parkinsonism in the elderly. *Lancet*, *ii*, 1082–1083.

VEERING, B. T. H., BURM, A. G. L., SOUVERIJN, J. H. M., *et al* (1990) The effect of age on serum concentrations of albumin and alpha$_1$ acid glycoprotein. *British Journal of Clinical Pharmacology*, **29**, 201.

VESTAL, R. E., MCGUIRE, E. A., TOBIN, T. D., *et al* (1977) Ageing and ethanol metabolism. *Clinical Pharmacology*, **21**, 343–354.

————, WOOD, A. J. J. & SHAND, D. G. (1979) Reduced beta adrenoreceptor sensitivity in the elderly. *Clinical Pharmacology and Therapeutics*, **26**, 181–186.

WALKER, J. M., MATSUMOTO, R. R., BOWEN, W. D., *et al* (1988) Evidence for a role of haloperidol-sensitive opiate receptors in the motor effects of antipsychotic drugs. *Neurology*, **38**, 961–965.

WOLTERS, E. C., HURWITZ, T. A., PEPPARD, R. F., *et al* (1989) Clozapine: an antipsychotic agent in Parkinson's disease. *Clinical Neuropharmacology*, **12**, 83–90.

WOODHOUSE, K. W. (1991) Disorders of temperature regulation. In *Textbook of Adverse Drug Reactions (4th Edition)* (ed. D. M. Davies), pp. 766–772. New York: Oxford University Press.

———— & JAMES, O. F. W. (1990) Hepatic drug metabolism and ageing. *British Medical Bulletin*, **46**, 22–35.

———— & WYNNE, H. A. (1991) Age-related changes in hepatic function: implications for drug therapy. *Drugs and Ageing*, (in press).

WYNNE, H., COPE, L., HERD, B., *et al* (1990) The association of age and frailty with paracetamol conjugation in man. *Age and Ageing*, **19**, 410–424.

————, ————, MUTCH, E., *et al* (1989) The effect of age upon liver size and liver blood flow in man. *Hepatology*, **9**, 297–301.

YESAVAGE, J., HOLMAN, C. & COHN, R. (1981) Correlation of thiothixine levels with age. *Psychopharmacology*, **74**, 170–172.

II. Functional disorders

8 The nature, frequency and relevance of depressive delusions

R. C. BALDWIN

This chapter focuses on four areas: firstly, the frequency of delusions in late-life depression; secondly, the phenomenology of these delusions; thirdly, the evidence that delusional depression in the elderly may be a distinct subtype of depressive illness; and lastly, the evidence for and against the suggestions that ageing and/or brain pathology play a part in the pathogenesis of delusional depression in later life.

Before returning to these themes, a little historical background will help set the scene.

Historical background

The historical background of late-life delusional depression is inseparable from the history of affective disorders in general, and the manner in which ageing came to be regarded as an explanatory factor in the pathogenesis of insanity. These and other issues are covered in a recent fascinating review (Berrios, 1991), and are beyond the scope of this chapter. Suffice to say that, to a significant degree, our notions of ageing have been influenced by sociodemographic change as much as by an understanding of age-related neurophysiological or neuroanatomic processes. Hence, during the formative years of psychiatric nosology, old age was deemed to begin at around the age of 50 years. This presents a problem as most studies of delusional depression have been concerned with subjects whose average age has been around 50 years, in keeping with the influence of the now unfashionable concept of 'involutional melancholia' at the turn of the century. The literature on subjects in their 70s is relatively meagre, although it is growing.

A landmark early study was that of Hoch & MacCurdy (1922). Their 67 cases of 'involution melancholia', as they termed it, had a mean age of 55 years. Their category of malignant (that is, poor outcome) cases included those patients with 'absurd ideas' and 'ridiculous hypochondriac delusions'.

However, these and other clinical terms which they used suggest that it is difficult to make direct comparisons with depression as diagnosed by current classificatory systems – the earlier cases may well have included patients nowadays regarded as suffering from schizophrenia, schizoaffective psychosis or delusional disorder. Even so Hoch & MacCurdy highlighted that of two particular forms of delusion – 'death and poverty' and 'severe hypochondria' – the latter appeared to be associated with a bad prognosis.

In an important review, Kantor & Glassman (1977) suggested that in the pre-electroconvulsive therapy (ECT) era the small percentage of depressives who failed to recover were delusional, in keeping with the findings of authors such as Hoch & MacCurdy. With the arrival of ECT, all types of severe depression were equally responsive so that the delusional/non-delusional distinction lost its significance. The modern pharmacological era then highlighted that delusional depressions seemed less responsive to tricyclics. This gave rise to two modern notions: firstly that ECT might be the treatment of choice for deluded depressives, and secondly that delusional depression might be a distinct clinical subtype.

The frequency of delusions in late-life depression

How common are delusional forms of depressive illness in later life? The answer is it all depends on where you look. Although there are now many community-based prevalence studies of depression in later life, I have only been able to find one, by Kivela & Pahkala (1989), which specifically ascertained the prevalence of delusional depression in a defined (Finnish) community of older people. The overall prevalence of delusional depression in the over 60s was only 1% in this study (12/1000 women and 6/1000 men). There were no community members in hospital with delusional depression at the time to artificially lower this figure. Although this seems a very low prevalence, it has to be placed in the context of the figure usually quoted for the prevalence of major depressive disorder in later-life community residents, namely 3% (Baldwin, 1988a).

In specialised psychogeriatric services the figures are, not surprisingly, much higher. Thus, Murphy (1983) calculated that 24% of patients referred to two psychogeriatric services were delusional. In two further UK studies, of in-patients only, the figures were 53% (Post, 1972) and 44% (Baldwin & Jolley, 1986). In Australia, Burvill et al (1991) calculated that 35% of their depressed group, who were mainly in-patients, were delusional. In the USA, Meyers & Greenberg (1986) reported that 45% of 161 consecutively admitted depressives to several psychogeriatric wards were deluded, and Nelson et al (1989) reported a figure of 36% deluded for consecutive admissions for depression of patients aged over 60 years. Recently I found that 34% of all patients over the age of 65 with major depression referred to me over a five-year period were deluded. Generally, these figures are within the range quoted by Eagles (1983) in a study of secular trends of mixed-aged delusional depressives. He found a significant decline over time in the proportion of admitted depressives with delusions. Between 1892 and 1942 there was a reduction from 66% to 36%, with a further non-significant reduction to 28% in 1981/2. Eagles believed that it was unlikely that there had been a true decline in the prevalence of delusional depression. Hence, the use of in-patient figures to calculate the prevalence of delusional depression may be misleading.

In summary, delusional depression among the elderly is an uncommon condition in the community. In old-age psychiatric services it comprises between a quarter and a third of all depressed referrals and between two-fifths and a half of all admitted elderly depressives. Delusional depression is thus an important clinical challenge to psychiatrists working with older patients.

The figure of 34% which was quoted comes from a new study of patients referred to the author in Manchester. Since it will be referred to intermittently, the main features will be outlined now. The study was based on patients who were referred over a five-year period, during which time a case register was kept. The total number of depressed referrals was 134 (mean age at referral 75.4 years, range 65–96) of whom 100 were non-delusional (mean age 75.4, range 65–96), and 34 were deluded (mean age 75.5, range 65–89). There were 30 age- and sex-matched controls (mean age 75.3, range 65–88). The rating of major depressive disorder, as in DSM–III–R (American Psychiatric Association, 1987), or before that the Feighner criteria for depression (Feighner *et al*, 1972), a physical health rating, cognitive screen, and the 17-item Hamilton Rating Scale for Depression (HRSD; Hamilton, 1960) were all made prospectively. The presence of delusions was recorded, the definition being that of the Present State Examination (PSE) (Wing *et al*, 1974). Patients were included if they had mood-incongruent delusions, provided that they also met criteria for major depression. Patients with organic brain syndromes were excluded.

This is a very strictly defined group of depressives and obviously comprises only a modest proportion of total clinical workload. If the number of delusional depressives seems small this is because the health authority in which these patients reside is much smaller than average. Extrapolating to an average Health District of 200 000 with 15% elderly and with similar referral patterns gives an equivalent referral rate, very roughly, of one patient over the age of 65 referred every two weeks with delusional depression – in other words, it is by no means a rare condition.

The phenomenology of late-life delusional depression

Is late-life delusional depression associated with any differences in symptoms compared with non-delusional depression, except the obvious one regarding delusions? This question is part of the wider issue of whether there are types of depression peculiar to the elderly. This has been vigorously debated and will not be discussed in any detail here. A few authors have looked for differences in symptoms other than delusions. Glassman & Roose (1981), studying a mixed-aged group of patients, found that delusional depressives had more retardation than non-deluded cases, and that this difference persisted after correcting for severity of depression. In the Finnish community study of late-life delusional depression, Kivela & Pahkala (1989) found symptoms of guilt, hypochondriasis, loss of insight, depersonalisation and paranoid thinking, as assessed by the HRSD (Hamilton, 1960), to be more severe in deluded patients, but one would expect this given the structure of the HRSD.

Retardation is a very 'biological' symptom within depression, and some overlap has been observed between it and basal ganglia disease (Rogers *et al*, 1987), and this might be relevant when considering recent studies, shortly to be discussed, which have implicated subcortical pathology in the pathogenesis of delusional depression. In the recent Manchester series, 30 patients for whom a complete 17-item HRSD score was available (four cases being too ill to cooperate fully) were compared with 30 age- and sex-matched controls. The only significant findings were of more guilt and less insight in the deluded group – similar to the Finnish study – although additionally the deluded group had more psychic anxiety than the controls, but at borderline significance levels ($P = 0.05$). Unlike Glassman & Roose (1981) there was no difference in retardation. This then casts doubt on a specific link between delusional depression and retardation.

What types of delusion occur in late-life depression? The findings for the recent Manchester series are shown in Table 8.1. A number of patients had more than one type of delusion so they were categorised according to which one dominated the clinical picture. Persecutory beliefs topped the bill, although hypochondriacal delusions were not far behind. Interestingly, delusions of guilt were not prominent as a main delusion, although they were the most common second type of delusion in those patients with more than one type of delusion (guilt 6, persecution 3 (including two

TABLE 8.1
Types of delusions in delusional depression

Main delusion	No of patients
Persecutory	12[1]
Hypochondriacal	11
Nihilistic	4
Guilt	3
Poverty	3
Other	1

1. Includes 4 'non-congruent'.

mood-incongruent type), hypochondriasis 3, and delusions of reference 2). Only five patients had more than two types of delusion. In men the most frequent delusion (main type only) was hypochondriasis (7/16) and in women it was persecution (7/18). These results are similar to those of Kivela & Pahkala (1989), who found that hypochondriacal delusions predominated in men, and guilt and paranoid delusions in women, and those of Meyers & Greenberg (1986) who found delusions of persecution and hypochondriasis were the most common types, followed by delusions of guilt. That delusions of guilt were not more common in this group of psychotic depressives seems surprising, but there is evidence that older depressed adults, especially men, express less guilt than their younger counterparts (Small *et al*, 1986). The prominence of hypochondriacal and persecutory delusions rather than guilty ones in older depressives might lead to inexperienced clinicians missing the diagnosis, given the prominent position which is traditionally accorded to guilty ideas in depression. Perhaps this should be highlighted more in teaching.

Some studies have excluded depressed cases with mood incongruent delusions on the grounds that these may represent cases of 'schizoaffective psychosis'. I did not exclude such cases. Four patients had non-congruent delusions (main type only). Three are still under supervision, and the average follow-up for all four patients to date is 26 months. For two patients, the depression represented a single episode and no other psychiatric morbidity has ensued. One patient developed a persistent persecutory state not long after the depression and a fourth developed multi-infarct dementia after a longer interval. No such changes occurred to the eight patients with mood-congruent persecutory delusions. One tentative conclusion might be that the presence of mood-incongruent delusions in depression is associated with the emergence, either in the short- or long-term, of another psychiatric disorder in some cases, and that such patients should be carefully followed up. On the whole, however, the diagnosis of delusional depression in this series seemed to be a reliable one, which is at odds with the proposal of Leuchter & Spar (1985) that non-organic forms of late-onset psychoses are inherently unreliable from a diagnostic point of view.

Some of the demographic findings were suprising. For the cohort as a whole the sex ratio was as one would expect for depression, with an excess of women (2.45F:1M), but for the deluded cases it was unusual: there were 18 women and 16 men, giving a near equal sex ratio (1.13F:1M). Secondly, single people were highly significantly over-represented in the deluded group, of whom 44% were single compared with 12% of the non-deluded patients ($\chi^2 = 16.6$, d.f. = 3, $P < 0.001$). There were rather more single men (56%) than single women (33%). Interestingly, Kivela & Pahkala (1989) found that 58% of their deluded sample were unmarried compared with only 8% of their controls, a figure which was not commented upon because, given their small numbers, it was not a statistically significant finding. It seems that the larger sample here has confirmed this result. These very basic findings may have as much bearing on the tendency to delusions in depression as the more biological explanations which will be outlined later. Some years ago Kay *et al* (1976) and Post (1967) emphasised the association between never having been married and later-life schizophrenia. Perhaps being single is also a risk factor for other psychoses in later life and possibly this has been overlooked in inquiry into delusional depression. Clearly simple findings of this sort need to be replicated.

Is delusional depression in late-life a distinct entity?

Two main areas are relevant to this question. The first concerns whether the two forms of depression are associated with different prognoses, and the second considers treatment differences between delusional and non-delusional depressions.

Prognostic considerations

Professor Elaine Murphy's work (1983) is particularly relevant here as she demonstrated an especially dire outcome for delusional depressives. Of the 30 deluded depressed patients in her cohort, only 10% had fully recovered by the end of one year, and almost a quarter had died. In an earlier study of the outcome of old-age depression which I carried out with Dr David Jolley (Baldwin & Jolley, 1986) there was no statistical relationship between delusions and outcome, but we did note that six out of seven patients who had pursued an unremitting course had presented with delusions.

In view of this, in a later study of delusional depression (Baldwin, 1988*b*) the outcome of the deluded and the non-deluded depressives, all late-onset, was evaluated. As the results have been published, the findings will be summarised only briefly. The study was retrospective and used the same cohort of in-patients previously examined by myself and David Jolley in an outcome study (Baldwin & Jolley, 1986). The entry criteria were: (a) aged over 65 years, (b) no previous psychiatric history, (c) in-patient status, and (d) Feighner's criteria for unipolar

TABLE 8.2
Characteristics at entry to 1986 study

	Deluded (n = 24)	*Controls* (n = 24)
Age: years	74.2	75.4
Sex ratio	5:1	5:1
Severity: HRSD score*	29.9[1]	25.7

1. Excludes one stuporose patient.
*$P = 0.01$ (Mann–Whitney U-test).
(From Baldwin, 1988*b*).

depression. All patients were late-onset depressives and the characteristics of the two groups of 24 patients at entry are summarised in Table 8.2. The sex ratio is strongly in favour of women in both groups, which is at odds with my more recent data, but as the latter was a study of all referrals and not only in-patients they are not directly comparable groups. The deluded patients were clearly more severely depressed, a finding also replicated in the more recent study (median HRSD score for deluded group = 23 and for controls = 20; $P < 0.01$).

The overall follow-up for both groups was approximately five years and there were eight deaths in each group. Table 8.3 illustrates the outcome groupings, utilising categories from the earlier study of Baldwin & Jolley (1986). Clearly there are no substantial differences (χ^2 tests were not significant).

A similar analysis of the 34 most-recently studied delusional patients has also been carried out. However, outcome categories were not rated blindly, so I would not claim the same rigour for this analysis as for the 1988 study. Also, it transpired that the deluded group had been followed through for an average period of 22 months compared with only 10 months on average for the control group, a statistically significant difference. Nevertheless, 31 of the 34 deluded patients were followed up comprehensively; of these 48% were judged to be well throughout, 19% had relapses with subsequent recovery, 23% were thought to be depressively invalided and 10% remained unchanged. For the control group, the proportions in each of the follow-up categories were virtually identical.

Taken together, these data do not support the view that delusional depression in old age is associated with a different prognosis compared with depression without delusions. They are also in agreement with the recent study of Burvill *et al* (1991), who were unable to demonstrate any association of delusions with outcome. It has been argued elsewhere (Baldwin, 1988*a*) that treatment differences may be important here, especially in the usage of ECT which seemed to be prescribed rather sparingly among those patients studied by Murphy (1983). Also, the Manchester findings are in line with the work of Coryell & Tsuang (1982) on mixed-aged patients who found that with longer periods of follow-up the prognostic importance of delusions disappeared.

TABLE 8.3
Delusional and non-delusional depression: long-term outcome (percentages)

	Deluded (n = 24)	Controls (n = 24)
Well throughout	33	21
Relapse(s) + recovery	42	42
Depressive invalidism	21	33
Depressed throughout	4	4
Total	100	100

Treatment response

The evidence that delusional depression is a distinct subtype derives mainly from studies of treatment which demonstrate that delusional depression has a poorer response to tricyclic antidepressants than non-delusional depression (Hordern *et al*, 1963; Glassman *et al*, 1975; Glassman & Roose, 1981; Charney & Nelson, 1981; Frances *et al*, 1981; Perry *et al*, 1982; Spiker *et al*, 1985). Further evidence for a difference between the two types of depression comes from studies comparing real and simulated ECT. These have demonstrated particular benefit (Brandon *et al*, 1984), or benefit only, (Clinical Research Centre, 1984) for deluded depressives. Also, delusional depressives rarely undergo spontaneous recovery (Glassman & Roose, 1981) and, lastly, it has been observed that the presence or absence of delusions in younger depressives tends to run true through repeated episodes (Charney & Nelson, 1981).

These studies have been on mixed-aged patients or those under the age of 65. It may therefore be unwise to extrapolate data from younger depressed patients to older ones, especially given current notions suggesting that brain changes may be a factor in later-life depressions (Alexopoulos, 1989). In the 1988 study, I undertook to examine the question of treatment response of delusional depressives in an older patient group. One patient from the deluded group was found to have a pancreatic cyst soon after admission and was transferred for surgery, resulting in only 23 in the deluded group. It can be seen (Table 8.4) that deluded patients responded less often to antidepressant drugs, were often given ECT and required significantly more major tranquilliser usage to improve them. Secondly, more patients in the deluded group required combinations of antipsychotic drugs and anti-depressants, resulting in the deluded group having higher total treatment scores. Lastly, the period of hospital admission of the deluded group was significantly longer.

Because those in the deluded group were significantly more depressed than the controls on the HRSD, a matched-pair analysis was conducted on 11 patients with identical HRSD scores. All the differences in Table 8.4 disappeared, with the exception of length of stay which remained significantly

TABLE 8.4
Delusional and non-delusional depression: treatments given

	Deluded (n = 23)	Controls (n = 24)	Significance
Antidepressant alone	4	11	$P<0.05$[1]
ECT: total use	15	8	$P<0.05$[1]
Major tranquilliser use	12	4	$P=0.01$[1]
Combination treatment	15	6	$P<0.01$[1]
Total treatment scores	24.7	11.7	$P<0.01$[2]
Hospital admission: weeks	11.2	6.9	$P=0.01$[2]

1. Fisher exact test.
2. Mann–Whitney U-test.

longer for delusional depressives (9.9 weeks) than controls (6.6 weeks) (Wilcoxon signed-rank test, $0.025 < P < 0.05$).

In 1981, Glassman & Roose proposed two hypotheses for understanding delusional depression. The first argues that delusional depression is merely a more severe form of depression. This is a state model. Thus, given a severe enough illness, any patient with depression might develop delusions. The second suggests that delusions arise in a depressive illness because of a distinct pathological vulnerability. This is a trait model. However, many severe depressions are not delusional, and Glassman & Roose (1981) did not demonstrate a severity effect – deluded patients were still poor responders to antidepressants after controlling for severity. Glassman & Roose therefore opted for the vulnerability model.

My findings are somewhat at odds with those of Glassman & Roose (1981) because the matched-pair comparison which controlled for severity suggested that the treatment differences might be explained by the effect of severity of depression. Does this mean that the vulnerability theory does not apply to elderly subjects? Not necessarily. Firstly, the difference in length of hospital admission, which was longer for the deluded group, was not explained by severity of depression. Although this might reflect natural caution in discharging patients who have been deluded it might equally point to an inherent property of delusional depression, namely slower recovery. Certainly it is known that delusions and depression do not always recover at the same rate. Secondly, two of the controls, but none of the deluded patients, recovered spontaneously, in keeping with literature from younger subjects (Charney & Nelson, 1981).

The third argument in favour of the vulnerability model requires a little more detail. If delusional depression is indeed a reflection of an inherent vulnerability to psychotic symptoms then one might expect future episodes to 'run true'. Such was the finding of Charney & Nelson (1981) in a retrospective study of mixed-aged patients. Thus, of 54 patients with delusional depression, 95% had at least one prior episode characterised by delusions, whereas this was true of only 8% of the 66 non-deluded patients. I therefore carried out a blinded analysis of subsequent relapses which resulted in readmission. At first relapse 7 out of 11 of the patients from the original deluded group had delusional relapses whereas this did not occur in any of the patients who relapsed from the control group (all 6 relapses here were non-delusional). For second relapses, the figures are similar: five out of 10 relapses from the deluded group were delusional but none out of the seven relapses from the controls. So delusional depressions in late life do indeed seem to 'run true'.

In summary, the evidence from this study suggests that some of the treatment differences which undoubtedly exist between delusional and non-delusional elderly depressives may arise because delusional depression is a more severe form of depression. However, there is some quite compelling evidence from the nature of subsequent relapses that delusional depression may be a reflection of a specific pathological vulnerability.

What might explain this vulnerability? An obvious contender is neurochemical imbalance involving the dopamine system. Thus, Meltzer *et al* (1976) found lower serum dopamine-Beta-hydroxylase (DBH) in younger psychotically depressed patients but not in controls, schizophrenics, manics or 'neurotic' depressives, and Sweeney *et al* (1978) found an imbalance in the ratio of dopamine to noradrenalin metabolites in deluded depressives but not non-deluded depressives under the age of 65. Furthermore Schatzberg *et al* (1985) have proposed a specific dysregulation of the hypothalamic–pituitary axis in deluded depressives resulting in raised glucocorticoid levels, which, they suggest, enhances dopaminergic activity. An important point is that the enzymes which control DBH and tyrosine hydroxylase are thought to be under genetic control. Moreover, Coryell *et al* (1982) have suggested that familial subtypes of primary unipolar depression are significantly associated with the presence of delusions, which also suggests a genetic influence towards delusionality.

These findings relate to younger groups of depressives and suggest that for younger patients there may be a genetic component involved in the expression of delusions within depressive illnesses, acting via the dopaminergic system. Given what we know about the reduced influence of genetic factors in the aetiology of late-life depressions (e.g. Mendelwicz, 1976), a genetic component towards delusionality in late-life depression seems much less likely.

Thus, in older delusional depressives the crucial factor affecting the dopamine system may not be genetic but some intrinsic cerebral factor, related either to ageing or structural brain damage. I shall now examine the evidence for this, but before doing so it is worth pointing out that the fundamental neurochemical observations concerning delusional depression from the 1970s have been relatively neglected. Dr Barnett Meyers of the New York Hospital, whose treatment findings on the immediate prognosis of delusional depression are, incidentally, very similar to my own (Meyers *et al*, 1985), is the only person I know of who is exploring the Schatzberg hypothesis in an elderly group of delusional depressives. So far he has demonstrated similar rates of escape from dexamethasone suppression in deluded and non-deluded depressives (70%) (Meyers, 1985), but his findings for the DBH enzyme assay are not yet reported.

Delusional depression and the factors of ageing and structural brain changes

The above considerations lead naturally to a discussion of the relevance of the factor of ageing and of brain pathology in the pathogenesis of late-life delusional depression. Firstly the factor of ageing will be considered; particularly in relation to age at onset of delusional depression.

If it could be demonstrated that delusions become more frequent in depressions arising in later life, and that delusional depression is associated with a later age of onset compared with non-deluded patients then this would support ageing as an aetiological factor. The evidence for this from mixed-aged or middle-aged depressives is weak. For example, Hordern *et al* (1963) found a trend for depressions over the age of 50 to be delusional but this did not reach statistical significance, and Brown *et al* (1984) in their review of 'involutional melancholia' did not find differences in the prevalence of depressive delusions before and after the age of 50. However, Meyers & Alexopoulos (1988) have argued that these studies 'wash out' associations that may be present in older patients, and suggested that studies specifically of older patients are needed. Meyers & Greenberg (1986) have produced evidence of an increase in delusional forms of depression with increasing age at onset (Fig. 8.1). It can be seen that there does seem to be a trend

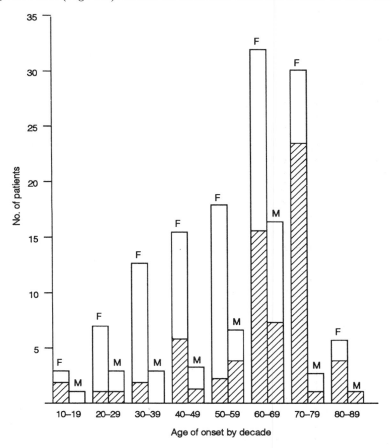

Fig. 8.1. Age of onset and proportion of deluded patients (▨) by decade, separated by sex (from Meyers & Greenberg (1986), reproduced with permission of the authors)

for more cases to be delusional with increasing age of onset – most notably for women. Furthermore they found evidence that the deluded cases had a significantly later age of onset than those without delusions.

These findings are very important as they suggest that: (a) delusional depression in later life may be a specific subtype; (b) age of onset may influence the presentation of depression; and (c) cerebral ageing and/or age-related pathology in the brain may modify the presentation of depression. As can be seen in Table 8.5, Nelson *et al* (1989) were unable to corroborate these findings. Because of the importance of Meyers' results I have performed a similar analysis on my recent cohort of 134 patients. Regrettably, I too have not been able to replicate Meyers' work (Table 8.5). Meyers also found that patients whose age at onset was above the median value of 60 years were significantly more likely to be deluded. Using the same median age, I found for my cohort that the proportions were 27% delusional for those with onset of depression over the age of 60 and 33% for those under it; clearly very similar. A similar calculation was carried out utilising the median age of onset for my own cohort, which was 72. The findings are little different: 23% delusional for onset above the median value and 30% for those below it – again these are very similar.

However, all may not be lost. Meyers and colleagues deliberately employed very restrictive entry criteria. Patients with marked physical illness or indeed anything likely to be associated with secondary depression were excluded (in fact 110 patients in all were excluded), whereas my criteria and those of Nelson and colleagues were less restrictive. Although such narrow criteria do not fit with the real world of old age psychiatric practice they may be justified in order to address the scientific question raised by age of onset. There may therefore be a case for trying to replicate the Cornell group's findings on a physically very robust elderly group of depressives, if practicable, given the importance of the hypothesis.

If the factor of age at onset has produced conflicting data, what of the role of structural brain damage? Some evidence has accumulated over recent years suggesting an association between depression in late life and subtle brain changes in at least a proportion of depressives. It would be inappropriate to rehearse all the evidence for this here, as it is well known and has been reviewed in a number of recent articles (Alexopoulos *et al*, 1988; Meyers & Alexopoulos, 1988; Alexopoulos, 1989).

TABLE 8.5
Age at onset of depression

Authors	n	Age at referral		Age at onset		Early/late
		deluded	*non-deluded*	*deluded*	*non-deluded*	
Meyers (1986)	161	72.6	70.9	62.4	51.5*	>60
Nelson (1989)	109	68.5	69.9	51.1	55.2	>60
Baldwin (1991)	134	75.5	75.4	68.8	70.5	>65

*Difference between deluded/non-deluded *P*<0.001.

The early imaging studies generally involved CT scanning. They did not specifically address issues relevant to delusional depression, with the exception of one study of much younger deluded depressed patients which did demonstrate mildly increased ventricular brain ratios in the deluded group (Targum *et al*, 1983). Jacoby *et al* (1981) have identified a subgroup of depressives with enlarged ventricles who were older, had late-onset depression, except one, a more 'endogenous' picture and a higher mortality rate. It would be interesting to be able to report that they were also characterised by being more likely to have delusions, but this was not the case (Jacoby, personal communication). These CT scan findings have not so far been associated with gross neuropathological change (Ferrier & McKeith, 1991).

The use of different technology, in the form of magnetic resonance imaging (MRI) and single photon emission computerised tomography (SPECT), has begun to generate new and very interesting data. The work originates mainly from North America. I will summarise only those studies where delusions have been mentioned as a variable.

In 1989, Coffey *et al* from Duke University reported on 51 severely depressed patients over the age of 60 who had been referred for ECT. Using MRI scanning they found subcortical white matter hyperintensity in all patients and changes in the subcortical grey matter nuclei in a half. Many patients had more than one lesion. In the authors' view, vascular disease was the most likely cause of these lesions. Of the group, 29% were delusional depressives. The authors do not state whether the lesions in these patients were different in any way from non-delusional cases, save for the finding that psychotic symptoms were less common in patients who had basal-ganglia lesions. They speculate that there may be a special relationship in depressed patients between psychotic symptoms, structural brain changes and dopaminergic dysfunction in the basal ganglia.

I am only aware of one study which specifically addressed delusional depression in the context of MRI and SPECT imaging. Lesser *et al* (1991), in California, compared 14 delusional depressives with a mean age of 57 with 72 non-psychiatrically ill controls. Two-thirds of the deluded depressives had evidence of brain abnormalities on MRI compared with only 10% of controls. Again, vascular-related white-matter lesions were the most common abnormalities. I was interested to note that the patient group had significantly lower mean Mini-Mental State Examination (MMSE) (Folstein *et al*, 1975) scores (28.1) than the controls (29.5). Pearlson *et al* (1989) had also noted, in a CT scan study, that depressed subjects with what they termed 'dementia of depression', defined by a MMSE score of less than 24, were more often found to be delusional than those with higher scores (40% compared with 9% of those above the cut-off of 24), although the difference was not statistically significant, perhaps because of very small numbers. I have not been able to demonstrate a difference in cognitive test scores between the deluded and non-deluded groups in my most recent cohort. However, there were problems caused by a change from the Blessed & Roth test (Blessed *et al*, 1968) to the MMSE during the study period. Also, ceiling effects were a problem, so it would be extremely useful to perform more sophisticated cognitive testing on deluded depressives and compare the results with non-deluded cases.

Earlier, in 1987, Coffey *et al* reported four cases of severe depression with white-matter lesions who responded to ECT. These patients were elderly. The origin of the lesions was again thought to be vascular, but only one patient was regarded as demented. I was struck by the fact that all four patients had delusional symptoms as part of their depression. However, the onset of depression in three cases was early rather than late, and different factors may operate in early-onset cases.

An obvious problem with the American study by Lesser *et al* is that there was no comparison group comprising non-delusional depressives. In a more recent study yet to be published, the Californian group (Miller *et al*, 1992) evaluated SPECT scans, an indication of function rather than structure, in older psychotic patients. They studied 18 patients with late-onset schizophrenia, 12 with late-onset delusional depression and 30 normal controls. The mean age of the depressed group was 56 years. They found abnormal SPECT patterns in 72% of the psychotics and 75% of the 12 delusional depressives, compared with only 13% of the controls – both study groups differing significantly from the control group. Because of Cumming's suggestion (1985) that frontal and temporal dysfunction in particular may be important in psychosis and depression, they evaluated perfusion to these areas and found that 83% of both the late-onset schizophrenics and the delusional depressives had hypoperfusion affecting one or other area, compared with only 27% of controls.

A word of caution is necessary. One-third of the late-onset delusional depressives had, on detailed evaluation, evidence of early degenerative brain disease, although this was not originally suspected; in other words, their mental states may have been a prodrome of organic brain damage, something which does not appear to be the case with the 34 delusional depressives I have recently studied, save for the one patient already mentioned. So, in addition to being somewhat younger than patients typical of old age psychiatry, selection bias may also have influenced the results.

Clearly, however, this sort of research does implicate brain pathology, principally white matter lesions, as an aetiological factor in at least a subgroup of late-onset delusional depressives. However, similar considerations seem to apply to late-onset schizophrenia and to non-psychotic late-onset depressive illnesses too (Zubenko *et al*, 1990), with little indication, as yet, as to how the pathological processes differ between them.

These deep white-matter changes seem similar to what Hachinski *et al* (1987) have dubbed 'leuko-araiosis', a condition known to be associated with a variety of conditions, including Binswanger's disease (Janota, 1981), non-specific neurological symptoms, dementia, stroke (Kinkel *et al*, 1985), and psychosis (Lesser *et al*, 1991). Such changes are not therefore specific pathological markers for delusions. Furthermore, white matter lesions are by no means uncommon in the normal elderly (Steingart *et al*, 1987). Nevertheless, this kind of research in older psychiatric patients is only in its infancy and holds out promise of identifying specific pathological processes in at least a proportion of delusional depressions occurring in late-life.

Summary and conclusions

Delusional depression in the elderly is not uncommon in old-age psychiatric practice, and ageing may exert a pathoplastic effect on the content of delusions. Patients with mood incongruent delusions should be carefully followed up. Treatment of delusional depression differs from non-delusional forms, and evidence from treatment data suggests that this is partly because it is a more severe illness. However, evidence from follow-up supports the view that there is an intrinsic vulnerability to the development of delusions in some patients with depression.

The search for a link between either ageing or pathology within the brain and late-life delusional depression has been inconclusive in the case of age of onset, but there is evidence to suggest that brain pathology, in the form of white-matter change, probably of vascular causation, may be important in a proportion of such cases. However, as yet, the pathology lacks specificity with regard to psychiatric diagnosis. It would be most valuable to look for linkages between neuropathological change and neurochemical markers, particularly of the dopamine system. Finally, the relevance of rather more mundane variables, such as the patient's sex and civil status, especially being single, should not be overlooked, as these too may exert an important influence on the expression of delusions within later-life depressive illness.

References

ALEXOPOULOS, G. S. (1989) Late-life depression and neurological brain disease. *International Journal of Geriatric Psychiatry*, **4**, 187–190.
——, MEYERS, B. S., YOUNG, R. C., *et al* (1988) Brain changes in geriatric depression. *International Journal of Geriatric Psychiatry*, **3**, 157–161.
AMERICAN PSYCHIATRIC ASSOCIATION (1987) *Diagnostic and Statistical Manual of Mental Disorders* (3rd edn, revised) (DSM–III–R) Washington, DC: APA.
BALDWIN, B. (1988a) Late life depression – undertreated? *British Medical Journal*, **296**, 519.
—— (1988b) Delusional and non-delusional depression in late life: evidence for distinct subtypes. *British Journal of Psychiatry*, **152**, 39–44.

———— & JOLLEY, D. J. (1986) The prognosis of depression in old age. *British Journal of Psychiatry*, **149**, 574–583.

BERRIOS, G. E. (1991) Affective disorders in old age: a conceptual history. *International Journal of Geriatric Psychiatry*, **6**, 337–346.

BLESSED, G., TOMLINSON, B. E. & ROTH, M. (1968) The association between quantitative measures of dementia and of senile change in the cerebral grey matter of elderly subjects. *British Journal of Psychiatry*, **114**, 797–811.

BRANDON, S., COWLEY, P., MCDONALD, C., *et al* (1984) Electroconvulsive therapy: results in depressive illness for the Leicestershire trial. *British Medical Journal*, **288**, 22–25.

BROWN, R. P., SWEENEY, J., LOUTSCH, E., *et al* (1984) Involutional melancholia revisited. *American Journal of Psychiatry*, **141**, 24–28.

BURVILL, P. W., HALL, W. D., STAMPFER, H. G., *et al* (1991) The prognosis of depression in old age. *British Journal of Psychiatry*, **158**, 64–71.

CHARNEY, D. S. & NELSON, J. C. (1981) Delusional and nondelusional unipolar depression: further evidence for distinct subtypes. *American Journal of Psychiatry*, **138**, 328–333.

CLINICAL RESEARCH CENTRE (1984) The Northwick Park ECT trial: predictors of response to real and simulated ECT. *British Journal of Psychiatry*, **114**, 227–237.

COFFEY, C. E., HINKLE, P. E., WEINER, R. D., *et al* (1987) Electroconvulsive therapy of depression in patients with white matter hyperintensity. *Biological Psychiatry*, **22**, 629–636.

————, FIGIEL, G. S., DJANG, W. T., *et al* (1989) White matter hyperintensity on magnetic resonance imaging: clinical and neuroanatomic correlates in the depressed elderly. *Journal of Neuropsychiatry*, **1**, 139–144.

CORYELL, W. & TSUANG, M. T. (1982) Primary unipolar depression and the prognostic importance of delusions. *Archives of General Psychiatry*, **39**, 1182–1184.

————, GAFFNEY, G., BURKHARDT, P. E., *et al* (1982) Hypothalamic-pituitary-adrenal axis activity: the importance of delusions and familial subtyping. In *Biological Markers in Psychiatry and Neurology* (eds E. Usdin & I. Hanin), pp. 261–267. Oxford: Pergamon Press

CUMMINGS, J. L. (1985) Organic delusions: phenomenology, anatomic correlations and review. *British Journal of Psychiatry*, **146**, 184–197.

EAGLES, J. M. (1983) Delusional depressive in-patients, 1892 to 1982. *British Journal of Psychiatry*, **143**, 558–563.

FEIGHNER, J. P., ROBINS, E., GUZE, S. B., *et al* (1972) Diagnostic criteria for use in psychiatric research. *Archives of General Psychiatry*, **26**, 57–63.

FERRIER, I. N. & MCKEITH, I. G. (1991) Neuroanatomical and neurochemical changes in affective disorders in old age. *International Journal of Geriatric Psychiatry*, **6**, 445–451.

FOLSTEIN, M. F., FOLSTEIN, S. E. & MCHUGH, P. R. (1975) "Mini-Mental State": a practical method for grading the cognitive state of patients for the clinician. *Journal of Psychiatric Research*, **12**, 185–198.

FRANCES, A., BROWN, R., KOCSIS, J. H., *et al* (1981) Psychotic depression: a separate entity? *American Journal of Psychiatry*, **138**, 831–833.

GLASSMAN, A. H., KANTOR, S. J. & SHOSTAK, M. (1975) Depression, delusions and drug response. *American Journal of Psychiatry*, **132**, 716–719.

———— & ROOSE, S. P. (1981) Delusional depression: a distinct clinical entity? *Archives of General Psychiatry*, **38**, 424–427.

HACHINSKI, V. C., POTTER, P. & MERSKEY, H. (1987) Leuko-araiosis. *Archives of Neurology*, **44**, 21–23.

HAMILTON, M. (1960) A rating scale for depression. *Journal of Neurology, Neurosurgery and Psychiatry*, **23**, 56–62.

HOCH, A. & MCCURDY, J. T. (1922) The prognosis of involutional melancholia. *Archives of Neurology and Psychiatry*, **7**, 1–17.

HORDERN, A., HOLT, N. F., BURT, C. G., *et al* (1963) Amitriptyline in depressive states: phenomenology and prognostic considerations. *British Journal of Psychiatry*, **109**, 815–825.

JACOBY, R. J., LEVY, R. & BIRD, J. M. (1981) Computed tomography and outcome of affective disorder: a follow-up study of elderly patients. *British Journal of Psychiatry*, **139**, 288–292.

JANOTA, I. (1981) Dementia, deep white matter damage and hypertension: 'Binswanger's disease'. *Psychological Medicine*, **11**, 39–48.

KANTOR, S. J. & GLASSMAN, A. H. (1977) Delusional depressions: natural history and response to treatment. *British Journal of Psychiatry*, **131**, 351–360.

KAY, D. W. K., COOPER, A. F., GARSIDE, R. F., *et al* (1976) The differentiation of paranoid from affective psychoses by patients' premorbid characteristics. *British Journal of Psychiatry*, **129**, 207–215.

KINKEL, W. R., JACOBS, L., POLANCHINI, I., *et al* (1985) Subcortical arteriosclerotic encephalopathy (Binswanger's disease). *Archives of Neurology*, **42**, 951–959.

KIVELA, S.-L. & PAHKALA, K. (1989) Delusional depression in the elderly: a community study. *Zeitschrift fur Gerontologie*, **22**, 236–241.

LESSER, I. M., MILLER, B. L., BOONE, K. B., *et al* (1991) Brain injury and cognitive function in late-onset psychotic depression. *Journal of Neuropsychiatry*, **3**, 33–40.

LEUCHTER, A. F. & SPAR, J. E. (1985) The late onset psychoses: clinical and diagnostic features. *Journal of Nervous and Mental Disease*, **173**, 488–494.

MENDLEWICZ, J. (1976) The age factor in depressive illness: some genetic considerations. *Journal of Gerontology*, **31**, 300–303.

MELTZER, H. Y., CHO, W., CARROLL, B. J., *et al* (1976) Serum dopamine-Beta-hydroxylase activity in the affective psychoses and schizophrenia. *Archives of General Psychiatry*, **33**, 585–591.

MEYERS, B. S. (1985) Delusional depression in the elderly. In *Proceedings of the American Psychiatric Association Annual Conference*, New research abstracts, p. 68. Dallas, Texas.

——, GREENBERG, R. & MEI-TAL, V. (1985) Delusional depression in the elderly. In *Treatment of Affective Disorders in the Elderly* (ed. C. A. Shamoian), pp. 19–28. Washington, DC: APP.

—— & —— (1986) Late-life delusional depression. *Journal of Affective Disorders*, **11**, 133–137.

—— & ALEXOPOULOS, G. (1988) Age of onset and studies of late-life depression. *International Journal of Geriatric Psychiatry*, **3**, 219–228.

MILLER, B. L., LESSER, I. M., MENA, I., *et al* (1992) Regional cerebral blood flow in late-life-onset psychosis. *Neuropsychiatry, Neuropsychology and Behavioural Neurology* (in press).

MURPHY, E. (1983) The prognosis of depression in old age. *British Journal of Psychiatry*, **142**, 111–119.

NELSON, J. C., CONWELL, Y., KIM, K., *et al* (1989) Age at onset in late-life delusional depression. *American Journal of Psychiatry*, **146**, 785–786.

PEARLSON, G. D., RABINS, P. V., KIM, W. S., *et al* (1989) Structural brain CT changes and cognitive deficits in elderly depressives with and without reversible dementia (pseudodementia). *Psychological Medicine*, **19**, 573–584.

PERRY, P. J., MORGAN, D. E., SMITH, R. E., *et al* (1982) Treatment of unipolar depression accompanied by delusions. *Journal of Affective Disorders*, **4**, 195–200.

POST, F. (1967) Aspects of psychiatry in the elderly. *Proceedings of the Royal Society of Medicine*, **60**, 249–254.

—— (1972) The management and nature of depressive illnesses in late life: a follow-through study. *British Journal of Psychiatry*, **121**, 393–404.

ROGERS, D., LEES, A. J., SMITH, E., *et al* (1987) Bradyphrenia in Parkinson's disease and psychomotor retardation in depressive illness. *Brain*, **110**, 761–776.

SCHATZBERG, A. F., ROTHSCHILD, A. J., LANGLAIS, P. J., *et al* (1985) A corticosteroid/dopamine hypothesis for psychotic depression and related states. *Journal of Psychiatric Research*, **19**, 57–64.

SMALL, G. W., KOMANDURI, R., GITLIN, M., *et al* (1986) The influence of age on guilt expression in major depression. *International Journal of Geriatric Psychiatry*, **1**, 121–126.

SPIKER, D. G., WEISS, J. C., DEALY, R. S., *et al* (1985) The pharmacologic treatment of delusional depression. *American Journal of Psychiatry*, **142**, 430–436.

STEINGART, A., HACHINSKI, V. C., LAU, C., *et al* (1987) Cognitive and neurologic findings in subjects with diffuse white matter lucencies on computed tomographic scan (leuko-araiosis). *Archives of Neurology*, **44**, 32–35.

SWEENEY, D., NELSON, C., BOWERS, M., *et al* (1978) Delusional versus non-delusional depression: neurochemical differences. *Lancet*, **ii**, 100–101.

TARGUM, S. D., ROSEN, L. N., DeLISI, L. E., *et al* (1983) Cerebral ventricular size in major depressive disorder: association with delusional symptoms. *Biological Psychiatry*, **18**, 329–336.

WING, J. K., COOPER, J. E. & SARTORIUS, N. (1974) *The Measurement and Classification of Psychiatric Symptoms*. London: Cambridge University Press.

ZUBENKO, G. S., SULLIVAN, P., NELSON, J. P., *et al* (1990) Brain imaging abnormalities in mental disorders of late life. *Archives of Neurology*, **47**, 1107–1111.

9 Status and investigation of body image delusions

CORNELIUS KELLY

"Man is a synthesis of the infinite and the finite, of the temporal and the eternal, of freedom and necessity, in short it is a synthesis." (Kierkegaard, 1849)

The interface between psychiatry and neurology is perhaps best illustrated by the central position of body image in brain-mind relationships. Neurologists who observed changes in the body image in patients with cerebral pathology were foremost in suggesting we each possess an internal diagram of our bodies. Several terms have been used including body concept, body percept or perceived body, body schema, and body image. In an attempt to clarify their usage, Smythies (1953) defined body concept as the beliefs and knowledge we instinctively have about our bodies. The 'perceived body' described the neurophysiological events that created the image in the brain and which may be damaged by neurological dysfunction. Body schema, a term introduced by Head & Holmes (1911), referred to the subconscious models we have of our body. Smythies reserved 'body image' to "describe a visual, mental, or memory image of the human body". For the purposes of this paper the definition used by Lukianowicz (1967) seems more appropriate

"a tridimensional concept of the body as a physical object, possessing a certain shape, size and mass, and occupying a certain space and position in the external world."

Body image in health: development and distortion

'Coenaesthesia', as used by 19th century French psychiatrists, such as Janet, referred to bodily sensations both internal and external. Patients exhibiting bizarre ideas relating to bodily sensation were said to show délire cenesthesiques. In England, Head & Holmes (1911) were the first to focus attention on this

115

subject based on their clinical experience as neurologists (at the National Hospital for Nervous Diseases, Queen Square). In their seminal paper they suggested that the sensory cortex acts as a store room of past impressions which become organised into models of ourselves. These they called 'schemata'. Incoming visual, tactile but especially proprioceptive impulses are modified by these schemata such that the final conscious sensation reflects past and present information. While emphasising the role of proprioceptive stimuli with visual and tactile impulses of secondary importance, they admitted that no one of the three elements was essential and, by way of illustration, showed how the blind have their own kind of body image. Moreover all three may be obliterated and yet an image remains (e.g. phantom limb).

Paul Schilder (1935) in his book *The Image and Appearance of the Human Body* used his observations from children's drawings to deduce a close relationship between optical development and the understanding of spatial relations in the body image. He also remarked that "there is no body image without personality" and clearly recognised the part played by maturational and emotional factors. Four years later, L'hermitte (1939) stressed the importance of factors operating during infancy in the development of a body image. These included painful stimuli, visual impressions, the repetition of kinaesthetic activities in play, and libidinous factors. It takes some years before the body image attains an adult pattern. For this reason, phantom limbs are rarely seen after amputations in childhood. Equally, the body image usually lags behind the physical changes of advancing years. Consequently, it is not uncommon for elderly people to believe they look younger than their age!

Psychoanalysts from Freud onwards have made useful contributions to our understanding of the body image. Freud (1933), in discussing the emergence of the ego, highlights the primary role of body ego development. This view was extended by Scott & Clifford (1948) who drew together the neurological and psychological views of 'the body schema' and the psychoanalytic concept of the ego. Linn (1954), reviewing the work of Bender (on double simultaneous cutaneous stimulation), concluded that the body image emerges through a repetition of the process of infantile separateness. More recently two German psychiatrists (Schmoll & Koch, 1989) examining disturbances of body perception in schizophrenic psychosis, argued that in health we move safely on a continuum, at one end of which we know we *have* a body and at the other, we know we *are* a body. These positions, they suggest, are worked out early in life. If this early resolution fails, then body dissolution is an ever-present risk. It follows that, however we regard it, the body image has a developmental history.

Distortion

The incorporation of inanimate objects into one's body image has been commented on by several authors. Flugel (1930) drew attention to the use of clothing and jewellery to enhance and transform the image to the onlooker as well as oneself. MacDonald Critchley (1950) suggested that a motor-car driver, a cyclist and an airline pilot, all temporarily alter their body image to include their vehicle, as do a soldier with a gun, a surgeon with a scalpel, and a blind man with a white stick. In apparently normal people who experience states of near ecstasy, the body image may lose its sense of cohesiveness.

"And there was no more me as a separate being. I was part of the tall grass, and the tiny sounds it made when it crinkled in the sun sounded within myself also, as truly did the beating of my heart." (Agnes Sanford, 1972)

Here she describes a classical pan-enhenic experience, i.e. the feeling of complete union with the surrounding environment which may extend to include the cosmos. Similar accounts are found in the writings of nature mystics including Tennyson and Symonds, philosophers such as Karl Joel, and Aikido practitioners. Such experiences may be regarded as depersonalisation phenomena. The relationship between depersonalisation (when an individual feels as if he is unreal) and body image, has both fascinated and puzzled writers of different disciplines. Transient depersonalisation experiences, as above, are not uncommon in normal subjects. A study of university students (Myers & Grant, 1972) showed a female preponderance and an association with agoraphobia in women and *déjà vu* in men. Disturbances in body image occurred significantly more often in hypnagogic than in waking depersonalisation. Such students reported:

"I feel my big toe, thumb or any portion of my anatomy swell up to gigantic proportions."
"I can see my body in the dark and it seems to be immensely long."
"I felt disembodied . . . only my mind seemed to exist. . . . I would have to pinch myself to reassure myself that I did exist."

Similar experiences have been recounted after severe fatigue, prolonged sleep deprivation (Bliss *et al*, 1959) and hallucinogenic drugs (Sedman & Kenna, 1964). Huxley (1954) in *Doors of Perception* describes his experience with mescalin "it was odd of course that 'I' was not the same as these arms and legs out there as this wholly objective trunk and neck and even head. It was odd; but one soon got used to it". Children as well as adults may be similarly affected (Salfield, 1958).

Mayer-Gross (1935), in his study of 26 patients, supported the Jacksonian view that depersonalisation could be viewed as " a preformed functional response of the brain". This response reflected activity of a lower level of evolution which was uncovered by removal of higher levels. (Psychoanalysts would regard this as regression to an earlier stage of development.) Of his 26 patients, 12 experienced bodily change. Similarly, Henry Ey (1950) argued that all psychic life is arranged on a number of structural levels and can disintegrate or dissolve to produce mental illness or more commonly a dream in sleep. That the essence of depersonalisation is elusive further confounds our ability to categorise it. Patients grapple for words, often resorting to simile in an attempt to convey the irreducible and indescribable quality of their experience. Ackner (1954) concluded that the "criteria of the salient features themselves are often in doubt or lacking in the clarity necessary for the establishment of their presence".

The association between depersonalisation and organic brain dysfunction has prompted some authors to suggest a primary role for clouding of consciousness. Feelings of unreality are commonly reported by patients with temporal lobe disorder including tumour, epilepsy and direct stimulation (experiments of Penfield). Sedman & Kenna (1965), however, failed to substantiate this link in a series of patients who had either epilepsy or an organic psychosis.

Feelings of bodily change are not invariably reported by those who experience depersonalisation. Consequently authors differ on whether to invoke body-image terminology. Schilder believed that somatic depersonalisation generated hypochondriacal delusions while Mayer-Gross saw a similarity between depersonalisation in young people and hypochondriacal delusional psychosis in middle-aged people. Ackner however, argued that to "explain all feelings of change of the self and the outside world by deriving them from a disturbance of the 'body scheme' would seem to stretch the concept to such extremes as to render it valueless".

Although some controversy remains as to the nature of the body image, from the above studies we can infer that the concept of the body image is an acquired composite structure, generated through psychological and physiological mechanisms, influenced by early developmental experiences, and in normal daily life the image is subject to expansion, contraction and distortion.

Body image in neurological disorders

Anosognosia

Denial of disease or disability was first observed by Von Monakow (1885) in patients with cortical blindness. Anton (1899) more accurately showed the connection with localised cerebral lesions including cortical blindness and deafness (bilateral lesions of the occipital and temporal lobes respectively) and in cases of left hemiplegia. Although Pick recognised the condition, it was Babinski (1914), reporting two patients who ignored their left hemiplegias, who named this phenomenon 'anosognosia', i.e. lack of knowledge or recognition of disease.

Thus patients with hemiplegia have been described who deny the defect, neglect the affected side, and insist it is normal and retains normal function. Hallucinatory and delusional elaboration and confabulation sometimes ensues in an attempt to explain away the problem (Gerstmann, 1942). Ownership of the affected part may be denied or attributed to another person, for example a patient described by Potzl (1925) said, when asked about the affected limb, "I don't know where it comes from; it is so long and lifeless and dead as a snake". Another reported by Ives & Nielsen (1937) stated "someone is substituting this arm (the paralysed one) for my left arm".

A woman of 39, reported by Critchley (1964) had left hemiplegia, hemianaesthesia and hemianopia. She denied she was paralysed and claimed that her left arm and leg belonged to her daughter. When asked to demonstrate her left limbs she searched in a bemused fashion over her left shoulder.

An association with left homonymous hemianopia causing impairment of the left visual field has been noted. In some patients the eyes show conjugate deviation to the right while others turn the whole body away from the affected side. Roth (1949) cites the case of a 61-year-old woman with left hemiparesis who ignored her left side and kept her eyes turned to the right. On the hospital ward she consistently failed to take left turnings. Her left hand felt as if it was not hers and at times she was seen searching for it. A ventriculogram showed the appearance of a tumour in the parietal region lying close to the midline. Visual neglect can occur, however, in the absence of hemianopic defects which implies a mechanism other than simple visual sensory defect.

Fredericks (1985) believed that some patients who deny their disability experience kinaesthetic hallucinations, i.e. they falsely believe they retain function because of hallucinatory experiences connected with the affected part.

Most documented cases have been associated with a right cerebral lesion, though there have been some notable exceptions. Brain (1941) was among the first to observe that the aphasia and other agnostic symptoms in those with right hemiplegias obscured the disordered awareness of the right half which he argued is identical to that seen in left hemiplegias. Stone and colleagues (1991) recently showed that visuo-spatial neglect was equally common in patients with right and left hemisphere strokes (72% compared with 62%) in patients assessed on day 3.

Cutting (1978) examined 100 consecutive hemiplegic patients (0–8 days from the onset of the hemiplegia) in an attempt to correlate deficits of higher mental function with the emergence of anosognosia and its phenomena. An association between laterality and the development of anosognosia was not proven. There was a significant correlation, however, between deficits in higher mental functioning and visual field defects, and the presence of anosognosia.

Pathology

Potzl, from two cases, deduced the phenomena resulted from the coincidence of lesions in the right parietal lobe and right optic thalamus. Gerstmann, reviewing the post-mortem data on these patients, concludes that the phenomenon is most likely to occur from lesions affecting the right optic thalamus or right thalamoparietal radiation or the parietal cortex in the minor hemisphere.

Authors agree that the parietal lobes play a crucial part in the elaboration of the body image. While lesions of the right parietal lobe cause anosognosia, lesions of the left produce Gerstmann's syndrome which is bilateral in distribution. In its complete form the patient displays finger agnosia, acalculia, agraphia, loss of right/left discrimination and constructional apraxia.

Partial paralysis

Enhancement of the body image occasionally occurs in partial paralysis. A patient with multiple sclerosis stated ''some days my left leg seems bigger than the right . . . as if pumped up tight''. Generalised painful experiences such as electric shocks brought the following description ''my head seemed to enlarge and burst with pain . . . my body, legs and feet seemed to shrink to nothing until I could stand on a ten cent piece''. (Critchley, 1950)

Phantom phenomena

Perhaps the best evidence for the existence of a body image is the abundant data on phantom limb sensations which occur in the majority of amputees, unless the limb was lost in childhood. Military surgeons were at one time the experts in this field. Sensory and motor sensations occur such that the phantom may appear heavy, cold, numb or painful. Although most commonly seen after amputation of a limb, loss of any extruding part of the anatomy (e.g. ear, breast, or penis) can be followed by phantom sensations. Occasionally they are reported after severe lesions of the nervous system. A 72-year-old man with a right brachial monoplegia following a left sub-cortical parietal haematoma described prolonged feelings of amputation of the right upper limb and foot (Cambier *et al*, 1984).

From these studies we can postulate that:

(a) the loss of afferent sensory input alone cannot explain these disorders of corporeal awareness
(b) an intact specific and complex physiological system, chiefly represented in the parietal lobe of the right cerebral hemisphere, is essential in maintaining an inner diagram of one's body: its size, shape, position, structure and function.

Body image in psychiatric disorder

Disturbance of body image seems inextricably linked to psychiatric disorder. Lukianowicz (1967), in a study of 200 consecutive psychiatric admissions, found that approximately one in four patients experienced some kind of body-image disorder. Depressed patients tended to have disturbance in its mass while those with schizophrenia exhibited bizarre changes in its shape. Burton & Adkins (1961) showed that schizophrenic patients perceived the size of their body parts in a more grandiose fashion that non-schizophrenic controls. They also noted that improvement in such patients undergoing psychotherapy was often accompanied by a reorganisation of the body image. Bruch (1962) described '' a disorder of delusional proportions in the body image and body concept'' among anorexics; this area has been extensively reviewed by Slade (1985). Body image misidentification and duplication have been described in a variety of psychiatric conditions but will not be discussed further.

Body image and 'melancholy'

Complaints of body change or dysfunction associated with melancholy have been recognised for centuries (Bright, 1586; Burton, 1621). Mandeville (1711), a London practitioner, in his book on mental illness (written primarily for his patients), described his own episode of melancholy complete with the delusion that he had syphilis '' it is no longer ago, than last winter, That I could not be persuaded, but that I was pox'd to all intents and purposes. . . . The losing of my nose, my palate, my Eyes, and all the Fright and shameful Consequences of that Disease possess'd my fancy''.

Morbid preoccupation with physical health or body came to be recognised separately in the 19th century as 'hypochondria' (Falret, 1822). Males are more commonly affected and some suggest hysteria may be the female equivalent. Usually it is seen as a non-delusional state although the distinction between hypochondriasis and hypochondriacal delusion is often of little use (Gull & Anstey, 1868). Lewis (1934) in his classic study of primary depressive disorder, examined 61 patients in great clinical detail. Of these, 25 had marked hypochondriacal preoccupation although it was difficult to distinguish those with delusions on the basis of conviction alone. While Gillespie (1928) believed that ''overt anxiety is no part of a purely hypochondriacal state'', the affect being ''better described as a type of interest'', Bleuler (1924) argued that a depressive mood was fundamental to the development of delusional hypochondriacal ideas.

The link with depersonalisation was clearly stated by Lewis (1934) ''. . . it is an observation which cannot but force itself, even on the casual observer, that there is a close connection between hypochondriacal delusions and those feelings of bodily change which are called depersonalization phenomena''. The underlying psychodynamic meaning was commented on by Ferenczi (1912) in a letter to Freud: ''the whole

E

hypochondriacal delusional system serves to defend [the patient] against the realization of anal erotic tendencies''.

The chronicity of the hypochondriacal state and the persistent negativistic attitude of such patients occupied the minds of many 19th century European psychiatrists.

Cotard's syndrome

In 1880 Jules Cotard presented a paper to the Societé Medicopsychologique entitled ''Du délire hypochondriaque dans une forme grave de la Melancholie anxieuse''. In it he described a particular type of hypochondriacal delusion in which the patient alleged that all that was left of her was the skin and bones of a disorganised body. She no longer had a soul, God did not exist, she would never be able to die a natural death; she would exist eternally, death by burning being the only possible end. She was in a state not of life or death but of a living death. Cotard concluded by outlining six characteristics of these patients:

(a) anxious melancholy
(b) ideas of damnation or of possession
(c) propensity towards suicide and self-mutilation
(d) analgesia
(e) hypochondriacal ideas of non-existence or, of destruction of various organs, the entire body, the soul, God, etc.
(f) ideas of never being able to die.

Regis (1893), who proposed the title ''Cotard's syndrome'' to describe such patients, along with Seglas (1897), expanded his ideas describing a variety of patients with what we now regard as classical Cotard features. From this group of patients he deduced that the condition is of sudden onset, usually in late middle life, is more common in women, and is accompanied by diffuse anxiety which leads to despair and 'involutional type' depression, which often becomes chronic. He suggested that hypochondriacal ideas appeared in the prodrome and could be regarded as a rough sketch on which the nihilistic delusions later appeared. These similarities he wrote (1891) were clearly seen in the hypochondriacal delusions characteristic of patients with syphilis. This view was supported by Bianchi (1924).

However, from the outset, several of these Cotard features have been contested. Lewis, in his study of depressed patients, wisely acknowledged that nihilistic delusions may be ''quite absent from the agitated melancholic of the involutional period and present in young people''. Likewise in Stenstedt's study (1959) of 'involutional melancholia' such delusions were present in only 10% of cases and could not be shown to have aetiological significance. Henne (1961) described the syndrome in a manic patient who showed excitation, insomnia, and declared she wanted to commit suicide to end her immortality.

While Cotard emphasised the underlying melancholy, and had differentiated his group of patients from those with persecutory delusions, nihilistic delusions have been described in schizophrenia as well as epilepsy, encephalitis, general paralysis, and acute and chronic confusional states. Despite this, psychopathologists have emphasised the necessity of an underlying melancholic state for the development of the complete Cotard's syndrome, i.e. the characteristic ideas of immortality and damnation or possession emerge only out of melancholia. The occurrence of nihilistic delusions in other forms of mental illness is consequently viewed independently. Although rare, Cotard's syndrome has been reported in adolescence and early adulthood (Mignot & Lacassagne, 1937; Halfon *et al*, 1985). Degiovanni *et al* (1987), described two cases, one of whom, a 19-year-old girl, asked to have her chest opened so her lack of organs could be seen. The other, a cachectic girl of 22 years believed that she was dead, neither she nor her parents existed. In both cases there was a past history of anorexia.

Aetiology

The relationship to depersonalisation was discussed by Henderson & Gillespie (1944) who, among others, emphasised the non-delusional quality of the latter and hence the retention of insight. ''Ideas of unreality are probably sometimes psychologically related to nihilistic delusions, but they are not usually delusional, the patient recognising their abnormality and complaining of the distress they occasion''. The nihilistic patient states ''I do not exist'' while the depersonalised patient says ''I feel I do not exist'' or ''it's as if I do not exist''. That Cotard's syndrome is the expression of an extreme depersonalised state was equally criticised by Agostini & Wenzel (1954). Failla *et al* (1962) suggested there were three types of depersonalisation, autopsychic (in which the ego is detached from reality), somatopsychic (in which there is negation of parts of the body), and allopsychic (in which the individual is detached from all perceptions). In their view, Cotard's syndrome could be best understood as a somatopsychic depersonalisation.

An organic aetiology has also been proposed. Baillarger (1860) described patients with general paralysis who believed they no longer had a stomach, a brain or a head. This view was adhered to by Ahleid (1966) who described a case of progressive paralysis with delusions of infestation and features of the Cotard syndrome. He hypothesised that lesions in the thalamus and hypophysis formed the organic explanation in this case. Later (1968) he reported nihilistic delusions in three patients with atherosclerosis, progressive paralysis, and alcohol abuse, again suggesting that these delusions were secondary to an organic psychotic syndrome. More recently, Drake (1988) described three patients with transient Cotard features. In all three, right frontotemporal pathology was demonstrated; this was neoplastic in one, atrophic and post-traumatic in the second, and post-infarction in the third. Despite these reported anomalies, Cotard's syndrome passed into psychiatric language, the concept being handed down from one generation of psychiatrists to another. With the advent of improved treatments however, clinical observations suggested that Cotard's original concept might no longer be appropriate. It was therefore decided to study two representative samples of psychiatric patients, one expressing hypochondriacal delusions, the other, nihilistic delusions, in an attempt to confirm Cotard's original phenomenological description, and to compare the two groups using standard measures.

Study

It was postulated that a relationship existed between the body image disorder seen in cases of anosognosia and the altered bodily experience of those expressing nihilistic delusions. As studies had shown a link with parietal lobe pathology in the former, the following hypothesis was formed:

"Patients with nihilistic delusions show more evidence of organic brain disease than age-, sex-, and primary-diagnosis-matched controls".

Thus, the aims of the study were:

(a) to describe the frequency and diagnostic distribution of nihilistic delusions in a psychiatric hospital population a century after Cotard described his syndrome
(b) to describe the clinical attributes and prognosis of these patients
(c) to determine whether possession of these symptoms is a marker of covert organic disease
(d) to compare this group with those expressing hypochondriacal delusions for the presence of any distinguishing variables.

Method

All patients admitted to the acute wards of five psychiatric hospitals (serving a total catchment population of 1.12 million people), over one year, who expressed nihilistic or hypochondriacal delusions, were assessed. For the study a hypochondriacal delusion was defined as "an unrealistic fear or belief, of delusional intensity, of having a disease which persists despite medical reassurance and evidence to the contrary and causes impairment in social and occupational functioning". A nihilistic delusion was defined as "a fixed delusional belief in which the patient denies the existence of part or all of self (e.g. I have no stomach . . . no blood; I am a ghost . . . I am dead) or the outside world (e.g. the world does not exist, everything is nothing)". Assessment consisted of four parts.

(a) A full formal psychiatric history and examination, substantiated by information from a family member or independent informant. This included (i) a chronological account to explore the temporal relationship of the delusions to the onset of psychiatric disorder, (ii) the treatment(s): type, length and response, (iii) mental state examination using the Present State Examination (Wing *et al*, 1974).

(b) A physical examination & haematological testing including erythrocyte sedimentation rate, full blood count, urea & electrolytes, liver and thyroid function tests, and syphilis serology. Patients routinely had a chest X-ray and an electrocardiogram.

(c) Psychometric screening was performed using the Middlesex Elderly Assessment of Mental State (MEAMS).

(d) Neuroradiological investigation (computerised tomography of the brain) was sought in all patients.

Case report: nihilistic delusions

A 76-year-old man was transferred to a psychiatric unit from a medical ward where he was being investigated for urinary retention. Until two months before admission he was a 'happy go lucky' man who enjoyed cricket and regularly went to Lords and the Oval. He was worried by pins and needles in his feet and felt "as though" he was "walking on fur". He complained further "I can't swallow, can't eat, can't open my bowels". He had lost two and a half stone (16kg) in weight, had early morning wakening and expected to die at any moment. Treatment with prothiaden, 150 mg nocte, improved his mood, although his nihilistic ideas remained. After two months at home he was readmitted with marked nihilistic delusions. "I've never been born . . . my brain is all gone . . . there's nothing there . . . I can't swallow anymore . . . there's nowhere for the food to go; my legs are dead . . . useless". He again developed urinary retention although no physical cause could be found. When questioned he said "If I pee I'll flood the Royal Free (the hospital)". Cotard (1888) describes similar paradoxical beliefs in his series of patients.

Case report: hypochondriacal delusions

A 78-year-old man was referred to the psychiatric service with a one-month history of anxiety and obsessional symptoms. When examined he was depressed, agitated and believed he had contracted venereal disease during

World War II (he had been with the 8th army in North Africa). He was convinced he had passed this on to the entire household with catastrophic consequences. Over four years he was admitted five times and treated with ECT. Only on one occasion did his delusions resolve. When I interviewed him he was firmly of the conviction that he was about to die, that doctors would not tell him the truth and he 'knew' his illness was due to venereal disease.

Results

In this paper I will focus on the clinical findings for the two groups of patients. A total of 18 hypochondriacal (HD) and 25 nihilistic (ND) patients were referred by fellow psychiatrists for assessment. For clinical reasons only 16 HD and 15 ND patients were included in the study. Of the 10 nihilistic patients who were referred but not included, two had hypochondriacal delusions and were added to that group, three had no delusional beliefs, while five had probable nihilistic delusions (from case note examination and discussion with ward staff). Examples include: "I've no insides, my backbone has been taken away", " bits of my body are not there . . . the cleaning woman has hoovered up my legs and arms". The latter group were similar in age and sex distribution to those included in the study; there were four females and one male with a mean age of 54 years and a range of 22–70 years. The prevalence rate for each delusion among psychiatric admissions – taken from five psychiatric units with a catchment population (all ages) of 1.12 million people – was 5.6 per 1000 for HD and 7.7 per 1000 for ND. Taking only those included in the study, the prevalence of HD was 4.9 per 1000 admissions per year while that for ND was slightly less at 4.6 per 1000 admissions per year.

Table 9.1 shows the prevalence of classical Cotard symptoms among the nihilistic group. All patients denied the existence of part of themselves, for example "I haven't got any intestines or stomach"; "there's nothing inside my skin"; " A man strangled me two years ago and ever since I've no organs, no brain, no blood . . . I've just dried up"; "I'm a living skeleton . . . all my head is a block of wood, my eyes no longer move or see".

TABLE 9.1
Prevalence of classical Cotard symptoms in the nihilistic group (n = 15)

Symptom	No. of patients
Deny part of self	15
Deny existence of self	14
Ideas of immortality	10
Deny existence of external world	2
Ideas of enormity	1

The majority of the nihilistic group believed they were dead or did not exist in the real, external world, for example "look at that dead wrist . . . I am dead . . . I was buried on January 5th"; "I'm dead, I've no body . . . I ain't got nothin' ''; "I'm a non-person . . . the walking dead". Paradoxically two-thirds of the patients also believed they would live forever: "I'm a zombie . . . it will always be like this for eternity". A particularly distressed Afro-Caribbean lady stated: "Take me to the operating theatre and take my head off and bury me. I'm suffering so bad . . . I know I can't die but I'd be better off if you took off my head"; "I'd like to die but it's impossible . . . doctors told me years ago I'd never die". Another patient who had contemplated suicide said "Without my spirit I'll have an eternal hell; even if I die I'll never find peace. Suicide for me wouldn't be a way out . . . I'm trying to hang on to life because without that I'll be tortured for eternity".

Only two patients overtly denied the existence of the external world: "Look out there [into hospital grounds] there used be life there; now there's nothing, like me . . . nothing". This patient had associated Capgras phenomena. The second patient believed she would never leave hospital as her family and "everything outside" had gone, all that was real was the hospital and her torment. One patient, although denying he ever existed, paradoxically believed that if he urinated, he would flood not only the hospital but also the world.

The clinical diagnoses, given by the patients' consultant, are shown in Fig. 9.1; in both groups depression was the commonest underlying condition

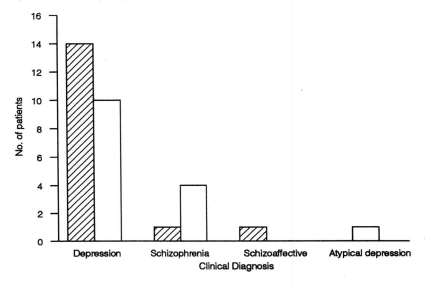

Fig. 9.1. Clinical diagnoses for hypochondriacal (▨) and nihilistic (□) patients

with a greater number of ND diagnosed as having schizophrenia. The sex distribution of both groups indicated that the hypochondriacal patients were mostly male (10 male : 6 female) while the nihilistic group were predominantly female (12 female : 3 male). This finding is statistically significant ($\chi^2 P < 0.05$). Examining the age of onset of psychiatric illness (Fig. 9.2), there was a trend for the ND group to have more members in the middle-aged range while the HD group was more represented by those over 60 years ($P < 0.02$). The length of illness (Fig. 9.3), duration of delusions (Fig. 9.4), interval from onset to appearance of delusions (Fig. 9.5) and number of psychiatric admissions (Fig. 9.6), were comparable in both groups.

Self-harm occurred in four (25%) of those expressing HD and three (20%) of those with ND. Two nihilistic patients who self-mutilated did so in an attempt to establish body existence.

Electroconvulsive therapy (ECT), antidepressants, and neuroleptic medication were used similarly in both groups (Fig. 9.7). In seven of the HD group and five of the ND group, the delusions had subsided with treatment. Of those, the majority had been given ECT either alone or in combination therapy (Fig. 9.8).

Discussion

A century after Cotard's original description, two representative samples of patients with hypochondriacal and nihilistic delusions have been examined

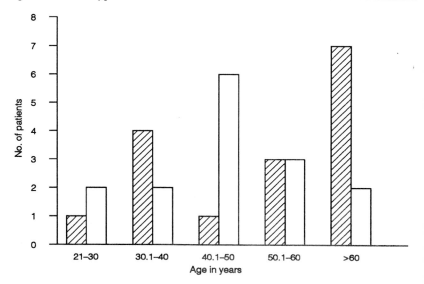

Fig. 9.2. Age of onset of illness for hypochondriacal (▨) and nihilistic (▢) patients

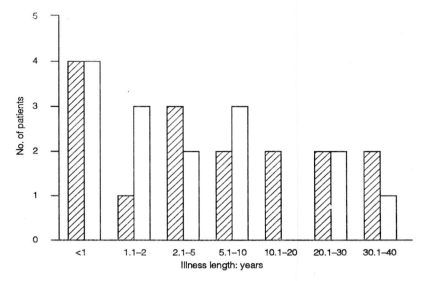

Fig. 9.3. Length of illness of hypochondriacal (▨) and nihilistic (☐) patients

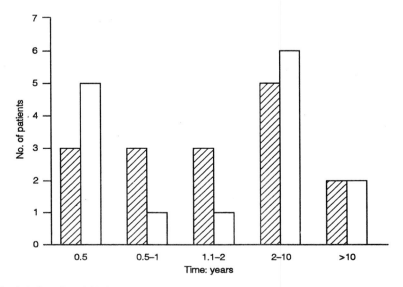

Fig. 9.4. Duration of delusions in hypochondriacal (▨) and nihilistic (☐) patients

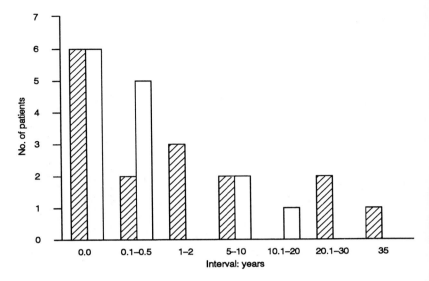

Fig. 9.5. Interval from onset of illness to delusions in hypochondriacal (▨) and nihilistic (□) patients

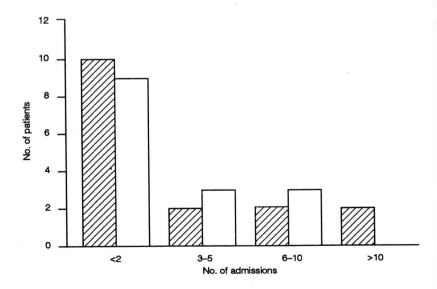

Fig. 9.6. Number of psychiatric admissions for hypochondriacal (▨) and nihilistic (□) patients

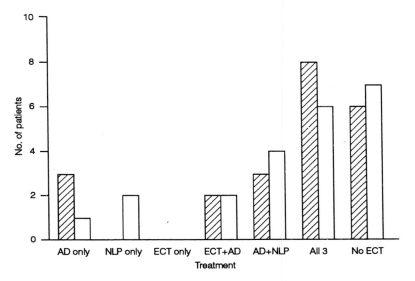

*Fig. 9.7. Treatment regime (antidepressant (AD), neuroleptic (NLP) or electroconvulsive therapy (ECT))
for hypochondriacal (▨) and nihilistic (□) patients*

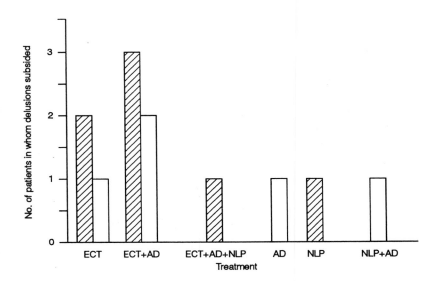

Fig. 9.8. Response to treatment by hypochondriacal (▨) (n = 7) and nihilistic (□) (n = 5) patients

to determine whether a sharp division could be found between the two. Based on the clinical findings alone the two groups show similarities in the chronicity of the condition, the underlying diagnosis and the resistance to treatment. Those who do respond appear to require ECT, a finding in keeping with studies on delusional depression in late life (Baldwin, 1988). Interestingly, a sizeable proportion of the resistant cases had not received ECT up to the time of assessment (Fig. 9.7). On two variables, however, the two groups differ substantially. Those with ND were chiefly female and mostly middle-aged, in keeping with Cotard's original description. The HD patients, by contrast, were mostly male and their illness began predominantly in late life. There is some evidence that patients move from being hypochondriacal to nihilistic, three of the nihilistic group had clearly documented hypochondriacal delusions in the past. The sex and age difference between the two groups, however, appears to contest the view that nihilistic delusions are simply an extreme or exaggerated form of hypochondriacal delusions.

Despite this, the clinical findings argue for, rather than against, the preservation of the original Cotard concept, i.e. a particular type of patient, mostly middle-aged and female, suffering from a chronic illness, principally depression, which is characterised by profound nihilistic beliefs. To be effective the treatment regime needs to be aggressive and almost certainly should include ECT.

A further study is planned which will examine the issue of organicity in these two patient groups and relate the psychotic beliefs of those with anosognosia to those who deny their very existence.

Conclusions

Disturbance of body image in health, and in neurological and psychiatric disorders, has been reviewed to provide a framework on which we might better understand hypochondriacal and nihilistic delusions. The denial of defects seen in some discrete neurological states, and the sense of body dissolution accompanying depersonalisation experiences, appear to be phenomenologically related to nihilistic delusions. The clinical findings of a study looking at patients expressing nihilistic and hypochondriacal delusions are presented. While these results give some credence to the original Cotard concept, the view that nihilistic delusions are an exaggerated version of hypochondriacal delusions is contested.

References

ACKNER, B. (1954) Depersonalization: 1. Aetiology & phenomenology. *Journal of Mental Science*, **100**, 838–853.

AGOSTINI, L. & WENZEL, U. (1954) Considerazioni psicopatologoche su un caso di sindrome di Cotard. *Rivista di Neurologia*, **24**, 476–481.

AHLEID, A. (1966) Sindrome di Cotard e delirio di zoopatia interna in un paralitico progressivo. *Il Lavoro Neuropsichiatrico*, **38**, 221–234

—— (1968) Considerazioni sull' esperienza nichilistica e sulla sindrome di Cotard nelle psicosi organiche e sintomatiche. *Il Lavoro Neuropsichiatrico*, **43**, 927–945.

ANTON, G. (1899) Ueber Selbstwahrnehmungen des Herderkrankungen des Gehirns durch den Kranken bei Rindenblindheit und Rindentaubheit. *Archiv fur Psychiatrie und Nervenkrankheiten*, **32**, 86–127.

BABINSKI, J. (1914) Contribution a l'etude des troubles mentaux dans l'hemiplegie orgabique cerebrale (anosognosie). *Revue Neurologique*, **27**, 845–848.

BAILLARGER, J. P. (1860) *Note sur le Delire Hypochondriaque*. Academie des Sciences.

BALDWIN, R. C. (1988) Delusional and non-delusional depression in late life. *British Journal of Psychiatry*, **152**, 39–44.

BIANCHI, L. (1924) *Trattato di Psichiatria*. III ed. Naples: Idelson.

BLEULER, E. (1924) *Textbook of Psychiatry*, 4th edition. London: George Allen & Unwin.

BLISS, E. L., CLARKE, L. D. & WEST, C. D. (1959) Studies of sleep deprivation – relationship to schizophrenia. *Archives of Neurology & Psychiatry*, **81**, 348–359.

BRAIN, W. R. (1941) Visual disorientation with special reference to lesions of the right cerebral hemisphere. *Brain*, **64**, 244–272.

BRIGHT, T. (1586) *A Treatise of Melancholie*. London.

BRUCH, H. (1962) Perceptual & conceptual disturbance in anorexia nervosa. *Psychosomatic Medicine*, **24**, 187–194.

BURTON, A. & ADKINS, J. (1961) Perceived size of self image body parts in schizophrenia. *Archives of General Psychiatry*, **5**, 39–48.

BURTON, R. (1651) *The Anatomy of Melancholy*, (eds F. Dell & R. Jordan-Smith). New York: Tudor Publishing, 1955.

CAMBIER, J., ELGHOZI, D., GRAVELEAU, PH., *et al* (1984) Hemiasomatognosie droite et sentiment d'amputation par lesion gauche sous-corticale, role de la disconnexion calleuse. *Revue Neurologique*, **140**, 256–262.

COTARD, J. (1880) Du délire hypochondriaque dans une forme grave de la melancholie anxieuse. *Annales Medico-Psychologiques*, **4**, 168–174.

—— (1882) Clinique mentale: du délires de negations. *Archives de Neurologie*, **4**, 152–170, 282–296.

—— (1888) Du délire d'enormité. *Annales Medico-Psychologiques*, **4**, 465–487.

—— (1891) *Maladies Cerebrales et Mentales*. Paris: Bailliere.

CRITCHLEY, M. (1950) The body image in neurology. *Lancet*, *i*, 335–341.

—— (1964) Psychiatric symptoms and parietal disease: differential diagnosis. *Proceedings of the Royal Society of Medicine*, **57**, 422–428.

CUTTING, J. (1978) Study of anosognosia. *Journal of Neurology, Neurosurgery & Psychiatry*, **41**, 548–555.

DEGIOVANNI, A., FAURE, M. & LEVEQUE, J. P. (1987) Le syndrome de Cotard chez le jeune: a propos de deux observations. *Annales Medico-Psychologiques*, **145**, 874–876.

DRAKE, M.E. (1988) Cotard's syndrome and temporal lobe epilepsy. *Psychiatric Journal of the University of Ottawa*, **13**, 36–39.

EY, H. (1950) Délires de négations. *Etudes Psychiatriques, Paris* (ed. Desclée de Brower), **11**, etude 16, 427–452.

FAILLA, E., COPPOLA, C. F. & SINISI, C. (1962) A proposito della sindrome di Cotard. *Rassegna di Neuropsichiatria*, **16**, 331–380.

FALRET, J. P. (1822) *De l'Hypochondrie et du Suicide*. Paris.

FERENCZI, S. (1912, pub. 1949) Ten letters to Freud. *International Journal of Psychoanalysis*, **30**, 244–246.

FREDERICKS, J. A. M. (1985) Disorders of body schema. In *Handbook of Clinical Neurology* (eds P. J. Vinken, G. W. Bruyn & H. L. Klawans) Vol 1, 45, pp. 373–393. Amsterdam: Elsevier.

FLUGEL, J. C. (1930) *Psychology of Clothes*. London: Hogarth Press.

FREUD, S. (1933) *New Introductory Lectures on Psychoanalysis*. London: Hogarth Press.

GERSTMANN, J. (1942) Problem of imperception of disease and of impaired body territories with organic lesions. *Archives of Neurology and Psychiatry*, **48**, 890–913.

GILLESPIE, R. D. (1928) Hypochondria: its definition, nosology, and psychopathology. *Guy's Hospital Reports*, **78**, 408–460.

GULL, W. W. & ANSTEY, E. (1868) Hypochondriasis. In *A collection of the Published Writings of Sir William Gull*. London, 1894.

HALFON, O., MOUREN-SIMEONI, M. C. & DUGAS, M. (1985) Le syndrome de Cotard chez l'adolescent. *Annales Medico-Psychologiques*, **143**, 876–879.

HEAD, H. & HOLMES, G. (1911) Sensory disturbances from cerebral lesions. *Brain*, **34**, 102–254.

HENDERSON, D. K. & GILLESPIE, R. D. (1944) *Textbook of Psychiatry*. 6th edition. London: Oxford University Press.

HENNE, M., TONNEL, M. & HENNE, S. (1961) A propos des états mixtes. Une observation de syndrome de Cotard maniaque. *Annales Medico-Psychologiques*, **119**, 318–324.

HUXLEY, A. (1954) *The Doors of Perception*. London: Chatto & Windus.

IVES, E. R. & NIELSEN, J. M. (1937) Disturbance of body scheme: Delusion of the absence of part of body in two cases with autopsy verification of lesion. *Bulletin of the Los Angeles Neurological Society*, **2**, 102–125.

KIERKEGAARD, S. (1849) *The Sickness unto Death*. (Ed. and transl. Howard V. Hong & Edna H. Hong, 1980). Princeton: Princeton University Press.

LEWIS, A. J. (1934) Melancholia: a clinical survey of depressive states. *Journal of Mental Science*, **80**, 277–378.

L'HERMITTE, J. (1939) L'image de notre corps. *Nouvelle Revue Critique*, Paris.

LINN, L. (1955) Some developmental aspects of the body image. *International Journal of Psychoanalysis*, **36**, 36–42.

LUKIANOWICZ, N. (1967) Body image disturbances in psychiatric disorders. *British Journal of Psychiatry*, **113**, 31–47.

MANDEVILLE, B. (1711) *A treatise of the Hypochondriack and Hysterick Passions*. London.

MAYER-GROSS, W. (1935) On depersonalisation. *British Journal of Medical Psychology*, **15**, 103–122.

MEAMS (1989) *Middlesex Elderly Assessment of Mental State* (Constructed and validated by Evelyn Golding). England: Thames Valley Test Company.

MIGNOT, M. & LACASSAGNE, A. M. (1937) Syndrome de Cotard chez une jeune fille de 20 ans. *Annales Medico-Psychologiques*, **95**, 246 –251.

MYERS, D. H. & GRANT, G. (1972) A study of depersonalization in students. *British Journal of Psychiatry*, **121**, 59–65.

POTZL, O. (1925) Ueber Storungen der Selbstwahrnehmung bei linksseitiger Hemiplegie. *Zeitschrift fur die gesamte Neurologie und Psychiatrie*, **93**, 117–168.

REGIS, E. (1893) Note historique et clinique sur le délire des negations. *Gazette Medicale de Paris*, **2**, 61–64.

ROTH, M. (1949) Disorders of the body image caused by lesions of the right parietal lobe. *Brain*, **72**, 89–111.

SALFIELD, D. J. (1958) Depersonalization and allied disturbances in childhood. *Journal of Mental Science*, **104**, 472–476.

SANFORD, A. (1972) *Sealed Orders*. New Jersey: Logos International.

SCHILDER, P. (1935) *The Image and Appearance of the Human Body*. London: Kegan Paul, Trench, Trubner.

SCHMOLL, D. & KOCH, T. (1989) Leibgefuhlsstorungen in der schizophrenen psychose. *Der Nervenartz*, **60**, 619–627.

SCOTT, W. & CLIFFORD, M. (1948) Some embryonic, neurological, psychiatric, psychoanalytic implications of the body scheme. *International Journal of Psychoanalysis*, **29**, 141–155.

SEDMAN, G. & KENNA, J. C. (1964) The occurrence of depersonalization phenomena under L.S.D. *Psychiatrie et Neurologie* (Basel), **147**, 129–139.

—— & —— (1965) Depersonalization in temporal lobe epilepsy and the organic psychoses. *British Journal of Psychiatry*, **111**, 293–299.

SEGLAS, J. (1897) Le delire des negations dans la melancholie. In *Les Maladies Mentales et Nerveuses*, pp. 457–494. Paris: Masson.

SLADE, P. (1985) A review of body image studies in anorexia nervosa and bulimia nervosa. *Journal of Psychosomatic Research*, **19**, 225–265.

SMYTHIES, J. R. (1953) The experience and description of the human body. *Brain*, **76**, 132–145.

STENSTEDT, A. (1959) Involutional melancholia: an aetiological, clinical and social study of endogenous depression in later life with special reference to genetic factors. *Acta Psychiatrica et Neurologica Scandinavica*, **34** (suppl. 127), 1–71.

STONE, S. P., WILSON, B., WROOT, A. *et al* (1991) The assessment of visuo-spatial neglect after acute stroke. *Journal of Neurology, Neurosurgery and Psychiatry*, **54**, 345–350.

VON MONAKOW, C. (1885) Experimentelle und pathologisch-anatomische Untersuchungen uber die Beziuehungen der sogenannten Sehsphare zu den infrakortikalen Opticuscentren und N. opticus. *Archive fur Psychiatrie und Nervenkrankheiten*, **16**, 151, 317.

WING, J. K., COOPER, J. E. & SARTORIUS, N. (1974) *Measurement and Classification of Psychiatric Symptoms*. Cambridge: Cambridge University Press.

10 Schizophrenic, schizoaffective and affective disorders in the elderly: a comparison

A. MARNEROS, A. DEISTER and A. ROHDE

As many authors – including some contributors in this volume – have pointed out, psychosis or psychotic features, affectivity, and reactivity in the elderly have properties distinguishing them from the mental disorders of younger people (Pitt, 1982; Jeste & Zisook, 1988; Müller, 1989; Berrios, this volume, pp. 3–14; Pichot, this volume, pp. 15–24; Post, this volume, pp. 43–49). This was one of the most important reasons why the creators of modern psychiatry reserved a special place for the disorders of old people. Kraepelin (1896), for instance, assumed that melancholia was the depressive illness of old people distinguishable from other forms of manic–depressive insanity. But he changed his mind after the work of some of his pupils, especially Dreyfus (1907). Concepts, including paraphrenia and presbyophrenia, are based mainly on the criterion of 'special features' of mental disorders in the elderly.

Psychiatrists, especially European psychiatrists, have paid a lot of attention to the so-called 'late-onset schizophrenia' (Harris & Jeste, 1988) and 'late-onset depression' (Murphy, 1989), but there has been practically no work on schizoaffective disorders in the elderly, with the exception of that carried out by Felix Post (1966, 1971) and, more recently, of Holden (1987) and Pitt (1990).

One of the most difficult questions in the research into late-onset mental disorders is what is 'late' and what is 'non-late'. So the terms 'late schizophrenia' or 'late-onset schizophrenia' are problematical. In an earlier publication (Marneros & Deister, 1984) we pointed out the lack of agreement as to what age at first manifestation should be regarded as the boundary for classification as 'late-onset schizophrenia'. Many authors, in agreement with Bleuler, classify those schizophrenic psychoses first clinically manifested at the age of 40 or above as 'late-onset schizophrenia' (Klages, 1961; Siegel & Rollberg, 1970; Berner et al, 1973; Huber et al, 1975, 1979; Gabriel, 1978). Others take the view that the pathological effects of old age must also be considered, and that only in this way can late-onset schizophrenia begin to acquire a clear profile (Sternberg, 1972). According to Sternberg's findings, the age-dependent modifications of a psychosis can be found at the earliest after the age of 50.

DSM–III (American Psychiatric Association, 1980) lays down an age of under 45 years at first manifestation as a *conditio sine qua non* for schizophrenia. This statistical boundary can be accepted as a guideline, based on the findings of most large studies of schizophrenia reporting a mean age at onset which is much lower than 45, mainly in the third decade of life (Häfner, 1990; Marneros *et al*, 1991; Häfner *et al*, 1991).

Another problem regarding earlier European work on late-onset schizophrenia is the broad definition of schizophrenia. Most studies are based on Kurt Schneider's or Eugen Bleuler's criteria, which are either much broader or less specific than modern operational criteria.

In an earlier study (Marneros & Deister, 1984) we evaluated the case records of 1208 patients with the discharge diagnosis of schizophrenia admitted to hospital for the first time in their life. The diagnostic criteria used at that time were broadly those of Schneider. The age at first admission, which in some cases is not identical to age of onset, is shown in Fig. 10.1.

We found that 23% of the investigated population met the criteria of late onset schizophrenia. That is a very big proportion, but mainly created by the broad definition.

Another weakness of this and similar studies – apart from the broad definitions – is that they consider only the cross-sectional aspect (Marneros & Deister, 1984).

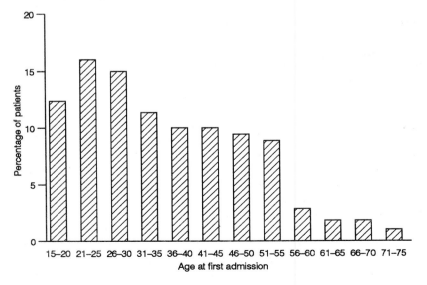

Fig. 10.1. Age at first admission for schizophrenic disorder (broad definition, n = 1208)

In the study reported below we tried to eliminate these shortcomings by using very narrow diagnostic criteria based on modified DSM–III criteria, considering the longitudinal aspect and incorporating long-term observation.

Method

The present study is part of the Cologne Study on the long-term course and outcome of patients with functional psychoses (Marneros *et al*, 1986, 1988, 1989, 1991). We examined and longitudinally investigated 402 patients. The original study population was 950 patients diagnosed between 1950 and 1979 at the university hospitals of Cologne and Bonn as having 'endogenous depression', 'mania', 'schizophrenia', 'suspected schizophrenia' and 'schizoaffective psychoses' ('cases-in-between' according to Schneider's nomenclature). During this period the diagnoses were made consistently according to Schneider's criteria. No age limit was imposed.

All available information about the patients was evaluated for the whole course (case records, personal interviews, interviews with the relatives, etc.). At the time of follow-up, 523 patients were still alive, 121 of whom refused investigation. The remaining 402 patients were followed-up for a mean observation time of more than 27 years.

The diagnostic criteria used in this study distinguish between 'episode' (defined cross-sectionally) and 'disorder' or 'illness' (defined longitudinally). The diagnostic criteria for episodes are based on DSM–III orientated criteria and definitions. The following types of episodes were defined: schizophrenic, schizodepressive, schizomanic, schizomanic–depressive mixed, melancholic, manic, manic–depressive mixed and uncharacteristic. The criteria are described in detail in the Appendix.

Patients were diagnosed using very narrow criteria (see Appendix). A schizophrenic disorder was diagnosed if only schizophrenic episodes occurred during the whole observation time, with no affective and no schizoaffective episodes. An affective disorder was diagnosed if only affective episodes occurred. The diagnosis of a schizoaffective disorder required the presence of schizoaffective episodes *or* the occurrence of both schizophrenic *and* affective episodes during the whole course.

Of the 402 longitudinally investigated patients, 148 were diagnosed as having schizophrenia, 101 as having a schizoaffective disorder and 106 as having an affective disorder. The remaining 47 patients did not fulfil the criteria of any of these diagnoses, but instead showed organic psychoses or personality or neurotic disorders. Some features of the study population are shown in Table 10.1. The instruments of evaluation are shown below:

Present State Examination (PSE; Wing *et al*, 1974)
Modified version of PSE for follow-up
Global Assessment Scale (GAS; Spitzer *et al*, 1976)
Disability Assessment Schedule (WHO/DAS; World Health Organization, 1988)
Psychological Impairments Rating Schedule (WHO/PIRS; Biehl *et al*, 1989*a,b*)
General sociodemographic schedule based on items of:
Psychiatric and Personal History Schedule (PPHS; WHO)
Follow-up History and Sociodemographic Description Schedule (FU-HSD; WHO)
Past History and Sociodemographic Description Schedule (PHSD; WHO)
Own items of social consequences of the illness (Marneros *et al*, 1991)

In the first part of the study, patients with late-onset disorder were compared with the patients with a non-late onset. For the definition of 'late-onset' schizophrenia we applied the DSM–III age criterion for schizophrenia, namely onset after the age of 45 years. It was a great problem to decide what is a 'late-onset schizoaffective' and a 'late-onset affective' disorder. However, considering the mean age at first manifestation and aiming at a fair comparison between the three categories of disorders, we decided to apply the same criterion for schizoaffective and affective disorders as for schizophrenia.

In the second part of the study, in each of the three diagnostic groups, patients who became older than 60 years at the end of the observation time were compared with those under 60 years.

TABLE 10.1
Features of the study population

	Schizophrenic disorders (n = 148)	Schizoaffective disorders (n = 101)	Affective disorders (n = 106)
Sex distribution: %			
male	58.1	36.6	24.5
female	41.9	63.4	75.5
Age at onset: years			
mean (s.d.)	27.7 (10.6)	30.4 (10.4)	36.1 (11.0)
median	24.0	29.0	35.0
range	14–64	15–58	15–63
Duration of observation time: years			
mean	25.0	27.5	29.9
median	27.0	27.0	27.0
range	12–52	12–63	12–58
Age at the end of observation time: years			
mean	52.7	57.9	66.0
median	53.0	56.0	68.0
range	29–86	29–89	34–89

The groups were compared on four levels. (a) Sociodemographic and premorbid variables consisted of: sex distribution, educational level, occupational level at onset, marital status at onset, premorbid personality, premorbid social interactions, stable heterosexual relationship before onset (>6 months), broken home, mental illness in the family, original social class (social class of parents), social class at onset, and highest achieved social class.

(b) Symptoms during the whole course consisted of: suicidal symptoms, productive psychotic symptoms, paranoid symptoms; and for schizophrenic and schizoaffective disorders only, depressive symptoms, hallucinations, psychotic passivity symptoms, and incoherence.

(c) Variables of long-term course was made up of: life events before onset, prodromal symptoms, number of episodes (hospital admissions), type of initial episode, type of episodes during course; and for schizoaffective and affective disorders only, annual frequency of episodes, number of cycles, average length of episodes, average length of intervals, average length of cycles, and polarity.

(d) Variables of long-term outcome consisted of: period without remanifestation before the end of observation time, frequency of persisting alterations, type of phenomenological constellations, social consequences (occupational mobility, social mobility, premature retirement, impairment of autarky); and for schizophrenic disorders only, frequency of permanent hospital admission.

A statistical analysis based on χ^2-test or similar tests was not carried out in cases of very asymmetrical distributions.

Results

Late onset compared with non-late onset

Applying the criteria outlined above we had very small numbers of patients with late onset (Fig. 10.2). Only 8% of the schizophrenic patients could be classified as having late-onset schizophrenia, and only 12% of schizoaffective disorders, and 24% of affective disorders were late onset (Fig. 10.3). These small proportions are compatible with other studies recently reported by Jeste & Zisook (1988), for instance the UCLA (Miller & Lesser, 1988), UCSD (Jeste *et al*, 1988), Johns Hopkins (Pearlson & Rabins, 1988) and Montreal (Yassa *et al*, 1988) studies, and in Germany the Mannheim-Heidelberg-Neckar epidemiological study (Häfner *et al*, 1991), but differ remarkably from the results of our former study using broad criteria and only cross-sectional definitions, in which we found that 23% of the patients had late-onset schizophrenia (Marneros & Deister, 1984).

Late-onset schizophrenia v. non-late-onset schizophrenia

The relevant differences between the schizophrenic patients with late onset and those with a non-late onset are shown in Table 10.2.

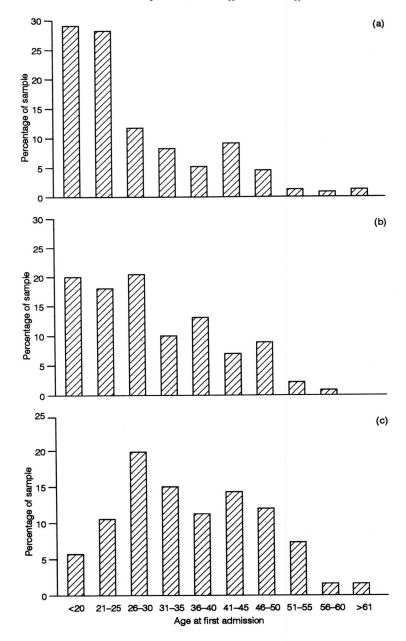

Fig. 10.2. *Age at first admission in (a) schizophrenic (n = 148), (b) schizoaffective (n = 101) and (c) affective disorders (n = 106) (narrow definitions)*

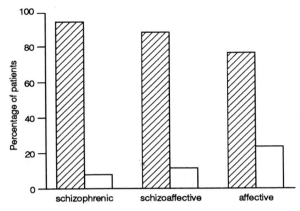

Fig. 10.3. Proportions of late-onset (□) and non-late-onset (▨) patients in the three diagnostic groups

TABLE 10.2
Schizophrenic disorders: relevant differences between patients with late and non-late onset

	Patients with non-late onset ($\leqslant 45$ years; n = 136) No. (%)	Patients with late onset (> 45 years; n = 12) No. (%)
Sociodemographic and premorbid variables		
Stable heterosexual relationship before onset (> 6 months)	42 (30.9)	9 (75.0)
Mental illness in the family	68 (50.0)	–
Variables of long-term course		
Type of course		
monoepisodic (1 hospital admission)	14 (10.3)	3 (25.0)
oligoepisodic (2 or 3 admissions)	52 (38.2)	9 (75.0)
polyepisodic (4 and more admissions)	70 (51.5)	–
Type of initial episode		
positive initial episode	55 (40.4)	8 (66.7)
negative initial episode	46 (33.8)	–
Type of episodes during course		
only positive episodes during long-term course	20 (14.7)	8 (66.7)
only negative episodes during long-term course	10 (7.4)	–
Symptoms during course		
delusions	122 (89.7)	12 (100)
hallucinations	77 (56.6)	8 (66.7)
incoherence	86 (63.2)	4 (33.3)
psychotic passivity symptoms	44 (32.4)	1 (8.3)
depressive symptoms	82 (60.3)	10 (83.3)
suicidal symptoms	76 (55.9)	4 (33.3)
Variables of long-term outcome		
Permanent hospital admission	34 (25.0)	1 (8.3)

Patients with late onset more often had a stable heterosexual partnership before onset, more often had only positive episodes during the long-term course and therefore more often had delusions and hallucinations. In addition, depressive symptoms were found more frequently in late-onset schizophrenia, but this is not melancholia because, with our definition, melancholic symptoms impose a diagnosis of schizoaffective disorder. Patients with late-onset schizophrenia less frequently have mental illness in the family, and less frequently have a polyepisodic course (i.e. more than four episodes during the course). In late-onset schizophrenia, no purely negative courses (with no positive episodes) were found. Psychotic passivity symptoms and suicidal symptoms were also rarely found. Patients with late-onset schizophrenia only exceptionally needed permanent hospital admission (more than three years continuously).

Late-onset schizoaffective disorders v. non-late-onset schizoaffective disorders

Comparing the schizoaffective disorders with 'late onset' and those with non-late onset (Table 10.3), we found far fewer differences than between the corresponding groups in schizophrenia. Patients with late onset more frequently had a stable heterosexual partnership before onset (unsurprisingly) and less frequently had pure paranoid syndromes. This means that late-onset schizoaffective disorders more frequently display a richness of psychotic symptoms like hallucinations or psychotic passivity symptoms.

Late-onset affective disorders v. non-late-onset affective disorders

The comparison of late-onset and non-late-onset affective disorders (Table 10.4) shows a higher frequency of stable heterosexual partnerships before onset in the late-onset group, as in the other two diagnostic categories. This was expected. Monoepisodic (or monophasic) course and unipolar course (i.e. only melancholic episodes) were found more frequently.

TABLE 10.3
Schizoaffective disorders: relevant differences between patients with late and non-late onset

	Patients with non-late onset ($\leqslant 45$ years; n = 89) No. (%)	Patients with late onset (> 45 years; n = 12) No. (%)
Sociodemographic and premorbid variables		
Stable heterosexual relationship before onset (> 6 months)	58 (65.2)	11 (91.7)
Variables of long-term course		
Pure paranoid syndromes during course	33 (37.1)	1 (8.3)

TABLE 10.4
Affective disorders: relevant differences between patients with late and non-late onset

	Patients with non-late onset (≤ 45 years; n = 81) No. (%)	Patients with late onset (> 45 years; n = 25) No. (%)
Sociodemographic and premorbid variables		
Stable heterosexual relationship before onset (> 6 months)	64 (79.0)	25 (100)
Variables of long-term course		
Type of course		
monoepisodic (1 episode)	2 (2.5)	6 (24.0)
oligoepisodic (2 or 3 episodes)	32 (40.0)	10 (40.0)
polyepisodic (4 and more episodes)	46 (57.5)	9 (36.0)
Polarity		
unipolar	55 (67.9)	21 (84.0)
bipolar	26 (32.1)	4 (16.0)

Therefore polyepisodic course (four and more episodes) and bipolar courses were less frequent. But one must consider that polyepisodic course and bipolar course are dependent variables. This is true also for monoepisodic course and unipolar course.

Younger patients compared with older patients

Again, we have to answer the trivial question: what is old and what is young? The answer can only be a compromise. For our investigations we drew the borderline – more or less arbitrarily – at the age of 60 years.

Currently, 26% of our schizophrenic patients, 42% of the schizoaffective patients, and 65% of patients with affective disorders are aged over 60 years (Fig. 10.4).

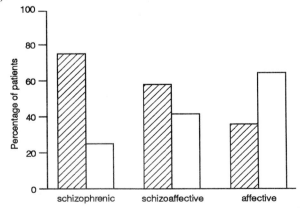

Fig. 10.4. Percentage of patients above (□) and below (▨) 60 years of age at the end of the observation time

Older v. younger schizophrenic patients

Comparison of those schizophrenic patients over 60 years of age with those 60 years and under revealed two significant differences (Table 10.5): Firstly, the older schizophrenic patients had a longer period without remanifestation of episodes before the end of the observation time. This can be interpreted as indicating that clinical activity of the disorder becomes milder with age, confirming the findings of earlier investigations (Ciompi & Müller 1976; Müller, 1989) that schizophrenic disorders became in old age more 'peaceful'. Secondly, the finding that older schizophrenic patients less frequently have suicidal symptoms can be explained as indicating a kind of 'peace with the illness'. It seems that confrontation with the schizophrenic disorder and its consequent deficits and impairments is the most relevant factor for suicidal behaviour; in the course of the illness, schizophrenic patients become more able to live with the deficits, or because of depletion they do not have the strength and the motivation for suicide (Marneros & Prentkowski, 1985; Rohde *et al*, 1989*a,b*, 1990; Marneros *et al*, 1991; Marneros *et al*, 1992).

Older v. younger schizoaffective patients

The comparison of the schizoaffective patients (patients who became older than 60 years with those who were still younger, Table 10.6) showed, as in schizophrenic patients, that a longer period without remanifestations of the illness before the end of the observation time was found in the older patients. Hallucinations were found more frequently and pure paranoid syndromes less frequently in this group. These last findings are, however, dependent on each other.

Older v. younger affective patients

Affective patients who were older than 60 years at the end of the observation time showed only two differences from the younger patients (Table 10.7):

TABLE 10.5
Schizophrenic disorders: statistically significant differences between patients 60 years and under and patients over 60 years at the end of the observation time

	Patients 60 years and under (n = 110) No. (%)	Patients over 60 years (n = 38) No. (%)
Variables during course		
Period without remanifestations before the end of observation time: months		
mean[1]	8.4	16.3**
median[2]	6.0	13.0**
Suicidal symptoms during course[3]	66 (60.0)	14 (36.8)*

*P<0.05 **P<0.01.
1. *t*-test.
2. Mann-Whitney *U*-test.
3. χ^2-test.

TABLE 10.6

Schizoaffective disorders: statistically significant differences between patients up to 60 years and patients older than 60 years at the end of the observation time

	Patients up to 60 years (n = 59) No. (%)	Patients older than 60 years (n = 42) No. (%)
Period without remanifestations before the end of observation time: months		
mean[1]	8.3	14.4**
median[2]	5.0	11.5**
Hallucinations during course[3]	22 (37.3)	26 (61.9)*
Pure paranoid syndromes during course[3]	26 (44.1)	8 (19.0)*

1. *t*-test.
2. Mann-Whitney *U*-test.
3. χ^2-test.
*$P < 0.05$ **$P < 0.01$.

TABLE 10.7

Affective disorders: statistically significant differences between patients up to 60 years and patients older than 60 years at the end of the observation time

	Patients up to 60 years (n = 37) No. (%)	Patients older than 60 years (n = 69) No. (%)
Variables of long-term course		
Suicidal attempts (at least once during course)[1]	4 (10.8)	19 (27.5)**
Variables of long-term outcome		
Phenomenological constellations[1]		
Slight asthenic insufficiency syndrome	8 (21.6)	14 (20.3)*
Chronic subdepressive syndrome	2 (5.4)	12 (17.4)
Chronic hyperthymic syndrome	2 (5.4)	0
Full remission	25 (67.6)	43 (62.3)

1. χ^2-test.
*$P < 0.10$, **$P < 0.05$.

they attempted suicide more frequently and also more frequently had chronic subdepressive syndromes; these findings are perhaps dependent on each other. A comparison with other studies such as those of Post (1962), Angst (1966), and Müller (1989) showed only partial similarities. The differences in definitions, study designs and methods may limit comparability.

Conclusions

Late-onset functional disorders fulfilling narrow criteria for schizophrenia, criteria for the melancholic type of major depression, the narrowly defined bipolar disorder, and also narrowly defined schizoaffective disorders are relatively rare. A possible explanation is that, in addition to a genuine relative rareness, most of the functional disorders in the elderly are 'atypical', including symptoms from other domains of psychopathology such as 'organic' or 'reactive' symptoms, so that they do not fulfil the criteria of 'typical disorders'. This could also explain the fact that earlier studies using broad definitions reported more voluminous populations. But as recently pointed out by Häfner and co-workers (1991), the distinction between pure late-onset schizophrenia and non-schizophrenic paranoid syndromes in the elderly is necessary because of the great theoretical relevance.

Regarding symptoms, it can be concluded that late-onset schizophrenia is a syndrome with rich productive psychotic symptoms and depressive elements. The prognosis of late-onset schizophrenia is similar to that of non-late-onset schizophrenia, but somewhat better in that frequency of episodes and the number of patients needing permanent hospital admission is lower. There are no differences between the two kinds of schizophrenia in other important aspects of prognosis, such as disability, psychological deficits, phenomenological constellations of persisting alterations, social consequences of the illness, etc.

Similarly, schizoaffective disorders with late onset have more, and more florid, symptoms than non-late-onset schizoaffective disorders. However, no other relevant differences in course, outcome and sociodemographic parameters are found between the two groups of schizoaffective disorders.

The only relevant difference between late-onset and non-late-onset affective disorders is that unipolar forms of the disorder are found much more frequently in the older group.

The most impressive characteristic of older schizophrenic patients is a kind of 'peace' with the illness; they have fewer remanifestations and less frequently exhibit suicidal symptoms. Older schizoaffective patients also showed fewer remanifestations. The older affective patients do not show the above-mentioned 'peace with the illness'; rather they more frequently display suicidal symptoms and subdepressive syndromes.

Appendix

Definitions of diagnostic criteria

Schizophrenic episode

1 . At least one of the following during the episode:

  (a) delusions of being controlled, thought broadcasting, thought insertion, thought withdrawal
  (b) delusions of persecution or jealousy, somatic, grandiose, religious, nihilistic, or other delusions, if accompanied by at least one of the following:

     (i) hallucinations
    (ii) blunted, flat, or inappropriate affect
   (iii) catatonic or other grossly disorganised behaviour

(c) auditory hallucinations in which either a voice keeps up a running commentary on the individual's behaviour or thoughts, or two or more voices converse with each other, or the patient hears his own thoughts spoken aloud

(d) auditory hallucinations on several occasions with content of more than one or two words, having no apparent relation to depression or elation

(e) incoherence, marked loosening of associations, markedly illogical thinking, or marked poverty of speech if associated with at least one of the following:

     (i) blunted, flat or inappropriate affect
    (ii) delusions or hallucinations
   (iii) catatonic or other grossly disorganised behaviour.

2. Duration of at least one week.
3. Absence of a melancholic, manic or manic–melancholic mixed episode – as defined in this paper – during, immediately before, or immediately after (without free interval) the presence of the symptoms of 1.
4. Not due to any mental organic disorder.

Melancholic episode

1. Loss of pleasure in all or almost all activities.
2. Lack of reactivity to usually pleasurable stimuli.
3. At least three of the following:

(a) distinct quality of depressed mood, i.e. the depressed mood is perceived as distinctly different from the kind of feeling experienced following the death of a loved one

(b) the depression is regularly worse in the morning

(c) early morning awakening (significantly earlier than ususal)

(d) marked psychomotor retardation or agitation

(e) significant anorexia or weight loss

(f) excessive or inappropriate guilt, or excessive or inappropriate feelings of insufficiency.

4. Duration of at least one week.
5. Absence of the criteria of the schizophrenic, manic or manic–depressive mixed episode, during, immediately before or immediately after (without free interval) the melancholic episode.
6. Not due to any organic mental disorder.

Manic episode

1. One or more distinct periods with a predominantly elevated, expansive, or irritable mood.
2. Duration of at least one week (or any duration if hospital admission is necessary), during which, for most of the time, at least three of the following symptoms have persisted (four if the mood is only irritable) and have been present to a significant degree:

   (a) increase in activity (either socially, at work, or sexually) or physical restlessness
   (b) more talkative than usual or pressure to keep talking
   (c) flight of ideas or subjective experience that thoughts are racing
   (d) inflated self-esteem (grandiosity, which may be delusional)
   (e) decreased need for sleep
   (f) distractibility, i.e. attention is too easily drawn to unimportant or irrelevant external stimuli
   (g) excessive involvement in activities that have a high potential for painful consequences which is not recognised, e.g. buying sprees, sexual indiscretions, foolish business investments, reckless driving.

3. Absence of the symptoms of the schizophrenic, melancholic, or manic–melancholic mixed episode, during, immediately before or immediately after (without free interval) the manic episode.
4. Not due to any organic mental disorder.

Manic–melancholic mixed episode

1. The episode involves the symptomatic picture of both melancholic and manic episode intermixed or alternating without free interval.
2. Not due to organic mental disorder.

Schizodepressive episode

1. The episode involves the symptomatic picture of both schizophrenic *and* melancholic episodes intermixed or alternating without free interval.
2. Not due to organic mental disorder.

Schizomanic episode

1. The episode involves the symptomatic picture of both schizophrenic *and* manic episode intermixed or alternating without free interval.
2. Not due to organic mental disorder.

Schizomanic–depressive mixed episode

1. The episode involves the symptomatic picture of both schizophrenic *and* manic–depressive mixed episodes intermixed or alternating without free interval.
2. Not due to organic mental disorder.

Uncharacteristic episodes

Episodes not fulfilling the criteria of the episodes mentioned above have been defined as uncharacteristic.

Schizoaffective disorder

During the whole course:

(a) presence of at least one schizoaffective episode, i.e. schizodepressive, schizomanic or schizomanic–depressive mixed episode, as defined in this paper

or

(b) if schizophrenic episodes and affective episodes change from one to another independently of their number, sequence or proportional representation

(c) if (a) or (b) positive, uncharacteristic episodes can occur within the course. Their presence does not have any influence on the diagnosis.

Schizophrenic disorder

During the whole course:

(a) presence of schizophrenic episodes
(b) absence of schizoaffective or affective episodes, as defined in this paper
(c) if (a) and (b) are positive during the whole course, the presence of uncharacteristic episodes does not have any influence on the diagnosis.

Affective disorder

During the whole course:

(a) presence of affective episodes
(b) absence of schizoaffective and schizophrenic episodes, as defined in this paper
(c) if (a) and (b) positive, the occurrence of uncharacteristic episodes does not have any influence on the diagnosis.

References

AMERICAN PSYCHIATRIC ASSOCIATION (1980) *Diagnostic and Statistical Manual of Mental Disorders* (3rd edn) (DSM-III). Washington, DC: APA.

AMERICAN PSYCHIATRIC ASSOCIATION (1987) *Diagnostic and Statistical Manual of Mental Disorders* (3rd edn – revised) (DSM-III-R). Washington, DC: APA.

ANGST, J. (1966) *Zur Ätiologie und Nosologie endogener depressiver Psychosen. Eine genetische, soziologische und klinische Studie.* Berlin, Heidelberg, New York: Springer.

BERNER, P., GABRIEL, E. & NASKE, R. (1973) Verlaufstypologie und Prognose bei sogenannten Spätschizophrenien. In *Verlauf und Ausgang schizophrener Erkrankungen* (ed. G. Huber). Stuttgart: Schattauer.

BIEHL, H., MAURER, K., JABLENSKY, A., *et al* (1989*a*) The WHO Psychological Impairments Rating Schedule (WHO/PIRS). I. Introducing a new instrument for rating observed behaviour and the rationale of the psychological concept. *British Journal of Psychiatry*, **155** (suppl. 7), 68–70.

――――, ――――, JUNG, E., *et al* (1989*b*) The WHO Psychological Impairments Rating Schedule (WHO/PIRS). II. Impairments in schizophrenics in cross-sectional and longitudinal perspective. *British Journal of Psychiatry*, **155** (suppl. 7), 71–77.

CIOMPI, L. & MÜLLER, C. (1976) *Lebensweg und Alter der Schizophrenen.* Berlin, Heidelberg, New York: Springer.

DREYFUS, G. L. (1907) *Die Melancholie. Ein Zustandsbild des manisch-depressiven Irreseins.* Jena: Fischer.

GABRIEL, E. (1978) *Die langfristige Entwicklung der Spätschizophrenien.* Basel: Karger.

HÄFNER, H. (1990) New perspectives in the epidemiology of schizophrenia. In *Search for the Causes of Schizophrenia, II* (eds H. Häfner & W. F. Gattaz). Berlin, Heidelberg, New York: Springer.

――――, MAURER, K., LÖFFLER, W., *et al* (1991) Schizophrenie und Lebensalter. *Nervenarzt*, **62**, 536–548.

HARRIS, M. J. & JESTE, D. V. (1988) Late-onset schizophrenia: an overview. *Schizophrenia Bulletin*, **14**, 39–55.

HOLDEN, N. L. (1987) Late paraphrenia or the paraphrenias? A descriptive study with a 10-year follow-up. *British Journal of Psychiatry*, **150**, 635–639.

HUBER, G., GROSS, G. & SCHÜTTLER, R. (1975) Spätschizophrenie. *Archiv Für Psychiatrie und Nervenkrankheiten*, **221**, 53.

――――, ―――― & ―――― (1979) *Schizophrenie.* Berlin, Heidelberg, New York: Springer.

JESTE, D. V. & ZISOOK, S. (1988) *Psychosis and Depression in the Elderly* (Psychiatric Clinics of North America, Vol. 11, Number 1). Philadelphia: Saunders.

――――, HARRIS, M. J., PEARLSON, G. D., *et al* (1988) Late-onset schizophrenia: studying clinical validity. In *Psychosis and Depression in the Elderly* (eds D. V. Jeste & S. Zisook). Philadelphia: Saunders.

KLAGES, W. (1961) *Die Spätschizophrenie.* Stuttgart: Enke.

KRAEPELIN, E. (1896) *Lehrbuch der Psychiatrie.* 5. Auflage. Leipzig: Barth.

MARNEROS, A. & DEISTER, A. (1984) The psychopathology of 'late schizophrenia'. *Psychopathology*, **17**, 264 –274.

―――― & PRENTKOWSKI, B. (1985) Suizidalität bei ersthospitalisierten schizophrenen Patienten. *Psychiatrie, Neurologie und Medizinische Psychologie*, **37**, 205–214.

――――, DEISTER, A. & ROHDE, A. (1986) The Cologne study on schizoaffective disorders and schizophrenia suspecta. In *Schizoaffective Psychoses* (eds A. Marneros & M. T. Tsuang). Berlin, Heidelberg, New York: Springer.

――――, ――――, ――――, *et al* (1988) Long-term course of schizoaffective disorders. Part I: Definitions, methods, frequency of episodes and cycles. *European Archives of Psychiatry and Neurological Sciences*, **237**, 264–275.

――――, ――――, ――――, *et al* (1989) Long-term outcome of schizoaffective and schizophrenic disorders: a comparative study. Part I: Definitions, methods, psychopathological and social outcome. *European Archives of Psychiatry and Neurological Sciences*, **238**, 118–125.

――――, ―――― & ―――― (1991) *Affektive, schizoaffektive und schizophrene Psychosen. Eine vergleichende Langzeitstudie.* Berlin, Heidelberg, New York: Springer.

——, —— & —— (1992) Phenomenological constellations of persisting alterations in functional disorders: a comparison. In *Nosology in Contemporary Psychiatry* (eds A. E. Haynal & F. Ferrero) (in press).

MILLER, B. L. & LESSER, I. M. (1988) Late-life psychosis and modern neuroimaging. In *Psychosis and Depression in the Elderly* (eds D. V. Jeste & S. Zisook). Philadelphia: Saunders.

MÜLLER, C. (1989) Altersveränderungen vorausgegangener psychischer Erkrankungen. In *Alterspsychiatrie* (Psychiatrie der Gegenwart, vol. 8, eds K. P. Kisker, H. Lauter, J. E. Meyer, *et al*). Berlin, Heidelberg, New York: Springer.

MURPHY, E. (1989) Depressionen im Alter. In *Alterspsychiatrie* (Psychiatrie der Gegenwart, vol. 8, eds K. P. Kisker, H. Lauter, J. E. Meyer *et al*). Berlin, Heidelberg, New York: Springer.

PEARLSON, G. & RABINS, P. (1988) The late-onset psychoses: possible risk factors. In *Psychosis and Depression in the Elderly* (eds D. V. Jeste & S. Zisook). Philadelphia: Saunders.

PITT, B. (1982) *Psychogeriatrics. An Introduction to the Psychiatry of Old Age.* Edinburgh: Livingstone.

—— (1990) Schizoaffective disorders in the elderly. In *Affective and Schizoaffective Disorders* (eds A. Marneros & M. T. Tsuang). Berlin, Heidelberg, New York: Springer.

POST, F. (1962) *The Significance of Affective Symptoms in Old Age.* Maudsley Monograph 10. London: Oxford University Press.

—— (1966) *Persistent Persecutory States of the Elderly.* Oxford: Pergamon Press.

—— (1971) Schizo-affective symptomatology in late life. *British Journal of Psychiatry*, **118**, 437–445.

ROHDE, A., MARNEROS, A. & DEISTER, A. (1989a) Suicidal behaviour in schizophrenic patients – a follow-up investigation. In *Current Research on Suicide and Parasuicide* (eds N. Kreitman & S. D. Platt). Edinburgh: Edinburgh University Press.

——, —— & —— (1989b) Schizoaffective disorders and suicidal behaviour: a long-term follow-up study. In *Current Research on Suicide and Parasuicide* (eds N. Kreitman & S. D. Platt). Edinburgh: Edinburgh University Press.

—— & —— (1990) Suizidale Symptomatik im Langzeitverlauf schizoaffektiver Psychosen. Symptomkonstellationen und soziale Faktoren. *Nervenarzt*, **61**, 164–169.

SIEGEL, E. & ROLLBERG, I. (1972) Über Spätschizophrenien. *Wiener Zeitschrift Für Nervenheilkunde*, **28**, 145–151.

SPITZER, R. L., GIBBON, M. & ENDICOTT, J. C. (1976) The Global Assessment Scale. *Archives of General Psychiatry*, **33**, 768.

STERNBERG, E. (1972) Neuere Forschungsergebnisse bei spätschizophrenen Psychosen. *Fortschritte Neurologie Psychiatrie*, **40**, 631–646.

WING, J. K., COOPER, J. E. & SARTORIUS, N. (1974) *Measurement and Classification of Psychiatric Symptoms.* London: Cambridge University Press.

WORLD HEALTH ORGANIZATION (1988) *WHO Psychiatric Disability Assessment Schedule* (WHO/DAS). Geneva: WHO.

YASSA, R., NAIR, N. P. V. & ISKANDAR, H. (1988) Late-onset bipolar disorder. In *Psychosis and Depression in the Elderly* (eds D. V. Jeste & S. Zisook). Philadelphia: Saunders.

11 Psychotic symptoms and the paraphrenic brain

H. FÖRSTL, R. HOWARD, O. P. ALMEIDA and G. STADTMÜLLER

"At sunt morosi et anxii et iracundi et difficiles senes. contemni se putant, despici, illudi; praeterea in fragili corpore odiosa omnis offensio est." (Cicero, Cato maior)

Elaborate, bizarre and persistent persecutory delusions with an onset in adulthood were reported in early psychiatric texts (Moritz, 1783–1793; Haslam, 1810; Anonymous, 1853). Emil Kraepelin (1913) distinguished what he called the 'paraphrenias' or 'paranoid dementias' ('paranoide Verblödungen') from 'dementia praecox' with an earlier onset and, as Kraepelin first thought, different course. The paraphrenics were described as a small group of patients, who shared some features of dementia praecox, but whose affect, will and personality was largely preserved. The paranoid delusion dominates the clinical picture. Kraepelin differentiated four forms of paraphrenia: *paraphrenia systemica* with an extremely insidious development of a steadily progressive persecutory delusion and consecutive ideas of grandiosity without a disintegration of personality; and the smaller groups of *paraphrenia expansiva* with overt delusions of grandiosity, primarily elated mood and mild excitation; *paraphrenia confabulatoria* typically with falsifications of memory; and *paraphrenia (dementia) phantastica* with abundant production of extraordinarily adventurous, incoherent, changeable delusional ideas. Kraepelin observed disorders of perception, primarily auditory hallucinations later in the course of paraphrenia systemica, expansiva and phantastica. In his paragraphs on perceptive disturbances in paraphrenia systemica (Appendix I, p. 163) Kraepelin presented a clear description of audible thoughts, voices commenting, voices arguing and discussing, thought insertion, thought withdrawal, passivity of volition and somatic passivity (delusions of alien penetration). These auditory hallucinations, thought disorders and passivity experience

---

"But one has to say: the elderly are grumpy and peevish and irascible and obstinate. They feel rejected, disdained and mocked; moreover, one is susceptible to the least offence if the body is frail."

153

F

were later listed among the first-rank symptoms (FRS) and considered diagnostic of schizophrenia (Schneider, 1959). Kraepelin mentioned (1913) that the initial diagnosis of paraphrenia could not be sustained in a large number of his patients. He admitted to the diagnostic difficulties and to his uncertaintly about the biological basis of these illnesses.

Wilhelm Mayer (1921) undertook a follow-up examination of Kraepelin's original patients (Appendix II, p. 164). His results were disappointing. Only a small proportion of the patients from Kraepelin's remaining sample had not yet exhibited sufficient evidence for another diagnosis, mostly dementia praecox. Mayer surmised that the later age of onset might be the only truly different factor of paraphrenia and schizophrenia, which could possibly account for all other symptomatic differences. This suggestion is in agreement with recent epidemiological research on schizophrenia (Häfner et al, 1991). The diagnostic categories became blurred. We will make no philological attempt to clarify primarily terminological issues, but concentrate on possibly associated brain changes.

Kleist (1913) examined the evidence for an organic illness as the basis for what he called 'involutional paranoia' (Appendix III, p. 165). He concluded that involutional paranoia could neither be due to primary degenerative or vascular dementia nor to alcoholism, neurosyphilis, etc., but that a more subtle and specific deficit, possibly a neuroendocrinological change, was not unlikely.

Bleuler (1943) reviewed the post-mortem findings of 17 patients with 'late-onset schizophrenia' (Appendix IV, p. 166). Pathological changes which could account for the clinical symptoms were only obtained in four cases and these patients had shown confusional states with catatonic features. Irrespective of their age, these patients would not have fitted into Roth's concept of late paraphrenia (1955) – patients over the age of 60, who present with a well organised system of delusions, with or without hallucinations, existing in the setting of a well preserved personality and affective response. This concept is advantageous, because it does not rely on nosological assumptions, which are difficult to prove in the early stages of illness; it was, however, not unequivocally accepted (Post, 1966). Quantitative neuropathological investigations based on this diagnosis could not demonstrate characteristic brain changes (Blessed et al, 1968).

At present, the biological heterogeneity of late paraphrenia can hardly be disputed (Almeida et al, 1991; Häfner et al, 1991). Holden's (1987) catamnestic study has shown that a variety of different clinical syndromes can be observed on re-examination of patients initially diagnosed as late paraphrenics. Thirteen of 39 cases progressed to dementia within only three years. Ten of the remaining 24 cases presented FRS.

Our study and literature review on late paraphrenia tries to investigate whether the presence or absence of FRS can contribute to a meaningful distinction which is further characterised by neuroradiological differences.

The frequency and significance of first-rank symptoms

First-rank symptoms are common in schizophrenia (Schneider, 1959) and they discriminate between schizophrenia and non-schizophrenic psychoses almost independently of the cultural background (Carpenter & Strauss, 1974; Chandrasena, 1987; Radhakrishnan *et al*, 1983). They can therefore be considered as hallmarks of schizophrenia, even if they are not pathognostic for this disease (Carpenter *et al*, 1973; Mellor, 1982). Grahame (1984) observed FRS in 14 out of 25 late paraphrenics and concluded that late paraphrenia should therefore be regarded as 'one of the schizophrenias'. Rabins *et al* (1984) found FRS in 22 of 35 patients who fulfilled their criteria for late-onset schizophrenia and in three of 35 depressed patients. In their study, severe cognitive impairment had been ruled out. No attempt was made to characterise the differences between paraphrenics with and without FRS.

Several authors have studied the occurrence of FRS in other 'functional' psychiatric illnesses and in organic mental syndromes. Cummings (1985) observed FRS in four of 20 patients with organic delusions; one suffered from hepatic encephalopathy, others from post-encephalitic Parkinson's disease, post-traumatic encephalopathy and idiopathic calcification of the basal ganglia. Table 11.1 lists four studies which compared the frequency of FRS in patients with schizophrenia and with organic mental syndromes. Cutting (1987) found FRS in 56 of 74 schizophrenics and in only two of 74 patients with organic psychosis. Johnstone *et al* (1988) reported the frequency of 'nuclear schizophrenic features', which correspond closely to Schneider's FRS, in a sample of 328 consecutively admitted psychotic patients. Their results showed the smallest difference of all studies regarding the prevalence of FRS in schizophrenia and organic mental syndromes. The large study of Marneros (1988) demonstrated that FRS can be found in a small percentage of patients with organic mental syndromes and that their occurrence is inversely related to the state of consciousness: 20% of the patients with clear consciousness had FRS, but only 1.5% of the patients with clouded consciousness. Cutting (1980) had reported similar rates of 29% versus 2% of 'nuclear schizophrenic syndrome' in psychiatric patients with physical illness depending on the absence or presence of cerebral

TABLE 11.1

The occurrence of first-rank symptoms (FRS) in schizophrenia and in organic mental syndromes (OMS)

Author (year)	Schizophrenia number of patients (% with FRS)		OMS number of patients (% with FRS)	
Cutting (1987)	74	(76)	74	(3)
Johnstone *et al* (1988)	43	(74)[1]	22	(50)[1]
Marneros (1988)	1208	(47)	1698	(7)
O'Grady (1990)	15	(73)	4	(25)

1. 'Nuclear symptoms' (see reference).

dysfunction. O'Grady (1990) observed FRS in five of 34 patients with affective disorders and in one of four patients with organic mental syndrome. He demonstrated that the specificity of FRS for schizophrenia increased if a narrower definition for FRS was used.

First-rank symptoms and neuroimaging: our study

First-rank symptoms have been observed more frequently in schizophrenia than in organic mental syndromes. Pathological computerised tomography (CT) findings, e.g. cerebral atrophy, infarcts, space occupying lesions, etc. are more common in patients with organic psychosis than in 'functional' psychosis. This suggests the hypothesis that the CT-scans reveal less abnormal findings in late paraphrenics with FRS than in elderly patients with schizophrenia-like illness lacking FRS (who are more likely to suffer from an organic mental syndrome). The following study was undertaken to investigate this hypothesis.

We examined the case notes and CT-scans of patients with a diagnosis of late paraphrenia who attended the Maudsley Hospital between 1978 and 1990. The criteria of inclusion and exclusion are outlined below (Förstl *et al*, 1991c; Howard *et al*, 1992).

(a) Presence of fantastic, persecutory or grandiose delusions. Delusions of reference with or without hallucinations.
(b) Absence of a primary affective disorder.
(c) Intellectual capacity in keeping with that of normal ageing. Documented evidence of a Mini-Mental State score of at least 25 out of 30.
(d) No clouding of consciousness.
(e) Onset of symptoms over the age of 60.
(f) No history or clinical evidence of medical or neurological illness. No history of alcohol abuse.
(g) Normal full blood count, electrolytes, liver and thyroid function tests, vitamin B12 and folate. Normal chest X-ray. Negative syphilis serology.

Most of the patients were examined with an EMI 1010 scanner, a smaller number with a high resolution CT-scanner (GE 9800). The changes of the following parameters were rated blindly and independently by two raters according to standards developed at the Institute of Psychiatry, London (Jacoby *et al*, 1980; Förstl *et al*, 1991c): cortical atrophy, ventricular enlargement, leuko-araiosis, basal ganglia calcification and cerebellar atrophy. The inter-rater reliability for each item was 0.83 or higher. Non-parametric tests were used for the comparisons of these semi-quantitative variables (Förstl *et al*, 1991c).

Computer-assisted planimetric measurements of ventricle and brain areas were carried out on the 14 scans performed with a high-resolution scanner (for details see Förstl *et al*, 1991*a*; Howard *et al*, 1992). The planimetric measurements were corrected for differences of skull size (Förstl *et al*, 1991*a*). Comparisons between the paraphrenic patients and normal elderly controls have been published elsewhere (Förstl *et al*, 1991*c*; Howard *et al*, 1992). In the present study, the quantitative neuroradiological findings were compared with the findings in sex-matched and age-approximated groups of elderly depressives and patients with probable Alzheimer's disease satisfying NINCDS-ADRDA criteria (McKhann *et al*, 1984), who were drawn from corollary studies (Beats *et al*, 1991; Förstl *et al*, 1991*a*). The quantitative measurements between the different patient groups were compared with one-way analyses of variance using Duncan's multiple range test ($P < 0.05$; Norusis, 1988).

Visual comparisons

Nineteen late paraphrenics (3 men; 16 women; mean age 73.8 (s.d. 7.7) years) had one or more FRS, 29 patients (3 men; 26 women) did not have FRS. Their mean age was higher (77.4 (s.d. 5.2) years). The duration of illness at the time the patients underwent the CT-scans was between three months and 20 years (mean four years).

The CT-findings are summarised in Table 11.2. Mild or moderate cortical atrophy was significantly more common in the patients without FRS. No single paraphrenic patient showed severe cortical atrophy. Mild ventricular enlargement was present in 76% and 69% of the late paraphrenics and slightly more common than in individually age- and sex-matched elderly controls (data not shown). White matter changes, cerebellar atrophy and basal ganglia calcification were not different between the groups nor between the paraphrenics and the controls.

TABLE 11.2
CT findings in paraphrenics with and without first rank symptoms (FRS)

	FRS (n = 19) No. (%)		No FRS (n = 29) No.(%)	
Cortical atrophy	8	(42)	22*	(76)
Ventricular enlargement	14	(76)	20	(69)
Leuko-araiosis	4	(21)	5	(17)
Basal ganglia calcification	3	(16)	2	(7)
Cerebellar atrophy	2	(10)	4	(14)

*$P < 0.01$ (Mann–Whitney U-test)

Computer-assisted planimetric measurements

Seven (4 men; 3 women; mean 72.7 (s.d. 8.1) years) of the 14 patients in whom high-resolution CT-scans were available had FRS. The mean age of the seven patients (1 man; 6 women) without FRS was higher (78.7 (s.d. 7.3) years). The results of planimetric measurements in late paraphrenics with and without FRS are shown in Table 11.3 and compared with measurements in groups of elderly depressives and of patients with clinically diagnosed Alzheimer's disease.

The left and right anterior horns in paraphrenics with FRS, but not in paraphrenics without FRS, were significantly smaller than in Alzheimer's disease. Both frontal lobes of paraphrenics with FRS and of depressives were significantly larger than in primary degenerative dementia. Similar results were obtained for measurements of the temporo-parieto-occipital areas, but the differences did not reach statistical significance. Paraphrenics without FRS held an intermediate position between depressives and paraphrenics with FRS on one side and Alzheimer's disease on the other side. Their ventricles were slightly enlarged and the frontal brain areas were slightly reduced.

Conclusions from the study

In the past, most neuroimaging studies have not differentiated between late paraphrenia – or late-onset schizophrenia – with and without FRS. A comparison of our total group of late paraphrenics (with and without FRS) with elderly depressives and senile dementia yielded only one significant difference: the area of the left frontal lobe was larger in late paraphrenia than in senile dementia. None of the other differences could be detected when the paraphrenics with and without FRS were collapsed into one group.

TABLE 11.3

Computer-assisted measurements of ventricular and brain areas in paraphrenics with and without first rank symptoms (FRS), in elderly depressives and in patients with clinically diagnosed Alzheimer's disease (AD). The groups were matched for gender and approximated for age.

| | | Paraphrenia | | | One-way ANOVAs | |
| | *Depression* | *FRS* | *no FRS* | *AD* | | |
Area in cm^2: mean (s.d.)	*(n = 14)*	*(n = 7)*	*(n = 7)*	*(n = 14)*	*F (d.f. = 3)*	*P*
3rd ventricle	1.3 (0.6)	1.1 (0.6)	1.5 (0.4)	1.8 (0.6)	2.4	NS
left anterior horn	2.9 (0.8)	2.5 (1.4)[1]	3.4 (1.3)	3.8 (1.2)	2.1	NS
right anterior horn	2.6 (0.6)	2.2 (1.2)[1]	3.3 (1.2)	3.4 (1.1)	2.8	NS
left anterior lobe	33.0 (4.1)[1]	33.4 (3.8)[1]	29.3 (3.2)	27.5 (5.6)[2]	4.5	0.008
right anterior lobe	33.7 (3.0)[1]	34.4 (4.3)[1]	30.2 (4.1)	29.3 (5.6)	3.5	0.02

1. Contrast with AD (Duncan's test for repeated measures (*P* < 0.05)).
2. The only significant difference between AD and the combined group of paraphrenics with and without FRS (Duncan's test for repeated measures (*P* < 0.05)).

TABLE 11.4
Computerised tomography (CT) and magnetic resonance imaging (MRI) in late paraphrenia and late-onset schizophrenia

Author (year)	CT or MRI	n	Age of onset	Findings
Miller *et al* (1986)	CT	5	>67	'occult organic disorder' (leuko-araiosis, infarction, normal pressure hydrocephalus)
Naguib & Levy (1987)	CT	43	>59	lateral ventricle enlargement
Rabins *et al* (1987)	CT	29	>44	increased ventricle–brain ratio
Harris *et al* (1988)	MRI	5	>45	mild atrophy and leuko-araiosis
Kohlmeyer (1988)	CT	98	?	leuko-araiosis (in a few cases with atrophy, infarction and BGC; see text)
Burns *et al* (1989)	CT	42	>59	mild ventricular enlargement (no cortical atrophy)
Breitner *et al* (1990)	MRI	8	>74	leuko-araiosis and infarction
Flint *et al* (1991)	CT	16	>59	subcortical or frontal (and parieto-occipital) infarction
Miller *et al* (1991)	MRI	24	>45	leuko-araiosis, infarction, tumour

Neuroimaging in late paraphrenia and late-onset schizophrenia

Table 11.4 summarises neuroimaging studies carried out on patients with late paraphrenia or late-onset schizophrenia.

CT studies

Our results (Förstl *et al*, 1991c; Howard *et al*, 1992) demonstrated that paraphrenics with FRS show features similar to elderly controls or elderly depressives, whereas paraphrenics without FRS showed no significant differences to patients with Alzheimer's disease, even though the signs of cerebral atrophy were less pronounced. Patients with clinical or neuroradiological evidence of further underlying brain disease had been excluded from our investigation.

Miller *et al* (1986) examined five cases with 'late-life paraphrenia', four of whom had unexpected CT-findings (subcortical hypodensities, infarcts and normal pressure hydrocephalus) which may have contributed to the manifestation of illness. Rabins *et al* (1987) observed an increase of the ventricle–brain ratio in a sample of late-onset schizophrenics. Naguib & Levy (1987) found mild ventricular enlargement in late paraphrenics and suggested that this may represent a non-specific risk factor for the development of late paraphrenia. Burns *et al* (1989) confirmed this result and noted that the degree of ventricular enlargement was uncoupled from the degree of cortical atrophy; cortical atrophy did not appear to be more severe than in the control sample. Kohlmeyer (1988), who did not differentiate between patients with depression and paraphrenia (because their CT-findings were so similar) reported isolated leuko-araiosis in 72.2%, leuko-araiosis accompanied by brain atrophy in 5.1% or by infarcts in 18.4% and by basal ganglia calcification in 4.1%. Flint *et al* (1991) made a promising attempt to revive Kraepelin's (1912) concepts of paraphrenia (delusions and hallucinations) and of paranoia (well organised delusions without hallucinations). Only one of 12 paraphrenic patients had a cerebral infarct, whereas all four patients with paranoia had clinically unsuspected brain infarcts. The authors concluded that brain lesions may act as risk factors for late-onset paranoia and that this may imply a prognosis worse than in paraphrenia.

MRI studies

Three of five patients from Harris *et al*'s (1988) sample with late-onset schizophrenia showed periventricular and subcortical signal hyperintensity, one other patient showed mild cortical atrophy and ventricular widening. Leuko-araiosis or vascular pathology, most pronounced in the temporo-parietal and occipital areas, was found in eight of eight patients with late-onset paranoid psychosis (Breitner *et al*, 1990). Miller *et al* (1991) observed brain abnormalities in 10 (42%) of 24 patients with late life psychosis and in only 8% of their 72 controls. Vascular lesions were found in 25% of the psychotic patients; in two patients, functional neuroimaging studies indicated early stages of Alzheimer's or Pick's disease, one had a large tumour in the cerebellopontine angle. The ventricles were only insignificantly wider than in the controls. The temporal, frontal and occipital white matter lesions were four to six times larger than in the controls.

The mind and brain-imaging problem in late paraphrenia

To abbreviate a long-winded discussion: we believe that our findings are meaningful. But the retrospective evaluation, the clinical data, and the relatively small number of patients are insufficient to establish a simple and firm distinction between late-onset schizophrenia (FRS, no cortical atrophy) and a second category of 'organic late paraphrenia' (no FRS, more cortical atrophy). Replication in a prospective longitudinal study with refined neuropsychological and neuroimaging standards will be necessary (and is currently under way). In the meantime, a critical consideration of the relevance of neuroimaging findings reported by other authors and ourselves may be worthwhile.

The clinical significance of abnormal and pathological neuroimaging findings

Only one of the studies listed in Table 11.4 (Flint *et al*, 1991) made an attempt to correlate clinical symptoms and CT-findings in two different subgroups of late paraphrenics. These results and their interpretation correspond to some extent with our data. Both studies reported a higher rate of abnormal CT-findings in the patients without hallucinations or FRS. The other authors merely reported the type and extent of abnormal and pathological features revealed by CT and MRI: atrophy, infarction, basal-ganglia calcification, unexpected normal pressure hydrocephalus or tumours, and leuko-araiosis. White matter changes are frequently observed with sensitive modern imaging methods such as high resolution CT and particularly MRI. Their diagnostic value for the individual patient is most doubtful (Hunt *et al*, 1989), their aetiology and nature is still under discussion (Janota *et al*, 1989; Leys *et al*, 1991; van Swieten *et al*, 1991), but their importance for subtle neuro-physiological (Kato *et al*, 1990), neuropsychological (Kertesz *et al*, 1990) or psychopathological (Merriam *et al*, 1989) changes can not be disregarded. The possible influence of basal-ganglia mineralisation on psychiatric and neurological disease has recently been examined and was reported as mild and of questionable clinical importance (Förstl *et al*, 1991*d*, 1992). When cortical atrophy was observed it was generally mild and non-focal. Only one patient from all the studies showed ventricular enlargement compatible with a diagnosis of normal pressure hydrocephalus. Other coarse brain changes (infarction, tumour) did not necessarily bear an apparent relationship to the psychopathological presentation. None of the authors was keen to assign *diagnostic* importance to the observed brain changes. The results did not point to the presence of any common, subtle and specific brain lesion one would hope to find if the organic change in itself determined distinctive clinical symptoms. This raises the question whether the observed changes are 'incidental' or chance findings whose observed prevalence is related to the selection criteria and not to an association with late paraphrenia.

Schizophrenia as a functional psychosis is not typically associated with organic illness. The rate of some, for example cerebrovascular diseases, may even be lower than in the general population (Harris, 1988). In a recent series, 15 of 268 patients with a diagnosis of first episode schizophrenia, who had already been screened by physicians to exclude physical illness, eventually had organic diseases of a potential aetiological significance (Johnstone *et al*, 1987): syphilis, sarcoidosis, alcohol and drug abuse, cerebral cysticercosis, previous head injury, etc. In three of these cases, the CT scans were reported to be abnormal. The age range of these patients was 17 to 59 years.

A slightly higher percentage of pathological CT-findings was reported in 8.8% of 136 patients with chronic schizophrenia, aged between 41 and 71 years (Cunningham Owens *et al*, 1980): seven had cerebral infarctions, two subdural haematomas, one a porencephalic cyst, one a meningioma and one a cystic enlargement of the pineal gland. Related clinical symptoms were found in only two of these patients. Hoffmann *et al* (1991) found evidence of past cerebrovascular accidents in 10 of 29 schizophrenic patients over the age of 55, basal ganglia calcification in two and extreme ventriculomegaly in one. Only three of these patients showed corresponding clinical symptoms. Incidental infarctions, neoplasms and chronic subdural haematomas have also been reported in senile dementia and – with lower frequency – in elderly depressives and controls (Jacoby *et al*, 1980; Jacoby & Levy, 1980). The prevalence of the reported abnormalities appears to be age-related and not disease-related.

The value of such incidental neuroradiological findings has been further challenged by Feinstein & Ron (1990), who could not discover a relationship between the site of coarse-brain pathology and the type of psychotic disorder in 12 patients with affective psychosis and in 53 patients with a syndrome indistinguishable from schizophrenia. Such criticism, however, does not affect the present study and the results of Flint *et al* (1991) which both demonstrated an association of clinical and neuroradiological differences between subgroups within the heterogeneous group of late paraphrenia, thereby fulfilling Wing's (1978) first criterion of a possible disease entity.

Delusions, hallucinations and the paraphrenic brain

At present, the potential relationship between morphological brain changes and clinical symptoms has to be viewed with caution and can at best serve as a source of speculation. Modern concepts about potential mechanisms underlying delusions and hallucinations have gained considerable complexity (Slade & Bentall, 1988 (for review); Doty, 1989; Gray *et al*, 1991) and have lost the simplistic strength of earlier models. Meynert felt that persecutory delusions were the consequence of subcortical irritation, whereas Wernicke believed that they were due to cortical excitation. Iwanow-Smolenski (1926) combined these ideas in his Pavlovian model of paranoia: hyperirritability of subcortical centres, normally responsible for the unconditioned defence reflex, lead to continuous cortical stimulation and this leads to a constant conditioned 'defence complex' including a pathological language reflex, i.e. delusions. The generalisation of these stimuli takes place in the sensory areas. In Kleist's involutional paranoia (Appendix III, p. 165) this disinhibition of self-defence, the strongest instinct of man, is facilitated by cortical wearing and tearing. Later in the course of illness and with further cortical decay, these symptoms are mitigated (Iwanow-Smolenski, 1926).

The simplistic argument of this outdated model relates to some of the observed brain changes. Subcortical changes, e.g. ventricular enlargement – which did not reach statistical significance in our samples – subcortical infarction, and leuko-araiosis were described in several studies (Table 11.4), pronounced cortical atrophy was only observed in our sample of paraphrenics without FRS (Table 11.2).

Cummings (1985), not unlike Iwanow-Smolenski (1926), suggested that subcortical dysfunction could predispose to abnormal experiences that can be elaborated by an intact hemispheric cortex and that this could lead to complex delusions. This is in agreement with reports gathered by Davison (1983) which showed that schizophrenia-like illness can be caused by a variety of basal ganglia diseases. An increased rate of paranoid illness in basal ganglia mineralisation has recently been demonstrated (Förstl *et al*, 1991*d*). This effect was unrelated to other cerebral pathology or to age. Psychopathological similarities between basal ganglia or other brainstem lesions and schizophrenia were attributed to a comparable disruption of ascending aminergic pathways (Trimble & Cummings, 1981; Doty, 1989).

As pointed out by Cummings (1985) and Iwanow-Smolenski (1926), the development of delusions and hallucinations may depend on an intact cerebral cortex. Nasrallah (1986) offered the explanation for FRS that they were intrusions of 'unintegrated right hemisphere consciousness' into the verbally expressive, largely intact, left hemisphere. Jacoby & Levy (1980) reported an inverse relationship between cortical atrophy and paranoid delusions in senile dementia. Burns *et al* (1990) found fewer complex delusions in Alzheimer patients with more severe cerebral atrophy. The localisation of hemispheric atrophy may influence the nature of the delusions in Alzheimer's disease (Förstl *et al*, 1991*b*). The bearing of these findings in Alzheimer's dementia upon the 'paranoid dementias' (Kraepelin, 1913) will have to be examined further.

Appendices

I. E. Kraepelin: The paranoid dementias ('paraphrenias')

"Generally, after several years of this highly tormenting state of suspicion, uncertainty and tension, real *misperceptions* namely of vision occur. The patient hears whistling, discordant eerie sounds, derogatory remarks, abuse and threats. These are whispered, telegraphed or spoken through the telephone. One patient discovered that the misperceptions stopped when he plugged his ears, another that they were only present at his home, but never when he went out for a walk; both drew the false conclusion that this made the experience real. Jews yell after the patient in the street; people talk about him, call him a fool, carrion, a dirty pig, a hag, a 'snow-goose', courtesan, pig-priest, spinach, scamp, criminal; he is accused of masturbation, of murder, of being impotent, that he has committed dirty sexual acts, has driven his parents into the grave, or has killed his son. One patient heard her husband and son wailing 'as if they were being crucified in purgatory'; another one felt that she was mocked everywhere because of her alleged sexual insatiability; the gossip spreads very quickly. Everybody scolds, and instigates and knows exactly the patient's situation. Sometimes there are no sensory misperceptions, but 'spiritual calls' ('geistige Zurufe'), 'inspirations', 'spiritual games' ('Gedankenspiel'), or a 'spiritual dialogue'

('Gedankenzwiegespräch'). The patients are prepared by hypnosis, are mentally cross-examined and give a spoken or internal answer. Sometimes they also feel that their thoughts become audible ('Gedankenlautwerden') so that others can hear them. A patient believes that his neighbours have become very annoyed by his audible thoughts; another one hears his thoughts echoed by the locomotives' whistle. Voices interfere with the patient's thoughts, they criticise and accompany his doings with comments. The misperceptions in other sensory modalities are far less important. The patient is 'fooled by visions', sees skeletons, the devil, dead, the mother of god, a bleeding host, naked females; one patient felt that peoples' faces were changed, she believed they could wear masks or other heads. Food tastes disgusting, it stinks; the flat is filled with strange smells; the clothes smell like a pharmacy. A patient complains about unnatural, embarrassing sensations, he feels secret stabs of a dagger, believes that satan spits on him; another one feels that things are thrown on him, knocked over, kicked; a woman feels that she was photographed with X-rays. Female patients have sensations, tickling in their genitals, they feel spiritually inseminated. The idea of hypnotic, magnetic or electrical influences, which is not uncommon, can frequently be combined with unpleasant physical sensations, tearing, twitching, pulling or being drenched.

Some patients mention influences on their volition ('Willensbeein-flussungen'). Suggestions are made via magnetism. People want to take their thoughts; the dead dictate what they have to do. A patient felt that an Earl had power over her; she was paralysed, had to follow him, could not eat her meals, became hungry at the wrong time, was forced to buy clothes against her will; she could not love her lady any more, had to be impolite to her. One patient explained that he was forced to do things, but that he would only allow when the circumstances seemed unimportant.'' (Kraepelin, 1913, pp. 976–978)

II. W. Mayer: on paraphrenic psychoses

''Kraepelin's separation of the group of paraphrenias from dementia praecox was based on a large number of observations in his department. I have collected and followed-up all these patients. I have, with very few exceptions, eliminated all those patients in whom the diagnosis of paraphrenia was made at their first admission and who dropped out from the follow-up examinations. Seventy-eight cases remained.

This raises the question whether these cases are something special. Are we allowed to consider them as a subgroup of dementia praecox in their own right (they doubtlessly belong there)? Is their course characteristic and can it clearly be distinguished from other psychoses, e.g. schizophrenia?

Let me review briefly all the cases to answer this question. I have followed-up the course of 78 cases as good as possible who had been diagnosed as paraphrenia. . . . The number of cases who followed the course of paraphrenia in Kraepelin's sense was 28. Fifty of the cases had to be disregarded on the basis of their further course. Thirty of these 50 certainly belonged to the group of dementia praecox. Therefore the number of paraphrenic illnesses, which had not been very large from the beginning, became even smaller (I would also like to mention that the diagnosis of paraphrenia has, to my experience, scarcely been made during the last six years). A whole series of paraphrenics have later developed a schizophrenic defect after the course has been typically paraphrenic for years. These are all the cases which I have eliminated and included with schizophrenia. One could argue that a number of the remaining 28 cases could show a similar course after longer observation. This may be true for a few of them, but most have remained stable for many years.

Considering that Kraepelin on viewing a large number of cases with chronic delusions found that 40% developed signs of dementia praecox during a few years, that 50% of the rest represent forms of paraphrenia and that more than half of these cases also have to be rediagnosed as dementia praecox after a short time, we have to ask ourselves whether . . . it is legitimate to insist on a cut-off between these illnesses.

In the majority of cases the onset of paraphrenia is in the fourth decade (other cases represent an exception). This late onset may perhaps contribute to the course of this psychosis and explain the predomination of complex delusions and the relative unimportance of disturbances of will. It has been pointed out for a long time and recently also by Kraepelin (in: Erscheinungsformen des Irreseins) that the disturbances of will recede in those years, because the fundamentals of will have already become rigid, whereas frequent and elaborate delusions predominate and suppress the intellect. Therefore one might think that the course of paraphrenia is different from the course of dementia praecox simply because the age of onset is much later." (Mayer, 1921, pp. 191, 203–205)

III.   K. Kleist: is involutional paranoia due to an organic-destructive brain process?

"In all women the illness begins in the years of sexual involution in close temporal relationship to the climacterium. Therefore one would primarily think that the illness may be caused by the physical changes following the end of functioning of the sexual organs. But as this disease reaches its height only several years after the cessatio mensium, it is quite possible that other changes occurring in late life contribute to this illness or that they even represent its genuine cause. In one patient a fast deterioration followed a brainstem infarct, another one ended up in a dementia of probably arteriosclerotic origin, while two others showed an at least minor memory impairment in the later years of their lives. And yet, the illness cannot be understood as an expression of arteriosclerotic or senile brain disease. Firstly, in the three cases just mentioned the signs of dementia occurred after the illness had been present for 20, 12 and nine years. Secondly, signs of dementia have not yet been observed in the other six cases, although the illness had lasted for 37, 18 and 16 years in three of the cases. In my opinion an illness cannot be considered as an expression of senile or arteriosclerotic brain changes if symptoms which are typical of arteriosclerotic or senile changes do not occur fairly soon (disturbances of memory, of orientation, of learning, general loss of knowledge, focal symptoms). Even if one assumes that our patients suffer from early forms of senile dementia – analogous to the peculiar disease of later age that Alzheimer first described – one would have to expect that a dementia would occur similar to Alzheimer's cases, but this is not a feature of our disease. Admittedly there are known cases of senile or arteriosclerotic brain disease, which begin with paranoid states and these paranoid states show several essential parallels to our patients. . . . But the development of delusions in the incipient paranoid senile and arteriosclerotic dementias is less developed than in the majority of our cases; the individual delusional ideas change more frequently and, most of all, the signs of the underlying disease process – memory impairment, disturbance of orientation, focal symptoms, etc. – soon predominate. Even if the signs of the underlying process may in rare cases occur later in the course of illness, it will never be possible that – as in some of my patients – decades go by without the development of a defect. Moreover, I believe that until now late paranoid illness has frequently and without justification been diagnosed as senile or arteriosclerotic dementia.

After all that we know, we finally have to ask whether there is or even whether there can be an organic brain process underlying involutional paranoia. There are undoubtedly peculiar brain diseases of old age other than senile or arteriosclerotic dementia, e.g. rare disorders described by Spielmeyer, Huntington's chorea or shaking palsy. The last two disorders in particular frequently generate paranoid states. Therefore we cannot rule out that an as yet unknown, peculiar organic brain change may underlie involutional paranoia. But it would have to be a genuinely different kind of organic brain change, because all known organic brain changes are of a progressive or destructive nature. They cause intellectual deficits (dementia or confusion), whereas we find a stationary change without defects in our cases. There is the question whether physical changes, perhaps the drying up of the functions of the sexual organs (neuroendocrinological changes?) could represent an organic cause for the change of brain functions.'' (Kleist, 1913, pp. 36–40)

IV.   M. Bleuler: post-mortem findings in late-schizophrenia

''I have considered the question to which extent post-mortem findings can shake or support our diagnosis of late schizophrenia, and if we have mistaken cases as late schizophrenia which at post-mortem turn out to be organic. With regard to this question, we have screened all female deaths in the Friedmatt, Basel, since the year 1929, when Prof. J. E. Staehelin became director. Among 267 deaths, we found only 17 with a psychiatric diagnosis of schizophrenia and with an onset of illness after age 40.

In 10 of these cases pathological findings were observed, but in view of the course of disease they had to be considered as mere complications which began later than the late-schizophrenic psychosis. In seven cases we found senile or arteriosclerotic brain changes in patients who died in old age, who had become psychotic several years, mostly even decades earlier; in one case a cerebral embolus was found in a patient, who had become depressive–paranoid 13 years before; two cases died of acute meningitis after several years of late schizophrenia.

Three late schizophrenics whose psychosis had lasted six to 12 years died of intercurrent pneumonia. The post-mortems yielded normal brains.

In four cases, however, the postmortem (and earlier observations) proved that the diagnosis late schizophrenia, which had been made earlier-on, was wrong or doubtful: in four cases with acute confused (*verworren*) catatonic excitation, the post-mortem revealed underlying disorders, which preceded the mental illness. It appeared certain (two cases) or possible (two cases) that these were conditions of amentia (*amentielle Zustände*) due to severe physical illness and not late schizophrenias. It was severe glomerulonephritis with cardiac insufficiency in one case; in one case severe endo- and myocarditis; and in one case the catatonic excitation occurred together with a compression of the struma and it remained unclear whether excitation or the compression of the struma was the primary cause of death; in the fourth patient catatonic excitation occurred after the onset of pulmonary carcinoma, but this patient had always been a schizoid psychopath and had gone through an episode diagnosed as schizophrenia.

If we look at these post-mortem findings, we must not forget that late schizophrenics who died in an asylum are in no way representative of the total sample of late schizophrenia: forms leading to dementia and severe excitatory states are over-represented, whereas the mild, chronic paranoid forms with preserved personality are almost completely missed. The latter cases are only rarely taken care of in the asylum until their death, but they evade the post-mortem in homes for the elderly, nursing homes or in their families. The schizophrenics who underwent post-mortems are undoubtedly the ones who are the most likely to be misdiagnosed as organic psychotics. A cautious interpretation of the post-mortem findings would permit the following conclusions: we can not provide evidence that mentally insane whose psychosis was of an organic nature, would have been diagnosed as late-schizophrenics. *But there is a greater danger that states of acute catatonic excitiation which is in reality a condition of amentia ('amentieller Natur'), are first diagnosed as schizophrenic.''* (Bleuler, 1943, pp. 284–285)

Acknowledgements

The help of B. Beats, A. Burns, M. Derrick and R. Levy is gratefully acknowledged. This work was supported by a grant from the Deutsche Forschungsgemeinschaft (DFG) and by a Parke-Davis Research Fellowship. Dr Osvaldo P. Almeida is sponsored by the CNPq (Brazil).

References

ALMEIDA, O. P., HOWARD, R., FÖRSTL, H., *et al* (1992) Should the diagnosis of late paraphrenia be abandoned? *Psychological Medicine*, **22**, 11–14.

ANONYMOUS (1853) *Nothschrei eines Magnetisch-Vergifteten* (Outcry of a victim of magnetic-poisoning). Stuttgart.

BEATS, B., LEVY, R. & FÖRSTL, H. (1991) Ventricular enlargement and caudate hyperdensity in elderly depressives. *Biological Psychiatry*, **30**, 452–458.

BLESSED, G., TOMLINSON, B. E. & ROTH, M. C. (1968) The association between quantitative measures of dementia and of senile change in the cerebral grey matter of elderly subjects. *British Journal of Psychiatry*, **114**, 797–811.

BLEULER, M. (1943) Die spätschizophrenen Krankheitsbilder. *Fortschritte der Neurologie und Psychiatrie*, **15**, 259–290.

BREITNER, J. C. S., HUSAIN, M. M., FIGIEL, G. S., *et al* (1990) Cerebral white matter disease in late-onset paranoid psychosis. *Biological Psychiatry*, **28**, 266–274.

BURNS, A., CARRICK, J., AMES, D., *et al* (1989) The cerebral cortical appearance in late paraphrenia. *International Journal of Geriatric Psychiatry*, **4**, 31–34.

——, JACOBY, R. & LEVY, R. (1990) Psychiatric phenomena in Alzheimer's disease. I. Disorders of thought content. *British Journal of Psychiatry*, **157**, 72–76.

CARPENTER, W. T., STRAUSS, J. S. & MULEH, S. (1973) Are there pathognomic symptoms in schizophrenia? *Archives of General Psychiatry*, **28**, 847–852.

—— & —— (1974) Cross-cultural evaluation of Schneider's first-rank symptoms of schizophrenia: a report from the international pilot study of schizophrenia. *American Journal of Psychiatry*, **131**, 682–687.

CHANDRASENA, R. (1987) Schneider's first rank symptoms: an international and interethnic comparative study. *Acta Psychiatrica Scandinavica*, **76**, 574–578.

CUMMINGS, J. L. (1985) Organic delusions: phenomenology, anatomical correlations, and review. *British Journal of Psychiatry*, **146**, 184–197.

CUNNINGHAM OWENS, D. G., JOHNSTONE, E. C., BYDDER, G. M., *et al* (1980) Unsuspected organic disease in chronic schizophrenia demonstrated by computed tomography. *Journal of Neurology, Neurosurgery and Psychiatry*, **43**, 1065–1069.

CUTTING, J. (1980) Physical illness and psychosis. *British Journal of Psychiatry*, **136**, 109–119.

—— (1987) The phenomenology of acute organic psychosis. Comparison with acute schizophrenia. *British Journal of Psychiatry*, **151**, 324–332.

DAVISON, K. (1983) Schizophrenia-like psychoses associated with organic cerebral disorders: a review. *Psychiatric Developments*, **1**, 1–34.

DOTY, R. W. (1989) Schizophrenia: a disease of interhemispheric processes at forebrain or brainstem levels? *Behavioural Brain Research*, **34**, 1–33.

FEINSTEIN, A. & RON, M. A. (1990) Psychosis associated with demonstrable brain disease. *Psychological Medicine*, **20**, 793–803.

FLINT, A. J., RIFAT, S. L. & EASTWOOD, M. R. (1991) Late-onset paranoia: distinct from paraphrenia? *International Journal of Geriatric Psychiatry*, **6**, 103–109.

FÖRSTL, H., BURNS, A., JACOBY, R., *et al* (1991a) Quantitative CT-scan analysis in senile dementia of the Alzheimer type: I. Computerized planimetry of cerebrospinal fluid areas. *International Journal of Geriatric Psychiatry*, **6**, 709–713.

——, ——, ——, *et al* (1991b) Neuroanatomical correlates of misidentification and misperception in senile dementia of the Alzheimer type. *Journal of Clinical Psychiatry*, **52**, 268–271.

——, HOWARD, R., ALMEIDA, O. P., *et al* (1991*c*) Cranial computed tomography findings in late paraphrenia with and without first rank symptoms. *Nervenarzt*, **62**, 274–276.

——, KRUMM, B., EDEN, S., *et al* (1991) What is the psychiatric significance of bilateral basal ganglia mineralization? *Biological Psychiatry*, **29**, 827–833.

——, ——, ——, *et al* (1992) Neurological disorders in 166 patients with basal ganglia calcification: a statistical evaluation. *Journal of Neurology*, **239**, 36–38.

GRAHAME, P. S. (1984) Schizophrenia in old age (late paraphrenia). *British Journal of Psychiatry*, **145**, 493–495.

GRAY, J. A., FELDON, J., RAWLINS, J. N. P., *et al* (1991) The neuropsychology of schizophrenia. *Behavioral and Brain Sciences*, **14**, 1–84.

HÄFNER, H., MAURER, K., LÖFFLER, W., *et al* (1991) Schizophrenie und Lebensalter (Schizophrenia and the life cycle). *Nervenarzt*, **62**, 536–548.

HARRIS A. E. (1988) Physical disease and schizophrenia. *Schizophrenia Bulletin*, **14**, 85–96.

HARRIS, M. J., CULLUM, C. M. & JESTE, D. V. (1988) Clinical presentation of late-onset schizophrenia. *Journal of Clinical Psychiatry*, **49**, 356–360.

HASLAM, J. (1810) *Illustrations of Madness*. London: G. Hayden.

HOLDEN, N. L. (1987) Late paraphrenia or the paraphrenias? A descriptive study with a 10-year follow-up. *British Journal of Psychiatry*, **150**, 635–639.

HOFFMAN, W. F., BURRY, M. T., KEEPERS, G. A., *et al* (1991) Unexpected intracerebral pathology in older schizophrenic patients. *American Journal of Psychiatry*, **148**, 3.

HOWARD, R., FÖRSTL, H., ALMEIDA, O. P., *et al* (1992) Computer-assisted measurements in late paraphrenia with and without Schneiderian first rank symptoms: a preliminary report. *International Journal of Geriatric Psychiatry*, **7**, 35–38.

HUNT, A. L., ORRISON, W. W., YEO, R. A., *et al* (1989) Clinical significance of MRI white matter lesions in the elderly. *Neurology*, **39**, 1470–1474.

IWANOW-SMOLENSKI, A. G. (1926) Über die Biogenese der Paranoia vom Standpunkte der modernen Grosshirn-Physiologie (On the biogenesis of paranoia: the view of modern cerebral physiology). *Allgemeine Zeitschrift für Psychiatrie*, **85**, 240–256.

JACOBY, R. J. & LEVY, R. (1980) Computed tomography in the elderly. 2. Senile dementia: diagnosis and functional impairment. *British Journal of Psychiatry*, **136**, 256–269.

——, —— & DAWSON, J. M. (1980) Computed tomography in the elderly. 1. The normal population. *British Journal of Psychiatry*, **136**, 270–275.

JANOTA, I., MIRSEN, T. R., HACHINSKI, V. C., *et al* (1989) Neuropathologic correlates of leuko-araiosis. *Archives of Neurology*, **46**, 1124–1128.

JOHNSTONE, E. C., COOLING, N. J., FRITH, C. D., *et al* (1988) Phenomenology of organic and functional psychoses and the overlap between them. *British Journal of Psychiatry*, **153**, 770–776.

——, MACMILLAN, J. F. & CROW, T. J. (1987) The occurrence of organic disease of possible or probable aetiological significance in a population of 268 cases of first episode schizophrenia. *Psychological Medicine*, **17**, 371–379.

KATO, H., SUGAWARA, Y., ITO, H., *et al* (1990) White matter lucencies in multi-infarct dementia: a somatosensory evoked potentials and CT-study. *Acta Neurologica Scandinavica*, **81**, 181–183.

KLEIST K. (1913) Die Involutionsparanoia. *Allgemeine Zeitschrift für Psychiatrie*, **70**, 1–64.

KERTESZ, A., POLK, M. & CARR, T. (1990) Cognition and white matter changes on magnetic resonance imaging in dementia. *Archives of Neurology*, **47**, 387–391.

KOHLMEYER, K. (1988) Periventrikuläre Dichteminderungen des Grosshirnhemisphärenmarks in Computertomogrammen von neuropsychiatrischen Patienten in der zweiten Lebenshälfte. Diagnostische Bedeutung und Pathoenese. *Fortschritte der Neurologie und Psychiatrie*, **56**, 279–287.

KRAEPELIN, E. (1912) Über paranoide Erkrankungen. *Zentralblatt für die gesamte Neurologie und Psychiatrie*, **11**, 617–638.

—— (1913) *Psychiatrie, eine Lehrbuch für Studierende und Ärzte*. (8th edn, Vol. III, Part 2). Leipzig: Johann Ambrosius Barth.

LEYS, D., PRUVO, J. P., PARENT, M., *et al* (1991) Could Wallerian degeneration contribute to "leuko-araiosis" in subjects free of any vascular disorder? *Journal of Neurology, Neurosurgery and Psychiatry*, **54**, 46–50.

MARNEROS, A. (1988) Schizophrenic first-rank symptoms in organic mental disorders. *British Journal of Psychiatry*, **152**, 625–628.

MAYER, W. (1921) Über paraphrene Psychosen. *Zeitschrift für die gesamte Neurologie und Psychiatrie*, **71**, 187–206.

MELLOR, C. S. (1982) The present status of first-rank symptoms. *British Journal of Psychiatry*, **140**, 423–424.

MCKHANN, G., DRACHMAN, D., FOLSTEIN, M., *et al* (1984) Clinical diagnosis of Alzheimer's disease: report on the NINCDS-ADRDA work group under the auspices of the Department of Health and Human Services Task Force on Alzheimer's disease. *Neurology*, **34**, 939–944.

MERRIAM, A. E., HEGARTY, A. & MILLER, A. (1989) A proposed etiology for psychotic symptoms in white matter dementia. *Neuropsychiatry, Neuropsychology and Behavioral Neurology*, **2**, 225–228.

MILLER, B. L., BENSON, D. F., CUMMINGS, J. L., *et al* (1986) Late-life paraphrenia: an organic delusional syndrome. *Journal of Clinical Psychiatry*, **47**, 204–207.

―――, LESSER, I. M., BOONE, K. B., *et al* (1991) Brain lesions and cognitive function in late-life psychosis. *British Journal of Psychiatry*, **158**, 76–82.

MORITZ, K. P. (1783–1793) *GNOTHI SAUTON, Magazin zur Erfahrungsseelenkunde*. Berlin: Mylius. Part I translated by H. Förstl & R. Howard (1992) *History of Psychiatry*, **3**, 95–115.

NAGUIB, M., & LEVY, R. (1987) Late paraphrenia: neuropsychological impairment and structural brain abnormalities on computed tomography. *International Journal of Geriatric Psychiatry*, **2**, 83–90.

NASRALLAH, H. A. (1986) Cerebral hemisphere asymmetries and interhemispheric integration in schizophrenia. In *Handbook of Schizophrenia* (eds H. A. Nasrallah & D. R. Weinberger) Vol. I, The Neurology of Schizophrenia, pp. 157–174. Amsterdam: Elsevier.

NORUSIS, M. J. (1988) *SPSS/PC + V2.0*. Chicago: SPSS Inc.

O'GRADY, J. C. (1990) The prevalence and diagnostic significance of Schneiderian first-rank symptoms in a random sample of acute psychiatric in-patients. *British Journal of Psychiatry*, **156**, 496–500.

POST, F. (1966) *Persistent Persecutory States in the Elderly*. Oxford: Pergamon Press.

RABINS, P., PAUKER, S. & THOMAS, J. (1984) Can schizophrenia begin after age 44? *Comprehensive Psychiatry*, **25**, 290–293.

RABINS, P., PEARLSON, G., JAYARAM, G., *et al* (1987) Increased ventricle-to-brain ratio in late-onset schizophrenia. *American Journal of Psychiatry*, **144**, 1216–1218.

RADHAKRISHNAN, J., MATHEW, K., RICHARD, J., *et al* (1983) Schneider's first rank symptoms – prevalence, diagnostic use and prognostic implications. *British Journal of Psychiatry*, **142**, 557–559.

ROTH, M. (1955) The natural history of mental disorders in old age. *Journal of Mental Science*, **101**, 281–301.

SCHNEIDER, K. (1959) *Klinische Psychopathologie*. Stuttgart: Thieme.

SLADE, P. D. & BENTALL, R. P. (1988) *Sensory Deception: A Scientific Analysis of Hallucination*. London: Croom Helm.

TRIMBLE, M. R. & CUMMINGS, J. L. (1981) Neuropsychiatric disturbances following brainstem lesions. *British Journal of Psychiatry*, **138**, 56–59.

VAN SWIETEN, J. C., VAN DEN HOUT, J. H. W., VAN KETEL, B. A., *et al* (1991) Periventricular lesions in the white matter on magnetic resonance imaging in the elderly. *Brain*, **114**, 761–774.

WING, J. K. (1978) *Reasoning about Madness*. Oxford: Oxford University Press.

12 Delusional disorders (of earlier onset) in old age

E. GABRIEL

At the meeting of the European Association for Geriatric Psychiatry in 1988, I presented data on affective symptoms in delusional disorders of midlife and their presentation and course in old age (Gabriel, 1989). The present chapter on the presentation of delusional disorders of earlier onset (in midlife) in old age is connected with that previous study.

The empirical data have been collected as part of the 'Enquête de Lausanne'[1] and are included there – following diagnostic habits in Switzerland according to the concept of schizophrenia of the Zürich school – in the group of schizophrenias (Ciompi & Müller, 1976). The data correspond to the data on so-called late schizophrenias (Bleuler, 1943) of the 'Enquête de Lausanne' which have been published previously (Gabriel, 1978). Recently, I have undertaken several re-evaluations of these data emphasising particular aspects (Gabriel, 1987, 1989; Gabriel & Schanda, 1990, 1991). The present paper on the presentation of delusional disorders of midlife in old age is one of these re-evaluations.

The theoretical background of the study corresponds to the positions of the Vienna Working Group on paranoid disorders of the last two decades with its main interest in the analysis and classification of delusional disorders by means of descriptive psychopathology and the concept of axis syndromes (Berner et al, 1986, 1992) and in course and outcome of delusional disorders of different kinds (Berner, 1965, 1969; Gabriel, 1978; Schanda, 1987; Gabriel & Schanda, 1990, 1991).

One should bear in mind that the British notion of late paraphrenia focusing on delusional disorders of the elderly is different from the notion of late schizophrenia of the Zürich school and from the descriptive notion of paraphrenia used by the Vienna group as well.

---

1. An inquiry on the influence of age on schizophrenia symptomatology conducted by Prof. Christian Müller and his collaborators.

Method

In the material of the 'Enquête de Lausanne', 553 former patients of the Psychiatric Clinic of the Hôpital de Cery in Lausanne, (which is also a University Department and a regional psychiatric Hospital) fulfilled the criteria of late schizophrenia with onset after age 40 but before age 65 (Bleuler, 1943). At the time of the follow-up investigations (1965–1969) 110 of these initial probands, (19.8%) were found to be alive and seen in personal follow-up examinations at their actual place of residence, the mean age at follow-up being 75 years, and the mean follow-up time 26 years. At first evaluation, 98 of that group of survivors were deluded. These 98 probands are the subject of this chapter (for details see Ciompi & Müller, 1976; Gabriel, 1978).

Psychopathological outcome and course are described under the following categories:

presence of delusions
delusional activity
structure of delusions
particular delusional symptoms
other psychopathological symptoms
syndrome diagnoses
course after age 65.

Results

Presence of delusions

At follow-up, at a mean age of 75 years and after a mean follow-up time of 26 years, 65 of the initial 98 probands (66.3%) were found to be still deluded. The item frequency had significantly decreased compared to the index evaluation ($P<0.001$). The item stability from index evaluation to follow-up (which may vary from 0.0 to 1.0) was found to be 0.66.

Delusional activity

Even those who were found to be still deluded usually showed a decrease in delusional activity ($n = 36$, 55.3%) (as assessed by the researchers using frequency and intensity of delusional symptoms) at follow-up. Of those whose delusions had not decreased, 25 (38.4%) were unchanged, three (4.6%) showed an increase in delusional activity, and in one the extent of delusional activity was unclear.

TABLE 12.1
The change in particular delusional items from index evaluation to follow-up evaluation

Item	Frequency at follow-up	Direction of change in frequency	Level of significance: P<	Item stability
Hallucinations	44	–	0.001	0.51
Acoustic hallucinations	39	–	0.001	0.53
Coenesthetic hallucinations	11	–	0.001	0.12
Acoustic and coenesthetic hallucinations	10	–	0.01	0.16
Experiences of reference and of being influenced	7	–	0.001	0.12
Depersonalisation	4	–	–	0.33
Interpretations	44	–	0.001	0.48
Delusions of persecution	51	–	0.001	0.57
Delusions of grandeur	13	+	–	0.66
Erotic delusions	9	–	0.01	0.4

Structure of delusions

With regard to the organisation of the delusions, 45 of the 65 still-deluded probands experienced some kind of loss in structure as compared with index evaluation. Only 24 of the probands still showed a high level of organisation of their delusions at follow-up, the item frequency being significantly decreased as compared with index evaluation ($P = 0.001$) and the item stability from index evaluation to follow-up evaluation being relatively low (0.42).

At index evaluation, polarisation[2] was the most frequent kind of insertion of delusions into reality, found in 53 of those 65 probands who remained deluded from index evaluation until follow-up evaluation. The frequency of polarisation was found to have decreased significantly (14 out of 53 still showed polarisation $P < 0.001$) at follow-up, the item's stability from index evaluation to follow-up evaluation being very low (0.18). Of the remaining 39 polarising patients, 27 now showed juxtaposition and 12 autism.

Particular delusional symptoms

Table 12.1 shows that all but one (delusions of grandeur) of the items in the series were found to be less frequent at follow-up than at index evaluation, the item stability being sometimes very low but more often of a medium level.

---

2. 'Polarisation' is a term derived from French structuralist psychopathology. Three forms of an individual's relationships with the delusions can be distinguished, (a) polarisation in which delusion and reality are intricately interwoven, (b) juxtaposition in which delusions and reality co-exist but are separated and (c) autism (e.g. Berner *et al*, 1986)

TABLE 12.2
The change of general psychopathology from index evaluation to follow-up evaluation

	Frequency at follow-up	Direction of change in frequency	Level of significance: P<	Item stability
Schizophrenic axis syndrome	18	+	0.01	0.66
Cyclothymic axis syndrome	32	–	0.001	0.43
manic type	10	–	–	0.28
depressive type	14	–	0.001	0.25
dysphoric type	14	–	0.01	0.77

Other psychopathological symptoms

With regard to axis syndromes

Apart from delusional symptoms, the Vienna group has been most interested in the classification of the so-called general psychopathology using the concept of axis syndromes (Gabriel, 1985; Berner *et al*, 1992). In Gabriel's (1978) study, the axis syndromes were defined by the leading symptoms.

Table 12.2 shows that formal disorders of thought (taken as leading symptoms of the schizophrenic axial syndrome) increase with time whereas affective symptoms decrease, usually significantly. However, one should stress that not less than 38 of the probands showed affective disturbances at follow-up – dysphoric disturbances showed high item stability from index evaluation to follow-up evaluation (Gabriel, 1987; Schanda, 1987; Gabriel & Schanda, unpublished data).

With regard to organic brain syndrome and dementia

One of the main purposes of the Enquête de Lausanne was to find out whether patients suffering from different psychiatric disorders have a different tendency to develop organic brain syndromes or dementia in their senium. The question is of great interest in psychiatric disorders of relatively late onset occurring in midlife which are often interpreted as early presentations of the dementing process (Sternberg, 1972).

Table 12.3 shows that the frequencies of different severity of organic brain syndrome/dementia as assessed following the rules of the 'Enquête de Lausanne' did not differ in the whole group of schizophrenics (Ciompi & Müller, 1976) or in the subgroup of delusional disorders of midlife which are called late schizophrenias by that school.

Syndrome diagnoses

Syndrome diagnoses at follow-up were assessed using a variant of Huber's classification (1966) proposed by Berner (1969).

TABLE 12.3
Prevalence of different intensities of organic brain syndrome in the whole group of 553 schizophrenics in the 'Enquete de Lausanne' and in those with late schizophrenia

| | Late schizophrenia[1] | | All schizophrenics |
	n	%	%
Intensity			
severe	8	11.2	8.0
marked	12	16.9	16.9
mild	30	42.2	34.9
any	16	22.5	22.8
unclear	5	7.0	17.3

1. 71 'late schizophrenics' had organic brain syndrome at follow-up, direction of change in frequency was positive, $P < 0.001$, item stability 0.9.

TABLE 12.4
The syndrome presentation of the 65 still-deluded patients at follow-up evaluation using a variant of Huber's (1966) classification

Syndrome	n	%	Direction of change in frequency	Level of significance	Item stability
Chronic schizophrenia	4	6.1			
Mixed residual state	16	24.6			
Paraphrenic syndrome	32	49.2	–	$P < 0.001$	0.5
Paranoic syndrome	5	7.6	–	NS	0.33
Others	8	12.3			

Table 12.4 shows that about one-half of the probands that were found to be still deluded suffered from the more or less systematised delusional syndrome which is called paraphrenic, and approximately one-quarter suffered from a residual state mixed with some delusional symptoms and therefore called mixed residual state, whereas schizophrenic and paranoic (delusional) syndromes were rare.

Course after age 65

Most of the probands have taken a chronic course in the senium which was stable ($n = 50$, 66.6%) or regressive ($n = 19$, 25.3%) in symptom presentation (seven (7.1%) were progressive). This result was also found in those who remained deluded ($n = 60$) with a chronic course after age 65, of whom 43 (71.6%) were stable, 15 (25.0%) were regressive and two (3.3%) were progressive.

Conclusions

Some general conclusions may be derived from these results. Even though most functional delusional disorders first appearing in midlife showed a remarkable decrease in symptoms after the age of 65, up to two-thirds of patients remained deluded in old age, and almost all had a chronic course. In these chronically deluded patients, decrease in symptom presentation was found in terms of the following: delusional activity, structure of delusions, symptoms, and syndromes. Organic brain syndrome/dementia in the elderly occurs as frequently as in the whole schizophrenic population of the same origin (Enquête de Lausanne) and probably no more frequently than in the general population. The course after the age of 65 may most often be described as chronic–stable, less often chronic–regressive and seldom progressive; a chronic course was found for affective cyclothymic disturbances. In these affective cyclothymic disturbances, dysphoric mood may justify particular interest.

References

BERNER, P. (1965) *Das paranoische Syndrom*. Berlin: Springer.
—— (1969) Der Lebensabend der Paranoiker. *Wien, Z. Nervheilk.*, **27**, 115–161.
——, GABRIEL, E., KIEFFER, W., *et al* (1986) Paranoid psychoses. New aspects of classification and prognosis coming from the Vienna Research Group. *Psychopathology*, **19**, 16–29.
——, ——, KATSCHNIG, H., *et al* (1992) *Diagnostic Criteria for Functional Psychoses*. Cambridge: Cambridge University Press.
BLEULER, M. (1943) Die Spätschizophrenen Krankheitsbilder. *Fortschritte der Neurologie-Psychiatrie*, **15**, 259–290.
CIOMPI, L. & MÜLLER, C. (1976) *Lebensweg und Alter der Schizophrenen*. Berlin: Springer.
GABRIEL, E. (1978) *Die langfristige Entwicklung von Späschizophrenien. Zugleich ein Beitrag zum langen Verlauf von Wahnbildungen der Lebensmitte*. Basel: Karger.
—— (1985) The concepts of axis syndromes 1965–1983. *Psychopathology*, **18**, 106–110.
—— (1987) Dysphoric mood in paranoid psychoses. *Psychopathology*, **20**, 101–106.
—— (1989) Affektive Störungen in Wahnerkrankungen der Lebensmitte und ihr Verlauf bis in das hohe Lebensalter. In *Depression in Old Age* (ed. J. U. Postma). Neuss: Janssen.
—— & SCHANDA, H. (1990) Are there differences in the course of delusional disorders in different periods of time? *Psychopathology*, **23**, 125–128.
—— & —— (1991) Why do the results of follow-up studies in delusional disorders differ? *Psychopathology*, **24**, 304–308.
HUBER, G. (1966) Reine Defektsyndrome und Basisstadien endogener Psychosen. *Fortschritte der Neurologie-Psychiatrie*, **34**, 409–426.
SCHANDA, H. (1987) *Paranoide Psychosen*. Stuttgart: Enke.
STERNBERG, E. (1972) Uber psychotische ('funktionelle') frühstatien seniler Geistesstörungen. *Psychiatrie Neurologie und Medizinische Psychologie*, **24**, 318–325.

13 Late chronic delusions – psychopathology and nosography

JOSÉ D. CORDEIRO

The psychopathology of the elderly mentally ill is very often the expression of a variety of simultaneous problems involving physical, psychological and cognitive aspects. This chapter focuses on the late-onset delusional states, particularly those starting after the age of 65. The delusional states of old age are more frequently paranoid; although erotomanic, prejudicial, dermatozoic and, of course, manic and depressive are also observed. Further understanding of such states involves the clarification of three main points. Firstly, should the delusional states emerging for the first time in late life be considered analogous to those with onset in younger ages, or are they the expression of distinct pathogenetic mechanisms? Secondly, what is the importance of the physical and sensorial deterioration in the development of such psychotic states? Thirdly, would the psychological distress associated with old age together with isolation and the absence of social support have a pathogenetic role in the appearance of late-onset delusional states?

A study on late-onset delusional states being conducted at the clinic Bel-Air, University of Geneva, and at the Medical School of Lisbon since 1968 is outlined, which attempts to answer these questions.

Epidemiology

The sample ($n = 180$) was made up of patients with no evidence of previous psychiatric morbidity, who represented 6.7% of our elderly in-patient population. Patients with psychotic phenomena secondary to either affective or organic disorders were excluded.

Kay & Roth (1964) reported that 10% of all the patients admitted over the age of 60 in both a Swedish and an English mental hospital were late paraphrenics. Blessed & Wilson (1982) found 8.7% of late-paraphrenics in a Newcastle-upon-Tyne population over the age of 65. Lower percentages have been reported for elderly psychiatric admissions in England and Wales (5.6%) as well as in the United States (3.2%).

The existence, in Portugal, of a traditional family structure constitutes an important social support for the elderly. Symptoms such as amnesia, confabulation and delusional ideas are usually well tolerated by the patient's relatives and rarely come to psychiatric attention. It is, therefore, likely that our 6.7% prevalence rate underestimates the real magnitude of the problem in the Portuguese elderly population. We believe that only those patients with very disruptive behaviour come to psychiatric attention, all the others being considered a 'normal' expression of the ageing process.

The mean age of the subjects in our sample was 73 years (range 65–95), with a female:male ratio of 3.3:1. This preponderance of females has been described by others, although the proportion of females to males reported varies widely with rates from 3:1 to 22.5:1.

In our sample, 76% of the patients had no psychiatric family history. Delusional syndromes in other family members were reported by 8%, while 10% reported the presence of other psychiatric disorders. We were not able to obtain reliable information from 6% of our patients.

Of the women in the sample, 43% were widowed, 9% married, 24% divorced, and 24% single (65% had no children). Of the men, 45% were widowed, 27% married, 18% divorced, and 10% single (30% had no children).

Onset of paraphrenic symptoms in 46% was acute or sub-acute, and in 54% was gradual. Schooling levels varied, 83% had undergone primary education only, 12% had reached level 7 – secondary education – and 5% had achieved a university degree. During their working lives 72% had a low income, 22% had an average income and 6% had an above average income. Since retirement, 74% had had no occupation and 26% reported some occupation. However, 77% of our sample reported having a hobby of some kind.

Premorbid personality

Personality abnormalities have been reported in patients with late-onset delusional states. However, their importance as the source for the later development of psychotic symptoms remains unclear.

Kay & Roth (1964) reported that 45% of their late-paraphrenic patients showed evidence of paranoid or schizoid personality traits. They were described as suspicious, quarrelsome, cold-hearted, eccentric, unsociable and religious. Hirschmann & Klages (1957) emphasised the difficulties of these patients' interpersonal relationships.

We could not find any clear evidence of personality disturbance in 69% of our patients; whereas 12% showed obsessive, 11% depressive, 6% sensitive, and 2% histrionic premorbid personality traits. At least 76% of these subjects showed an adequate premorbid adjustment with stable work and social life before the onset of their illnesses. Our findings are in agreement with those of Janzarik (1957) and Barontini & Fossi (1962), who suggested that true paranoid or schizoid traits were only rarely found in late-onset paranoid cases.

Among our patients, 66% of the women and 69% of the men had no close social contacts, even though 78% of them had lived in the same place since they were born.

Very little has been written about the physical make-up of these patients. Post (1966) could not find any significant association between psychiatric diagnosis and physical characteristics in an elderly population. Conversely, Janzarik (1957) and Hirschmann & Klages (1957) reported an excess of pyknic body build among their patients. Of our sample 63% were pyknic, 19% leptosomatic and 18% of athletic build.

Clinical features and psychopathology

The delusional syndromes of our elderly patients were often associated with other psychiatric symptoms. We found that 78% of the subjects were anxious, 45% were hypochondriac and 18% exhibited non-psychotic depressive symptoms. Auditory and visual impairment were present in 36% of the patients in this sample. Delirium in association with a physical illness was noticed in 19% of our patients. Formal thought disorder was observed in 24% of the patients.

The relationship between the patient and the medical staff was considered adequate in 80% of the cases.

One or more types of hallucinations were experienced by 69% of the subjects, the most frequent being auditory (46%). The patients reported elementary (such as noises) and verbal hallucinations. Visual illusions or hallucinations were present in 21% of the patients and were often associated with delirium or visual impairment. Tactile hallucinations were reported by 21% of the subjects, in 6% of the cases similar to those described in the dermatozoic syndrome. The olfactory hallucinations (10.5%) were usually associated with other modalities of hallucinations.

The late delusional states can be, as in early onset cases, acute, chronic, reactive or symptomatic. The content of the delusional ideas was most frequently paranoid, although a variety of other themes could also be found. The mechanism involved in the development of the delusions could be either interpretative, intuitive and/or secondary to hallucinations.

None the less, some characteristics seemed to be associated with late-onset delusions and could help to differentiate them from early-onset cases.

(a) Transient delusions and chronic delusional states were often associated with organic syndromes, physical illness (symptomatic psychosis), or sensorial impairment.

(b) Polythematic delusional ideas were common. Even in those patients who were clearly paranoid we could usually observe other themes, such as hypochondriacal, depressive, erotomanic, or prejudicial.

(c) Most symptoms are 'understandable' from the existential and psychodynamic perspective of ageing.

Prejudicial ideas were very frequent, often referring to the patient's reputation or personal belongings. The association of such beliefs with memory impairment is common. However, as in the case of Kraepelin's (1913) presenile prejudicial delusion, the true prejudicial belief is not based on amnesia.

Erotomanic ideas were frequent in both sexes. In late-onset cases, however, the idea that one is loved is not as stable as in younger age groups, and did not reach in any of our patients the disruptive social behaviour described by de Clérambault (1942) in adult cases.

The denial of the consort's death can appear either immediately after the death of the spouse or some years later. We believe, as do others (Capgras *et al*, 1933), that this condition is not based on a memory loss, but on a refusal to remember. Some of our patients were able to describe in detail the funeral of their spouses, but would still insist that the consort was alive somewhere else.

The association between sensory impairment and delusional states has been frequently reported. Kraepelin (1919) described what he called 'deaf paranoia' and Seglas (1888) reported the case of a patient with unilateral auditory hallucinations associated with homolateral hearing impairment. A high prevalence of hearing deficits has been reported in patients with late-onset delusional states when compared with normal age-matched controls or elderly patients with affective disorder.

Cooper (1976) suggested that the characteristics of deafness likely to be of aetiological significance in late-onset paranoid states were early age of onset, chronicity and severity. Deafness could act as a trigger to the psychotic phenomena in individuals with predisposed personality traits. This could be less important in those patients without such characteristics or with typical schizophrenic symptoms (Post, 1967; Holden, 1987).

The real pathogenic role of deafness in late onset delusional states is not yet clear. Nevertheless, a patient with late paraphrenia was reported to have improved dramatically after adjustment to a hearing aid (Eastwood *et al*, 1981).

Deafness is not thought to be a direct source of delusions, but a phenomenon provoking social isolation and loneliness. The disruption of communication with others would motivate an indirect change in personality with the emergence of suspiciousness, instability, sensitivity and paranoia.

Another condition associated with late-onset delusions is dementia. Delusions can be the first evident manifestation of dementia. However, we do not consider that dementia itself is a direct source of delusions. Conversely, we would suggest that such an organic syndrome is a precipitating factor. An organic syndrome induces changes in the personality structure and is often associated with anxiety, and reduction of the sense of reality, judgement, and insight. In fact, some sensitive patients who develop dementia show an exacerbation of such premorbid traits, which could facilitate the development of full paranoid psychotic symptoms.

We have observed that patients with organic delusional syndromes did not exhibit any specific delusional structure. The delusional themes were comparable to those reported in our late-onset deluded patients.

The therapeutic response of both functional and organic deluded patients was similar. The psycho-organic syndrome might weaken the memory, judgement and mental synthesis abilities of the patients. Such dissolution could facilitate the appearance of day-dreams, fabulation and the amnestic delusion described by Delay (1970).

Functional psychosis

We find all sorts of delusional structures in old age. They can be acute, reactive and chronic. Most patients exhibit delusional intuitions, interpretations and hallucinations. Some of them would correspond to what the french called 'chronic hallucinatory psychosis'.

The deterioration of the personality has been, for a long time, considered an important criterion to distinguish schizophrenia from other paranoid syndromes. We have hardly observed deterioration of the personality among our 'functional' patients. These patients were often anxious, but not perplexed, and very concerned with their belongings. They would describe envious people trying to steal things from their flats. Those patients who hallucinated frequently reported two different current sorts of 'voices': (a) hostile and threatening and (b) pleasant, encouraging and flattering.

Nosology

The nosological status of late-onset delusional states is still uncertain. The relationship between what is called 'late paraphrenia' in the UK and schizophrenia remains the subject of dispute.

Erwin Bleuler (1911*a,b*) reported that he was never able to establish that the onset of 'late schizophrenia' would not be before the age of 65. Would late schizophrenia be just a late form of schizophrenia? Halberstadt (1925) suggested that those patients without clear 'splitting' of the personality should not be considered schizophrenics.

Kleist (1913) described 10 patients with involutional paranoia with onset between 60 and 70 years of age. Some of them would correspond to what Kraepelin called 'paraphrenia'. Mayer (1921), after a follow-up of Kraepelin's paraphrenics, suggested that such patients would show a deterioration in line with that reported in schizophrenics. Roth (1955) used the term late paraphrenia to describe a group of late-onset delusional syndromes with a "well organised system of paranoid delusions with or without auditory hallucinations existing in the setting of a well preserved personality and affective response . . . clinical observations had made it clear that in the great majority of these patients, the illness commences after the age of 60''.

Fish (1960) did not accept the new term and stated that late paraphrenia was equivalent to Bleuler's "late schizophrenia", which was a very rare condition. Christian Müller (1969) found only four patients with onset after the age of 60 in a sample of 101 old schizophrenics.

Some authors, including myself, prefer not to make a diagnosis of schizophrenia in old age. Along with the deterioration of the personality, typical schizophrenic symptoms do not improve only with admission to an institution (which is often the case with late paraphrenics; Post, 1966). Almeida *et al* (personal communication) have recently suggested that "in our current state of knowledge, the attempt to classify late paraphrenic patients as schizophrenics may be premature".

The nosological difficulties with the delusional late-onset states are due to various problems. The age of onset, for instance, is not clearly defined in many works. Also, the terminology employed varies in different countries and even within the same country. Some consider all persistent paranoid syndromes as schizophrenia. Others base their diagnoses on the presence or absence of deterioration of personality, making use of a variety of different terms such as 'schizophrenia' for the former, and 'chronic hallucinatory psychosis', 'bouffée délirante' and 'paraphrenia' for the latter.

There are now studies available showing that some patients diagnosed as schizophrenics did not show deterioration of their personalities and, in contrast, patients considered non-schizophrenics exhibited such deterioration with time.

Several attempts have been made to establish a nosological classification for late-onset psychosis.

Kraepelin (1919)

Pre-senile prejudicial delusion
Senile persecutory delusion

Delusions associated with dementia (persecutory, megalomaniac, hypochondriacal, denial)
Delusional melancholia

Naudascher (1939)

Pre-senile psychosis
(a) Paranoid psychosis
    (i) Prejudicial delusion (Kraepelin, 1919)
    (ii) Involutional paranoia (Kleist, 1913)
    (iii) Jealousy delusion
        Ekbom's ectoparasitic psychosis (Ekbom, 1938)
(b) Paranoid and paraphrenic psychosis
(c) Good prognosis psychosis
    (i) Late chronic interpretative delusion
        Late chronic hallucinatory psychosis
    (ii) Senile dementia with delusions
    (iii) Involutive delusional melancholia

Janzarik (1957)

(a) Senile schizophrenias
    (i) Acute delusional psychosis
    (ii) Persecutory chronic psychosis
    (iii) Hallucinatory psychosis
(b) Catatonia

Fish (1960)

Paranoid syndrome
Psychogenic paranoid reaction
Schizophrenia
Organic psychosis
Paranoid depression

Post (1966)

Paranoid development of the personality
Paranoid acute reaction
Functional paranoid psychosis
    (i) Paranoid auditory hallucinosis
    (ii) Schizophreniform syndrome
(iii) Schizophrenic syndrome
Catatonic schizophrenia

Paranoid syndrome associated to organic syndrome or sensory impairment
Delusional melancholia
Delusional mania

Müller (1969)

Schizophrenia-like psychosis
Psycho-organic delusional psychosis
Delusional mania
Delusional depression

Mayer-Gross *et al* (1969)

Late paraphrenia
Paranoid psycho-organic syndrome
Paranoid syndrome in depression

In 1972 we introduced the following classification:
(a) Late acute psychosis

    (i) Delusional acute psychosis
   (ii) Delusional reactions
  (iii) Symptomatic psychosis

(b) Late chronic psychosis

    (i) Without deterioration
       Late schizomorph psychosis (associated or not to sensory impairment) – includes paranoid, prejudicial, paraphrenic, erotomanic, dermatozoic and denial delusions (associated or not)
   (ii) With deterioration
      Late schizophreniform psychosis
  (iii) Psycho-organic delusional states
  (iv) Affective delusional psychosis (late delusional melancholia, late delusional mania).

With reference to the psychopathology of late-onset delusional states, four main questions arise.

(a) Are they nosologically and pathogenetically similar to those states described in younger patients?
(b) Why would people with no previous psychiatric history and who have always been considered normal and adequate develop psychotic symptoms after the age of 60?

(c) What is the role of the physical, psychological and sensorial conditions of these patients in the development of psychotic symptoms?

(d) Has the vulnerability of the ageing personality, particularly at the level of coping mechanisms, in association with isolation, loneliness and lack of social support, a pathogenic role in the emergence of delusional states in ageing people approaching death?

Both the DSM–III–R (American Psychiatric Association, 1987) and the ICD–9 (World Health Organization, 1978) show an incomplete and reductive nosology, since they were primarily designed for young adults and psycho-organic syndromes. I believe we could all agree that there are some delusional states emerging in late life (not due to dementia) that do not have, necessarily, a direct counterpart in younger ages.

We believe that, psychologically, people depend not only on the genetic constitution but also on their biopsychosocial development. The ageing process is characterised by profound changes, with the emergence of fatigue, pain, insomnia, physical illnesses, reduction of the libido, sensorial and social isolation, retirement, and insecurity.

These changes are psychologically very demanding on the elderly. We think that the anxiety and the psychological, physical and social vulnerability of these patients mobilise adaptive coping mechanisms of the personality, some of them pathological – such as projection and denial.

Most late-onset delusional psychosis without any personal or familial psychiatric history can be regarded as an active, but pathological, reaction of the patient's personality against the new and often frightening physical, psychological and social reality, characterised by several deficits, losses, mournings and lack of future perspective.

References

BARONTINI, F. & FOSSI G. (1962) Sulle psicosi paranoide della está involutiva. *Rivista di Patologia Nervosa et Mentale*, **LXXXII**, 4.

BLESSED, G. & WILSON, D. (1982) The contemporary natural history of mental disorders in old age. *British Journal of Psychiatry*, **141**, 59–67.

BLEULER, E. (1911a) *Dementia Praecox or the Group of Schizophrenias* (translated by J. J. Zinkin, 1950). New York: International Universities Press.

——— (1911b) *Traité de Psychiatrie*. Aschafferburg:

CAPGRAS, JOAKI & ELLENBERGER (1933) Psychose présénile. Négations systématiques et érotomanie. *Annales Médico Psychologiques*, **2**, 209–224.

CLERAMBAULT, G. de (1942) *Oeuvre Psychiatrique*. Paris: PUF.

COOPER, A. F. (1976) Deafness and psychiatric illness. *British Journal of Psychiatry*, **129**, 216–226.

DELAY, J. (1970) *Les Maladies de la Memoire*. Paris: PUF.

EASTWOOD, M. R., CORBIN, S. & REED, M. (1981) Hearing impairment and paraphrenia. *Journal of Otolaryngology*, **10**, 306–308.

EKBOM, K. A. (1938) Der praeseniler Dermatozoenwahn. *Acta Psychiatrica et Neurologica*, **13**, 227–259.

G

FISH, F. J. (1960) Senile schizophrenia. *Journal of Mental Science*, **106**, 938–946.

HALBERSTADT, G. (1925) La schizophrénie tardive. *L'encéphale*, **9**, 655–662.

HIRSCHMANN, J. & KLAGES, W. (1967) Konstitutionspezifishe leitlinien bei den psychosen des hoheren lebensalter. *Archiv. Psychiat. Nervenkr.*, **196**, 254–264.

HOLDEN, N. L. (1987) Late paraphrenia or the paraphrenias? A descriptive study with a 10-year follow-up. *British Journal of Psychiatry*, **150**, 635–639.

JANZARIK, W. (1957) Zur problematik schizophrener psychosen im hoheren lebensalter. *Nervenarzt*, **28**, 535–542.

KAY, D. W. & ROTH, M. (1964) Old age mental disorders in Newcastle upon Tyne. *British Journal of Psychiatry*, **110**, 668–682.

KLEIST, K. (1913) The involution paranoia. *Allgemeine Zeitschrift fur Psychiatrie*, **70**, 1–134.

KRAEPELIN E. (1913, 1915) *Psychiatrie* (8ᵉ éd.) Vol. III, Vol. IV. Berlin: Springer.

——— (1919) *Dementia Praecox and Paraphrenia* (translated by R. M. Barclay from the eighth German edition of the ''Text Book of Psychiatry'', Vol. III, part II, section on the Endogenous Dementias, 1919). Edinburgh: Livingstone.

MÜLLER, Ch. (1969) *Manuel de Géronto-Psychiatrie*. Paris: Masson.

NAUDASCHER, J. (1939) *Les Psychoses Délirantes D'involution*. Paris: Thèse de Paris.

POST, F. (1966) *Persistent Persecutory States of the Elderly*. Oxford: Pergamon Press.

——— (1967) The schizophrenic reaction-type in late life. *Proceedings of the Royal Society of Medicine*, **60**, 249–254.

ROTH, M. (1955) The natural history of mental disorder in old age. *Journal of Mental Science*, **101**, 281–301.

SEGLAS, E. (1888) Les psychoses séniles tardives. *Le Progrès Médical*, **43**, 289–292.

14 Charles Bonnet syndrome and musical hallucinations in the elderly

THOMAS FUCHS and HANS LAUTER

In organic mental disorders, a plain organic substrate can usually be identified, and a comparatively simple pathogenesis may be assumed – destruction of brain tissue by degeneration, infarct or tumour, disconnection of pathways, etc. There are, however, two rare forms of organic hallucinosis in which the lack of a demonstrable substrate and the connection with peripheral sensory deficits suggest a more complex pathogenesis: visual hallucinations with impaired vision, commonly referred to as 'Charles Bonnet syndrome', and musical hallucinations in deafness. Situated on the borderline between different medical specialities, their frequency probably surmounts by far their publicity.

Since the late 19th century, mainly French psychiatrists have contributed to the description and investigation of organic hallucinations, above all Régis, L'Hermitte, Hécaen, Ey, and De Morsier. De Morsier (1938) coined the term 'Charles Bonnet syndrome' for complex visual hallucinations in otherwise mentally unimpaired old persons. For musical hallucinations a similar eponym does not yet exist. Recently, the literature on Charles Bonnet syndrome and musical hallucinosis has been reviewed by Podoll (1989) and Berrios (1990). Since both syndromes are associated with sensory impairment, they must be in some way analogous. By comparing their epidemiological, psychopathological, and pathogenetic features we will examine to what extent this parallel is justified. To this end, a more precise definition of the two syndromes is required.

Definition

Here we meet a dilemma and a corresponding dissent in the literature. If the two syndromes belong to the organic hallucinoses, then what is their underlying 'specific organic factor', required, for example, by DSM–III–R? Most cases do not show any demonstrable brain pathology, but only peripheral sensory impairment – an 'organic factor' thus, but not in the usual sense. This distinguishes the two syndromes from complex visual hallucinations occuring with lesions at any level of the visual tract and cortex, for example, in Chiasma syndrome, 'peduncular hallucinosis' or hemianopia through occipital lobe lesion (Gold & Rabins, 1989; Weller & Wiedemann, 1989; Kölmel, 1991); from musical hallucinations caused by temporal lobe epilepsy or tumours, brainstem lesions, encephalitis or brain intoxication (Rozanski & Rozen, 1952; Cambier *et al*, 1987; Berrios, 1990); and from hallucinations in dementia or delirium. This distinction would be lost if all those hallucinations of demonstrable organic origin were included in the definition, as suggested by some authors (Hecaen & LeGuen, 1960; Burgermeister *et al*, 1965; Gold & Rabins, 1989). The interesting question is indeed, how hallucinatory experiences are possible in spite of intact visual or acoustic tracts, well functioning brain, and mental sanity. After all, there are good reasons to suppose a pathogenesis quite different from the hallucinations triggered by localised lesions and commonly explained as 'irritative' phenomena. The possible mechanism may rather be a disinhibition or release of stored visual and acoustic material as a result of sensory deafferentation (West, 1962).

Should brain pathology therefore be excluded altogether? This would lead into another dilemma: how can we explain the rarity of the two syndromes in contrast to the apparent frequency of visual or hearing loss in the elderly? Obviously 'central' but more subtle factors have still to be searched for which in combination with the peripheral disorder could account for the peculiarity of these hallucinations.

In our opinion, a possible solution for this dilemma lies in delimiting the two syndromes from dementia, delirium, and specific neurological disorders without, however, excluding slighter cerebral dysfunctions. This approach has been taken by Podoll *et al* (1990), following DSM–III–R, and we prefer their criteria of the Charles Bonnet syndrome (listed below) to the purely symptomatic definition of Gold & Rabins (1989).

(a) Visual hallucinations in elderly persons with normal consciousness are the predominant clinical signs.
(b) No delirium, dementia, organic affective or delusional syndrome, psychosis, intoxication or neurological disorder with lesions of the central visual pathways or cortex.
(c) Reduced vision resulting from eye disease in most cases, but not obligatory.

It seems doubtful, yet, whether the syndrome in the sense of (a) and (b) occurs without ophthalmic disorder. Podoll names a few examples from the first half of this century which, however, had not been subjected to instrumental diagnostics excluding specific brain lesions.

Turning to musical hallucinosis, no formal definition has yet been attempted; apparently the peculiarity of content is regarded as a sufficient characterisation. Thus, in his overview Berrios has included cases with brain tumour, infarction, epilepsy, depression, and other diseases, which unfortunately renders a comparison with the Charles Bonnet syndrome quite difficult. However, if analogous diagnostic criteria are used for musical hallucinosis, a second look at the literature leaves only 19 cases without relevant psychiatric or neurological disorders, especially without temporal lobe lesions (David *et al*, 1944, case 1; Rozansky & Rosen, 1952; Hecaen & Ropert, 1963, case 1–7; Ross *et al*, 1975, case 1 & 2; Miller & Crosby, 1978; Raghuram *et al*, 1980; Hammeke *et al*, 1983, case 1 & 2; Allen, 1985; Jonas, 1986; Patel *et al*, 1987; Wagner & Gertz, 1991). This means that musical hallucinations also occur independently of such disorders, thus allowing a comparison with the Charles Bonnet syndrome. Musical hallucinosis (MH) in this paper is defined as an organic hallucinosis analogous to the Charles Bonnet syndrome (CBS).

The following comparison is divided into epidemiological, psychopathological, and pathogenetic aspects; it follows the surveys and case publications available so far. The figures are based on the 46 cases of CBS surveyed in Podoll *et al* (1989) and the 19 cases of MH mentioned above. Of special interest regarding the analogy is the fact that in two cases the syndromes occurred simultaneously in the same patient (Patel *et al*, 1987; Wagner & Gertz, 1991).

Epidemiology and course

In CBS, the patients' age varies between 59 and 92 years, the mean being 76 years; in MH the age ranges from 37 to 89, with a mean of 69 years.

TABLE 14.1
Epidemiology and course of Charles Bonnet syndrome and musical hallucinosis

	CBS (n = 46)	MH (n = 19)
Age	59–92 years; mean 76 years	37–89 years; mean 69 years
Sex	men:women = 48%:52%	men:women = 16%:84%
Prevalence	1–2% of psychiatric elderly out-patients	no information
Peripheral sensory impairment	loss of vision in 87%; (of these:) cataract 41% glaucoma 20%	loss of hearing in 100%; (of these:) otosclerosis or specific infections 37%
Latency	mostly years	mostly years or decades
Onset	sudden > gradual	sudden ≈ gradual (9:10)
Course (as far as observed)	mostly continuous (1–8 years) 22% episodical or periodical	predominantly continuous (months to years)
Therapy	successful cataract operation in 6 out of 7 cases	successful operation of otosclerosis in 1 case

Thus, even with omission of the mostly younger patients with brain lesions included by Berrios, the average age in MH is still lower than in CBS. Nevertheless, it is justified to classify both syndromes as disorders of later life (Table 14.1).

Charles Bonnet syndrome is equally distributed between the sexes, whereas MH is more frequent in women. However, Norton-Willson & Munir (1987), in their series of examinations in psychogeriatric patients, found CBS to be also unequally distributed (men/women = 1/7), as would be expected demographically. Studies concerning prevalence have only been carried out in CBS: it was diagnosed in 1.3% and 1.8% of psychogeriatric out-patients (Berrios & Brook, 1984).

The peripheral sensory impairment consisted of a more or less marked loss of vision to the point of blindness in 87% of patients with CBS; cataract or glaucoma were the most frequent ophthalmic disorders. A partial or complete loss of hearing was met in all cases of MH, caused mainly by presbyacusis, specifically also by otosclerosis or infections such as lues. The latency from the beginning of sensory impairment until the onset of hallucinations varied from months to years, in MH even to decades. Onset was sudden in most cases of CBS, while it was gradual in approximately 50% of MH. Accordingly, the course of MH, as far as observed, was mostly continuous and extended over years, whereas episodic or periodic courses are not infrequent in CBS.

The only successful therapy described in both syndromes was a surgical intervention restoring vision or hearing, which in six out of seven cases of CBS and in one case of MH lead to a disappearance of the hallucinations (Hecaen & Ropert, 1963, case 2; Podoll *et al*, 1989; Siatkowsky *et al*, 1990). Pharmacological or psychotherapeutic treatment was found to be ineffective.

Psychopathology

To begin with, the hallucinations differ in their mode of appearance: in CBS, they occur suddenly, often several times a day, but mostly in evening or night hours, and last only seconds or minutes; whereas the musical hallucinations accompany two-thirds of the patients through the whole day and cease only during sleep (Table 14.2).

The visual hallucinations are always located by the patients into external space, in 9% unilaterally to the side of poorer vision or into the area of existing scotomas. In the musical hallucinations, spatial projection is less definite; sometimes they are perceived like the tinnitus in the patient's own head, in 16% also unilaterally corresponding to the different degree of hearing loss.

In both syndromes, the hallucinations are of a very intense quality; in CBS they are mostly coloured. Patients often describe a much more vivid and distinct perception than their advanced impairment of vision or hearing otherwise permits.

TABLE 14.2

Psychopathological characteristics of Charles Bonnet syndrome and musical hallucinosis

	CBS (n = 46)	MH (n = 19)
Mode of appearance	mostly paroxysmal (seconds or minutes); often several times a day; predominantly in evening or at night	68% continuous 32% intermittently
Localisation	into external space	spatial projection less definite
Lateralisation	in 9%	in 16%
Quality	very intense, mostly coloured	very intense and distinct; often very loud
Content	37% elementary (11% changing into complex hallucinations) 83% human figures 50% animals 46% plants 48% inanimate objects often fragmented objects	37% elementary (32% changing into complex hallucinations) 63% instrumental music 63% vocal music 11% bird songs or bells 37% voices often pieces of melodies or sentences
	predominantly no relationship to conscience and memory; 13% acquaintances or deceased persons 13% religious contents	predominantly familiar melodies mostly stemming from childhood 26% religious music
Changes over time	often scenical course, motions *en bloc*; less often 'mechanical' sequences and repetitions	often monotonous rhythms or repetitions
Modification	9% modifiable voluntarily 11% motions following eye movement 17% vanishing with lid closure	26% content modifiable voluntarily
Insight	65% yes 7% no 28% no information	95% yes 5% no
Reaction	65% rather positive 24% rather negative	first predominantly positive; later increasing distress

As regards the content of the hallucinations, about one-third are partially or predominantly elementary – photisms and geometric patterns in CBS, whistles, motor and water noises in MH. In some cases, these elementary hallucinations change into complex ones, in the course of the illness as well as during single hallucinatory experiences (Hecaen & Ropert, 1963; Podoll *et al*, 1989). Complex objects in CBS are mainly human figures, less often animals, plants and various inanimate things. Thus, the CBS appears in manifold forms, whereas the musical hallucinations show but a few variations: instrumental and vocal music are almost equally represented, less frequently bird songs or bells, and in 37% non-melodic human voices are heard. The latter differ from psychotic acoustic hallucinations mainly by the monotonous repetition of words or fragmented sentences which to the patient are not threatening but familiar from his memory. This corresponds to the character of the melodic hallucinatory experiences. The frequent fragmentation of content is indeed a common feature of both syndromes; in CBS this shows in the form of isolated parts of the body, busts and others. Different, however, is the congruence of the phenomena with the contents of conscious memory. The melodies heard are nearly always familiar to the patient and he often feels carried back into his childhood; only one case of a new combination of 'nonsense-melodies' has been reported (Hammeke 1983, case 1). On the other hand, *déjà-vu* experiences are rare in CBS; only 13% of the patients recognised the figures as acquaintances or deceased. Certainly this does not exclude a connection of the other hallucinations with unconscious memories.

As regards the changes of the phenomena over time, the visual hallucinations mostly appear scenically moving; typical are motions *en bloc*, with the figures gliding through the room without internal change. Sometimes the same phantoms follow each other repeatedly, giving the impression of filing soldiers. In the same way, the musical hallucinations are characterised by monotonous repetitions of refrains like haunting tunes or by uniform rhythms. Hence, in both syndromes the phenomena are of a rather mechanical, stereotyped character and lack real spontaneity.

In some of the patients this is compensated by the ability to modify the hallucinations voluntarily: movements like pushing, blowing, turning the eyes, closing the lids, and in two cases even conscious thinking, e.g. 'orders', make the figures in CBS move, shrink, or vanish; still more frequently, patients with musical hallucinations succeed in sounding a melody by just imagining it.

Insight into the unreality of the hallucinations is the rule in both syndromes, and therefore was sometimes included in their definitions (e.g. Damas-Mora, 1982; Gold & Rabins, 1989). But mostly this correct judgement is only achieved after initial deception in a process of reality testing, perplexity and search for possible causes, not infrequently even only after information given by the examining physician. Understandably, insight is often accompanied by a certain uneasiness and fear of mental illness; whereas the visions or melodies as such are experienced predominantly as positive, i.e. amusing or fascinating. However, the constant repetition of the musical hallucinations sooner or later may lead to feelings of annoyance, helplessness or depression; in a quarter of patients with CBS the imagery arouses anger, anxiety or even mild paranoid reactions.

Pathogenesis

So far the comparison has shown a substantial similarity between CBS and MH in many respects. Clear differences were only found in the mode of appearance (more continuous in MH, more paroxysmal in CBS) and in their relationship to conscious memory (familiar melodies in MH, more unknown images in CBS). Yet only a similar pathogenesis could complete the analogy between the two syndromes. Little, however, can be said with certainty about their origin. The possibility remains to apply to both syndromes the theories and models which have been previously advanced as explanations.

The 'perceptual-release' theory

The pathogenetic role of the sensory impairment is mostly interpreted in terms of the 'perceptual-release' theory put forward by West (1962) and Cogan (1973). The continuous input of sensory stimuli is thought to inhibit the memory traces stored in neuronal circuits, always ready for reactivation. If this input is reduced below a certain threshold level, with sufficient cortical arousal and hence consciousness preserved at the same time, this results in a disinhibition, release and conscious perception of those engrams. This theory is supported by the experiments with sensory deprivation during which healthy persons experience visual and, although more rarely, musical hallucinations (Freedman *et al*, 1961; West, 1962; Zubek, 1969). The occurrence of 'memory hallucinations' in most cases of MH and some of CBS also points to the applicability of the model. Moreover, it allows an explanation of the therapeutic effect of operations restoring vision or hearing ability.

Cerebral dysfunction

Considering, however, the evident frequency of sensory impairment in later life, the model of deafferentation alone seems insufficient to account for the scarcity of hallucinations in mentally sane elderly persons. Also the fact that both syndromes are almost specific to old age points to local or generalised cerebral dysfunctions as the basis for a disinhibition in normal wakefulness. Thus, electroencephalogram (EEG)-examinations showed local or diffuse dysrhythmias in four out of 15 cases of CBS, and in four out of nine cases of MH (Miller & Crosby 1978; Hammeke *et al*, 1983, cases 1 & 2; Olbrich, 1987, cases 1–4; Wagner & Gertz, 1991, case 1) (see Table 14.3). Many reports of both syndromes provide clues as to disturbances of brain perfusion in the patients (Dejean, 1939; Sizaret *et al*, 1971; Olbrich, 1987; Podoll *et al*, 1989; Fuchs, 1990; Wagner & Gertz, 1991). Furthermore, the most frequent underlying diseases of the sensory organs, namely senile cataract and presbyacusis, are related to impaired micro- and macrocirculation (Böhme, 1989). As manifest central lesions are eliminated by definition, several CT-Scans showed at most mild atrophy (Table 14.3). Nevertheless, local metabolic dysfunction without detectable structural correlates might

TABLE 14.3
Technical findings in Charles Bonnet syndrome and musical hallucinosis

	CBS (n = 46): %	MH (n = 19): %
EEG		
abnormal	9	21
normal	24	26
no information	67	53
CT scan		
mild atrophy	4	25
normal	7	5
no information	69	69

still be present, for instance in the occipital or parieto-temporal cortex, leading to a dissociation of circuits in the association cortex. Also interesting in this context is the occurrence of both visual and musical hallucinations in vertebro-basilar insufficiency (Price *et al*, 1983) as well as in the so-called peduncular hallucinosis (L'Hermitte, 1922; Cambier *et al*, 1987). The close relationship of these disorders, especially to the CBS, suggests a diencephalic or thalamic dysfunction as another locus of aetiology in both CBS and MH.

A dysregulation of the sleep-wake-centre was discussed as a further pathogenetic mechanism in vertebro-basilar and peduncular hallucinosis: a dysfunction of the activating reticular formation would allow a breakthrough of dream elements into awareness (L'Hermitte, 1922; Scheibel & Scheibel, 1962; Caplan, 1980). Visual and auditory hallucinations in hypnagogic states are also relevant in this respect. Correspondingly, temporary disturbances of vigilance, as they are frequent in old age, also seem to play a role for the emergence of CBS: decreased alertness, retardation, reduced state of health or internal diseases were often described (Morax, 1922; Dejean, 1939; Sizaret *et al*, 1971; Olbrich, 1987; Podoll *et al*, 1989, 1990; Fuchs, 1990). The predominant appearance of the hallucinations in the evening or at night points to the same direction. Similar results were also obtained by sensory deprivation, research showing reduced vigilance to be favourable to the occurrence of hallucinatory experiences (Ziskind, 1964).

However, the picture of an episodically occurring, absence-like 'hallucinatory state' matches the CBS but not the musical hallucinations. Although they are modified by external stimuli and fade, for example, during vivid conversation, thus indicating an influence of alertness, the mostly continuous appearance of these hallucinations cannot be explained by fluctuations of vigilance. Here we are perhaps faced with an important pathogenetic difference between CBS and MH.

Personal quality

Release of memory traces as a result of sensory impairment in coincidence with a cerebral dysfunction – this could well be the common pathogenetic basis of CBS and MH. However, a third principle still seems to be missing in order to explain the fascinating vividness of the imagery or the familiarity of the melodies from childhood – in short: their personal quality. If both perception and reminiscence in themselves are processes of active construction and formation, then their combination in 'hallucinated recollections' of images and melodies must be more than just stored-up pieces of memory which are set free by leakage. According to Henry Ey (1972), normal perception is built up by a concurrence and amalgamation of 'centripetal' input on the one hand, and 'centrifugal', 'gestalt-forming' organisation on the other. In this way, incomplete sensory data are constantly supplemented and moulded into complete and meaningful entities. When the afferent input becomes increasingly blurred and outlines the 'gestalt' no more than roughly, the centrifugal activity is stimulated vicariously. This phenomenon also underlies the illusionary experiences of children in the darkness, and of some patients with CBS (Morax, 1922; Podoll *et al*, 1989; Fuchs, 1990; Wagner & Gertz, 1991). Another example is sensory deprivation, where hallucinations emerge in a 'white noise' or unpatterned sensory field, i.e. with monotonous or homogeneous rather than with missing stimuli (Ey, 1973).

Thus, the hallucinations in CBS and MH could be explained by a predominance of the centrifugal part of the perception process which becomes dissociated and independent from the input. The principle of disinhibition would have to be supplemented by the principle of elaboration and 'gestalt formation'. This is supported by the frequent transition from elementary to complex hallucinations, which occurs as a transformation and superposition of simple photisms or sounds. From rhythmic noises, first bird songs, then melodies, and finally singing may develop (Hécaen & Ropert, 1963). This progression is also found in sensory deprivation (Heron, 1961). The fragmentation of figures or melodies would then be equivalent to an incomplete elaboration of primary, rudimentary, or archetypal material.

This gradual 'gestalt formation' is apparently subjected to still other influences stemming from personal reminiscence, imagination and emotion. Musical hallucinations mostly originate from childhood or religious experiences and show a strong emotional emphasis or a dependency on affect (Ahlenstiel, 1963; Ross *et al*, 1975). Many cases of CBS are clearly associated with bereavement or social isolation (Alroe & McIntyre, 1983; Patel *et al*, 1987; Adair & Keshavan, 1988). The patients frequently have vivid imaginative faculties (Damas-Mora *et al*, 1982), in MH they are often musically talented (e.g. Ross *et al*, 1975; Jonas, 1986). Particularly in a sensitive and interested person, not sensory deprivation alone, but a more general loss of access to the world seems to facilitate the formation of a 'substitute world'. This personal world is furnished with fascinating images or familiar music.

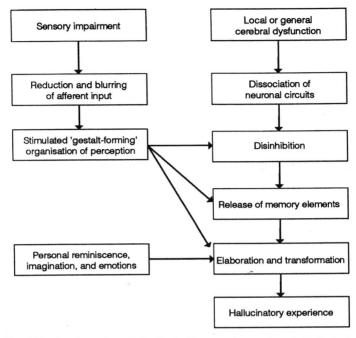

Fig. 14.1. A pathogenetic model for Charles Bonnet syndrome and musical hallucinosis

If we now try to integrate all these considerations and hypotheses into a speculative, but nevertheless plausible pathogenetic model, we arrive at a picture (Fig. 14.1): peripheral sensory impairment leads to constant reduction and blurring of afferent input. This in turn stimulates the centrifugal 'gestalt-forming' organisation of perception. In combination with local or general brain dysfunction and dissociation of neuronal circuits, this results in a disinhibition and release of stored-up visual or acoustic memory elements. Their dynamic elaboration and transformation into complex hallucinations is continuously influenced by personal reminiscence, imagination and emotion.

Regarding both syndromes, empirical evidence and theoretical considerations are compatible with this general model. An explanation is required, however, for their psychopathological differences. In any case, the pathogenetic model also points to a relationship of CBS and MH, so that, in conclusion, the analogy between the two syndromes is confirmed.

The principal common feature of these rare phenomena is that they bring into appearance something which normally remains latent and escapes conscious experience. It may well be that we are facing here, as it were, a form of the Platonic ideas and the Pythagorean harmony of spheres: a stream of archetypal images and sounds constantly flowing below the threshold of awareness, usually concealed by the sensations of the real world, and yet serving as a foil and measure for these sensations to be adjusted and organised into full perceptions.

References

ADAIR, D. & KESHAVAN, M. S. (1988) The Charles Bonnet syndrome and grief reaction. *American Journal of Psychiatry*, **145**, 895–896.

AHLENSTIEL, H. (1963) Den Sinnengedächtnis-Erscheinungen nahestehende, langdauernde akustische Halluzinationen. *Archiv für Psychiatrie und Zeitschrift für die gesamte Neurologie*, **204**, 86–95.

ALLEN, J. R. (1985) Salicylate-induced musical perceptions. *New England Journal of Medicine*, **313**, 642–643.

ALROE, C. J. & McINTYRE, J. N. M. (1983) Visual hallucinations – the Charles Bonnet syndrome and bereavement. *The Medical Journal of Australia*, **10/24**, 674–675.

BERRIOS, G. E. (1990) Musical hallucinations. A historical and clinical study. *British Journal of Psychiatry*, **156**, 188–194.

—— & BROOK, P. (1984) Visual hallucinations and sensory delusions in the elderly. *British Journal of Psychiatry*, **144**, 662–664.

BÖHME, G. (1989) Zerebrovaskuläre Erkrankungen und Hörfunktion. In *Sinnesorgane und zerebrovaskuläre Erkrankungen* (ed. G. Böhme), pp. 104–135. Stuttgart, New York: Thieme.

BURGERMEISTER, J. J., TISSOT, R. & DE AJURIAGUERRA, J. (1965) Les hallucinations visuelles des ophtalmopathes. *Neuropsychologia*, **3**, 9–38.

CAMBIER, J., DECROIX, J. P. & MASSIN, C. (1987) Hallucinose auditive dans les lésions du tronc cérébral. *Revue Neurologique*, **143**, 255–262.

CAPLAN, L. R. (1980) "Top of the basilar" syndrome. *Neurology*, **30**, 72–79.

COGAN, D. G. (1973) Visual hallucinations as release phenomena. *Albrecht von Graefes Archiv klinischer und experimenteller Ophtalmologie*, **188**, 139–150.

DAMAS-MORA, J., SKELTON-ROBINSON, M. & JENNER, F. A. (1982) The Charles Bonnet syndrome in perspective. *Psychological Medicine*, **12**, 251–261.

DAVID, M. M., HÉCAEN, H. & COULONJOU, R. (1944) Hallucinations auditives sans délire par affections neurologiques. *Annales Médico-Psychologiques*, **102**, 139–143.

DEJEAN, M. C. (1939) Les phantopsies de truc. Trois nouvelles observations. *Revue Otoneuroophtalmologique*, **17**, 248–253.

EY, H. (1973) *Traité des Hallucinations*. Paris: Masson et Cie.

FREEDMAN, S. J., GRUNEBAUM, H. U. & GREENBLATT, M. (1961) Perceptual and cognitive changes in sensory deprivation. In *Sensory Deprivation* (eds P. Solomon, P. H. Leiderman, P. E. Kubzansky, *et al*), pp. 58–71. Cambridge/Mass.: Harvard University Press.

FUCHS, T. (1990) Zur Psychopathologie und Pathogenese des Charles-Bonnet-Syndroms. *Fundamenta Psychiatrica*, **4**, 181–185.

GOLD, K. & RABINS, P. V. (1989) Isolated visual hallucinations and the Charles Bonnet syndrome: a review of the literature and presentation of six cases. *Comprehensive Psychiatry*, **30**, 90–98.

HAMMEKE, T. A., McQUILLEN, M. P. & COHEN, B. A. (1983) Musical hallucinations associated with acquired deafness. *Journal of Neurology, Neurosurgery, and Psychiatry*, **46**, 570–572.

HÉCAEN, M. & LE GUEN, C. (1960) Hallucinations visuelles chez un ophtalmopathe (syndrome de Charles Bonnet). *Annales Médico-Psychologiques*, **118**, 152–156.

HÉCAEN, H. & ROPERT, R. (1963) Les hallucinations auditives des otopathes. *Journal de Psychologie Normale et Pathologique*, **60**, 293–324.

HERON, W. (1961) Cognitive and physiological effects of perceptual isolation. In *Sensory Deprivation* (eds P. Solomon, P. H. Leiderman, P. E. Kubzansky, *et al*), pp. 6–33, Cambridge/Mass.: Harvard University Press.

JONAS, W.R. (1986) Akustische Halluzinose bei Schwerhörigkeit. *Nervenarzt*, **57**, 252–254.

KOLMEL, H. W. (1991) Visuelle Halluzinationen als neurologisches Symptom. In *Grenzgebiete zwischen Psychiatrie und Neurologie* (eds K. J. Neumärker, M. Seidel, D. Janz, *et al*), pp. 186–198. Berlin, Heidelberg: Springer.

L'HERMITTE, J. (1922) Syndrome de la calotte du pédoncule cérébral. Les troubles psycho-sensoriels dans les lésions du mésencéphale. *Revue Neurologique*, **38**, 1359–1365.

MILLER, T. C. & CROSBY, T. W. (1978) Musical hallucinations in a deaf elderly patient. *Annals of Neurology*, **5**, 301–302.

MORAX, V. (1922) Sur les hallucinations visuelles survenant au cours des altérations retiniennes. *Progrès Medical*, **50**, 652–654.

MORSIER, G. DE (1938) Les hallucinations, Étude oto-neuro-ophtalmologique. *Revue Otoneuroophtalmologique*, **16**, 244–352.

NORTON-WILLSON, L. & MUNIR, M. (1987) Visual perceptual disorders resembling the Charles Bonnet syndrome. A study of 434 consecutive patients referred to a psychogeriatric unit. *Family Practice*, **4**, 27–31.

OLBRICH, H. M. (1987) Optische Halluzinationen bei älteren Menschen mit Erkrankungen des Auges (Charles Bonnet-Syndrom). In *Halluzination und Wahn* (ed. H. M. Olbrich), pp. 34–41. Berlin, Heidelberg: Springer.

PATEL, H. C., KESHAVAN, M. S. & MARTIN, S. (1987) A case of Charles Bonnet syndrome with musical hallucinations. *Canadian Journal of Psychiatry*, **32**, 303–304.

PODOLL, K., OSTERHEIDER, M. & NOTH, J. (1989) Das Charles Bonnet-Syndrom. *Fortschritte der Neurologie und Psychiatrie*, **57**, 43–60.

——, SCHWARZ, M. & NOTH, J. (1990) Charles Bonnet-Syndrom bei einem Parkinson-Patienten mit beidseitigem Visusverlust. *Nervenarzt*, **61**, 52–56.

PRICE, J., WHITLOCK, F. A. & HALL, R. T. (1983) The psychiatry of vertebrobasilar insufficiency with the report of a case. *Psychiatria Clinica*, **16**, 26–44.

RAGHURAM, R., KESHAVAN, M. D. & CHANNABASAVANNA, S. M. (1980) Musical hallucinations in a deaf middle-aged patient. *Journal of Clinical Psychiatry*, **41**, 357.

ROSS, E. D., JOSSMAN, P. B., BELL, B., *et al* (1975) Musical hallucinations in deafness. *Journal of the American Medical Association*, **231**, 620–622.

ROZANSKI, J. & ROSEN, H. (1952) Musical hallucinosis in otosclerosis. *Confinia Neurologica*, **12**, 49–54.

SCHEIBEL, M. E. & SCHEIBEL, A. B. (1962) Hallucinations and the brain stem reticular core. In *Origin and Mechanism of Hallucinations* (ed. L. J. West), p. 66. New York: Plenum Press.

SIATKOWSKY, R. M., ZIMMER, B. & ROSENBERG, P. R. (1990) The Charles Bonnet syndrome. Visual perceptive dysfunction in sensory deprivation. *Journal of Clinical Neuro-Ophthalmology*, **103**, 215–218.

SIZARET, P., DEGIOVANNI, E., DEGIOVANNI, A., *et al* (1971) Un cas de syndrome de Charles-Bonnet. *Revue Otoneuroophtalmologique*, **43**, 117–121.

WAGNER, S. & GERTZ, H. J. (1991) Musikalische Halluzinationen bei Schwerhörigkeit-Fallbericht. *Zeitschrift für Gerontopsychologie und -psychiatrie*, **4**, 189–193.

WELLER, M. & WIEDEMANN, P. (1989) Visual hallucinations. An outline of etiological and pathogenetic concepts. *International Ophthalmology*, **13**, 193–199.

WEST, L. J. (1962) A general theory of hallucinations and dreams. In *Hallucinations* (ed. L. J. West), pp. 275–291. New York: Grune & Stratton.

ZISKIND, E. (1964) A second look at sensory deprivation. *Journal of Nervous and Mental Diseases*, **138**, 223–232.

ZUBEK, J. P. (1969) *Fifteen Years of Sensory Deprivation*. New York: Appleton Century Crofts.

III. Organic disorders

15 Some hypotheses about the genesis of visual hallucinations in dementias

JEAN WERTHEIMER

Hallucinations and illusions occur at the borderline between reality and unreality, in that place where the critical faculties mobilised by these phenomena either erect their defence and proclaim their worthlessness, or collapse and open the way to interpretation and flights of fancy. They emerge furthermore from an interstice between impaired perception and the imagination, or the imaginary, which will either be deluded or not, as the case may be. Perception and imagination are no longer bound up with one another, insofar as a potentially critical distance is created by the unusual nature of the message perceived.

Perception is the faculty of converting the world around us, as well as our own bodies, into a reality in our conscious mind. It involves the harmonious operation of the five senses – sight, hearing, touch, smell, and taste. Imagination, or the imaginary, is the realisation in the conscious mind of what is and has been perceived. To quote the French philosopher, Taine (1870), the mind is a "polypary of images". Indeed, through the mechanism of the memory, the immediate brings with it the evocation of what is associated with it by similitude or analogy. It involves not only what the senses enable us to perceive, but also what is produced by the embellishing process. Sartre (1940) said:

> "The imagination is not an empirical power superadded by our consciousness, it is our consciousness in the round, insofar as it makes real; any concrete and real situation of our consciousness in the world is pregnant with the imaginary, insofar as it always appears as a transcending of the bounds of reality".

The imaginary and reality

The imaginary is submitted, on the other hand, to the test of reality, to the monitoring of which it is submitted on several levels. The first is that of cognition, and more specifically, its principal functions – attention, judgement and comprehension. The second level is affectivity, whose individual fluctuations, especially those of mood and emotion, imprint the peculiar colourations of subjectivity on what is perceived. The functioning of the senses is the third main factor monitoring reality, and the fourth, vigilance, or a state of wakefulness. In contrast to the waking world, in which the imagination is held in check by a constant stream of concrete perceptional messages, in the dream-world, spontaneously produced images succeed one other in a loose process of association, the links in this association being principally of an affective order. Finally, the monitoring of reality hinges upon the structure of the personality, in so far as the latter establishes a permanent relational system with the world. Psychosis produces a profound disturbance of the victim's relationship with reality, a relationship becoming increasingly subjective and incommunicable. It is within the matrix represented by these five levels of the monitoring of reality, that, according to whether a sole or associated lapses are involved, hallucinatory phenomena and visual illusions will occur. In fact, old people are more prone to be disturbed in these different areas than the younger generations.

Normal visual illusions

To begin with, we should recall that normal perception can fall prey to visual illusions, illusions which moreover do not spare those who have perceptional impairments. It is, on the other hand, possible that certain of these physiological phenomena may combine, in certain circumstances, in a pathological perceptional world. This may be the case with hypnagogic visual manifestations at the moment of waking, and hypnopompic ones, when falling asleep. Thus, it happens that everyone sometimes has the fleeting impression that a person who has just appeared in a dream remains present for a few moments at their side. Such an experience, when it happens to an old person suffering from an incipient psycho-organic syndrome, may give rise to the conviction that someone really was there. The same thing perhaps applies with pareidolias, those flights of fancy whereby we discern people's faces or the heads of animals in motifs of wall-paper or curtains. Such illusions may lend credence to a mistaken conviction, during, for example, lowered vigilance in a delirium.

Sensory deafferentation certainly plays a fundamental role in the genesis of hallucination, in general, and more specifically in its visual form. Physiologically too, it is evident that it will not take long for any healthy subject to hallucinate, if placed in conditions of total isolation from sensory stimuli, for example, in total darkness in a soundproof tank. It is also well known that a subject suffering from blindness or deafness will hallucinate in his specific deprivation register, i.e. visually, in a blind subject, or aurally, in a deaf subject.

If it is unlikely that the optogeometric illusions deriving from the biophysical laws of perception could produce pathological perceptions, the same probably does not apply in the cases of phosphenes and post-images. It is indeed possible that into the sparkling of these rudimentary illusions which are phosphenes, and equally into the designs of residual images, representations of objects, individuals, flowers or animals may be grafted. We should bear in mind, moreover, that the normal ageing of the visual function is accompanied by a greater sensitivity to dazzle and a longer-lasting post-image. It is also accompanied by an attenuated perception of blues and reduced sensitivity to contrast. All these factors have to be taken into account, when endeavouring to understand the mechanisms from which hallucination and visual illusion derive.

Visual hallucinatory activity

Visual hallucinatory activity implies three orders of fundamental facts. Firstly, it involves a discordance between the real and what is consciously perceived. Next, it reveals a slackening of the visual sensory register, whereby random images interfere with objective ones. Lastly, it reveals a disorganisation in the articulation between the various sensory functions, the visual function featuring in the foreground, either alone or associated with other processes which customarily remain in the background.

Visual hallucination and illusion occur under three conditions. Firstly, the destructuring of the field of consciousness, consequent upon a lowering of the level of vigilance. This is what one observes in the confuso-oneiric state, or delirium, a common clinical picture in old age, originating in a cerebral metabolic disturbance as a result of a general ailment or, not infrequently, a medicinal intoxication. Hallucination combines with illusions, the visual register predominating, although not to an exclusive degree, and the patient often being the actor in an oneiric scene, in which visual, auditory, cenesthetic, olfactory and gustative manifestations are combined. This state is characterised by its intensity, its extrareality and its affective projection into imagery. Anguish may indeed be very pronounced, in tandem with a perplexity directly associated with the destructuring of the field of consciousness. Once beyond this stage, the sick person for most of the time retains a hazy, nightmarish memory of it. It sometimes happens, however, that he does not succeed in keeping a critical distance, and that he incorporates what he experienced during this period into an encysted delirious system, restricted to this sole psychopathological experience.

The second condition under which visual hallucinatory activity and, in particular, a disorganisation of the relational system with the world, occurs, is schizophrenia. We shall speak here, of noetico–affective hallucinations (Ey, 1973), this author giving his definition, as follows:

"hallucinations, which inextricably combine delusional illusions, interpretations and beliefs. They form an integral part of the ideo-verbal work of chronic delusions and constitute its production process, insofar as it is, at the same time, a discourse and a conviction which, referring to a system or representation of the purely subjective world, contravene the system of reality."

Finally, the last of the conditions in which visual hallucinations and illusions appear concerns peripheral and central lesions of the visual system, i.e. lesions of the cornea, lens, retina, optical nerve and central visual pathways and centres. Ey calls these manifestations, 'hallucinotic eidolias' (*eidolon* = image), thereby emphasising that they are non-delirious hallucinatory phenomena. The best known example is that of the Charles Bonnet syndrome. In 1760, Bonnet, a Genevan naturalist and philosopher, described in his *"Essai analytique sur les facultés de l'âme"*, the 'strange experiences' of his grandfather, Charles Lullin. This 89-year-old man presented with highly variegated 'visions' in the form of individuals, fantastic objects and animals, visions which he was able to judge sanely without taking them for realities. The name, 'Charles Bonnet syndrome', was thus given to a clinical picture consisting of visual hallucinatory episodes, rich, coloured, animated and silent, in which the sick person is a witness, both neutral and capable of criticising the event. This phenomenon would primarily ensue from an ophthalmopathy, according to certain authors; an ophthalmopathy associated with cerebral lesions, according to others (Burgermeister *et al*, 1965).

Phenomenology of hallucinatory activity in old people

Visual hallucinations and illusions in old people often occur in the evening, but may also appear during the day, frequently in half-light. The frequency of the episodes is variable, from one to several, occasional or regular, and liable to extend over several months. Their content is often peopled by menacing and impassive individuals, frequently truncated and moving in a straight line, regularly from one side of the field of vision to the other. The scene, in which the patient is the spectator, frequently has sexual overtones. It sometimes happens that the individuals inhabiting their hallucinations are identified with the deceased, such as a husband, or any member of the community of deceased relatives. Sometimes the patient is gratified to see kindly children, or irritated to see others who are unruly. It is not uncommon for him to see animals such as rats or insects. Certain of them claim that their apartment is overgrown with branches, logs, or pine needles. Others are prey to illusions rather than hallucinations, labouring, for example, under the misapprehension that the people appearing on the television screen are really present in their homes; others again holding conversations with portrait photographs cut out from newspapers, even to the point of putting food on the mouths of the individuals represented – a phenomenon which some authors have named 'picture sign' (Berrios & Brook, 1984). Illusion is also predominant in those patients who see human figures in shrubs or big cats in bushes, a phenomenon whose genesis is probably, in part, the same as that of the pareidolias.

Gradations of insight

Criticism of an abnormal nature of what is taking place varies according to the influence of various factors, particularly the degree of demential deterioration, an attenuation of vigilance, or the presence of a magical thought of a psychotic type. A gradation in the critical register can thus be described. The first degree is that of a recognition of the episode as something abnormal, characterising the classical Charles Bonnet syndrome. The second is characterised by a temporary ascendancy of the hallucination over the subject, who will temporarily consider what he experiences to be real. In this context, two eventualities may arise. One is fear and anguish, the other is the temporary adoption of a behaviour adapted to the fantasised situation, but not to reality. This is the case with those patients who prepare a meal for their 'visitors'. The third of these degrees is that of defensive behaviour of the persecutory kind, which will spill over from the limited period of the hallucinatory episode to intrude into his daily life. The patient will arm himself with a stick to chase off intruders and will work out strategies to prevent their approach. Finally, the first degree may develop into the third, and *vice versa*.

Causes and conditions of visual hallucinations

In the genesis of visual hallucinations and illusions in old people, it is difficult to distinguish between the triggering factors and conditions. One of the general constants of psychogeriatric problematics is indeed the polymorbidity combined in the same subject, somatic organic and often cerebral disorders with problems of a psychiatric, psychological or social order. Thus, each of the fields which will be briefly explored may, according to the context in which they interact, be triggering factors or conditions.

Impairment of visual function

Mention has already been made of the visual function impairments associated with age. The high incidence of ocular pathologies is another of the possible causes of perceptional disorders. Cataracts, indeed, make the perceived image hazy, and macular degenerescence is the cause of a central scotoma in the field of vision. It is an undeniable fact that ophthalmopathies clearly predominate among old people afflicted with visual hallucinations. In her study dealing with 18 cases, Brand (1986) found a proportion of 78% of cases, as against 41% in a control group. Let us remember that recent blindness can produce visual hallucinations, a phenomenon which Bartlett (1951) (referred to by Post, 1965) compares to the phantom limb of amputees.

Localised cerebral lesions

When one considers the question of a possible aetiological link between a localised cerebral lesion and hallucination, one should distinguish between what may be the aspecific manifestation of a diffuse encephalic suffering produced by the lesion, and what results from the defect or focused irritation. In the field of cerebral tumours, for example, Ey (1973) summarised various statistical studies comprising 1021 cases, in which the localised distribution of the 93 cases suffering visual hallucinations was as follows: 27 temporal tumours, 18 meso-diencephalic tumours, 15 occipital tumours, 14 frontal tumours, and eight subtentorial tumours.

When cerebrovascular accidents cause visual hallucinations, this is usually in the context of confuso-oneiric states. An exception to this rule is the peduncular hallucinosis that sometimes occurs with thalamic lesions (de Morsier, 1969), and those mentioned by Caplan (1980) with high rostral basilar infarcts.

Dementias

The reported incidence of visual hallucination in Alzheimer's disease has varied widely. For example Burns *et al* (1990) assess it at about 5%, while Teri *et al* (1989) talk of an incidence of 20–30%. No mention is made in the literature of a possible association of visual hallucinations with Balint syndrome. Beats (1989) poses the question, concerning a case of Alzheimer's disease which had started with nocturnal visual hallucinations, of a possible link between Charles Bonnet syndrome and a demential disorder. The answer is probably to be found in the concept of polymorbidity, the degree of criticism of the phenomenon depending then on the relative integrity of the cognitive function. This would explain the discrepancy between the case mentioned, which developed into Alzheimer's disease with hallucinatory episodes triggering a defence by it, and the cases cited by Damas-Mora *et al* (1982) who describe the Charles Bonnet syndrome as occurring in healthy subjects with the full clarity of consciousness, undeluded, at the cognitive level. Another hallucinatory source in the demented person is delirium, more common it seems in the form of a vesperal confusion, in the vascular type.

The presence of a psycho-organic syndrome was discovered in 83% of the cases in the study of Brand (1986), cited earlier. On the other hand, a dual ocular and psycho-organic pathology occurs in 61% of cases. It is possible that hallucinatory phenomena are the resultants of a matrix of circumstances in which perceptional disorder, critical faculty impairment, and attention and comprehension difficulties coalesce. Dementia further, perhaps, fosters hallucinations through the passivity it produces, the lack of initiative and thus reduced activity, causing a relative sensory deafferentation. Finally, perhaps, as Post (1965) infers, through a release of the higher integrating controls, it leads to an access to the consciousness of visual imagery in the form of hallucinations.

The affective state

The affective state also plays its role in the make-up of the visual hallucinatory state. In physiological mourning, it is not uncommon for the widower or widow to believe that they hear their departed loved-one climbing the stairs, see their silhouette stretched out on the bed, and hear them breathing. This, at the same time, manifests the hallucinatory realisation of the desire to rediscover the departed, and the fantasised ambiguity of the absent presence. It is conceivable that, through the psychological mechanisms previously described in the context of dementia, the imaginary nature of these physiological phenomena may not be realised, but may assume a clearer hallucinatory consistency. On the other hand, the depressive state in itself, accompanied by loneliness, provides a matrix conducive to the hatching of aggressive fantasies, which may take concrete form when the contextual circumstances are favourable, in the projection of hostile and persecutory imagery. Of the cases described by Brand (1986), 72% presented with depressive signs or suffered from loneliness. Another interesting fact revealed in this work was the high incidence (56%) of conflictual situations.

Conclusion

The genesis of visual hallucination in an old person is very complex. It develops in an overall context in which the sensory and cognitive functions, state of wakefulness, affectivity, environment and relational world are involved – this overall context, at a given time, forming a situation propitious to the psychopathological manifestation. The problem thus requires an approach which is not restricted to psychopathology, but which opens the way to an understanding of the situation in which this psychopathology occurred.

References

BARTLETT, J. E. A. (1951) Hallucinations in an old man with cataracts. *Brain*, **74**, 363.

BEATS, B. (1989) Visual hallucinations as the presenting symptom of dementia – a variant of the Charles Bonnet syndrome? *International Journal of Geriatric Psychiatry*, **4**, 197–201.

BERRIOS, G. E. & BROOK, P. (1984) Visual hallucinations and sensory delusions in the elderly. *British Journal of Psychiatry*, **144**, 662–664.

BONNET, C. (1760) *Essai Analytique sur les facultés de l'âme*. Copenhagen: C. & A. Philibert.

BRAND, U. (1986) *Les Hallucinations Visuelles chez la Personne Âgée*. Thèse. Lausanne: Université de Lausanne, Faculté de médecine.

BURGERMEISTER, J. J., TISSOT, R. & DE AJURIAGUERRA, J. (1965) Les hallucinations visuelles des ophtalmopathes. *Neuropsychologia*, **3**, 9–38.

BURNS, A., JACOBY, R. & LEVY, R. (1990) Psychiatric phenomena in Alzheimer's Disease II: disorder of perception. *British Journal of Psychiatry*, **157**, 76–81.

CAPLAN, L. R. (1980) "Top of the basilar" syndrome. *Neurology*, **30**, 72–79.

DAMAS-MORA, J., SKELTEN-ROBINSON, M. & JENNER, F. A. (1982) The Charles Bonnet syndrome in perspective. *Psychological Medicine*, **12**, 251–261.

DE MORSIER, G. (1969) Les hallucinations visuelles diencéphaliques. *Psychiatria Clinica*, **2**, 167–184, 232–251.

EY, H. (1973) *Traité des Hallucinations*. Paris: Masson.

POST, F. (1965) *The Clinical Psychiatry of Late Life*. Oxford: Pergamon Press.

SARTRE, J. P. (1940) *L'imaginaire*. Paris: Gallimard.

TAINE, H. (1870) *De l'Intelligence*. Paris: Hachette.

TERI, L., LARSON, E. B. & REIFLER, B. U. (1988) Behavioural disturbance in dementia of the Alzheimer type. *Journal of the American Geriatrics Society*, **36**, 1–6.

16 The French concept of delusions of passion

J. M. LÉGER and J. P. CLÉMENT

This chapter reviews the phenomenon of the 'phantom boarder'[1] in dementia, and examines the issues of erotomania and morbid jealousy as described in French literature. It discusses their role in the elderly and their connections with cognitive function.

Delusions of passion in the French literature

The ideas date from Pinel (1801) who distinguished 'partial delusions' from 'global forms of madness' and Esquirol (1838) who divided melancholia into lypemania and monomania (he already had distinguished 'erotic monomania' from 'nymphomania' and satyriasis). In the latter, intellect is unaffected and there is no evolutionary deficit. The operational concept of *délire chronique* (chronic delusional state) was introduced by Lasègue (1881), Falret (1879) and Foville (1872) who included the notion of progressive evolution. Magnan (1833) also described chronic delusional state with a systematic evolution to a dementia. Between 1880 and 1911, Kraepelin (1909) distinguished between dementia praecox, manic–depressive psychosis, paranoia (delusions with internal logic based on persecutory themes) and the paraphrenias, on evolutionary criteria. Bleuler (1911) introduced the group of schizophrenias but left no place for non-schizophrenic delusional psychoses.

The first essential work was that of Serieux & Capgras (1909) who between 1902 and 1909 wrote about the *folies raisonnantes* based exclusively on the mechanism of interpretation. This *délire d'interprétation* was differentiated from Ballet's *psychose hallucinatoire chronique* (1911), from Dupré's

---

1. The most common equivalent in the English-speaking literature has been used although the literal translation would be 'imaginary companion'.

délire d'imagination (1925) and from de Clérambault's *psychoses passionelles* with delusions of injury, jealousy, and erotomania (1942). The French point of view did not change. It continued to distinguish between schizophrenia and chronic delusional states, the latter being lasting delusional states evolving in clear consciousness in late middle life and having a chronic evolution with static periods and periods of reactivation and above all not leading to a schizophrenic defect.

Dating from the writing of Claude and Nodet (1932–1937) (Claude & Ey, 1932; Nodet, 1937) a distinction was made between delusions with a paranoiac structure, those with a paraphrenic structure, and those considered paranoid. Grouped among those with a paranoiac structure were chronic hallucinatory psychosis, paranoiac psychosis with delusions of interpretation, sensitive delusions of reference and delusions of passion. Among the latter, the most well known are morbid jealousy and erotomania.

These paranoiac delusional states correspond to the category of 'paranoid disorders' in DSM–III (American Psychiatric Association, 1980). In this work, interpretative states do not appear and only themes of persecution and of jealousy are mentioned. The revised version (DSM–III–R; American Psychiatric Association, 1987) no longer refers to paranoid disorders but to 'delusional disorder whose type is based on the predominant delusional theme'. Five types are described which are roughly equivalent to the *folies raisonnantes* of Serieux & Capgras (1909). The somatic types are reminiscent of Morel's *folie hypochondriaque* (1860), the persecutory type resembles that of Lasegue, the grandiose type is like that of Foville (1871), and finally the jealous type corresponds to Trelat's (1839) description and the erotomanic type to the enamoured persecutors described by Falret (1864) and Pottier (1886) before the emergence of de Clérambault's syndrome. It is to Gaëtan Gatien de Clérambault (and later to Langfeldt, 1961) that we owe the best description of erotomania. It is the delusional belief of being loved by a person (usually of higher social rank) which often evolves in three stages over many years: hope, disillusion, and resentment. It usually affects single women who are affectively and/or sexually frustrated, unlike morbid jealousy which more often affects males who often also suffer from alcoholism. The mean age for both erotomania and morbid jealousy is between 40 and 55, and they are both associated with serious marital and social disturbance. The concept of erotomania as a disease entity has been challenged largely by authors from English-speaking countries (Hollander & Callahan, 1975; Lehman, 1985; Ellis & Mellsop, 1985) but it appears to have been restored as an autonomous disorder in DSM–III–R.

Delusions in the elderly in the literature

We have outlined elsewhere the deficiencies of DSM–III and DSM–III–R in relation to mental pathology in the elderly (Léger & Clément, 1990).

Nevertheless, the subject has a long history. Dating from one of the first descriptions of senile dementia by Esquirol in 1838, several authors have shown an interest in the psychoses of old age (Wille, 1873; Maudsley, 1879); Pécharman (1883) asserted that all dementia was delusional and that isolated dementia was a fiction.

Ritti (1896) and Séglas (1888) pointed to the importance which they attached to visual hallucinations, erotic and somatic preoccupations in systematic persecutory delusional states in the elderly, and distinguished between senile persecutory ideas developing on the basis of dementia, and late-onset persecutory delusions independent of any dementia. Kraepelin (1910) gave a good description of presenile delusions of prejudice with ideas of jealousy expressed towards the spouse and senile delusions of persecution.

Pascal & Courbon (1906) pointed to the attentional difficulties and the slowing of association of ideas which led them to consider delusions of prejudice as attenuated and early forms of senile dementia, a point of view later expressed by Guiraud (1956). These authors also singled out involutional delusions of jealousy without constitutional jealousy. Kleist (1913) described involutional paranoia with ideas of prejudice, interpretative mechanisms and a state of mental viscosity.

Capgras *et al* (1933) described a form of senile psychosis with nihilistic delusions, systematic misrecognition and erotomania on the basis of a disorder of mood. Naudascher (1939) also distinguished involutional delusional psychosis from senile dementia with a delusional onset while underlining the frequency of transitional forms and the polymorphism of the symptoms. Dias Cordeiro (1972) took a phenomenological and psychodynamic approach to late-onset delusional states. Attempting a classification like that of Halberstadt (1934), he drew a distinction between delusions with or without associated psychic disturbance and those associated with sensory disorders. He introduced the frequently encountered theme highlighted by Dias Cordeiro (1972) who termed it *délire du compagnon tardif* ('phantom boarder syndrome'). He spoke of 'narcissistic reactive psychosis' in order to highlight the depressive position and modification of defence mechanisms linked to the narcissistic injury. The delusion would thus be seen as a partial success in the struggle against depression.

The pre-senile delusion of injury was taken up by Bieder & Leduc (1977) who stressed three points: the injury was an attenuated form of persecution, the elderly did not go in for interpretative elaboration, ideas of jealousy were common and important, so much so that certain senile delusions of jealousy might be considered as disguised forms of delusions of injury.

Finally, Leboucher & Le Goues (1982), from a psychodynamic point of view, consider late-onset delusions as more or less successful compromises at re-establishing the libidinal equilibrium (see also Chapter 5). The delusion is seen in the context of intellectual deficit and allows the subject to avoid facing his losses. It wards off depression by inventing a neoreality.

Delusions of passion in the elderly

In 'delusions of passion', de Clérambault described a state of general exaltation, a prevailing idea emerging from a fundamental postulate and developing segmentally. Leaving aside delirious states, delusions of passion in the strictest sense always consist of an unshakable ideoaffective component which upsets psychic life through disturbances of mood, depersonalisation and impulsive acts. Themes of love and hate are intermingled. In the two main forms, there is no alteration of consciousness but rather the elaboration of a neoreality. This is a particular modality of old people's being which gives an erroneous meaning to their existence.

According to Dias Cordeiro (1970), late-onset erotomania follows the main phases described earlier in life – hope, disillusionment, and resentment. However, these are not always obvious and are experienced with less intensity and less protest. Erotomania appears as an attempt to restore and revalue the body. By his delusional belief of being loved, the elderly person tries to deny his physical deficiency.

The 'involutional form of morbid jealousy' (Guiraud's term) is an interpretative delusion of late onset and is often absurd. It is a jealousy which extends with accusations which are not limited to the credible or possible. The spouse may be accused of entertaining unceasing physical relations with neighbours both male and female and even with children or grandchildren.

In morbid jealousy, suspicion arises from a trifle (a smile, a handshake), or from a false postulate (being cuckolded). The coincidental occurrences are seen as proofs which then lead to interrogations and searches.

In relation to these two entities, we must consider the different contexts in which they may occur (a) affective disturbance, (b) evolving dementia, (c) sensory deficiency and deafferentation, (d) a feeling of loss. In depression, we know that there is a significant correlation between the presence of delusions and the first onset of a depressive episode after 60 or later (Meyers & Greenberg, 1986). The prevalence of delusions is high (40% in Post (1982) and 56% in Meyers *et al* (1984, 1985)). More often these are expressed through themes of hypochondria or injury.

Regarding dementia, Kahlbaum (1863), in his description of 'presbyophrenia', involving confabulation, false recognition and memory impairment, showed that delusional ideas were common, and this was confirmed by Berrios & Brook (1985). The most common delusions are of theft (Merriam *et al*, 1988), that one's home is not one's home, of abandonment or suspiciousness (Reisberg *et al*, 1987), and of unfaithfulness (Burns *et al*, 1990). We also need to include the misidentification syndromes taken up by Rubins *et al* (1988), 'people living in the house, misidentification of mirror images, of people on television and of relatives' (Burns *et al*, 1990). The latter are facilitated by the presence of sensory impairment but these do not appear to be prominent causes of delusions of passion.

As for situations of loss marked by loneliness, isolation and communication difficulties, these favour the development of delusional states sometimes with vivid hallucinations and persecutory interpretations.

Proposals

From the historical point of view, there are obvious differences of opinion about the place of these two entities within systems of classification and about their individual nosological status. It seems worthwhile to look at the problem across nosological groups. Erotomania and morbid jealousy appear to be relatively rare in old age, particularly within the framework of dementia. At most, certain traits and symptoms of jealousy may occur in the context of sensibility particularly with a background of marital disharmony where conjugal life has consisted of an uneasy compromise. Ageing may highlight underlying tensions as well as favouring physical disability. Cessation of sexual relations may lead to the expression of passion in other forms. One may consider that these symptoms are active adaptational responses rather than being purely passive deficiences. As far as erotomania is concerned, this is most often seen in old women with hysterical personalities tormented by 'matters of the flesh'. In the elderly with progressive intellectual impairment, these delusions must be seen as compensatory reactions at the beginning of the illness. In this transnosographic approach, taking account of affective and evolutional factors, we would like to suggest the following theoretical speculation: during the progression of dementia the emergence of delusions may be facilitated by affective features, sensory disturbance, isolation and conflict but also by the fragmentation of thought in the dement (Péruchon & Le Goues, 1991). The following sequence may occur: suspicion and mistrust may lead to morbid jealousy, then to misidentification of the spouse, and finally to the phantom boarder syndrome (and possibly later to hallucinations). The phantom boarder percept may be transferred on to a person, on to the subject's own mirror image or on to an intimate object. This may be followed by motor stereotypies and finally by death. There develops a relationship with an object which becomes more and more narcissistic and acts as a focus for the projection of libidinous and aggressive impulses of a very ambivalent nature. We have observed many patients who developed morbid jealousy during adult life but lost the delusions at the onset of a dementing illness. Equally erotomania may, during the course of a dementia, give way to isolation and anxiety with failure of recognition of the spouse and be followed by the 'phantom boarder syndrome'. The object of looking at the problem in this way allows us to examine the relationship between delusions and dementia which is the topic of this section.

The organic state which we should attempt to specify cannot in itself explain these forms of delusions but left to itself will develop relentlessly and may sometimes be accompanied by delusions which can result in two outcomes.

(a) The delusions may lead to abnormal behaviour which is damaging both to the patient and to his environment.

(b) The delusions may be seen as expressions of the patient's thought processes and as a defence against anxiety and a mechanism of narcissistic reinforcement. The first leads to medico-social intervention and an understanding of the underlying abnormal behaviour. The second may be more constructive and at any rate may lead to a better understanding of the form and content of the delusions and perhaps to a prediction of the course which the dementia may take.

References

AMERICAN PSYCHIATRIC ASSOCIATION (1980) *Diagnostic and Statistical Manual of Mental Disorders* (3rd edn) (DSM-III). Washington, DC: APA.
—— (1987) *Diagnostic and Statistical Manual of Mental Disorders* (3rd edn, revised) (DSM-III-R). Washington, DC: APA.
BALLET, G. (1912) La psychose hallucinatoire chronique. *L'Encéphale*, **2**, 401-411.
BERRIOS, G. E. & BROOK, P. (1985) Delusions and the psychopathology of the elderly with dementia. *Acta Psychiatrica Scandinavica*, **72**, 296-301.
BIEDER, J. & LEDUC, E. (1977) Le délire (pré) sénile de préjudice. *Annales Médico-Psychologiques*, **135**, 516-521.
BLEULER, E. (1911) Dementia Praecox oder Gruppe der Schizophrenien. In *Traité d'Aschaffenburg: Handbuch der Psychiatrie*. Liepzig und Wien: Franz Deuticke.
BURNS, A., JACOBY, R. & LEVY, R. (1990) Psychiatric phenomena in Alzheimer's disease. Disorders of thought content. *British Journal of Psychiatry*, **157**, 72-76.
CAPGRAS, JOAKI & ELLENBERGER (1933) Psychose présénile. Négations systématiques et érotomanie. *Annales Médico-Psychologiques*, **2**, 209-224.
CLAUDE, H. & EY, H. (1932) Hallucinose et hallucinations. *L'Encéphale*, **11**, 576-621.
DE CLERAMBAULT, G. (1942) *Oeuvres Psychiatriques*. Paris: P.U.F. Ed.
DIAS CORDEIRO, J. (1970) Les états délirants de préjudice. *Annales Médico-Psychologiques*, **128**, 719-734.
—— (1972) *Les États Délirants Tardifs, Approche Phénoménologique et Psycho-dynamique*. Thèse, Genève: No. 3270.
DUPRE, E. (1925) *Les Psychose Imaginatives Aiguës, Pathologie Mentale de l'imagination et de L'émotion*. Paris: Payot.
ELLIS, P. & MELLSOP, G. (1985) De Clérambault's syndrome. A nosological entity ? *British Journal of Psychiatry*, **146**, 90-95.
ESQUIROL, E. (1838) *Traité des Maladies Mentales*. Paris: Baillière.
FALRET, J. P. (1864) *Des Maladies Mentales et des Asiles D'aliénés*. Paris: Baillière.
—— (1879) La folie circulaire ou folie à formes alternes. In *Etudes Cliniques*, pp. 584-620. Paris: J. B. Baillière.
FOVILLE, A. (1871) *Etude Clinique de la Folie avec Prédominance du Délire des Grandeurs*. Paris: Baillière
—— (1872) Folie à double forme. *Nouveau Dictionnaire de Médecine et de Chirurgie Pratiques* (ed. Jaccoud), **15**, 321-331.
GUIRAUD, P. (1956) *Psychiatrie Clinique* (3ème edit.). Paris: Librairie Le Francais.
HALBERSTADT, G. (1934) Les psychoses préséniles. *Encéphale*, **XXIX**, 630-644, 722-737.
HOLLANDER, M. H. & CALLAHAN, A. S. (1975) Erotomania or de Clérambault's syndrome. *Archives of General Psychiatry*, **32**, 1574-1576.

KAHLBAUM, K. (1863) *Die Gruppirung der psychichen Krankheiten*. Berlin: Kafemann.
KLEIST, K. (1913) Die Involutions Paranoïa. *Allgemeine Zeitschrift fur Psychiatrie*, **70**, 1–134.
KRAEPELIN, E. (1909) *Psychiatrie*, 8ème édit, vol. 4. Leipzig: Johann Ambrosius, Barth.
—— (1910) *Ein lehrbuch für studerende und Artze*, 8th edition. Leipzig: Johann Ambrosius Barth.
LANGFELDT, G. (1961) The erotic jealousy syndrome. A clinical study. *Acta Psychiatrica et Neurologica Scandinavica*, suppl. 151.
LASEGUE, C. (1881) De l'évolution des délires de persécution. *Annales Médico-Psychologiques*, **39**, 272–277.
LEBOUCHER, H. & LE GOUES, G. (1982) Valeur économique des états délirants tardifs. *Actualités Psychiatriques*, Special psychogeriatrics supplement, **6**, 67–72.
LÉGER, J. M., GAROUX, R., TESSIER, J. F., *et al* (1986) Le compagnon tardif et l'objet non animé du sujet dément sénile. Essai de compréhension par une étude comparative avec des phénomènes rencontrés au cours de l'enfance. *Annales Médico-Psychologiques*, **144**, 341–355.
——, CLEMENT J. P. & TESSIER, J. F. (1989) Y a-t-il une spécificité des délires de l'âgé? *Rapport du Congrès de Psychiatrie et de Neurologie de Langue Française, Montréal 1989*, Paris: Masson.
—— & —— (1990) DSM–III, DSM–III–R et pathologie mentale du sujet âgé. Intérêts et limites. *Psychological Medicine*, **22**, 617–624.
LE GOUES, G. (1989) L'expérience du discontinu. *Annales de Psychiatrie*, **4**, 31–35.
MAGNAN, V. (1833) *Leçons Cliniques sur les Maladies Mentales*. Paris: Baillière.
MAUDSLEY, H. (1879) *The Pathology of Mind*. London: MacMillan.
MERRIAM, A. E., ARONSON, M. R., GASTON, P., *et al* (1988) The psychiatric symptoms of Alzheimer's disease. *Journal of the American Geriatrics Society*, **36**, 7–12.
MEYERS, B. S., GREENBERG, R. & MEI TAL, V. (1984) Late onset delusional depression. A distinct clinical entity ? *Journal of Clinical Psychiatry*, **45**, 347–349.
——, —— & —— (1985) Delusional depression in the elderly. In *Treatment of Affective Disorders in the Elderly* (ed. C. A. Shamoion), pp. 19–28. Washington, DC: American Psychiatric Press.
—— & —— (1986) Late life delusional depression. *Journal of Affective Disorders*, **11**, 133–137.
MOREL, B. A. (1860) *Traité des Maladies Mentales*. Paris: Masson.
NAUDASCHER, J. (1939) *Les Psychoses Délirantes D'involution*. Thèse, Paris, Jouve et Cie.
NODET, C. (1937) *La Groupe des Psychoses Hallucinatoires Chroniques*. Paris: G. Doin et cie, ed.
PASCAL, C. & COURBON, P. (1906) Les délires des préjudices séniles. *L'Encéphale*, **6**, 573–578.
PECHARMAN, A. (1883) *Essai sur les Psychoses de la Vieillesse*. Paris: Thèse.
PERUCHON, M. & LE GOUES, G. (1991) Les processus de pensée dans la maladie d'Alzheimer. Approche psychoanalytique. *Bulletin de Psychologie*, Tome XLIV, **398**, 11–14.
PINEL, P. (1801) *Traité Médico-Philosophique sur L'aliénation Mentale ou la Manie*. Paris: 2e edition (1809). Paris: Brosson.
POST, F. (1982) Affective disorders in old age. In *Handbook of Affective Disorders* (ed. E. Paykel), pp. 393–402. New York: Guilford Press.
POTTIER, P. (1886) *Etude sur les Aliénés Persécuteurs*. Paris: Ghesse.
REISBERG, B., BORENSTEIN, J., SALOB, S. P., *et al* (1987) Behavioral symptoms in Alzheimer's disease. Phenomenology and treatment. *Journal of Clinical Psychiatry*, **48** (suppl. 5), 9–15.
RITTI, A. (1896) Les psychoses de la vieillesse. In *Rapport au Congrès des Médecins Aliénistes et Neurologistes de Langue Française*, Bordeaux, pp. 3–48. Paris: Masson.
RUBINS, E., DREVETS, W. & BURKE, A. (1988) The nature of psychotic symptoms in senile dementia of the Alzheimer type. *Journal of Geriatric Psychiatry and Neurology*, **1**, 16–20.
SEGLAS J. (1888) Les psychoses séniles tardives. *Le Progrès Médical*, **VIII**, 43, 289–292.
SERIEUX, P. & CAPGRAS, J. (1909) *Les Folies Raisonnantes. Le Delire d'Interprétation*. Paris: Alcan.
TRELAT, U. (1838) *Recherches historiques sur la folie*. Paris: Baillière.
WILLE, L. (1873) Die psychosen des griesenalters. *Allgemeine Zeitschrift fur Psychiatrie*, **XXX**, 269–294.

17 Deceptions and delusions in Alzheimer's disease and frontal lobe dementia

LARS GUSTAFSON and JARL RISBERG

Patients with dementing diseases display a great variety of clinical manifestations related to the brain damage but also influenced by other factors such as the patient's previous personality, environmental factors, and the presence of other diseases and sensory impairments. Sensory deceptions, divided into hallucinations and illusions, and delusions, have been described in all types of dementia, although the reported frequencies vary markedly between different studies. There are several possible explanations for these discrepancies, such as differences between the patient samples in age, type and severity of dementia, and differences in the clinical assessment. The sources of information, with a distinction between observed and reported symptoms, are of vital importance. The clinical evaluation, which is influenced by the patient's degree of dementia, has to rely on a standardised assessment of a wide range of psychopathology. Amnesia, confabulation, dysphasia and emotional changes may easily lead to misunderstanding and underestimation of other symptoms. Symptoms such as hallucinations and illusions, which often appear in combination, may be difficult to recognise without a close examination of a certain duration.

In our prospective dementia study, several hundred cases have accumulated which have been studied from a clinical, neurophysiological and neuropathological point of view. This paper will mainly deal with clinical and neurophysiological findings in two types of primary degenerative dementia: dementia of Alzheimer type (DAT) and dementia with frontotemporal cortical degeneration (FTD). The latter group contains patients with Pick's disease, but the majority of cases in our catchment area suffer from frontal lobe dementia of non-Alzheimer type (FLD). This disease has been described by our group in Lund (Brun, 1987; Gustafson, 1987; Risberg, 1987; Englund & Brun, 1987; Johanson & Hagberg, 1989; Gustafson et al, 1990a) and by Neary and his colleagues in Manchester (Neary et al, 1988, 1990). About 50% of early as well as late-onset dementia was accounted for by DAT, and FLD and Pick's disease accounted for about

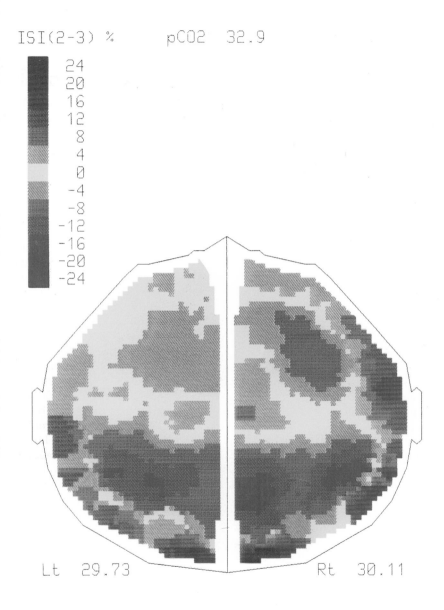

ISI(2-3) %   pCO2 32.9

24
20
16
12
8
4
0
-4
-8
-12
-16
-20
-24

Lt 29.73   Rt 30.11

Plate I. Cortical blood flow as measured with the xenon-133 inhalation method and a high resolution recording equipment (254 detector Cortexplorer equipment; Scan. Detectronic, Inc., Hadsund, Denmark) in a patient with DAT and Lilliputian hallucinations. The mean hemispheric flow levels (ISI-units) are shown in the lower part of the figure. The vertex projection shows all parts of the cortical mantel with a colour coding with the global mean flow level as reference. Orange and red shades indicate a regional value above the mean flow level as reference while green colours show values lower than the average

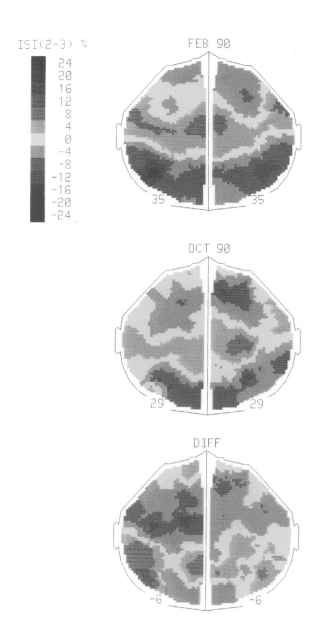

Plate II. Repeated high-resolution rCBF results in a patient with DAT and Lilliputian hallucinations. Symbols in the two upper flow maps as in Plate I. The lower 'DIFF' map shows the difference between the two flow distributions with the absolute differences between the hemispheric mean flows shown in the lower part of the map

ISI(2-3) %

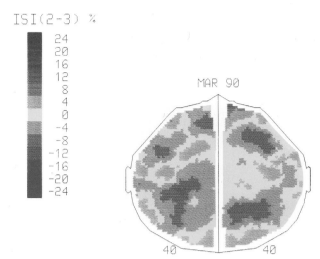

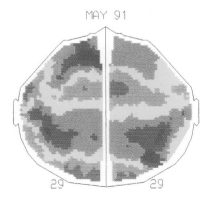

Plate III. Repeated high-resolution rCBF results in a patient with frontal lobe dementia and visual hallucinations. Symbols as in Plate I

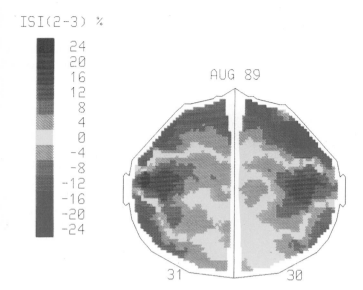

ISI(2-3) %

24
20
16
12
8
4
0
-4
-8
-12
-16
-20
-24

AUG 89

31   30

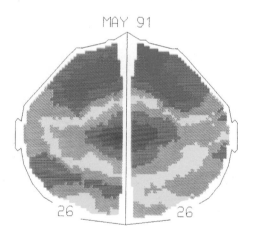

MAY 91

26   26

Plate IV. Repeated high-resolution rCBF results in a patient with frontal lobe dementia and hypochondriacal delusions. Symbols as in Plate I

12% of our patient material dominated by early-onset cases. Pick's disease and FLD were, however, extremely rare among late-onset dementias. Vascular dementia (VD) of multi-infarct type or Binswanger type was diagnosed in about 20% of deceased cases. Mixed VD and DAT was found in 10% of early-onset and 25% of late-onset dementia (Brun & Gustafson, 1988; Brun *et al*, 1991).

The factor-analytic approach to psychopathology offers the possibility to study not only a single symptom but also symptom constellations in different patient samples. In 1975, we published a factor analysis of symptoms rated in patients with different types of presenile dementia. No less than 14 symptom clusters – factors – were obtained (Gustafson & Hagberg, 1975) describing different cognitive, emotional and conative aspects of dementia. The patients' factor scores were used to calculate correlations between factors and regional cerebral blood flow (rCBF) measured in eight regions of the left hemisphere. The Xe clearance technique using arterial injection of the tracer was used to measure rCBF (Ingvar & Gustafson, 1970). All 14 symptom clusters showed significant and meaningful correlations to rCBF (Gustafson & Risberg, 1974). The amnesia–apraxia factor containing symptoms of pronounced mental deterioration such as amnesia, sensory aphasia, spatial disorientation and apraxia showed the largest negative correlations to rCBF and relative weight of grey matter in the temporoparietal association cortex. Symptoms of paranoia, which were found in patients on all levels of cognitive deterioration, showed significant positive correlations to grey matter flow in all cortical regions of the left hemisphere, except the posterior temporal region. Thus paranoid symptoms in presenile dementia of different severity appeared to require a relatively high functional activity of the grey matter especially frontally. The paranoid symptoms were looked upon as an effort to compensate for the failure of essential intellectual functions located in the posterior cortical regions, parallel to the relationship between paranoid reactions and hearing loss and other sensory deficits (Post, 1966). The conclusion is supported by computerised tomography (CT) findings by Jacoby & Levy (1980) that delusions in patients with dementia seem to require a relatively intact cerebral cortex. By contrast, depressive symptoms showed significant ($P < 0.001$) positive correlations to the cognitive functional level, and significant positive correlations to grey matter flow in the post-rolandic regions.

The prevalence of psychotic symptoms in demented patients depends to a large extent upon the selection criteria of the patient sample. We have studied frequency and type of illusions, hallucinations and delusions in 65 consecutive patients with dementia in our psychogeriatric day-care unit. The patients suffered from dementia or other organic brain disease, but they were still capable of living at home, alone or with a relative.

All 65 patients were diagnosed clinically, based on a thorough neuro-psychiatric examination including rCBF measurement, electroencephalogram

H

TABLE 17.1
Psychopathology in patients with dementia (n = 65) in psychogeriatric day care unit

Symptoms	Clinical diagnosis				
	DAT[1] (n = 21)	DAT + VD[2] (n = 11)	VD (n = 26)	FTD[3] (n = 2)	Other (n = 5)
Visual deceptions					
people		1	2		
Lilliputian	1	1			
animal	2				
objects			2		
television	1				
Auditory deceptions	1	1			
Delusions					
paranoid	4	4	4	1	
other	1	1	1		1
Prosopagnosia					
close relatives	5	4	3		
own face (mirror)	1				
Disinhibition					
aggressiveness	1	1	6	1	
fantastic confabulation		2	1	1	
Patients affected total	9	7	12	2	1

1. DAT = Dementia of Alzheimer type.
2. VD = Vascular dementia.
3. FTD = Frontotemporal degenerative dementia.

(EEG) and CT scan. The non-traumatic Xe inhalation technique was used for rCBF measurement (Risberg *et al*, 1990). There were 21 cases with DAT, 26 with VD, 11 with mixed DAT and VD, two cases with FTD and five patients with other diagnoses. The clinical information was obtained from the staff and collateral sources such as relatives and home service. Table 17.1 presents part of the psychopathology in different diagnostic groups. Deceptions, delusions, severe visual dysgnosia and signs of disinhibition were by no means uncommon in these subjects, who lived independently.

One patient with DAT and one with mixed DAT and VD spontaneously reported Lilliputian hallucinations during daytime and without any signs of clouding of consciousness. They observed tiny, silent people, on several occasions appearing in identical or similar situations. The hallucinations were usually not very frightening, although sometimes described as irritating. The differentiation between hallucinations and illusions was a difficult task, since the deceptions often appeared in dark and shady places. Four patients with VD described visual hallucinations. Two of them observed people and two patients saw tools, which were of special interest to them. Paranoid reactions were recorded in four DAT cases, in two of these probably due to severe prosopagnosia with misidentification of people. One of these patients also had visual and auditory hallucinations, and the other experienced disturbing illusions when watching the television. He easily became involved in the actions on the TV screen. He became frightened and agitated when accidents or violence were shown. One DAT patient displayed a combination of prosopagnosia and the peculiar 'mirror sign' (Stengel & Vienna, 1943). He often stood perplexed and anxious looking at his own image in a mirror. He said that he saw a familiar face: "It might be my brother". The paranoid delusions in two of the DAT cases were not associated with any illusions or hallucinations. The 'picture sign' (Berrios & Brook, 1984) was not found in this patient sample.

Thus, sensory deceptions, delusions and certain other alarming symptoms were frequent among patients with dementia in a day care unit. The results are in agreement with the prevalence numbers reported by Rubin *et al* (1988) and Burns *et al* (1990) in similar patient cohorts. It is important to recognise these symptoms as early as possible and to offer treatment, explanations and support to the patients and their relatives. The majority of patients suffered from DAT, VD or the combination of them. The limited number of patients with pure frontal lobe dementia in the day care unit does not allow comparison between FTD and DAT in this material.

The high prevalence of FTD in a longitudinal study of dementia has, however, made it possible to compare FLD and Pick's disease on the one hand and DAT on the other. The distribution of cortical degeneration is almost contrary in these two types of dementia. The degeneration in DAT is accentuated in temporal limbic structures and the temporoparietal association cortex with a relative sparing of frontal cortex, especially in early onset DAT (Brun & Gustafson, 1976). The degeneration in FLD and Pick's disease involves predominantly frontal or frontotemporal areas and cingulate gyrus in its anterior parts, while post-central cortical regions are better preserved (Brun, 1987). The pathological changes in FLD are unspecific, with neuronal loss, slight gliosis and spongiosis but no or few plaques or tangles. A reliable clinical differentiation between DAT and FTD can be based on a systematic evaluation of the clinical features (Gustafson *et al*, 1990*b*), psychometric testing (Johanson & Hagberg, 1989; Johanson *et al*, 1990) and functional brain imaging such as rCBF (Gustafson & Risberg, 1979; Gustafson *et al*, 1985), single photon emission computerised tomography (SPECT; Beats *et al*, 1991), and positron emission tomography (PET; Chase *et al*, 1987). EEG (Johannesson *et al*, 1977), CT, magnetic resonance imaging (MRI) and cerebrospinal fluid analysis (Minthon *et al*, 1990) may strongly contribute to the differential diagnosis.

The clinical features in AD and FTD and the differential diagnosis between the two types of dementia have been analysed elsewhere (Gustafson, 1987). Table 17.2 shows age at onset and duration of symptoms of dementia, and complementary information concerning hallucinations and delusions in three

TABLE 17.2

Clinical findings in presenile Alzheimer's disease (AD), senile dementia of Alzheimer type (SDAT), and frontotemporal degenerative dementia (FTD)

	AD (n = 21)	SDAT (n = 20)	FTD (n = 20)
Age at onset: years (mean (s.d.))	57(5)	76(6)	55(2)
Duration (onset to death): years (mean (s.d.))	11(3)	6(3)	9(4)
Hallucinations/illusions	5	9	2
Paranoid delusions	4	5	4
Confabulation	5	10	4
Vocally disruptive	10	2	0
Pain	2	?	5

? = insufficient information

groups of patients with post-mortem verified diagnoses. There were 21 cases of presenile AD, 20 cases with SDAT and 20 with FTD. The latter group contained 16 patients with FLD and four with Pick's disease. Hallucinations and delusions were reported in about 25% of FTD cases and early-onset DAT cases and in 50% of the late-onset DAT group. The clinical distinction between hallucinations and illusions was sometimes difficult and the two phenomena often alternated. There was no strong connection between hallucinatory experience and paranoia in presenile AD. The delusions seemed more strongly related to the cognitive impairment with memory failure, disorientation and prosopagnosia. Hallucinations and illusions in SDAT were more often associated with fluctuations of the clinical state and confusional episodes. The symptoms seemed precipitated by changes of the patient's somatic condition, and medication and by environmental factors. Moreover paranoid reactions in late onset DAT seemed more directly coupled to the hallucinatory experience. Insight into the clinical condition in general was however relatively preserved in DAT, even in patients with suspiciousness and paranoid ideas. The deceptions and delusions in DAT were often influenced by the patient's feelings of insecurity, anxiety and depression and therefore possible to ameliorate with psychological techniques.

Six out of the 20 patients with FLD and Pick's disease had psychotic episodes: in three cases an aggressive paranoid reaction, in two cases delusions of hypochondriacal type and in one case a paranoid, hallucinatory state. One psychotic case and two others manifested severe acts of easily provoked violence. Compulsive behaviour of psychotic dimension was observed in four cases. Thus, psychotic symptoms were not only common but also showed a high variability in patients with frontotemporal degeneration. The combination with other frontal lobe traits such as lack of insight, disinhibition, restlessness and mental rigidity made it difficult to handle these patients with psychological techniques. A possible reason for underestimation of psychotic symptoms in the FTD group is the communication difficulties due to deterioration of language and the emotional changes. The premorbid personality remains, however, a pathoplastic factor in the FTD group, contributing to the variability of psychotic symptoms with similarity to functional psychoses.

Generalised hyperalgesia has been reported in patients with Pick's disease with post-mortem verified diagnosis (Robertson *et al*, 1958). Sensory distortion, especially hyperaesthesia, was reported in five cases in the FTD group and in two presenile AD cases. The pain was more intense in the FTD group and in two cases coupled to bizarre hypochondriasis. The information concerning pain was rather inconsistent and difficult to evaluate in the SDAT group, partly due to presence of other possible explanations such as somatic disorders.

Thus, both hallucinations and delusions are prevalent in primary degenerative dementia and will probably be reported in a majority of cases, when followed closely from the early stage of the disease. The clinical analysis has to consider the complex interaction between symptoms and behaviour changes which are more directly determined by the brain damage and secondary reactions reflecting the patient's experience of, and reactions to, the consequences of the cerebral disorder. The first reported case of AD (Alzheimer, 1907) showed delusions of jealousy as an early symptom and auditory hallucinations later in the course. Psychotic symptoms in DAT have been described in a large series of post-mortem verified cases (Lauter, 1970) and delusions appearing in Pick's disease have been reviewed by van Mansvelt (1954). Eiden & Lechner (1950) pointed out the high prevalence of psychotic reactions in the early stages of AD and Pick's disease. Few studies, however, have compared deceptions and delusions in DAT and frontal lobe dementia in a wider sense. Our impression is that psychotic symptoms in early-onset DAT seem strongly related to the general cognitive failure with dysmnesia and visuospatial dysfunction in these patients. The delusions in the late-onset DAT, with a less focal temporoparietal symptom pattern, are more related to sensory deceptions and confusional traits. Delusions in DAT are, however, strongly influenced by the patient's emotional state and therefore accessible to psychological as well as pharmacological treatment.

The central psychopathology, the core syndrome, in both FLD and Pick's disease, is progressive personality change with early signs of disinhibition and loss of insight into the illness. Delusions and perceptual disturbances may also appear, with a great variability of these symptoms. The psychotic traits easily give the impression of functional psychosis, most often schizophrenia. The delusions in these patients are extremely difficult to divert and influence with psychological and pharmacological treatments. This association between psychosis and frontal lobe syndrome has also been described in DAT with a marked frontal lobe degeneration and in patients with ischaemic white matter lesions in the frontal lobes (Brun *et al*, 1992; Miller *et al*, 1991). Thus, there are reasons to believe that differences in psychotic symptoms between DAT and FTD are related to differences in localisation of the degenerative process. The clinical differences between early- and late-onset DAT are in agreement with other studies (Lauter, 1970; Blennow *et al*, 1991), and possibly related to differences in the distribution of grey-matter degeneration and the presence of white matter disease (Englund *et al*, 1989).

The complex relationship between symptoms in dementia and brain dysfunction will be further illustrated by four case reports also including rCBF findings.

Case reports

Case 1

This patient was a skilled worker with positive heredity for presenile dementia. A progressive mental deterioration with memory failure and general tiredness started in 1984, when he was 64 years old. Four years later he had difficulties in finding his way around the house where he had been living for about ten years. One year later he had a severe dysmnesia and difficulty in recognising his wife. When he took his dog for a walk, he sometimes only took the leash and left the dog at home. During 1990, at the age of 70, he started to complain of seeing tiny people gathering around his caravan in the garden. The small people were completely silent, moved rapidly and were possibly involved in some kind of repair work. He could never see their faces clearly. The patient was slightly disturbed but not frightened by their appearance. In addition to the Lilliputian hallucinations, he sometimes saw full-sized persons in dark and shady corners of the garden. He was more self-critical concerning these experiences. Also on a few occasions he had a feeling of being watched from a distance, probably by a Russian spy. Confusional episodes during the night started in February 1991 and the patient became more restless and anxious even during the daytime. He was examined by the psychogeriatric out-reach team and referred to the day-care unit. The clinical picture was clearly that of presenile AD with the typical combination of dysphasia, dysgnosia, dyspraxia, spatial disorientation, increased muscular tension with slight tremor and cog-wheel phenomena. He was a nice, humorous person with a well preserved capacity for social interaction and he is getting on very well at the day care unit. He is being treated with a small dose of haloperidol. His clinical condition has improved with normalisation of sleep, less anxiety and few hallucinations. The clinical diagnosis has been verified by psychometric testing, rCBF measurement and EEG. The high-resolution xenon inhalation technique was used to measure rCBF in 254 cortical regions of the two hemispheres (Risberg *et al*, 1990).

The rCBF measurement (Plate I) showed a subnormal average flow level in both hemispheres with accentuation in the temporoparietal regions, typical of DAT. The precentral cortical areas were less affected but showed a slight focal asymmetry with lower flow in the right frontal region. The occipital cortical flow was relatively spared. It should be pointed out that rCBF was measured in a resting situation and, as far as we know, when the patient was not hallucinating.

Thus, the visual hallucinations and illusions in this case started after six years of progressive AD. The deceptions were sometimes associated with anxiety and suspiciousness but the patient's attitude in general was trustful and self-critical and he seemed to appreciate reassuring comments and explanations. The rCBF measurement revealed cortical dysfunction with temporoparietal predominance and better preserved function in the occipital cortex. The effect of the combined therapeutic approach was satisfactory.

Case 2

This male patient became completely blind and slightly deaf in an accident when he was 39 years old. After the accident he was educated as an economist and worked as such until retiring aged 64 years. The patient's wife described a progressive mental deterioration that started in 1989 when he was 66 years old. The patient became forgetful, passive and anxious. He could no longer find his way at home and had difficulties in recognising his wife, who was mistaken for her sister or someone else. The patient sometimes woke up in the middle of the night quite convinced that he was not at home. He and his wife had to get dressed and leave the house. They could return to their flat after a short tour by car, and the patient felt at home again. The first rCBF measurement (Plate II) in February 1990 showed a moderate decrease in the average hemispheric flow with temporoparietal and frontal accentuations as in more advanced DAT. The patient was treated with a tricyclic antidepressant because of anxiety and depressed mood. Some clinical improvement was seen at first but two weeks later the patient started to experience visual hallucination. He saw a group of small, silent persons in gaudily coloured clothes, sometimes climbing on to his knees. The Lilliputian hallucinations disappeared for a while when the patient waved his hands at them.

A second rCBF measurement in October 1990 showed a further general flow reduction. In addition, however, there was an interesting regional flow increase in the temporo-occipital association cortex from the first to the second measurement, more marked on the left side. There might be a relationship between the hallucinations and the focal increase of rCBF in the visual association cortex. In October 1990, CT scan revealed no tumours or infarcts but slight cortical atrophy. The EEG showed general slowing. Single photon emission computerised tomography (SPECT) confirmed the rCBF findings but also showed increased activity in the periventricular white matter.

This patient illustrates the multifactorial aetiology of hallucinations in patients with dementia and sensory handicap. The development of hallucinations in this case seems to be precipitated by the combination of degenerative brain disease, total blindness and anticholinergic medication.

Case 3

This patient was a male, unskilled worker with a massive heredity for FLD, affecting the family for at least three generations. The first symptoms of the disease started when he was 43 years old. He became restless, anxious and tense, sometimes with aggressive outbursts against his children. Later he became apathetic and developed a marked expressive dysphasia and temporal disorientation. He also changed his oral and dietary behaviour with excessive smoking and drinking. Episodes of visual and tactile hallucinations were reported, beginning in 1985 when the patient was 53 years old. He called out the fire brigade on several occasions reporting that he saw burning houses, both nearby and at a long distance. He also complained of the sensation of being touched on different parts of the body. The patient was agitated and preoccupied by his deceptions and delusions. The medical examination, at the psychogeriatric department, revealed no somatic disorders. In March 1990, rCBF (Plate III) showed a global flow level at the border between normal and subnormal with a bilateral flow pathology in frontal areas indicating FTD. The frontal rCBF pathology was more marked at the second measurement in May 1991, and has been confirmed with SPECT and CT-scan. The progress of the rCBF pathology is typical of FTD. The hallucinations in this patient with progressive frontal lobe degeneration were thus both tactile and visual and reported with high intensity and without insight. It has been extremely difficult for the patient's family and later for the ward staff at the mental hospital to handle the situation, in spite of the fact that the patient's practical abilities and spatial orientation are still comparatively spared. The treatment strategy has been a firm regime with verbal and non-verbal guidance of the patient in his daily activities.

Case 4

This patient was a male unskilled worker, of previously good physical and mental health. Slow progressive personality changes started in 1976, when he was 51-years old. He became passive, careless, silent, and emotionally withdrawn. He also complained of severe pain, associated with a sensation of stiffness in different parts of the body such as the neck, chest and heart. The patient was convinced that the stiffness would spread to other parts of his body and lead to sudden death. He consulted doctors frequently, asking for examinations and treatment. The patient was well aware of the negative results of previous somatic examinations. Moreover, he did not dare to use the radio or TV because this might disturb his neighbours, who could also observe him through the walls. The patient stopped working referring to his severe pain, and his sisters and brothers had to care for him. In 1984, at 59 years of age, he was diagnosed as suffering from post-psychotic residual schizophrenia. In 1989, the patient was almost mute, and two years later he was described as restless, disinhibited, sometimes aggressive, disorientated and dyspractic. In August 1989, rCBF showed a general decrease of the average hemispheric flow with accentuation in frontal areas (Plate IV). In addition there was a bilateral relative hyperactivity in temporoparietal sensory and association areas, not at all typical of FLD. A second rCBF measurement one and half years later showed progress and accentuation of the focal frontal flow pathology and no post-central flow increase, supporting the diagnosis of FLD. CT-scan showed general cortical atrophy and the regional cortical pathology was confirmed by SPECT.

This patient with a progressive frontotemporal degenerative dementia of non-vascular type was first diagnosed as suffering from schizophrenic psychosis. This is a common misinterpretation of patients of this age with a combination of personality changes, progressive dysphasia and delusions. The rCBF pathology clearly indicated a frontal degenerative process and there might be a relationship between the delusional sensory distortion and the hyperactivity in sensory and post-central association cortex.

Conclusions

The analysis of the relationship between psychotic symptoms and brain function is a complex matter and alternative explanations and interpretations of research data have to be considered. It is tempting to suggest a relationship between the hallucinations and delusions, and the focal and asymmetric rCBF abnormalities observed in some but not all demented patients with these symptoms. This has also been reported in organic mental diseases such as alcoholic hallucinosis (Berglund & Risberg, 1981) and organic affective states (Silfverskiöld *et al*, 1983). The understanding of such clinicopathological correlates will hopefully improve not only the clinical diagnosis but also the treatment and care of patients with dementia.

Acknowledgements

This study was supported by the Swedish Medical Research Council (Projects No. 3950, 4969, 6606) and Greta & Johan Kocks Foundation. Special thanks to Dr Alf Johanson for valuable assistance, to Aniko Wolf for manuscript typing and to Helena Fernö for preparing the illustrations.

References

ALZHEIMER, A. (1907) Über eine eigenartige erkrankung der hirnrinde. *Allgemeine Zeitschrift für Psychiatrie*, **64**, 146-148.

BEATS, B., BURNS, A. & LEVY, R. (1991) Single photon emission tomography in dementia. *International Journal of Geriatric Psychiatry*, **6**, 57-62.

BERGLUND, M. & RISBERG, J. (1981) Regional cerebral blood flow during alcohol withdrawal. *Archives of General Psychiatry*, **38**, 351-355.

BERRIOS, G. E. & BROOK, P. (1984) Visual hallucinations and sensory delusions in the elderly. *British Journal of Psychiatry*, **144**, 662-664.

BLENNOW, K., WALLIN, A. & GOTTFRIES, C-H. (1991) Presence of parietotemporal symptomatology distinguishes early and late onset Alzheimer's disease. *International Journal of Geriatric Psychiatry*, **6**, 147-154.

BRUN, A. (1987) Frontal lobe degeneration of non-Alzheimer type. I. Neuropathology. *Archives of Gerontology and Geriatrics*, **6**, 193-208.

—— & GUSTAFSON, L. (1976) Distribution of cerebral degeneration in Alzheimer's disease. A clinico-pathological study. *Archiv für Psychiatrie und Nervenkrankheiten*, **223**, 15-33.

—— & —— (1988) Zerebrovaskuläre erkrankungen. In *Psychiatrie der Gegenwart, Band 6, Organische Psychosen* (eds K. P. von Kisker, H. Lauter, J.-E. Meyer, *et al*), pp.253-295. Berlin: Springer Verlag.

——, ——, SAMUELSSON, S. M., *et al* (1992) The neuropathology of late life. *Dementia* (in press)

BURNS, A., JACOBY, R. & LEVY, R. (1990) Behavioral abnormalities and psychiatric symptoms in Alzheimer's disease: preliminary findings. *International Psychogeriatrics*, **2**, 25-36.

CHASE, T. N., BURROWS, G. H. & MOHR, E. (1987) Cortical glucose utilization patterns in primary degenerative dementias of the anterior and posterior type. *Archives of Gerontology and Geriatrics*, **6**, 289-297.

EIDEN, H. - F. & LECHNER, H. (1950) Über psychotische zustandsbilder bei der Pickschen und Alzheimerschen krankheit. *Archiv für Psychiatrie und Zeitschrift Neurologie*, **184**, 393-412.

ENGLUND, E. & BRUN, A. (1987) Frontal lobe degeneration of non-Alzheimer type IV. White matter changes. *Archives of Gerontology and Geriatrics*, **6**, 235-243.

——, —— & GUSTAFSON, L. (1989) A white-matter disease in dementia of Alzheimer's type - clinical and neuropathological correlates. *International Journal of Geriatric Psychiatry*, **4**, 87-102.

GUSTAFSON, L. (1987) Frontal lobe degeneration on non-Alzheimer type. II. Clinical picture and differential diagnosis. *Archives of Gerontology and Geriatrics*, **6**, 209-223.

—— & RISBERG, J. (1974) Regional cerebral blood flow related to psychiatric symptoms in dementia with onset in the presenile period. *Acta Psychiatrica Scandinavica*, **50**, 516-538.

—— & HAGBERG, B. (1975) Dementia with onset in the presenile period. A cross-sectional study. *Acta Psychiatrica Scandinavica*, **257**, 9-71.

—— & RISBERG, J. (1979) Regional cerebral blood flow measurements by the 133-Xe inhalation technique in differential diagnosis of dementia. *Acta Neurologica Scandinavica*, **60**, 546-547.

——, BRUN, A., FRANCK HOLMKVIST, A., *et al* (1985) Regional cerebral blood flow in degenerative frontal lobe dementia of non-Alzheimer type. *Journal of Cerebral Blood Flow and Metabolism*, **5**, S141-S142.

——, —— & RISBERG, J. (1990a) Frontal lobe dementia of non-Alzheimer type. In *Alzheimer's Disease* (eds R. Wurtman, S. Corkin, J. Growdon, *et al*), pp.65-71. New York: Raven Press.

——, ——, JOHANSON, A., *et al* (1990b) Diagnostic criteria of Alzheimer's disease. In *Alzheimer's Disease. Epidemiology, Neuropathology, Neurochemistry, and Clinics* (eds K. Mauer, P. Riederer & H. Beckmann), pp.357-364. Berlin: Springer Verlag.

INGVAR, D. I. & GUSTAFSON, L. (1970) Regional cerebral blood flow in organic dementia with early onset. *Acta Neurologica Scandinavica*, **46** (suppl. 43), 42-73.

JACOBY, R. J. & LEVY, R. (1980) Computed tomography in the elderly: II Senile dementia: diagnosis and functional impairment. *British Journal of Psychiatry*, **136**, 256-269.

JOHANNESSON, G., BRUN, A., GUSTAFSON, L., *et al* (1977) EEG in presenile dementia related to cerebral blood flow and autopsy findings. *Acta Neurologica Scandinavica*, **56**, 89–103.

JOHANSON, A. & HAGBERG, B. (1989) Psychometric characteristics in patients with frontal lobe degeneration of non-Alzheimer type. *Archives of Gerontology and Geriatrics*, **8**, 129–137.

——, GUSTAFSON, L., SMITH, G. J. W., *et al* (1990) Adaptation in different types of dementia and in normal elderly subjects. *Dementia*, **1**, 95–101.

LAUTER, H. (1970) Über spätformen der Alzheimerschen krankheit und ihre beziehung zur senilen demenz. *Psychiatria Clinica*, **3**, 169–189.

MILLER, B., LESSER, I., BOONE, K., *et al* (1991) Brain lesions and cognitive function in late-life psychosis. *British Journal of Psychiatry*, **158**, 76–82.

MINTHON, L., EDVINSSON, L., EKMAN, R., *et al* (1990) CSF neuropeptide Y-like levels in dementia of Alzheimer type and dementia with frontotemporal degeneration of non-Alzheimer type. *Dementia*, **1**, 262–266.

NEARY, D., SNOWDEN J. S., NORTHEN, B., *et al* (1988) Dementia of frontal lobe type. *Journal of Neurology, Neurosurgery, and Psychiatry*, **3**, 353–361.

——, ——, MANN, D. M. A., *et al* (1990) Frontal lobe dementia and motor neuron disease. *Journal of Neurology, Neurosurgery, and Psychiatry*, **53**, 23–32.

POST, P. (1966) *Persistent Persecutory States of the Elderly*. Oxford: Pergamon Press.

RISBERG, J., GUSTAFSON, L. & BRUN, A. (1990) High resolution regional cerebral blood flow measurements in Alzheimer's disease and other dementia disorders. In *Alzheimer's Disease. Epidemiology, Neuropathology, Neurochemistry, and Clinics* (eds K. Maurer, P. Riederer & H. Beckmann), pp.509–516. Berlin: Springer Verlag.

RISBERG, R. (1987) Frontal lobe degeneration of non-Alzheimer type. III. Regional cerebral blood flow. *Archives of Gerontology and Geriatrics*, **6**, 225–233.

ROBERTSON, E. E., LE ROUX, A. V. S. & BROWN, J. H. (1958) The clinical differentiation of Pick's disease. *Journal of Mental Science*, **104**, 1000–1024.

RUBIN, E. H., DREVETS, W. C. & BURKE, W. J. (1988) The nature of psychotic symptoms in senile dementia of the Alzheimer type. *Journal of Geriatric Psychiatry and Neurology*, **1**, 16–19.

SILFVERSKIÖLD, P., GUSTAFSON, L. & RISBERG, J. (1983) rCBF changes following seizures in two cases of organic affective syndrome. In *Current Problems in Epilepsy I* (eds M. Baldy-Moulinier, D. H. Ingvar & B. S. Meldrum), pp.39–43. London, Paris: John Libbey & Co.

STENGEL, B. & VIENNA, M. D. (1943) Study on the symptomatology and differential diagnosis of Alzheimer's disease and Pick's disease. *Journal of Mental Science*, **374**, 1–20.

VAN MANSVELT, J. (1954) *Pick's disease. A Syndrome of Lobar, Cerebral Atrophy: its Clinico-anatomical and Histopathological Types*. Thesis. Enschede, Utrecht.

18 Psychosis in dementia of the Alzheimer type

ALISTAIR BURNS

There is a well recognised association between psychotic symptoms and neurological disorders (Cummings, 1985), particularly in patients with Alzheimer's disease (AD; Cummings & Victoroff, 1990; Burns *et al*, 1990*a*). There is increasing interest in this area, which is justified because features have become an important aspect of the investigation of AD. There are six main reasons why psychotic features in AD are important.

(a) They may be of help in the differential diagnosis of dementia, if their presence or absence is indicative of one or other type.
(b) Some of the changes may have implications for early diagnosis.
(c) The presence may indicate subtypes of the disorder, evidence for which may be gleaned from studies of the natural history and neuropathological/neurochemical correlates.
(d) AD is a useful paradigm by which brain/behaviour relationships can be investigated.
(e) They cause a great deal of strain on carers.
(f) They are, unlike the cognitive deficits, amenable to available treatment.

This chapter will review the current state of knowledge concerning psychotic features in AD. The term 'psychosis' includes delusions, hallucinations and misidentifications – affective symptoms will be mentioned only briefly as they may, at times, merit the label 'psychotic'. The review will start with a general overview and description of these features, followed by a summary of the possible aetiology of the disorders, an analysis of associations between these features and other aspects of dementia, a summary of the author's own work in this field and finally a note on treatment.

Early studies

Alzheimer's famous case was published on two occasions (Alzheimer, 1906, 1907). It is the latter paper which has received most attention and is the most widely quoted. In this, Alzheimer describes the case of a 51-year-old woman in whom focal cognitive deficits were associated with delusions of jealousy and auditory hallucinations, in conjuction with a particular neuropathological appearance. To quote a translation:

"A woman, 51 years old, showed jealousy towards her husband as the first notable sign of the disease. Soon a rapidly increasing loss of memory could be noticed. She could not find her way around in her own apartment. She carried objects back and forth and hid them. At times she would think that someone wanted to kill her and would begin shrieking loudly. . . . At times she greeted the doctor like a visitor and excused herself for not having finished her work; at times she shrieked loudly that he wanted to cut her, or she repulsed him with indignation, saying that she feared from him something against her chastity. Periodically, she was totally delirious, dragged her bedding around, called her husband and her daughter and seemed to have auditory hallucinations." (Wilkins & Brody, 1969)

Over the next five years, 15 cases of AD were described, the oldest sufferer being aged 67 years. Bonfiglio (1908) reported a case of a 60-year-old man who had delusions and hallucinations as did the cases described by Fuller (1912) and Ziveri (1912). Perusini and Lafora described cases with both delusions and hallucinations, and delusions, respectively (Perusini, 1909; Lafora, 1911). None of the remaining nine cases had either delusions or hallucinations and these symptoms were not mentioned in Alzheimer's second case of 1911 (Alzheimer, 1911, translated by Förstl & Levy, 1991). In addition to AD, delusions and hallucinations were well known to occur in elderly subjects with cognitive impairment (Berrios, 1990). Fischer (1907) used the term presbyophrenia in referring to cases of senile dementia in whom hallucinations (associated with rapid disease development, confabulation and serious memory disorder) were prominent.

Subsequent descriptions of psychotic symptoms in AD can be divided into two temporal categories – those before and those after the mid-1970s. Early studies relied on substantially anecdotal reports from clinical observers, usually in small and unrepresentative samples of patients (e.g. young patients referred to hospital for assessment). Later, instruments of proven validity and reliability were used to assess symptoms in more representative groups of patients.

Henderson & MacLachlan (1930) reported four female patients (mean age 57 years), only one of whom was without psychotic features. Of the other three, one had hallucinations (type unspecified), one had paranoid delusions and the third had both. Goodman (1953) noted that in his 23 autopsy-proven

AD cases that "hallucinations frequently occurred", visual being the most common type. Paranoid delusions "were fairly common early in the disease" and most were of a simple, unsystematised type.

Ziegler (1954) found in his sample of 40 psychiatric patients with idiopathic atrophy on pneumoencephalography, that 15% were 'paranoid', 15% were 'depressed', and the same proportion had 'neurotic symptoms'. However, although quoted in many articles as indicative of the prevalence of psychiatric symptoms in DAT (e.g. Liston, 1979), it is uncertain how many of these patients were suffering from primary dementia. Sim & Sussman (1962) reported on 46 patients referred to a department of Psychological Medicine, 22 of whom had AD diagnosed by cerebral biopsy. They reported that in this group, depressive symptoms occurred early in the disease and tended to disappear as the dementia became more severe; also that 'psychotic' features (not further defined) were a late manifestation. 'Agitation' was present in 29%. Coblentz *et al* (1973) examined ten subjects with histologically confirmed AD and described five as 'agitated' and two with psychotic features.

Gustafson & Hagberg (1975) studied 57 patients with pre-senile dementia. Extensive psychiatric assessments were performed on the patients and 50 had cerebral blood flow assessed by xenon-133. Seven factors were described based on a factor analysis of a standardised psychiatric interview – ixophrenia (an emotionally charged 'clinging' attitude), depression, explosive temper, hypochondriasis, paranoia, psychomotor overactivity and euphoria/affective liability. Associations were described between the presence of these symptoms, regional cerebral blood flow, and severity of dementia. Ixophrenia, depression and hypochondriasis were all found in subjects with mild dementia and relatively normal cerebral blood flow, although the first two were associated with slightly reduced flow. As such, these three symptoms were considered as 'compensatory' (both psychologically and physiologically) for mild impairment of cerebral function, but also possibly related to premorbid personality characteristics. Affective lability, explosive temper and overactivity were associated with severe cognitive impairment and were designated as signs of disinhibition relating to low frontal blood flow. Paranoia was said to be present at all levels of cognitive impairment – in mild dementia it was considered a psychological reaction to diminished comprehension of the environment and in the later stages, the result of direct brain damage. The authors stated that blood flow studies appeared to confirm this with high frontal flow in the early stages, reducing in the later stages. Gustafson & Risberg (1974) were the first to describe an association between blood flow and particular symptoms which went some way towards the elucidation of subtypes, i.e. different clinical manifestations (with different symptom complexes) were associated with pathophysiological markers (alterations in regional cerebral blood flow).

More recent work has used standardised and reproducible measures of assessing phenomenology. Three main types of psychiatric phenomena have been defined (*Lancet*, 1989) – disorders of thought content (delusions and paranoid ideation), disorders of perception (hallucinations and misidentifications) and disorders of affect (depression and elevated mood).

Disorders of thought content

It is recognised that delusions occur in association with AD. DSM–III–R (American Psychiatric Association, 1987) has a separate category, subsumed under the main heading 'Primary degenerative dementia of the Alzheimer type', for patients with delusions, but no such subheading occurs in ICD–10 (World Health Organization, 1986). Delusions are known to occur in patients with organic brain disease such as Huntington's Disease (Dewhurst *et al*, 1969) and post-encephalitic Parkinsonism (Fairweather, 1947). Regional localisation has suggested an association between delusions and temporal lobe damage as in temporal lobe epilepsy (Toone, 1981) and Herpes encephalitis (which preferentially affects temporal structures, Rennick *et al*, 1973). Schneiderian first rank symptoms of schizophrenia have also been related to temporal lobe atrophy (Trimble, 1990). Idiopathic basal ganglia calcification has been implicated in the genesis of delusions (Cummings & Benson, 1983).

Attempts have been made to subclassify delusions associated with organic brain damage. Cummings (1985) suggested that they be divided into four types – simple persecutory delusions, complex persecutory delusions, grandiose delusions and those delusions associated with specific neurological deficits. He identified delusional ideation in a prospective study of 20 male patients with organic disorders, four of whom had AD (representing 15% of all AD subjects seen in the service). Patients with mood-congruent delusions were excluded. Simple delusions were confirmed to subjects with AD or vascular dementia while the other delusions occurred in patients with a variety of neurological disorders such as tumours and encephalopathies. It was found that those with simple delusions were more cognitively impaired than those with any of the other three types. He also made the practical observation that simple delusions were more responsive to neuroleptic medication than complex delusions.

Cutting (1987) followed Cummings' (1985) scheme in an attempt to classify delusions in 74 patients with acute organic psychoses, 35 of whom were deluded. He was able to classify only 17 patients according to the Cummings (1985) classification – eight with simple persecutory delusions and nine with mood-congruent delusions (this category replacing that of grandiose delusions as described by Cummings, 1985). Seventeen of the remaining 18 were afforded a separate category described as 'complex, bizarre or multiple'. This category was similar to the 'complex persecutory' delusions described by Cummings (1985). In addition, one patient had a delusion "based on a specific neuropsychology deficit" (a phrase employed by Cutting to describe the concept suggested by Cummings).

There have been some studies specifically assessing the frequency with which delusions occur in AD. Cummings *et al* (1987) defined both delusions and AD using DSM–III criteria (American Psychiatric Association, 1980). They found that delusions had occurred, since the onset of illness, in 14 out of 30 AD subjects (average age 70.4 years) and that there was a trend (not statistically significant) for these patients to be less cognitively impaired. Although well characterised, the sample consisted of only 30 subjects who were referred from a variety of sources (out-patients or in-patients, geriatric, psychiatric or neurological) and thus cannot be considered a representative population of AD subjects. Rubin *et al* (1988) found 31% of their sample to be deluded, the commonest type of delusion being that of stealing (which would have been in the 'simple persecutory' category of Cummings, 1985). Although, in comparison to the sample of Cummings *et al* (1987), the number studied was large ($n = 110$), there was no definition of delusions. It can be inferred from the paper that the patients were diagnosed by a number of investigators, thus reducing the reliability of the results.

Berrios & Brook (1985) reported delusions in 37% of 100 demented patients referred to an out-patient clinic. Of 68 patients with AD, 23 were diagnosed as deluded. These subjects scored less than the non-deluded patients on the information, but not on the memory subscale of the Blessed Dementia Scale (Blessed *et al*, 1968). Patients with both vascular dementia and AD were included and it seems likely that some of the subjects had an intercurrent delirium at the time of examination. Also, 14 of the 37 deluded subjects had an additional diagnosis of a functional illness. This factor raises the suspicion that they had a previous psychiatric disorder, thereby casting doubt on the diagnosis of AD.

Common delusional themes include delusions of abandonment and impostering (Reisberg *et al*, 1987), suspicion and stealing (Berrios & Brook, 1985; Cummings *et al*, 1987; Rubin *et al*, 1988). None of these studies divided delusions in DAT into the subtypes described by Cummings (1985) and Cutting (1987).

Clues to the pathological substrate of delusions come from two lines of evidence. Firstly, delusional ideation seems to require relatively intact cerebral function. Jacoby & Levy (1980) and Gustafson & Risberg (1974) found delusions to be inversely related to both cerebral atrophy and cortical perfusion. Secondly, delusions have been associated with basal ganglia calcification (Cummings, 1985). There appears to be no difference in the prevalence of delusions in patients with vascular or degenerative dementia (Berrios & Brook, 1985; Cummings *et al*, 1987) suggesting that they are not specific to a particular pathological process but that they result from brain damage of diverse aetiology, perhaps localised to particular brain regions.

Paranoid ideation, held without delusional intensity, has not been examined specifically in DAT although Reisberg *et al* (1987) described 21% of his sample as exhibiting 'paranoia' (not further defined). Merriam *et al*

(1988) found 42% to have paranoid ideation "of a relatively minor nature" and 56% to have "more severe paranoid symptoms". It may be that the former finding represented paranoid ideation and the latter delusions, but this conclusion cannot be made with certainty. The relatively high rates suggest that some difference in definition is present or that a very biased sample has been studied. No definitions of the symptoms were given and the sample was drawn from patients referred to a neurology clinic and, as stated in the paper, not a clinic dealing particularly with psychiatric or behavioural problems. These factors make the high proportion of patients with psychopathology even more surprising. Most studies lack a precise definition of delusions (with the exception of Cummings *et al*, 1987) so it is possible that some patients have paranoid ideation which has been wrongly equated with ideas held with delusional intensity and *vice versa*. The absence of operational criteria for the diagnosis of such symptoms in dementia should be borne in mind when comparing different studies.

Disorders of perception

Perceptual disturbances can be divided into two types (Fish, 1985) – sensory distortions (changes in the intensity, quality or spatial form of perception) and sensory deceptions (illusions and hallucinations). Hallucinations occur in many psychiatric conditions such as schizophrenia, depression and acute organic psychoses (Cutting, 1987). Their presence in senile dementia was partly responsible for the condition being classified as a senile psychosis. There is a considerable French literature on hallucinations. L'hermitte (1951) noted that hallucinations (in particular, visual hallucinations) occurred in elderly patients with atherosclerosis and cerebral atrophy. Henry Ey (Ey, 1973) observed that clinicians had long been familiar with the tendency for the aged to experience hallucinations, especially those suffering from AD although rarely in-patients with Pick's disease. Both authors mention the 'Charles Bonnet syndrome' as an example of visual hallucinosis in the elderly. This syndrome has been well documented (Berrios & Brook, 1984; Damas-Mora *et al*, 1982) and is dealt with elsewhere in this book (Fuchs & Lauter, pp. 189–200). Characteristically, the sufferers have insight into their experiences, generally have poor vision, are not worried by the hallucinosis and remain cognitively intact, which makes a misdiagnosis of dementia unlikely.

Several studies have reported the prevalence of hallucinations in AD. For example, Sjögren *et al* (1952) reported a prevalence of 15%. More recently, Cummings *et al* (1987), in addition to diagnosing delusions, assessed hallucinations in their 30 AD patients (average age 70.4 years) and 15 with multi-infarct dementia (MID). Of the AD patients, only one had auditory and none had visual hallucinations; in MID, three experienced visual and one auditory hallucinations. The authors required that only those subjects reporting 'a sensory perception' would be regarded as suffering from hallucinations. The patients were interviewed directly to ascertain whether hallucinations were present but information was also sought from the case notes. Three of the four patients with these experiences had visual defects. The association between this type of hallucinatory experience and ocular pathology has been described previously (Berrios & Brook, 1984). Clinical subtypes of AD based on visual hallucinations, which do not take ocular pathology into consideration, cannot therefore be posited.

Reisberg *et al* (1987), in describing a new behavioural rating scale, found that 12% of their sample of 57 out-patients (mean age 75.0 years) had suffered visual hallucinations. Auditory hallucinations were not mentioned. Merriam *et al* (1988) examined 175 subjects with AD using the Schedule for Affective Disorders (Spitzer & Endicott, 1971) to assess depression and reported, incidentally, that 28% had experienced either visual or auditory hallucinations. Similarly, Teri *et al* (1988) reported that of 127 out-patients, 21% had hallucinations (type unspecified). There was a tendency (not statistically significant) for the proportion of subjects with these perceptual phenomena to be greater as severity of cognitive impairment increased.

The difference in frequency rates in various studies may be explained in three ways. Firstly, the sample studied: most reports from North America describe populations of patients referred to out-patient clinics or to AD research facilities. There may be differences in referral procedure to each centre and the patient group may be biased in favour of subjects suffering from psychiatric problems. No reports have yet described the rates of psychiatric symptoms for an epidemiologically representative population. Secondly, the definition and method of ascertainment of symptoms: for example, Cummings *et al* (1987) used a very stringent definition of hallucinations and relied mainly on direct interview with the patient. By contrast, Reisberg *et al* (1987) relied solely on review of medical case notes. Thirdly, the period of time to which the given rates refer: in the majority of studies, it is unclear whether the prevalence rates refer to symptoms occurring at any time since the onset of the illness, or if they are reserved for symptoms present at the time of the examination.

Misidentifications

The other main types of perceptual disturbances seen are misrecognitions and misidentifications which have been virtually ignored as symptoms of AD. There have been a number of case reports in the literature of mis-identification of relatives in dementia (some manifesting as the Capgras Syndrome, e.g. Burns & Philpot, 1987). Misidentification of mirror image has also been described and 'Signe du miroir' is the term used to refer to patients conversing with their own image (Mayer Gross *et al*, 1960). Rubin *et al* (1988) described three types of misidentification – imagining that other people were in the same house, the inability of a subject to recognise his or her own image in a mirror and treating events or people on the television as if in real three-dimensional space. Rubin *et al* (1988) reported that 23% of their 110 patients had experienced at least one type of misidentification (the belief that others were in the house being the most common). Merriam *et al* (1988) described these 'perceptual' symptoms and found that 49% of the patients misidentified other people and 41% misidentified places. The study by Merriam *et al* (1988) is, again, unusual in the very high rates of symptoms described (e.g. major depression was found in 86% of cases) and so the number of patients experiencing these disorders of perception may be falsely high.

Aetiology

The cause of psychotic symptoms in AD has been discussed by Berrios (1989) and Cummings & Victoroff (1990). Berrios (1990) postulated four different mechanisms by which non-cognitive symptoms would result. Firstly, an intercurrent delirium occurs not uncommonly in patients with dementia. Usually the symptoms are fleeting and the hallucinatory experiences are most often visual. However, it is unlikely that symptoms persisting for more than a few days are due to a delirium.

Secondly, Berrios invokes a theory of cortical disinhibition using Hughlings Jackson's model to justify the symptoms found following upper motor neuron lesions. The idea is that 'released behaviour' results from damage to mechanisms normally inhibiting behaviour. An associated hypothesis, common in France, is that psychotic phenomena are a type of dream activity which intrudes into consciousness.

Thirdly, the pathoplastic effect of personality, which Berrios dismisses as a cause of abnormal mental experiences such as delusions and hallucinations, but admits may have a part to play in features which can be regarded as exaggerations of normal personality, e.g. mood changes. The relationship between paranoid personality traits and subsequent dementia with paranoid beliefs has yet to be examined.

Fourthly, the possibility of a coexistence of two separate mental disorders, i.e. dementia and a coexisting functional psychosis. The tendency to discourage separate diagnoses of two mental disorders and the rigid stance of modern operational criteria make this position hard to defend and involve a hierarchical model of diagnosis.

Cummings & Victoroff (1990) take a practical view of possible aetiological mechanisms for delusions. They postulate five causes. Firstly, delusional ideation results from the subjects' (understandable) attempts to make sense of their environment. Simple accusatory beliefs (which may be held with delusional intensity) following misplacement of personal possessions might be explainable in terms of loss of memory. However, there is generally a poor association between delusional ideation and amnesia. Secondly, Cummings & Victoroff (1990) suggest that some changes may be secondary to mood disorders in AD. The phenomenology of delusions and the lack of association between disorders of mood and delusional ideas negate this theory. Thirdly, the possibility that dementia and psychosis arise by chance is not supported by the evidence of a high prevalence rate of delusions in patients with dementia compared with control groups. Fourthly, (and solely for hallucinations) is the possibility of sensory deprivation resulting in hallucinations. Berrios & Brook (1984) found fleeting visual hallucinations in patients with dementia and found these to be strongly associated with eye pathology. However, Burns *et al* (1990*a*) found no such association and it is unlikely that a satisfactory explanation for auditory hallucinations would be obtained in this way.

The final reason postulated by Cummings & Victoroff (1990) for psychotic phenomena is that they may be related to structural abnormalities found in the brain, whether these are neuropathological or neurochemical, and there is evidence that damage to the limbic system (common in AD) leads to a particular propensity for delusional ideation (*vide infra*).

It can be seen that while there are many competing reasons why psychotic phenomena are present in AD, there is no unitary theory to explain them all.

Associations

It is important, in order to investigate psychotic phenomena in dementia, to consider their association with other features of the dementia syndrome. Five main areas can be examined.

Previous history of psychiatric disorder

There have been no studies which have examined non-cognitive features as possible prodromata of dementia. Our own study (Burns *et al*, 1990*a*) suggested that patients with AD who had a previous history of depression may deteriorate cognitively less quickly than those without. However, Lopez *et al* (1990) performed a longitudinal study of 20 patients with AD (10 of whom also had major depression) and found no difference in base line or follow up neuropsychological test results at one year.

Neurological signs

Mayeux *et al* (1985) found an association between the presence of delusions and hallucinations and those with extrapyrimidal signs (bradykinesia and rigidity). They were also more likely to have poor cognitive function and a poorer functional capacity than those without.

Cognitive function

The relationship between psychotic phenomena in AD and the other major manifestation of dementia, the cognitive deficit, is most important. One of the reasons that non-cognitive features may have been neglected over the years was the automatic assumption that they were secondary to the cognitive changes, and therefore, of secondary importance. Generally speaking, research has found that while psychotic phenomena are associated with more severe dementia, correlations between individual symptoms and cognitive impairment are less obvious. Thus (as noted above), Cummings *et al* (1987) and Berrios & Brook (1985) found no difference in cognitive function in patients with and without hallucinations and delusions respectively. With regard to depression, the situation is slightly different and generally studies have reported (Reifler *et al*, 1982; Merriam *et al*, 1986; Cummings *et al*, 1987) that depression is associated with less severe cognitive impairment. There are four reasons why this may be so. Firstly, some symptoms may be easier to assess than others and patients may complain of depression more readily than they would admit to other experiences. Secondly, theoretically, there may be a protective effect of the cholinergic deficits seen in AD. Thirdly, it may be simply due to an insensitivity of the instruments in that the phenomenology of depression is difficult to assess in patients with even moderate cognitive impairment. Finally, the effects of advanced brain disease might not allow an individual to experience complex emotional changes such as those found in depression. Lopez *et al* (1991) examined 17 patients with AD who had experienced delusions and hallucinations and compared them with a carefully matched sample without these phenomena. Patients with AD appear to have a specific defect in receptive language as assessed by auditory comprehension, reading and token test. This is evidence that such phenomena are associated with a focal neuropsychological deficit.

Natural history

Delusions, misidentifications and hallucinations have been reported as being associated with an accelerated cognitive decline (Drevets & Rubin, 1989) and with a decreased death rate. Mayeux *et al* (1985) reviewed the records of 62 patients in a longitudinal study and found that those with 'psychosis' (inadequately defined as persistent or recurrent thought disorder) deteriorated more rapidly in both cognitive and functional abilities over time. Stern *et al* (1987) reported on the follow-up of 55 patients from Mayeux *et al*'s study. They reported that the sudden onset of psychosis was associated with a rapid decline in one of the 'benign' group (an intermittent delirium may have been present but there was no mention of it). Very little has been recorded about the pathological substrate of perceptual symptoms. However, one recent preliminary report has suggested that in cortical Lewy body disease, cholineacetyltransferase activity is lower in patients who have experienced hallucinations than in those who have not (Perry *et al*, 1990). Recently, Rosen & Zubenko (1991) described the results of prospective evaluations of 32 patients with AD. Psychosis emerged in 47%, its presence being associated with increasing dementia and more rapid cognitive decline. However, it was not associated with increased mortality. Lopez *et al* (1991) found that patients with delusions and hallucinations had a more rapid rate of cognitive decline (as assessed by the Mini-Mental State Examination, MMSE; Folstein *et al*, 1975). However, several studies (Drevets & Rubin, 1989; Burns *et al*, 1990*a*; Rosen & Zubenko, 1991) have found that patients with psychosis (localised to those with misidentification syndromes by Burns *et al*, 1990*a*) have a decreased mortality. The reasons for this are unclear.

Biological changes

The large study by Gustafson & Hagberg (1975) showing an association between cerebral blood flow and psychiatric symptoms has been previously outlined. Studies examining the associations between psychiatric phenomena and cerebral blood flow changes using modern single photon emission computerised tomography (SPECT) with new radiotracers such as hexamethylpropyleneamineoxime (HMPAO) imaging have yet to be performed. Lopez *et al* (1991) found in their 17 patients with delusions and hallucinations that these patients had a greater degree of cerebral dysfunction as evidenced by the greater proportion of abnormal electroencephalograms and an increased amount of delta and theta activity. Further studies in this important area are awaited. The results of computerised tomography (CT) scan changes in the author's own study are outlined below.

Zubenko *et al* (1991) described neuropathological and neurochemical correlates in 27 patients with autopsy-confirmed AD, of whom 14 had prominent delusions and hallucinations. The presence of psychosis was associated with: increased density of senile plaques in the prosubiculum, increased neurofibrillary tangle counts in the middle frontal cortex and a significant reduction of serotonin in the prosubiculum. There were trends towards increased plaque and tangle density counts elsewhere in the temporal cortex and hippocampus with a trend for relative preservation of noradrenalin in the substantia nigra, thalamus, amygdala, and caudate nucleus. These changes are distinct from those found in patients with depression and AD.

The Institute of Psychiatry Alzheimer cohort

In this study, 178 subjects with Alzheimer's disease were enrolled in a longitudinal prospective clinical study in an attempt to identify subtypes of AD. The sample has been well characterised (Burns *et al*, 1990*b*) and a high degree of accuracy for the neuropathological diagnosis of Alzheimer's disease has been confirmed in the sample (Burns *et al*, 1990*b*) using NINCDS/ADRDA criteria (McKhann *et al*, 1984). Particular attention was paid to non-cognitive phenomena. Delusions had occurred in 16% of the sample at some point since the onset of the illness and had occurred within the 12 months of entry to the study in 11%. The commonest types of delusions were delusions of theft and suspicion, with a greater proportion of men experiencing delusions of theft. Some patients had systematised delusions (six subjects) and these were associated with preservation of the lateral ventricles and with basal ganglia calcification. One-fifth of the sample had experienced persecutory ideation (not held with delusional intensity) since the onset of the illness. There was no association between cognitive function (either at baseline or follow-up) and delusions.

Visual hallucinations had been experienced by 13% of the sample and auditory hallucinations by 10% at some point since the onset of the illness. In total, 17% of the sample had experienced one or other form of hallucinosis since the onset of the disorder, of whom 11% had experienced it within the 12 months before entry to the study. Patients who had experienced hallucinations (particularly of recent onset and particularly auditory hallucinations) had a more rapid deterioration in cognitive function over the first year of the study. This was not related to neuroleptic medication. There was no sex difference in hallucinating patients.

Four misidentification syndromes were found in the sample – misidentification of other people (found in 12%), the belief that other people were living in the patient's house (17%), the belief that events on television were occurring in real three-dimensional space (6%), and the misidentification of the patient's own mirror image (4%). Misidentification of other people and the belief that people were in the house were more common in men. Some form of misidentification had been experienced by 30% of the sample since the onset of the dementia. Patients with these symptoms were younger and had a younger age of onset of the dementia compared with patients without these symptoms. An analysis of computerised tomography scans in 128 of the sample (of whom 40 showed misidentification phenomena) showed that patients with these syndromes had significantly larger right anterior horn areas of the lateral ventricles and larger left anterior brain areas than patients without the syndromes (Förstl *et al*, 1991). This may suggest that an accentuated degeneration of the right frontal lobe and relative preservation of the left frontal lobe may be associated with delusional misidentification. A previous study suggested that misidentification was associated with frontal lobe atrophy (Eslinger *et al*, 1984).

Treatment

It is hardly surprising that attention is now being paid to the treatment of non-cognitive features of dementia although practising clinicians have been doing this for many years. Attention has been largely directed towards control of agitation and aggression with neuroleptic and sedative medication and very little has been published on the use of antipsychotics specifically for psychotic phenomena. One would imagine that isolated psychotic beliefs in association with dementia would be treated as if they were part of a functional psychosis, whereas psychotic beliefs in association with agitation and aggression may be given more sedative medication. Tune *et al* (1991) recently reviewed 30 published studies, only one of which mentioned specifically an effect on persecutory ideation. This may partly reflect the absence of specific scales to measure psychotic phenomena in dementia. Transient psychosis in the setting of confusional states obviously merits treatment aimed at the underlying cause.

Conclusion

Psychotic phenomena in Alzheimer's disease are at last being recognised as being of considerable interest and importance from both a research and a clinical point of view. Elucidation of their frequency and biological correlates in dementia is a necessary step forward and one in which the psychiatrist has a unique role to play.

References

ALZHEIMER, A. (1906) Uber einen eigenartigen, schweran erkrankungsprozess der hirnrinde. *Neurol CBL. XXV*, (1906), 1134.
—— (1907) Uber eine Eigenartige Erkrankung der Hirnrinde. *Allegemeine Zeitschrift fur Psychiatrie und Psychisch – Gerichtlich Medicin*, **64**, 146–148.
—— (1911) Uber eigenartige Krankheitsfalle des spateren Alters. *Zeitschrift gesamte Neurologica und Psychiatrica*, **4**, 356–385.
AMERICAN PSYCHIATRIC ASSOCIATION (1980) *Diagnostic and Statistical Manual of Mental Disorders* (3rd edn) (DSM–III). Washington, DC: APA.
—— (1987) *Diagnostic and Statistical Manual of Mental Disorders* (3rd edn, revised) (DSM–III–R). Washington, DC: APA.
BERRIOS, G. (1989) Non-cognitive symptoms in the diagnosis of dementia: historical and clinical aspects. *British Journal of Psychiatry*: **154** (suppl. 4), 11–16.
—— (1990) Alzheimer's disease: a conceptual history. *International Journal of Geriatric Psychiatry*, **5**, 355–365.
—— & BROOK, P. (1984) Visual hallucinations and sensory delusions in the elderly. *British Journal of Psychiatry*, **144**, 662–664.
—— & —— (1985) Delusions and the psychopathology of the elderly with dementia. *Acta Psychiatrica Scandinavica*, **72**, 296–301.
BLESSED, G., TOMLINSON, B. & ROTH, M. (1968) The association between quantitative measures of dementia and of senile change in the cerebral grey matter of elderly subjects. *British Journal of Psychiatry*, **114**, 797–811.

BONFIGLIO, F. (1908) Di speciali reperti in un caso di probabile sifilide cerebrale. *Riv. Sper. Freniatria*, **34**, 196–206.

BURNS, A. & PHILPOT, M. (1987) Capgras' syndrome in a patient with dementia. *British Journal of Psychiatry*, **150**, 876–877.

——, JACOBY, R. & LEVY, R. (1990*a*) Psychiatric phenomena in Alzheimer's disease. *British Journal of Psychiatry*, **157**, 72–94.

——, LUTHERT, P., LEVY, R., *et al* (1990*b*) Accuracy of clinical diagnosis of Alzheimer's disease. *British Medical Journal*, **301**, 1026.

COBLENTZ, J., MATTINS, S., ZINGESSER, L., *et al* (1973) Presenile dementia: 1. Clinical aspects and evaluation of CSF dynamics. *Archives of Neurology*, **29**, 299–308.

CUMMINGS, J. (1985) Organic delusions: phenomenology, anatomical correlations and review. *British Journal of Psychiatry*, **146**, 184–197.

—— & BENSON, D. (1983) *Dementia: A Clinical Approach*. Boston: Butterworths.

—— & VICTOROFF, J. (1990) Non-cognitive neuropsychiatric syndromes in Alzheimer's disease. *Neuropsychiatry, Neuropsychology and Behavioural Neurology*, **3**, 140–158.

——, MILLER, B., HILL, M. A., *et al* (1987) Neuropsychiatric aspects of multi-infarct dementia and dementia of the Alzheimer type. *Archives of Neurology*, **44**, 389–393.

CUTTING, J. (1987) The phenomenology of acute organic psychosis: comparison with acute schizophrenia. *British Journal of Psychiatry*, **151**, 324–332.

DAMAS-MORA, J., ROBINSON, M. & JENNER, F. (1982) The Charles Bonnet syndrome in perspective. *Psychological Medicine*, **12**, 251–261.

DEWHURST, K., OLIVER, J., TRICK, K., *et al* (1969) Neuropsychiatric aspects of Huntington's Disease. *Confinia Neurologica*, **31**, 258–268.

DREVETS, W. & RUBIN, E. (1989) Psychotic symptoms in the longitudinal course of senile dementia of the Alzheimer type. *Biological Psychiatry*, **25**, 39–48.

ESLINGER, P., DAMASIO, H., RADFORD, N., *et al* (1984) Examining the relationship between CT and neuropsychological measures in normal and demented elderly. *Journal of Neurology, Neurosurgery and Psychiatry*, **47**, 1319–1325.

EY, H. (1973) Les hallucinations dans les psychoses et les neuroses. In *Traite des Hallucinations* (ed. H. Ey) Tome II, pp. 713–898. Paris: Masson.

FAIRWEATHER, D. (1947) Psychiatric aspects of the post-encephalitic syndrome. *Journal of Mental Science*, **93**, 201–254.

FISCHER, O. (1907) Miliare Nekrosen mit drusigen Wucherungen der Neurofibrillen, eine regelmaessege Verandaerung der Hirnrinde be seniler Demenz. *Monatsschrift für Psychiatrie und Neurologie*, **22**, 361–372.

FISH, F. (1985) *Fish's Clinical Psychopathology* (2nd edn) (ed. M. Hamilton), pp. 16–36. Bristol: John Wright and Sons.

FOLSTEIN, M., FOLSTEIN, S. & MCHUGH, P. (1975) Mini-Mental State Examination. *Journal of Psychiatric Research*, **12**, 189–198.

FÖRSTL, H. & LEVY, R. (1991) Certain peculiar diseases of old age. (A. Alzheimer). *History of Psychiatry*, **2**, 71–101.

——, BURNS, A., JACOBY, R., *et al* (1991) Neuroanatomical correlates of clinical misidentification and misperception in senile dementia of the Alzheimer type. *Journal of Clinical Psychiatry*, **52**, 268–271.

FULLER, S. C. (1912) Alzheimer's disease (senium praecox): The report of a case and review of published cases. *Journal of Nervous and Mental Disease*, **39**, 440–455, 536–557.

GOODMAN, L. (1953) Alzheimer's Disease: a clinical and pathologic analysis of 23 cases with a theory on pathogenesis. *Journal of Nervous and Mental Disease*, **117**, 97–130.

GUSTAFSON, L. & HAGBERG, J. (1975) Dementia with onset in the presenile period. *Acta Psychiatrica Scandinavica*, suppl. 257.

—— & RISBERG, J. (1974) Regional cerebral blood flow related to psychiatric symptoms in dementia with onset in the pre-senile period. *Acta Psychiatrica Scandinavica*, **50**, 516–538.

HENDERSON, D. K. & MACLACHLAN, S. (1930) Alzheimer's disease. *Journal of Mental Science*, **76**, 646–661.

JACOBY, R. J. & LEVY, R. (1980) Computed tomography in the elderly: II. Senile dementia: diagnosis and functional impairment. *British Journal of Psychiatry*, **136**, 256–269.

LAFORA, G. R. (1911) Beitrag zur Kenntnis der Alzheimerschen Krankheit oder prasenilen Demenz mit Herdsumptomen. *Zeitschrift fur die gesamte Neurologica Psychiatrica*, **6**, 15–20.

LANCET (1989) Psychotic symptoms in Alzheimer's disease. *Lancet*, *ii*, 1193–1194.

L'HERMITTE, J. (1951) *Les Hallucinations Clinique et Physiopathologie*. Paris: Doin.

LISTON, E. (1979) Clinical findings in pre-senile dementia. *Journal of Nervous and Mental Disease*, **167**, 337–342.

LOPEZ, O., BOLLER, F., BECKER, J., *et al* (1990) Alzheimer disease in depression: neuropsychological impairment and progression of the illness. *American Journal of Psychiatry*, **147**, 855–860.

——, BECKER, J. T., BRENNER, M. D., *et al* (1991) Alzheimer's disease with delusions and hallucinations: neuropsychological and electroencephalographic correlates. *Neurology*, **41**, 906–912.

MAYER-GROSS, W., SLATER, E. & ROTH, M. (1960) *Clinical Psychiatry*. London: Casell and Co. Ltd.

MAYEUX, R., STERN, Y. & SANO, N. (1980) Psychosis in patients with dementia of the Alzheimer type. *Annals of Neurology*, **18**, 144.

McKHANN, G., DRACHMAN, D., FOLSTEIN, M., *et al* (1984) Clinical diagnosis of Alzheimer's disease. Report on the NINCDS-ADRDA work group under the auspices of the Department of Health and Human Services Task Force on Alzheimer's disease. *Neurology*, **34**, 939–944.

MERRIAM, A., ARONSON, N., GASTON, P., *et al* (1988) The psychiatric symptoms of Alzheimer's disease. *Journal of the American Geriatrics Society*, **36**, 7–12.

PERRY, E. K., KERWIN, J., PERRY, R. H., *et al* (1990) Visual hallucinations and the cholinergic system in dementia. *Journal of Neurology, Neurosurgery and Psychiatry*, **53**, 88.

PERUSINI, G. (1909) Uber klinische und histologische eigenartigen, psychische Erkrankungen der spateren Lebensalters. *Nissle-Alzheimers Histol. histopatol. Arb.*, **3**, 297–351.

REIFLER, B., LARSON, E. & HARLEY, R. (1982) Co-existence of cognitive impairment and depression in geriatric outpatients. *American Journal of Psychiatry*, **139**, 623–626.

REISBERG, B., BORENSTEIN, J., SALOB, S., *et al* (1987) Behavioural symptoms in Alzheimer's disease: phenomenology and treatment. *Journal of Clinical Psychiatry*, **48** (suppl.), 9–15.

RENNICK, P., NOLAN, D., BAVER, R., *et al* (1973) Neuropsychological and neurological follow-up after herpes hominis encephalitis. *Neurology*, **23**, 42–47.

ROSEN, J. & ZUBENKO, G. S. (1991) Emergence of psychosis and depression in the longitudinal evaluation of Alzheimer's disease. *Biological Psychiatry*, **29**, 224–232.

RUBIN, E., DREVETS, W. & BURKE, W. (1988) The nature of psychotic symptoms in senile dementia of the Alzheimer type. *Journal of Geriatric Psychiatry and Neurology*, **1**, 16–20.

SIM, M. & SUSSMAN, I. (1962) Alzheimer's disease: its natural history and differential diagnosis. *Journal of Nervous and Mental Disease*, **135**, 489–499.

SJÖGREN, P., SJÖGREN, H. & LINDGREN, A. G. H. (1952) Morbus Alzheimer and Morbus Pick. *Acta Psychiatrica et Neurologica Scandinavica*, suppl. 82.

SPITZER, R. L. & ENDICOTT, J. (1971) The Schedule for Affective Disorders (SADS-C). *Archives of General Psychiatry*, **24**, 540–547.

STERN, Y., MAYEUX, R., SANO, M., *et al* (1987) Predictors of disease course in patients with probable Alzheimer's disease. *Neurology*, **37**, 1649–1653.

TERI, L., LARSON, E. B. & REIFLER, B. (1988) Behavioural disturbance in dementia of the Alzheimer type. *Journal of the American Geriatrics Society*, **36**, 1–6.

TOONE, B. (1981) Psychoses in epilepsy. In *Epilepsy in Psychiatry* (eds E. Reynolds & M. Trimble). New York: Churchill Livingstone.

TRIMBLE, M. (1990) First rank symptoms of Schneider. A new perspective? *British Journal of Psychiatry*, **156**, 195–200.

TUNE, L., STEELE, C. & COOPER, T. (1991) Neuroleptic drugs in the management of behavioural symptoms of Alzheimer's disease. *Psychiatric Clinics of North America*, **14**, 353–373.

WILKINS, R. H. & BRODY, I. A. (1969) Alzheimer's disease. *Archives of Neurology*, **21**, 109–110.

WORLD HEALTH ORGANIZATION (1986) *ICD – IO*. Draft of Chapter V. Geneva: WHO.

ZEIGLER, D. (1954) Cerebral atrophy in psychiatric patients. *American Journal of Psychiatry*, **111**, 54–58.

ZIVERI, A. (1912) Su di un caso annoverabile nella cosidetta 'malattia di Alzheimer'. *Rivista di Patologia Nervosa e Mentale*, **17**, 137–148.

ZUBENKO, G. S., MOOSSY, J. JULIO MARTINEZ, A., *et al* (1991) Neuropathologic and neurochemical correlates of psychosis in primary dementia. *Archives of Neurology*, **48**, 619–624.

Index

Compiled by Stanley Thorley